Contents

Acknowledgments

A lot of nice folks helped with this Fifth Edition and to all of them we say, "Thanks!"

Brown Pelican Antiques, Panama City, Florida
Eye of the Peacock, Pottstown, Pennsylvania
Delmar and Anita Goode, Lamoni, Iowa
Graham Silver, Omaha, Nebraska
RSVP Antiques, Cedarhurst, New York
Jennie D. Long, Kingsburg, California
Aluminum Collector's Books, Weatherford, Texas
Conway Barker, Dallas, Texas
Jim Frye, WHO Radio, Des Moines, Iowa
Lamplighter Books, Leon, Iowa
Caddo Trading Co., Murfreesboro, Arkansas
Debbie Hamm, Romney, Michigan
Dan Pickerel, Mount Shasta, California
Boone Trading Co., Brinnon, Washington
Veryl Marie Worth, Oakridge, Oregon
R. E. Burt, Dalton, New York
Arkies, Chillicothe, Missouri
Bob and Nancy Searjeant, Rochester, New York
N. Flayderman & Co., Inc., New Milford, Connecticut
Jacquie Greenwood, Mount Arlington, New Jersey
Ruth A. Forsythe, Galena, Ohio
Jobeco Books, Humble, Texas
Whirligig Antiques, Austin, Texas
Grandpa's Depot Caboose Antiques, Denver, Colorado
The Old Storefront Antiques, East Germantown, Indiana
Allen Koenigsberg, Brooklyn, New York
Ed Hyde, Santa Fe, New Mexico
Antique Americana Graphics, Costa Mesa, California
Stan and Peggy Hecker, San Diego, California
Iris L. Fischer, Woodbridge, Connecticut
Dori Miles, Remsen, New York
Warren Harris, Carmichael, California

Jo Cunningham, Springfield, Missouri
Holloway House, Lititz, Pennsylvania
Ray and Eilene Early, Westerville, Ohio
Royal Toy Store, Hammond, Louisiana
Continental Hobby House, Sheboygan, Wisconsin
Veeder's Antiques, Guilderland, New York
Mrs. Marion Cohen, Albertson, New York
Wood 'n Things, Jones, Oklahoma
Pat Beall, Michigan City, Indiana
Laughing Cat Antiques, Houston, Texas
Romex International, Polson, Montana
Bordertown Antiques, Texarkana, Arkansas
Dale C. Anderson Co., Hampton, New Hampshire
Phoneco, Ron and Mary Knappen, Galesville, Wisconsin
Glen B. Bowen, Glenview, Illinois
Jane Wood, Gas City, Indiana
Lone Star Autographs, Kaufman, Texas
E. Ruth Wood, Chicago, Illinois

A special thanks to Ted Hake's Americana & Collectibles in York, Pennsylvania. Subscribe to Ted's monthly catalog if you enjoy bidding by mail on thousands of collectibles. Send $8 for twelve issues or $5 for six issues to P. O. Box 1444, York, PA 17405.

Introduction

Welcome to the big, new Fifth Edition of the Wallace-Homestead *Flea Market Price Guide,* America's most popular publication to do with Flea Marketing, Collectibles, and Americana!

If you're buying, selling, or collecting anything that was mass-produced in America during the twentieth century that costs between a few pennies and hundreds of dollars then *you* are the person this price guide was written for!

Prices in the collectibles field are fairly well established, but the reason we pioneered the two-price system is because you probably won't buy or sell the same item in Ohio or Pennsylvania that you would in New York or California. Also, our prices are based on an item that's in good condition unless otherwise noted. Normal wear on any old item is to be expected.

Hopefully, "regional pricing" will become a thing of the past someday. There are too many price guides, trade journals, national clubs, and collectors' newsletters in national circulation to continue this nonsense called "regional interest" collecting.

This Fifth Edition of the *Flea Market Price Guide* is a GUIDE. Repeat, a G-U-I-D-E! If you're a collector with a few years' experience, you know that you're going to pay a fair market price for a particular item. If you're selling to a dealer (ask to see their tax license), you're going to get 60 or 70 percent of the net price. But FOR GOODNESS SAKE, DO NOT sell your merchandise for 35 or 40 percent of its value simply because certain price guides tell you to.

Please note that we do *not* have a special board of advisors. We have nothing against dealers who assist in making a price guide a better publication (see our "Acknowledgments" section). But we do not tell you, the collector, that you should have to sell your merchandise to another collector for 35 to 40 percent of its retail value. A dealer expects to buy at a discount. One collector to another — make your own deal. This especially holds true at flea markets and garage sales.

We are highly complimented that the competition has *finally* gotten around to listing clubs to join, publications to subscribe to, and periodicals to read. We know you appreciate this information because your letters have told us so.

To the countless thousands who rely on our Wallace-Homestead *Flea Market Price Guide* to keep them aware of what's going on in the field of Flea Markets, Collectibles, and Americana, we say a large "Thank you!"

We have always aimed our books at the beginning collector or dealer, and we want you to learn, but we refuse to make *our* price guide read like a textbook for Latin 107.

Always remember: If the price is right, *buy* it. If the price is right, *sell* it.

For years this editor has been the *only* one who personally answered your questions. If you'll write to him in care of the publisher, and include an SASE (self-addressed, stamped envelope), we'll do our best to provide a prompt, informative reply. Since you were kind enough to purchase this price guide, we'll certainly take a few minutes to answer your letters.

Repairs and Services

Here's another exclusive for you — hundreds of places where you can buy supplies, find that elusive piece of china, or get cherished pieces repaired or restored.

Always inquire first and **always** enclose an SASE (self-addressed, stamped envelope) if you expect a reply. This exclusive service is for **you** because we feel a Price Guide should do something more than just list a bunch of prices.

Note: If your firm isn't listed here it doesn't mean that you don't do quality work or sell a quality product. It does mean that we don't know about you. If you want to be included in the Sixth Edition of the Wallace-Homestead *Flea Market Price Guide,* write!

D

E

F

G

H

Q

R

S

T

U

V

W

1 B & L Antiquerie
25011 Little Mack
St. Clair Shores, MI 48080

2 Graham Silver
Box 6021
Omaha, NE 68106

3 T-K Michael Stained Glass
28200 Florence
St. Clair Shores, MI 48081

4 LEMiniatures
2615 Gravenstein Hwy.
Sebastopol, CA 95472

5 Studio Hannah
Star Route A, Box 93
Flemington, NJ 08822

6 Thompsons
Back Meadows Rd.
Damariscotta, ME 04543

7 Wilson Bergerud
30 Herring St.
Harrington Park, NJ 07640

8 Hector Olszewski
140 W. Houston
New York, NY 10003

9 Globes by Chick
328 Danville Pike
Hillsboro, OH 45133

10 Colonial "out-of-print" Book Service
23 E. 4th St.
New York, NY 10003

11 Horton Brasses
P. O. Box 95
Cromwell, CT 06416

12 Nowell's, Inc.
P. O. Box 164
Sausalito, CA 94965

13 The Antique Phonograph Shop
320 Jericho Turnpike
Floral Park, NY 11001

14 Gotham Book Mart & Gallery
41 W. 47th St.
New York, NY 10036

15 Al Meekins
P. O. Box 161
Collingswood, NJ 08108

16 "My Grandfather's Shop" Ltd.
940 Sligo Ave.
Silver Spring, MD 20910

17 Ronald's Woodcarving
434 W. 4th St.
W. Islip, NY 11795

18 Morgan, Dept. A03K11
915 E. Ky.
Louisville, KY 40204

19 Antique Trunk Supply Co.
3706 W. 169th St.
Cleveland, OH 44111

20 J & S Co.
P. O. Box 4840
Chattanooga, TN 37405

21 Sierra Studios
P. O. Box 1005
Oak Park, IL 60304

22 Paul W. Bowser
1618 W. Main St.
New Lebanon, OH 45345

23 Les Gould
391 Tremont Pl.
Orange, NJ 07050

24 The Genealogical Helper
526 N. Main St.
Logan, UT 84321

25 Mike Wells
30½ W. Wheelock St.
Hanover, NH 03755

26 The Bedpost
Rt. 1, Box 155
Pen Argyl, PA 18072

27 Schoepfer Eyes
138 W. 31st St.
New York, NY 10001

28 Wood & Leather Craft
Star Route
Callicoon, NY 12723

29 The Clarks
P. O. Box 434
Oceanside, CA 92054

30 Constantine
2050 Eastchester Rd.
Bronx, NY 10461

31 Whittemore-Durgin
P. O. Box H2065
Hanover, NH 02339

32 PECO
P. O. Box 777
Smithville, TX 78957

33 Replica Products
610 57th St.
Vienna, WV 26105

34 Trans World Trading Co.
509 S. Cross
Robinson, IL 62454

35 Appraisers Association of America, Inc.
60 East 42nd St.
New York, NY 10017
(Note: A Membership Directory is available at a cost of $4 to persons seeking the services of a professional appraiser.)

36 Mildred E. Webster
P. O. Box 37114
Los Angeles, CA 90037

37 Adams Antiques
426 Main Ave.
Northport, AL 35476

38 Doll & Craft World
125 8th St.
Brooklyn, NY 11215

39 Waymar, Inc.
6015 S. Lindbergh
St. Louis, MO 63123

40 Gaston Wood Finishes, Inc.
3630 E. 10th St.
Bloomington, IN 47401

41 Seeley's Ceramic Service, Inc.
9 River St.
Oneonta, NY 13820

42 Dolls By Rene
8228 Allport
Santa Fe Springs, CA 90670

43 Costume Quarterly
38 Middlesex Dr.
Brentwood, MO 63144

44 Jeannette Strauss
3705 Chapel Forge Dr.
Bowie, MD 20715

45 John J. Mesterhazy
12917 Westwood Lane
Omaha, NB 68144

46 Hess Repairs
200 Park Ave. S.
New York, NY 10003

47 Williams' Antiques
Albion, IL 62806

48 BMS Materials
P. O. Box 222
Windsor, NY 13865

49 Hardwood Grove Mfg.
Rt. 2, Box 200
West Fork, AR 72774

50 Pat & Hanks Antiques
410 Don Tyler
Dewey, OK 74029

51 DiPonziano & Associates
P. O. Box 23356
San Jose, CA 95153

52 Bill E. Berger
29 E. 12th St.
New York, NY 10003

53 Museum Services
P. O. Box 119
Hingham, MA 02043

54 American Assn. of Conservators
1250 E. Ridgewood Ave.
Ridgewood, NJ 07450

55 Graphics International
P. O. Box 13292, Station E
Oakland, CA 94661

56 Ms. Micheline Masse
Stock Market Information Services, Inc.
Montreal, Canada

57 Accelerated Indexing Systems, Inc.
3346 S. Orchard Dr.
Bountiful, UT 84010

58 Michael Sissman
Buttonshop Rd.
Williamsburg, MA 01096

59 Lorraine Boyce
15 Bruce Dr.
Newton, NJ 07860

60 Genealogical Bookshelf
P. O. Box 468
New York, NY 10028

61 John Crary
Rt. 1
Canton, NY 13617

62 W.H.M.
2686 McAllister
San Francisco, CA 94118

63 Donna Vernal
217 E. First
Waconia, MN 55387

64 Sandy Ritchie
Rt. 1, Box 17
Scottsville, VA 24590

65 Clark Mfg. Co.
Rt. 2
Raymore, MO 64083

66 Wallin Forge
Rt. 1, Box 65
Sparta, KY 41086

67 The Sobys
P. O. Box 180
W. Springs, IL 60558

68 Irvin Hoover
Rt. 1
Mt. Pleasant Mills, PA 17853

69 The Canery
250 Brookstown Ave.
Winston-Salem, NC 27101

70 Haviland Corner Matching Service
P. O. Box 82
Belmont, CA 94002

71 R. Wayne Reynolds
P. O. Box 28
Stevenson, MD 21153

72 Helt's Antiques
Durhamville, NY 13054

73 Strawflower, Inc.
801 W. Eldorado
Decatur, IL 62522

74 House of Antiques
202 N. 5th St.
Springfield, IL 62701

75 Helen Lawler
Rt. 1, Box 334
Blytheville, AR 72315

76 Antique Hardware Co.
P. O. Box 877
Redondo Beach, CA 90277

77 Porter Music Box Co.
5 Mound St.
Randolph, VT 05060

78 American International Galleries
17792 Fitch St.
Irvine, CA 92714

79 The Shade Tree
1318 S. Peoria Ave.
Tulsa, OK 74120

80 Peter Michaels
1922 South Rd.
Baltimore, MD 21209

81 Nicholas Fiscina
20-17 Jackson Ave.
W. Islip, NY 11795

82 Neumann Miller
5482 Lakeview
Yorba Linda, CA 92686

83 Karl Frick
940 Canon Rd.
Santa Barbara, CA 93110

84 Doe's Treasures
P. O. Box 6505
Providence, RI 02940

85 Marleda's
P. O. Box 2308
San Bernardino, CA 92406

86 Bob McCumber
201 Carriage Dr.
Glastonbury, CT 06033

87 Warden's Clock Supply
103 N. Boling
Claremont, OK 70017

88 Musical Americana
354 E. Campbell
Campbell, CA 95008

89 William D. Gilstrap
Rt. 2
Bevier, MO 63532

90 Vintage Patterns II
5304 Thrasher Dr.
Cincinnati, OH 45239

91 McKenzie Art Restoration Studio
2907 E. Monte Vista Dr.
Tucson, AZ 85716

92 Calligraphic Ink
Crystal City Underground
Arlington, VA 22202

93 Emerson Hardwood Co.
2279 NW Front Ave.
Portland, OR 90710

94 Glass Masters Guild
621 6th Ave.
New York, NY 10009

95 Paul Baron Co.
2825 E. College Ave.
Decatur, GA 30030

96 Grady Stewart
2019 Sansom St.
Philadelphia, PA 19103

97 All-Art Restorers
140 W. 57th St.
New York, NY 10019

98 Rikki's Studio
2256 Coral Way
Miami, FL 33145

99 Mr. William and Co.
14 Garfield Pl.
Cincinnati, OH 45202

100 Bostonia Furniture Co.
183 Friend St.
Boston, MA 02114

101 Marcey Medgepeth
Rt. 179
Ringoes, NJ 08551

102 W. B. Lewis
231 Chatham Ave.
Pooler, GA 31322

103 Dorothy Briggs
410 Ethan Allen Ave.
Takoma Park, MD 20012

104 Andrew Hurst
2423 Amber St.
Knoxville, TN 37917

105 Rosemary Evans
9303 McKinney
Loveland, OH 45140

106 Billard's Old Telephones
21710 Regnart Rd.
Cupertino, CA 95014

107 Ritter & Son
P. O. Box 907
Campbell, CA 95008

108 Heritage Clocks of Mass.
P. O. Box 336
Sturbridge, MA 01566

109 Antique Music Box
1015 S. Teljon
Colorado Springs, CO 80906

110 Larry G. Harmon
1731 Pine Knoll
Caro, MI 48723

111 Howard's Stained Glass
2602 S. 11th St.
Gadsden, AL 35901

112 American Lamp
100 Elm Hill Pk.
Nashville, TN 37210

113 Eleanor Sopp
15144 Chamisal
Ballwin, MO 63011

114 The Yankee Drummer
23 Burnham Rd.
Hudson, NH 03051

115 TEC Specialties
P. O. Box 909
Smyrna, GA 30081

116 Modern Technical Tools
Box 681
Hicksville, NY 11801
117 Wedgwood Studio
2522 N. 52nd St.
Phoenix, AZ 85008
118 Elaine L. Mooza
286 Wilson Ave.
Rumford, RI 02916
119 White's
P. O. Box 680
Newberg, OR 97132
120 Jacquelynn's China
4770 N. Oakland Ave.
Milwaukee, WI 53211
121 Oscar Black
1940 Old Taneytown Rd.
Westminster, MD 21157
122 Mrs. Emily Troutman
325 N. 6th St.
Reading, PA 19601
123 Bob Depenbrok
6638 Van Noord Ave.
North Hollywood, CA 91606
124 Pie Galinat
41 Perry St.
New York, NY 10014
125 Stephen W. Weston
Winthrop, ME 04364
126 Play It Again Sam's
5343 W. Devin
Chicago, IL 60646
127 James Broaddus
1635 S. 4th
Terre Haute, IN 47802
128 Silver Plated Flatware Matching Service
142 Hampshire Rd.
Waterloo, IA 50701
129 Zephyr Glassworks
P. O. Box 42
Santa Cruz, CA 95060
130 Ross Jasper
2213 W. 2nd St.
Davenport, IA 52802
131 Best Books
2034 Empire Blvd.
Webster, NY 14560
132 Oak Knoll Books
680 S. Chapel St.
Newark, DE 19713
133 Yankee Peddler Bookshop
94 Mill St.
Pultneyville, NY 14538
134 Bailes
P. O. Box 150
Eureka Springs, AR 72632
135 Ron-Dot Bookfinders
P. O. Box 44
Greensburg, OH 44232
136 Art Ltd.
Stonecroft 2210
Grafton, WI 53024
137 The Fan Man
4606 Travis
Dallas, TX 75205
138 Carolina Caning Supply
P. O. Box 2179
Smithfield, NC 27577
139 Pat's Etcetera Co.
P. O. Box 777
Smithville, TX 78957
140 The Finishing Touch
5636 College Ave.
Oakland, CA 94618
141 Nostalgia
McHenry, IL 60050
142 Berkley, Inc.
2011 Hermitage Ave.
Wheaton, MD 20902
143 Irene Foukes
5170 Kitson
Orchard Lake, MI 48033
144 Mariana Redwine
756 Bluebird Cyn. Dr.
Laguna Beach, CA 92651
145 Char-Mar's
909 N. 7th
Garden City, KS 67846
146 E. Black
6130 SW 12th St.
Miami, FL 33144

147 Busy "B" Antiques
Rt. 1, Box 99
Zumbro Falls, MN 55991
148 Blue Plate Antiques
P. O. Box 124
Sherborn, MA 01770
149 Leslie
1359 Williamsburg
Flint, MI 48507
150 Stained Glass School
1705 S. Pearl
Denver, CO 80210
151 J & L's Jewelry
1915 Central St.
Evanston, IL 60201
152 R & K Weenike Antiques
Rt. 7
Ottumwa, IA 52501
153 Chicago Old Telephone Co.
P. O. Box 189
Lemon Springs, NC 28355
154 Thomas Malone Studio
12 Ashwood Rd.
Port Washington, NY 11050
155 Family Tree Antiques
P. O. Box 93
Merrick, NY 11566
156 Timesavers
P. O. Box 171
Wheeling, IL 60090
157 Al Bar Wilmette Platers
127 Green Bay Rd.
Wilmette, IL 60091
158 Connecticut Cane & Reed Co.
P. O. Box 1276
Manchester, CT 06040
159 Helt's Antiques
Durhamville, NY 13054
160 Vera L. Phillips
6427 S. Prince
Littleton, CO 80120
161 Lynne-Art's Glass House
P. O. Box 54-6014
Miami Beach, FL 33154
162 Cordier's Fine Arts
1619 S. La Cienega Blvd.
Los Angeles, CA 90035
163 Daniel Zalles
580 Sutter St.
San Francisco, CA 94102
164 Simms & Associates
18311 SW 95th Ct.
Miami, FL 33157
165 Diamonds by Terry
Burnsville, MI 55337
166 19th Century Co.
P. O. Box 1455
Upland, CA 91786
167 Fagan's
P. O. Box 329
Piedmont, AL 36272
168 DB Musical Restorations
230 Lakeview Ave. NE
Atlanta, GA 30305
169 Peggy's Matching Service
P. O. Box 476
Ocala, FL 32670
170 Reed Arts & Crafts
233 W. 5th Ave.
Columbus, OH 43201
171 Inez Pianos, Inc.
2473 Canton Rd.
Marietta, GA 30066
172 Art Reblitz Pianos
3916 N. Azalea
Colorado Springs, CO 80907
173 American Billiards
Suffern, NY 10901
174 Den of Antiquity
810 Rangeline
Columbus, MO 65201
175 Rand & Openshaw
3222 Larga Ave.
Los Angeles, CA 90039
176 The Sterling Fox
P. O. Box 398
Richmond, KY 40475
177 The Silver Queen
778 N. Indian Rocks Rd.
Belleair Bluffs, FL 33540
178 Senti-Metal Co.
1919 Memory Lane
Columbus, OH 43209

179 Ron Steidinger
Forrest, IL 61741
180 Woodsmith Classics
4021 California Ave.
Carmichael, CA 95608
181 Phoneco
Rt. 2
Galesville, WI 54630
182 Pierre et Jacqueline
1223 Green Bay Rd.
Wilmette, IL 60091
183 Paul Jones
429 S. Fredonia
Longview, TX 75601
184 Gary Bradley
Rt. 3, Box 606
Corvallis, OR 97330
185 Sarah Bustle
1701 Central St.
Evanston, IL 60201
186 Triple X Chemical Co.
841 Skokie Highway
Lake Bluff, IL 60044
187 Herbert K. Goodkind
25 Helena Ave.
Larchmont, NY 10538
188 Park Place Antiques
Long Grove, IL 60047
189 McMaster Fine & Antique Oriental Carpets
997 Roxwood
Boulder, CO 80303
190 Specialized Repair Service
2406 Bryn Mawr
Chicago, IL 60659
191 Karekin Beshir Ltd.
1125 Madison Ave.
New York, NY 10028
192 Lead 'n' Glass
357 Stone Place
Wheeling, IL 60090
193 Midwest Burnishing
208 E. Main
Round Lake Park, IL 60073
194 The Little Corner
3939 W. Main
McHenry, IL 60050
195 Elizabeth Crumley
2208 Derby St.
Berkeley, CA 94705
196 Mountain Lumber
1327 Carlton Ave.
Charlottesville, VA 22901
197 Leslie Brooks
166-25 Powells Ave.
Beechhurst, NY 11357
198 Lafayette
111 Jericho Turnpike
Syosset, NY 11791
199 Michael J. Dotzel & Son
402 E. 63rd St.
New York, NY 10021
200 Radio Shack
2617 W. 7th St.
Fort Worth, TX 76107
201 Sam Faust
Changewater, NJ 07831
202 Musical Museum
Deansboro, NY 13328
203 Ross's Antiques
Rt. 6
Milford, PA 18337
204 Porter Music Box Co.
Randolph, VT 05060
205 Jukebox Junction
P. O. Box 1081
Des Moines, IA 50311
206 Gloria Kluever
P. O. Box 124
Sherborn, MA 01770
207 John Martin Antiques
Rt. 3
Clarksville, GA 30523
208 Paul N. Smith
408 E. Leeland Heights Blvd.
Lehigh Acres, FL 33936
209 K. Parry
17557 Horace
Granada Hills, CA 91344
210 Slot Machine Repair Service
2404 W. 111th St.
Chicago, IL 60655

211 Mort Jacobs Restorations
231 S. Green St.
Chicago, IL 60607

212 Mechanical Music Center
25 Kings Highway North
Darien, CT 06820

213 Harris Woodcarving
120 E. Main St.
Falconer, NY 14733

214 Art Scan, Inc.
310 State St.
Albany, NY 12210

215 Estes-Simmons Silverplating, Ltd.
1168 Howell Mill Rd. N.W.
Atlanta, GA 30318

216 Nu-Cane Seat Co.
P. O. Box 995
Lawrence, MA 01842

217 Landers Co.
429 Memorial Ave.
W. Springfield, MA 01089

218 Fan Motors
3901 Sapling
Mesquite, TX 75180

219 Art Essentials, Ltd.
P. O. Box 260
Monsey, NY 10952

220 19th Century Co.
P. O. Box 599
Rough and Ready, CA 95975

221 Ritter & Son Hardware
Dept. 923
Gualala, CA 95445

222 Antique Apparatus Co.
13355 Ventura Blvd.
Sherman Oaks, CA 91432

223 Burdoch Silk Lampshade Co.
3283 Loma Riviera Dr.
San Diego, CA 92110

224 MLB Novelty Works
P. O. Box 416
Exton, PA 19341

225 Chicago Antique Slot Machine Co.
1778 W. Algonquin Rd.
Arlington Heights, IL 60005

226 Tom Krahl
238 Hecker Dr.
Dundee, IL 60118

227 Charlotte Ford Trunks
P. O. Box 536
Spearman, TX 79081

228 Hamlin's Haviland
3510 W. 47th Terrace
Shawnee Mission, KS 66205

229 Joseph DeVoren, Silversmiths
6350 Germantown Ave.
Philadelphia, PA 19144

230 Weber Furniture Service
5704 N. Western Ave.
Chicago, IL 60659

231 International Silver Plating Co.
364 Park Ave.
Glencoe, IL 60022

232 Searjeant's Historical Print & Restoration
P. O. Box 23942
Rochester, NY 14692

233 New York Nautical Instrument & Service Corp.
140 W. Broadway
New York, NY 10012

234 New York Marble Works, Inc.
1399 Park Ave.
New York, NY 10029

235 The Lamp Shader
222 Waukegan Rd.
Glenview, IL 60025

236 Adourian Bros.
2114½ W. Lawrence Ave.
Chicago, IL 60625

237 Seven Acres Antique Village & Museum
Rt. 20 & S. Union Rd.
Union, IL 60181

238 Antique Bazaar
924 Ogden Ave.
Lisle, IL 60532

239 House of Martin, Inc.
4719 Woodward
Downers Grove, IL 60515

240 Midwest Stripping
102 E. Main St.
Round Lake Park, IL 60073
241 Village Strip Shop
211 S. Main St.
Wauconda, IL 60084
242 Yankee Stripper
1283 E. Oakwood
Des Plaines, IL 60016
243 F. P. Turnip & Co.
2566 Prairie Ave.
Evanston, IL 60201
244 The Oak Peddlers
Spring Rd. and Montrose
Elmhurst, IL 60126
245 Victorian House Antiques
320 N. York St.
Elmhurst, IL 60126
246 Klavier Music Roll
10520 Burbank Blvd.
N. Hollywood, CA 91601
247 QRS Music Rolls
1026 Niagara St.
Buffalo, NY 14213
248 Paul C. Burgess
P. O. Box 12
Friendship, MA 04547
249 Carl A. Tessen
1620 Columbia Ave.
Oshkosh, WI 54901
250 Dennis Devine
722 E. Pierce St.
Council Bluffs, IA 51501
251 Arthur Sanders
Musical Museum
Deansboro, NY 13328
252 Paul Crist Studios
14903 Marquardt Ave.
Santa Fe Springs, CA 90670
253 Richard Simonton
4209 Burbank Blvd.
Burbank, CA 91602
254 Sheffield Knifemakers Supplies
P. O. Box 141
DeLand, FL 32720
255 Knife & Gun Finishing Supplies
P. O. Box 13522
Arlington, TX 76013
256 Ben Kelley, Jr.
4726 Chamblee-Tucker Rd.
Tucker, GA 30084
257 Cecil E. Clark
10903 Sharondale Rd.
Cincinnati, OH 45241
258 Bob Cargill
14401 136 St.
Lockport, IL 60441
259 Adrian A. Harris
Rt. 1, Zion Lane
Columbia, TN 38401
260 American Assn. of Conservators & Restorers
1250 E. Ridgewood Ave.
Ridgewood, NJ 07450
261 Miss Louise G. Bluhm
Fogg Art Museum
Harvard University
Cambridge, MA 02138
262 Archival Restoration Associates, Inc.
510 School Rd.
Blue Bell, PA 19422
263 Miss Linda Shaffer
827 Ocean Front Walk
Venice, CA 90291
264 Ms. Wynne H. Phelan
3721 Ella Lee Lane
Houston, TX 77027
265 Insurance Information Institute
110 William St.
New York, NY 10038
266 Jordan Specialty Co., Inc.
95 University Place
New York, NY 10003
267 Ultra-Violet Products, Inc.
Walnut Grove Ave. at Grand
San Gabriel, CA 91776
268 Peters Antiques
110 Irving St.
Woodstock, IL 60098
269 The Hollinger Corp.
3810 S. Four Mile Run Dr.
Arlington, VA 22206

270 Musical Americana Talking
Machine Co.
561 Washington St.
Santa Clara, CA 95050

271 Mechanical Music Center
P. O. Box 88
Darien, CT 06820

272 A.P. S. Strippery
3421 W. Pearl St.
McHenry, IL 60050

273 Doyle H. Lane
Daniel Boone Village
Hillsborough, NC 27278

274 Forbes
1024 E. Willow Grove Ave.
Philadelphia, PA 19118

275 Antiques Etc. Ltd.
My Grandmother's Dolls
Rt. 47 and North St.
Huntley, IL 60142

276 The Carol Co.
612 S. Hawley Rd.
Milwaukee, WI 53214

277 Saf-Pak Sales Co.
P. O. Box 126
Oak Park, IL 60303

278 Mountain Lumber Co.
P. O. Box 285
Charlottesville, VA 22902

279 Victorian Reproductions, Inc.
1601 Park
Minneapolis, MN 55404

280 Mylan Enterprises, Inc.
P. O. Box 194
Morris Plains, NJ 07950

281 Wraptiques
P. O. Box 353
Larchmont, NY 10538

282 Dave Pierson
806 W. Market St.
Akron, OH 44303

283 Antique Slot Machine Co.
238 Hecker Dr.
Dundee, IL 60118

284 Jack T. Irwin, Inc.
601 E. Gude Dr.
Rockville, MD 20852

285 Reisch College of Auctioneering
P. O. Box 949
Mason City, IA 50401

286 Mason City College of
Auctioneering
P. O. Box 1463
Mason City, IA 50401

287 Missouri Auction School
1600 - 36 Genessee St.
Kansas City, MO 64102

288 Jim Graham School of
Auctioneering
204 U.S. 1
N. Palm Beach, FL 33408

289 Free Play
35 E. St. Joseph St.
Arcadia, CA 91006

290 Sandler Products, Inc.
2229 S. Halsted
Chicago, IL 60608

291 Silver & China Exchange
P. O. Box 4601
Springdale, CT 06907

292 Les McGinnis
P. O. Box 3411
Amarillo, TX 79106

293 The China Match
9 Elmford Rd.
Rochester, NY 14606

294 Wedgwood China Cupboard
740 N. Honey Creek Pkwy.
Milwaukee, WI 53213

295 Marvetia Jack
148 12th St.
Silvis, IL 61282

296 Dialcraft
305 N. High St.
Columbus Grove, OH 45830

297 Fred Catterall
54 Short St.
New Bedford, MA 02740

298 D. E. Myers
430 Virginia Ave.
Sanford, FL 32771

299 L. Hulphers
3153 W. 110th
Inglewood, CA 90303

300 Beverly Sims
421 Plymouth St.
E. Bridgewater, MA 02333

301 Victory Glass Co.
P. O. Box 119
Des Moines, IA 50301

302 Burns Forge
11 N. John St.
Pearl River, NY 10965

303 Timothy J. Somers Leathers
1340 W. School St.
Chicago, IL 60657

304 Van Parys Studio
6338 Germantown Ave.
Philadelphia, PA 19144

305 Antiques Mechanical Ltd.
605 Ethan Allen Hwy.
Ridgefield, CT 06877

306 Rawburn Hall
Rt. 341 at Brick School Rd.
Warren, CT 06754

307 Ruby Harrison Photographic Inventory
1916 Lee St.
Evanston, IL 60202

308 Home in Focus
1919 Colfax St.
Evanston, IL 60201

309 Schutte's Lamp Supply
503 W. Spring St.
Lima, OH 45801

310 Tom & Judy's Chair Caning
1201 Florence
Evanston, IL 60202

311 Jeffrey R. Husar
6159 N. Nassau
Chicago, IL 60631

312 Pro-Strip & Long Ago Antiques
132 S. Lincoln Ave.
Carpentersville, IL 60110

313 Colonial Strip Shop
22 N. 29 Pepper Rd.
Lake Barrington, IL 60010

314 Paul Crist Studios
14903 Marquardt Ave.
Santa Fe Springs, CA 90670

315 Galerie de Porcelain
520 Hillside Ave.
Glen Ellyn, IL 60137

316 Burdoch Silk Lampshade Co.
3283 Loma Riviera Dr.
San Diego, CA 92110

317 Guzzo's Crossland Studio
812 E. Main St.
St. Charles, IL 60174

318 Don Daley, Goldsmith
1210 E. State St.
Sycamore, IL 60178

319 Compleat Caning Workshop
4719 Woodward
Downers Grove, IL 60515

320 Nissan Oriental Rugs
7217 W. Lake St.
River Forest, IL 60305

321 Klug & Schumacher
3604 Waterfield P'Way
Lakeland, FL 33801

322 Weber Furniture Service
5704 N. Western Ave.
Chicago, IL 60645

323 The Crystal Cave
1141 Central Ave.
Wilmette, IL 60091

324 Antique Watch Co. of Atlanta
P. O. Box 450066
Atlanta, GA 30345

325 Vintage Cash Register & Scale Co.
13448 Ventura Blvd.
Sherman Oaks, CA 91423

326 Stock Search Services
6320 74th Ave.
Summit, IL 60501

327 Custom House
6 Kirby Rd.
Cromwell, CT 06416

328 The Metal Mender
7 Silver Spring Park Rd.
Ridgefield, CT 06877

329 Bryan Keysor
Main St.
Wolcott, NY 14590

330 Johnson Watch Repair
Box 121 F
Keenesburg, CO 80643
331 Freemont Glass Works
401 Bidwell Ave.
Freemont, OH 43420
332 Bob Patton
6400 Wurzbach #505
San Antonio, TX 78240
333 Joseph A. Flannery
219 W. Church St.
Galion, OH 44833
334 Master's Pieces Antique Cash Registers
418 N. El Camino
San Clemente, CA 92672
335 Chili Doll Hospital
4332 Buffalo Rd.
North Chili, NY 14514
336 Charles D. Pheiffer
514 Philadelphia Ave.
Takoma Park, MD 20012
337 Eldred Schutt
Clarion, IA 50525
338 M. Lynn Reid
110 Highland Dr.
Union, SC 29379
339 Bennett Antiques
417 Marine Blvd.
Suisun City, CA 94585
340 Ragola Piano Co.
1111 Las Vegas Blvd.
Las Vegas, NV 89101
341 Elbinger Laboratories, Inc.
220 Albert St.
E. Lansing, MI 48823
342 Craig Willardson
P. O. Box 8296
Spokane, WA 99203
343 Puett Electronics
P. O. Box 28572
Dallas, TX 75228
344 "Gold Ole Stuff" Antique Lamp Supply
610 N. Meridian St.
Lebanon, IN 46052
345 B & L Antiquerie
6217 S. Lakeshore Dr.
Lexington, MI 48450
346 Muffs Antiques
135 S. Glassell
Orange, CA 92666
347 E. R. Clair
Box 171, R.D. 2
Howard, PA 16841
348 Back Number Wilkins
Box 247
Danvers, MA 01923
349 Grandpa's Attic
112-A E. Washington
Goshen, IN 46526
350 PAB
2915A Atlantic
Atlantic City, NJ 08401
351 Eugene Brown
Box 477
Dodge City, KS 67801
352 Reggio Register Co.
Box 511
Ayer, MA 01432
353 The Consortium
5 S. Wabash, Suite 1210
Chicago, IL 60603
354 M. McDowell
Box 138
Granger, WY 82934
355 Handcrafted Walls
P. O. Box 844
New Canaan, CT 06840
356 The Clock Shop
806 Main St.
Lake Geneva, WI 53147
357 Judy Giangivli
R. D. 6, Box 152
New Castle, PA 16101
358 Gen. Finley
6331 Shields Dr.
Huntington Beach, CA 92647
359 S-E Repair Services
Rt. 7, Box 147
Marshall, TX 75670

360 Dolls, Inc.
Rt. 3, Box 64-C
Sandpoint, ID 83864

361 Barb Barker
18 Farmstead Dr.
S. Windsor, CT 06074

362 This 'N That Shoppe
721 Jackson Ave.
Dixon, IL 61021

363 McKenzie Art Restoration Studio
2907 E. Monte Vista Dr.
Tucson, AZ 85716

364 Old Hotel Antiques
68 Main St.
Sutter Creek, CA 95685

365 The Silver Lady
P. O. Box 792
Friday Harbor, WA 98250

366 Sterling Locators
3300 W. Mockingbird, Suite B-101
Dallas, TX 75235

367 Smith's Book Service
Sunsmith House
Brewster, MA 02631

368 Atticana
P. O. Box 437
Sidney, OH 45365

369 Vintage Silver
33 LeMay Ct.
Williamsville, NY 14221

370 Betty Maki
1155 Willow St. #2
Faribault, MN 55021

371 Maurer TV
29 S. 4th
Lebanon, PA 17042

372 The Treasure Hunter
3783 Vivian Rd.
Monroe, MI 48161

373 Old Mill Books
Box 12353
Charleston, SC 29412

374 Marcy's Antiques
6777 Dumeny Rd.
Greencastle, PA 17225

375 Yesterday's Yankee
Lakeville, CT 06039

376 L. Pergl
Colesville Rd., R.D. 6
Binghamton, NY 13904

377 Vince's Glass Refurbishing
73 Rivermount Terrace
Burlington, VT 05401

378 Dori Miles
P. O. Box 159
Remsen, NY 13438

379 Grey Owl Indian Craft Co.
113-15 Springfield Blvd.
Queens Village, NY 11429

380 Aiku Amber Center
760 Market St., No. 617
San Francisco, CA 94102

381 Anglo-American Brass Co.
Box 9792
San Jose, CA 95157

382 Keystone
P. O. Box 3292
San Diego, CA 92103

383 Ita H. Aber Co.
1 Fanshaw Ave.
Yonkers, NY 10705

384 Archival Conservation Co., Inc.
8225 Daly Rd.
Cincinnati, OH 45231

385 The Book Doctor
984 High St.
Harrisburg, OH 43126

386 Abercrombie & Co.
8227 Fenton St.
Silver Spring, MD 20910

387 Carrousel Midwest
Highway 83, Box 97
North Lake, WI 53064

388 Gray Sales, Inc.
P. O. Box 4732
Surfside Beach, SC 29577

389 Just Enterprises
2790 Sherwin Ave., Unit 10
Ventura, CA 93003

390 Rosene Green Associates, Inc.
1622A Beacon St.
Brookline, MA 02146

391 Harry A. Eberhardt & Son, Inc.
2010 Walnut St.
Philadelphia, PA 19103

392 Kromer's Carriage Shop
Box 115, R.R. 4
Hodgenville, KY 42748

393 Furniture Revival and Co.
P. O. Box 994
Corvallis, OR 97330

394 A. Beshar & Co.
49 E. 53rd St.
New York, NY 10022

395 Fred & Nancy Dikeman
42-66 Phlox Place
Flushing, NY 11355

396 Marc King
Rt. 5, Box 48
Bluntstown, TN 37617

397 L. Eagle Feathers
758 E. Yale St.
Ontario, CA 91764

398 J & J Chrome Plating & Metal Finishing Corp.
101 Orange Ave.
West Haven, CT 06516

399 The Wicker Shop
2011 Cleveland Rd.
Sandusky, OH 44870

400 Paxton Hardware Co.
Upper Falls, MD 21156

401 Custom Book Binding
1618 W. Main St.
New Lebanon, OH 45345

402 Clock Wheel Cutting
1039 Route 163
Oakdale, CT 06370

403 The Jukebox Junkyard
P. O. Box 181
Lizella, GA 31052

404 Wicker King
8241 Highway 70 South
Nashville, TN 37221

405 Trunks by Paul
411 Marion Dr.
Longview, TX 75602

406 George Studios
45-04 97th Place
Corona, NY 11368

407 R. Bruce Hamilton
551 Main St.
W. Newbury, MA 01985

408 Gary's Restorations
P. O. Box 3843
San Bernardino, CA 92413

409 Noel Bennett
P. O. Box 1175
Corrales, NM 87048

410 Century Glass & Mirror, Inc.
1417 N. Washington
Dallas, TX 75204

411 Crystal Mountain Prisms
P. O. Box 31
Westfield, NY 14787

412 Glassmasters Guild
621 Avenue of the Americas
New York, NY 10011

413 John Morgan
443 Metropolitan Ave.
Brooklyn, NY 11211

414 All-Tek Finishing Co.
355 Bernard St.
Trenton, NJ 08618

415 The Condon Studios
33 Richdale Ave.
Cambridge, MA 02140

416 Sandra Brauer/Stained Glass
235 Dean St.
Brooklyn, NY 11217

Antique, Collectible Clubs, Publications

Your many letters tell us that you find this section invaluable. Great! When corresponding, *always* enclose a self-addressed, stamped envelope (SASE).

Some of you are having your letters of inquiry returned and we're truly sorry for that. Many clubs change officers and post office boxes and don't tell us. The post office will not forward mail to another address for more than one year.

We are delighted to know that you're making new friends, but please don't hold us responsible for any situations arising between you and any of the organizations listed in this Price Guide.

Clubs

Airplanes
Antique Airplane Association
Route 2, Box 172
Ottumwa, IA 52501

Akro Agate
Akro Agate Art Association
P. O. Box 758
Salem, NH 03079

Aladdin Lamps
Mystic Light of the Aladdin Knights
c/o J. W. Courter
Simpson, IL 62985

Horatio Alger
Horatio Alger Society
1 Kirkland Drive
Andover, MA 01810

Alice in Wonderland
Lewis Carroll Society of North America
617 Rockford Road
Silver Spring, MD 20902

Amusement Parks
National Amusement Park Historical Association
P.O. Box 83
Mt. Prospect, IL 60056

Angels
Angel Collectors Club
11334 Earlywood Drive
Dallas, TX 75218

Animal Licenses
International Society of Animal License Collectors
4420 Wisconsin
Tampa, FL 33616

Antique Auto Racing
Antique Auto Racing Association
Route 1, Box 116
Ixonia, WI 53036

Antique Automobiles
Antique Automobile Club of America
501 W. Governor Road
Hershey, PA 17033

Horseless Carriage Club of America
9031 E. Florence Avenue
Downey, CA 90240

Veteran Motor Car Club of America
105 Elm Street
Andover, MA 01810

Antiques and Collectibles —free catalog
Wallace-Homestead Book Company
580 Water's Edge Road
Lombard, Illinois 60148

Autograph Collectors
Manuscript Society
350 N. Niagara Street
Burbank, CA 91505

Universal Autograph Collectors Club
P.O. Box 467, WH
Rockville Centre, NY 11571

Autumn Leaf China
National Autumn Leaf Collectors
4002 35th Street
Rock Island, IL 61201
(publishes a newsletter)

Aviation
American Aviation Historical Society
P.O. Box 99
Garden Grove, CA 92642

Bands (Music)
Big Band Collectors Club
P.O. Box 3171
Pismo Beach, CA 93449

Banks
Mechanical Bank Collectors of America
P.O. Box 128
Allegan, MI 49010

Still Bank Collectors Club
c/o Andrew Moore, Beverly Bank
1357 W. 103rd Street
Chicago, IL 60643

Barbed Wire
International Barbed Wire Historical Society
c/o Jack Glover
Sunset, TX 76270

Barbershop
Barbershop Collectibles
c/o Robert E. Powell
P. O. Box 833
Hurst, TX 76053

Beads
The Bead Society of Southern California
P. O. Box 605
Venice, CA 90219

Bears
Good Bears of the World
P. O. Box 8236
Honolulu, HI 96815

Teddy Bear Boosters
P. O. Box 814
Redland, CA 92373

Beatles
International Beatles Club
3310 Roosevelt Court N.E.
Minneapolis, MN 55418

Beer Cans/Breweriana
American Breweriana Association
Box 6082
Colorado Springs, CO 80934

Beer Can Collectors of America
747 Merus Court
Fenton, MO 63026

Eastern Coast Breweriana Association
14 Manor Drive
Mount Airy, MD 21771

National Association of Breweriana Advertising
P. O. Box 521
New Carlisle, IN 46552

World Wide Beer Can Collectors
P. O. Box 1852
Independence, MO 64055

Belleek
Belleek Collectors' Society
10002 Howe Drive
Leawood, KS 66206

Bells
American Bell Association
Route 1, Box 286
Natronia Heights, PA 15065

Bibles
International Society of Bible Collectors
P. O. Box 2485
El Cajon, CA 92021

Bicycles
Antique Bicycle Club
260 W. 260th Street
Bronx, New York, NY 10471

Wheelmen
1708 School House Lane
Ambler, PA 19002

Blotters
Blotter Collectors
c/o R. J. Romey
2222 S. Millwood
Wichita, KS 67213

Blue and White Pottery
Blue and White Pottery Club
P. O. Box 297
Center Point, IA 52213

Blue Willow China
Blue Willow Society
6543 Indian Trail
Fallbrook, CA 92028

The Willow Society
359 Davenport Road, Suite 6
Toronto, Ontario, Canada M5R 1K5

Boats
Antique and Classic Boat Society
15 Normandy Parkway
Morristown, NJ 07960

Bottle Openers
Figural Bottle Opener Collectors Club
11 Mark Drive
Port Chester, NY 10573

Just for Openers
63 October Lane
Trumbull, CT 06611

Bottles
Antique Bottle Collecting (British)
Chapel House Farm, Newport Road
Albrighton, NR Wolverhampton
Staffordshire, England

Federation of Historical Bottle Clubs
50001 Queen Avenue N.
Minneapolis, MN 55430

Genessee Valley Bottle Collectors Association
P. O. Box 7528
Rochester, NY 14615

International Association, Jim Beam Bottles
5120 Belmont Road, Suite D
Downers Grove, IL 60515

National Ezra Brooks Bottle Club
420 W. 1st Street
Kewanee, IL 61443

National Ski Country Bottle Club
1224 Washington Avenue
Golden, CO 80410

Pennsylvania Bottle Collectors Association
743 Woodberry Road
York, PA 17403

Bricks
International Brick Collectors
c/o Dr. R. P. Anjard, Sr.
10942 Montego Drive
San Diego, CA 92124

Buffalo Bill
Buffalo Bill/Western Americana
P. O. Box 203
Pocahontas, IA 50574

National Association of Buffalo Bill Collectors
P. O. Box 6554
Woodland Hills, CA 91365

Business Cards
Business Card Collectors International
P. O. Box 466
Hollywood, FL 33022

Buttons
National Button Society
2733 Juno Place
Akron, OH 44313

Buttonhooks
The Buttonhook Society
83 Loose Road, Maidstone
Kent, England MEIS 7DA

Cabs
American British Cab Society
P. O. Box 904
Stamford, CT 06904

Cambridge Glass
National Cambridge Glass Collectors
P. O. Box 416
Cambridge, OH 43725

Candlewick Crystal
Candlewick Crystal Collectors
2817 Appletree Lane
South Bend, IN 46615

Candy Containers
Candy Container Collectors of America
P. O. Box 184
Lucerne Mines, PA 15754

Carnival Glass
American Carnival Glass Association
P. O. Box 273
Gnadenhutten, OH 44629

International Carnival Glass Association
Route 1
Mentone, IN 46539

National Carnival Glass Association
3142 S. 35th Street
LaCrosse, WI 54601

Carousels
National Carousel Association
c/o Frederick Fried
875 West End Avenue
New York, NY 10025

National Carousel Roundtable
448 Riverside Drive
Honesdale, PA 18431

Carriages, Horse-drawn
The American Driving Society
79 Southgate Avenue
Hastings-on-Hudson, NY 10706

Carriage Association of America
P. O. Box 3788
Portland, ME 04104

Cars, Professional
The Professional Car Society
12505 Bennett Road
Herndon, VA 22070

Cats
Cat Collectors
c/o Marilyn Dipboye
31311 Blair Drive
Warren, MI 48092

Ceramics
The Glaze
Haf-A Productions
P. O. Box 4929, G.S.
Springfield, MO 65808

Chess
Chess Set Collectors
c/o George A. Dean, MD
1135 Charrington
Birmingham, MI 48010

The Verein Chess Society
P. O. Box 2066
Chapel Hill, NC 27514

Chrysler Cars
W.P.C. Club
P. O. Box 4705
N. Hollywood, CA 91607

Cigar Bands/Labels/Seals
International Seal, Label and Cigar Band Society
8915 E. Bellevue Street
Tucson, AZ 85715

Cigarette Packs
Cigarette Pack Collectors of America
61 Searle Street
Georgetown, MA 01833

Cigarette Pack Collector's Club
c/o Richard Elliot
5 Governors Avenue
Winchester, MA 01890

Circus Fans
Circus Fans Association of America
500 Kathy Drive
Mesquite, TX 75149

Circus Fans of America
P. O. Box 69
Camp Hill, PA 17011

Citrus Labels
The Citrus Label Society
16633 Ventura Blvd., #1011
Encino, CA 91436

Civil War
Civil War Token Society
6222 Little River T'pike
Alexandria, VA 22312

Clocks/Watches
American Watch Association
39 Broadway
New York, NY 10016

National Association of Watch and Clock Collectors
514 Poplar Street
Columbia, PA 17512

Cloissoné
Cloissoné Collectors Club
1631 Mimulus Way
La Jolla, CA 02037

Coats of Arms
Ship's Chandler
Wilmington, VT 05363

Coin-Operated Games/Machines
For Amusement Only
1853 Ashby
Berkeley, CA 94703

Coins
American Numismatic Association
P. O. Box 2366
Colorado Springs, CO 80901

American Numismatic Society
617 W. 155th Street
New York, NY 10032

"Coke"
Coca-Cola Collectibles
P. O. Box 36M01
Los Angeles, CA 90036

The Cola Clan
3965 Pikes Peak
Memphis, TN 38108

Cookie Cutters
Cookie Cutter Collector's Club
5426 27th Street, NW
Washington, DC 20015

Bing Crosby
Bing Crosby Historical Society
P. O. Box 8013
Tacoma, WA 98408

Crosley Cars
Crosley Automobile Club
3323 Eaton Road
Williamson, NY 14589

Cut Glass
American Cut Glass Association
P. O. Box 7095
Shreveport, LA 71107

Degenhart Glass
The Friends of Degenhart
P. O. Box 186
Cambridge, OH 43725

Depression Glass
International Depression Glass Club
2737 Wissemann Drive
Sacramento, CA 95826

National Depression Glass Association
721 Cambridge Drive
Lee's Summit, MO 64063

Dionne Quints
Dionne Quint Collectors
P. O. Box 2527
Woburn, MA 01888

Disneyana
Disney Collectors Society
Sherman Turnpike
Danbury, CT 06816

The Mouse Club
13826 Ventura Blvd.
Sherman Oaks, CA 91423

Dogs
Country Scottie
P. O. Box 1512
Columbus, IN 47202

Dolls
Doll Artisan Guild
35 Main Street
Oneonta, NY 13820

Doll Collectors of America
14 Chestnut Road
Westford, MA 01886

Madame Alexander Fan Club
P. O. Box 146
New Lenox, IL 60451

United Federation of Doll Clubs
2814 Herron Lane
Glenshaw, PA 15116

Doorknobs
Antique Doorknob Collectors of America
P. O. Box 3088
Sedona, AZ 86340

Dorflinger Glass
Christian Dorflinger Glass Study Group
8701 Georgia Avenue, Suite 406
Silver Spring, MD 20910

Duncan Glass
National Duncan Glass Society
P. O. Box 965
Washington, PA 15301

Elephants
National Elephant Collectors Society
Box CY — 7
400 Commonwealth Avenue
Boston, MA 02215

Elongated Coins
Elongated Coin Collectors
4872 NW 171st Terrace
Miami, FL 33055

Ephemera (Short-lived)
Ephemera Society
124 Elm Street
Bennington, VT 05201

The Ephemera Society
12 Fitzroy Grove
London, W1, England

The Ephemera Society
P. O. Box 333
Wilbraham, MA 01095

Expositions
Expo Collectors and Historians Organization
1436 Killarney Avenue
Los Angeles, CA 90065

Fans
East Bay Fan Guild
P. O. Box 1054
El Cerrito, CA 94530

Fan Circle
24 Asmuns Hill
London NW11 6ET, England

Fast-Food
Fast-Food Memorabilia
5000 Y Street
Sacramento, CA 95817

Fenton Glass
Fenton Art Glass Collectors
P. O. Box 2441
Appleton, WI 54911

Ferrandiz
The Ferrandiz Collectors' Club
29210 Crow
Elkhart, IN 46514

Fire Marks
Fire Mark Circle of the Americas
530 Cypress Street
Philadelphia, PA 19106

Fishing Lures
National Fishing Lure Collectors Club
P. O. Box 71
Point Lookout, MO 65726

Flags
Flag Research Center
3 Edgehill Road
Winchester, MA 01890

Ford V-8s
Early Ford V-8 Club of America
P. O. Box 2122
San Leandro, CA 94577

Fostoria Glass
Fostoria Glass Society of America
P. O. Box 826
Moundsville, WV 26041

R. Atkinson Fox
Fox Hunt
c/o Rita Mortenson
805 Mill #202
Lee's Summit, MO 64063

Franklin Mint
The Franklin Mint Collectors Society
Franklin Center, PA 19091

Gambling
Gambler's Book Club
630 S. 11th Street, Box 4115
Las Vegas, NV 89106

Gar Wood Boats
Gar Wood Society
P. O. Box 6003, Teal Station
Syracuse, NY 13217

Gas Station
OPEC
Box 25763
Colorado Springs, CO 80936

Genealogy
Accelerated Indexing Systems
3346 S. Orchard Drive
Bountiful, UT 84010

National Genealogical Society
1921 Sunderland Place NW
Washington, DC 20036

German Military
Imperial German Military Collectors
P. O. Box 651
Shawnee Mission, KS 66201

Glass, Early American
Antique & Historical Glass Association
P. O. Box 7413
Toledo, OH 43615

National Early American Glass Club
55 Cliff Road
Wellesley Hills, MA 02181

Golf
Golf Collectors' Society
638 Wagner Road
Lafayette Hill, PA 19444

Gone With the Wind
GWTW Collectors Club
1 West Old Liberty Road
Sykesville, MD 21784

Graniteware
American Graniteware Association
525 Hawthorne Place, Apt. 1201
Chicago, IL 60657

Greentown Glass
National Greentown Glass Association
1807 W. Madison
Kokomo, IN 46901

Greeting Cards
Prank Mark Society
American Life Foundation
Watkins Glen, NY 14891

Guns
National Rifle Association
1600 Rhode Island Avenue, NW
Washington, DC 20036

Handbags
The Costume Society of America
c/o Metropolitan Museum of Art
New York, NY 10028

Harmonicas
Society, Preservation and Advancement of the Harmonica
P. O. Box 865
Troy, MI 48099

Hatpins/Hatpin Holders
International Club, Collectors of Hatpins/ Hatpin Holders
15237 Chanera Avenue
Gardena, CA 90249

Heisey Glass
Heisey Collectors of America
P. O. Box 27
Newark, OH 43055

Hubcaps
Hubcap Collectors Club
P. O. Box 54
Buckley, MI 49620

Hummel
Goebel (Hummel) Collectors' Club
105 White Plains Road
Tarrytown, NY 10591

Hummel Collectors Club
P. O. Box 257
Yardley, PA 19067

Hymns
Hymn Society of America
Wittenberg University
Springfield, OH 45501

Ice Cream
Ice Cream Collectors
1042 Old Hickory Road
Lancaster, PA 17601

Imperial Glass
Imperial Glass Collectors Society
P. O. Box 4012
Silver Spring, MD 20904

Infant Feeders
American Collectors of Infant Feeders
16 Algonquin Avenue
Andover, MA 01810

Inkwells
Society of Inkwell Collectors
5136 Thomas Avenue S.
Minneapolis, MN 55410

Insulators
Glass Insulators
c/o A. L. Rash
Route 3, Box 669
Silsbee, TX 77656

National Insulator Association
3557 Nicklaus Drive
Titusville, FL 32780

Yankee Pole Cat Insulator Club
5 Brownstone Road
E. Granby, CT 06026

Japan
Occupied Japan Collectors Club
18309 Faysmith Avenue
Torrance, CA 90504

Japanese Swords
Japanese Sword Society, U.S.
5907 Deerwood Drive
St. Louis, MO 63123

Jazz
New Orleans Jazz Club of California
P. O. Box 1225
Kerrville, TX 78028

Jazz Records
International Association of Jazz Record Collectors
90 Prince George Drive
Islongton, Ontario
M9B 2X8, Canada

Al Jolson
International Al Jolson Society
2981 Westmoor Drive
Columbus, OH 43204

Jukeboxes
Jukebox Collector
2545 SE 60th Court
Des Moines, IA 50317

Jukebox Trader
P. O. Box 1801
Des Moines, IA 50311

Kewpies
International Rose O'Neill Club
P. O. Box 688
Branson, MO 65616

Keys
Key Collectors International
P. O. Box 9397
Phoenix, AZ 85068

Kitchen Equipment
Early American Industries Association
P. O. Box 2128
Empire State Plaza Station
Albany, NY 12220

Knives
American Blade Collectors
112 Lee Parkway Drive
Stonewall Building
Chattanooga, TN 37421

Ka-Bar Knife Collectors Club
434 North 9th Street
Olean, NY 14760

Knife Collectors Club
1705 Highway 71 North
Springdale, AZ 72764

National Knife Collectors Association
P. O. Box 21070
Chattanooga, TN 37421

Lace
International Old Lacers
5206 Olley Lane
Burke, VA 22015

License Plates
Automobile License Plate Collectors Association
P. O. Box 712
Weston, WV 26452

Michigan License Plate Collectors Association
601 Duchess Road
Milford, MI 48042

Lighters
Lighter (tobacco) Collectors International
829 Rockaway Street
Grover City, CA 93433

Charles A. Lindbergh
Charles A. Lindbergh Association
P. O. Box 63
Genevieve, MO 63670

Lithophanes
Lithophane Collectors' Club
Blair Museum of Lithophanes
2032 Robinwood
Toledo, OH 43620

Locks
American Lock Collectors Association
14010 Cardwell Street
Livonia, MI 48154

Magic Lanterns
Magic Lantern Society
819 14th Street NE
Auburn, WA 98002

Manuscripts, Old
The Manuscript Society
350 N. Niagara Street
Burbank, CA 91505

Marbles
Marble Collectors
c/o Gary Huxford
503 W. Pine
Marengo, IA 52301

Marble Collectors Society of America
P. O. Box 222
Trumbull, CT 06611

Matchcovers
Rathkamp Matchcover Society
1312 E. 215th Place
Carson, CA 90745

Medals
American Numismatic Association
P. O. Box 2366
Colorado Springs, CO 80901

American Numismatic Society
617 W. 155th Street
New York, NY 10032

Medals and Tokens
Token and Medal Society
611 Oakwood Way
El Cajon, CA 92021

Military
American Military Historical Society
1528 El Camino
San Carlos, CA 94070

American Society of Military Insignia Collectors
526 Lafayette Avenue
Palmerton, PA 18071

Military Vehicles Collectors Club
P. O. Box 33697
Thornton, CO 80233

Milk Bottles
The Milk Route
4 Ox Bow Road
Westport, CT 06880

MOO
P. O. Box 5456
Newport News, VA 23605

National Milk Glass Collectors
c/o Walt Sill
P. O. Box 25266
Nashville, TN 37202

Mills

Society for Preservation of Old Mills
P. O. Box 435
Wiscasset, MA 04578

Miniature Figures

Miniature Figure Collectors of America
102 St. Paul's Road
Ardmore, PA 19003

National Association of Miniature Enthusiasts
P. O. Box 2621
Brookhurst Center, CA 92804

Tom Mix

Tom Mix Straightshooters Club
P. O. Box 15553
Belleville, IL 62224

Model A's

Model A Ford Club of America
250 S. Cypress Street
La Habra, CA 90631

Model A Restorers Club
24712 Michigan Avenue
Dearborn, MI 48124

Model Cars

Model Car Collectors Association
6434 Amherst Avenue
Columbia, MD 21046

Model/Toy Soldiers

American Model Soldier Society
1528 El Camino
San Carlos, CA 94070
Miniature Figure Collectors of America
P. O. Box 1245
North Wales, PA 19454

National Capital Military Collectors
P. O. Box 166
Rockville, MD 20850

Model T's

Model T Ford Club of America
P. O. Box 7400
Burbank, CA 91510

Motor Bikes/Motorcycles

Antique Motorcycle Club of America
2411 Middle Road
Davenport, IA 52803

Historic Motor Sports Association
P. O. Box 30628
Santa Barbara, CA 93105

Vintage Motor Bike Club
330 E. North Street
Coldwater, OH 45828

Movies

Film Collector's World
Rapid City, IL 61278
Hollywood Studio Collectors Club
P. O. Box 5815
Sherman Oaks, CA 91403

Motion Picture Collectibles Association
P. O. Box 33433
Raleigh, NC 27606

National Film Society
7800 Couser Drive
Shawnee Mission, KS 66204

Old Time Western Film Club
P. O. Box 142
Silver City, NC 27344

Studio Collectors Club
P. O. Box 1566
Apple Valley, CA 92307

Music Boxes

Automatic Musical Instrument Collectors Association
P. O. Box 172
Columbia, SC 29202

Musical Box Society, International
Route 3, Box 202
Morgantown, IN 46160

Musical Instruments

American Musical Instrument Society
University of South Dakota, Box 194
Vermillion, SD 57069

Automatic Musical Instrument Collectors Association (AMICA)
P. O. Box 172
Columbia, SC 29202

Nails

Texas Date Nail Collectors
501 W. Horton Street
Brenham, TX 77833

Nautical

National Maritime Historical Society
2 Fulton Street
Brooklyn, NY 11201

Needlework
Collector Circle
1313 S. Killian Drive
Lake Park, FL 33403

Netsukes
International Netsuke Collectors Society
P. O. Box 10426
Honolulu, HI 96816

Newspapers
Newspaper Collectors Club
P. O. Box 7271
Phoenix, AZ 85011

Nippon
International Nippon Collectors
P. O. Box 102
Rexford, NY 12148

Occupied Japan
Occupied Japan Club
3536 Ramona Avenue
Louisville, KY 40220

The Occupied Japan Club
18309 Faysmith
Torrance, CA 90504

Old Sleepy Eye Pottery
Old Sleepy Eye Club
P. O. Box 12
Monmouth, IL 61462

Olds, Curved Dash
Curved Dash Oldsmobile Club
3455 Florida Avenue
Minneapolis, MN 55427

Owls
Owl Collectors Club
Box 5491
Fresno, CA 93755

Russell's Owl Collectors Club
P. O. Box 1292
Bandon, OR 97411

Pairpoint
Pairpoint Cup Plate Collectors of America
5906 Arbroath Drive
Clinton, MD 20735

Paper Money
Society of Paper Money Collectors
P. O. Box 4082
Harrisburg, PA 17111

Paper/Advertising
National Association of Paper & Advertising Collectors
P. O. Box 471
Columbia, PA 17512

Paperweights
Paperweight Collectors' Association
P. O. Box 128
Scarsdale, NY 10583

Paperweight Collectors' Society
P. O. Box 11
Bellaire, TX 77401

Pencils
American Pencil Collectors Society
1037 N. Main, Apt. C5
Brookings, SD 57006

Society for the Collection of Brand-Name Pencils
4601 W. 101st Street
Oak Lawn, IL 60453

Pens
The Pen Fancier's Club
1169 Overcash Drive
Dunedin, FL 33528

Pewter
Pewter Collectors Club of America
Old Bull House, Main Street
Centerbrook, CT 06409

Phonographs
Antique Phonograph Collectors Club
650 Ocean Avenue
Brooklyn, NY 11226

City of London Phonograph/Gramophone Society
157 Childwall Valley Road
Liverpool, England L16 1LA

Michigan Antique Phonograph Society
Lansing, MI 48909

Phonograph Society of South Australia
P. O. Box 253, Prospect 5082
Australia

Photographic
Photographic Historical Society
P. O. Box 1839, Radio City Station
New York, NY 10019

Western Photographic Collectors Association
P. O. Box 4294
Whittier, CA 90607

Pins
International Pin Collectors
P. O. Box 227
Marcy, NY 13403

Pipe Smokers
International Association of Pipe Smoker's Clubs
647 S. Saginaw Street
Flint, MI 48502

Universal Coterie of Pipe Smokers
20-37 120th Street
College Point, NY 11356

Planters Peanuts
Peanut Pal
P. O. Box 4465
Huntsville, AL 35802

Plates
International Plate Collectors Guild
5581 Sandoval Avenue
Riverside, CA 92509

The Plate Collector
P. O. Box 1041, ACC
Kermit, TX 79745

Plate Insider's Club
P. O. Box 981
Kermit, TX 79745

Playing Cards
Chicago Playing Card Collectors, Inc.
1559 W. Pratt Blvd.
Chicago, IL 60620

Playing Card Collector's Association
813 W. Orchard Street
Milwaukee, WI 53204

The Playing Card Society
188 Sheen Lane, East Sheen
London SW14 8LF, England

Police Insignia
Police Insignia Collector's Association
135 Tate Avenue
Buchanan, NY 10511

Political Items
American Political Items Collectors
1054 Sharpsburg Drive
Huntsville, AL 35803

The Political Collector
444 Lincoln Street
York, PA 17404

Postcards
Angels Flight Postcard Club
2027 Appletown Street, #5
Long Beach, CA 90803

Connecticut Postcard Club
P. O. Box 842
Shelton, CT 06484

Deltiologists of America
3709 Gradyville Road
Newton Square, PA 19073

Metropolitan Postcard Collector's Club
c/o Ben Papell
146 – 17 Delaware Avenue
Flushing, NY 11355

Postcard History Society
P. O. Box 3610
Baltimore, MD 21214
(publishes a newsletter before shows)

Pottery/Porcelain
American Art Pottery Association
P. O. Box 714
Silver Spring, MD 20901

Porcelain Club of America
P. O. Box 736
Syosset, NY 11791

Pre-Columbian Art
The Pre-Columbian Art Collectors of America
P. O. Box 11
Farmington, MI 55024

Prints, Historical
American Historical Print Collectors Society
555 Fifth Avenue
New York, NY 10017

Puppets
Puppeteers of America
2311 Connecticut Avenue NW, #501
Washington, DC 20008

Radios/Phonographs
Antique Radio Club of America
1 Steeplechase Road
Devon, PA 19333

Antique Wireless Association
Main Street
Holcomb, NY 14469

Association for Recorded Sound Collections
P. O. Box 1643
Manassas, VA 22110

Radio Club of America
P. O. Box 2112, Grand Central Station
New York, NY 10017

Vintage Radio and Phonograph Society
P. O. Box 5345
Irving, TX 75062

Railroadiana

American Association of Private Railroad Cars
224 Orr Drive
Somerville, NJ 08876

The Horn and Whistle
140 Forest Avenue
Glen Ridge, NJ 07028

Key, Lock and Lantern
P. O. Box 15
Spencerport, NY 14559

National Railway Society
P. O. Box 5181
Denver, CO 80217

Railroadiana Collectors Association
405 Byron Avenue
Mobile, AL 36609

Railroadiana Collectors Association
Box 365
St. Ignatius, MT 59865

Reamers

National Reamer Collectors Association
277 Highland Avenue
Wadsworth, OH 44281

National Reamer Collectors Association
112 S. Center
Lacon, IL 61540

Red Wing Pottery

Red Wing Collectors
c/o David A. Newkirk
Route 3, Box 141
Monticello, MN 55362

Norman Rockwell

Norman Rockwell Memorial Society
12109 Wasatch Street
Tampa, FL 33624

The Rockwell Society of America
Box B
Stony Brook, NY 11790

Rogers Statuaries

The Rogers Group
13 Oenoke Ridge
New Canaan, CT 06840

Royal Doulton

Royal Doulton International Collectors Club
U. S. Branch, P. O. Box 1815
Somerset, NJ 08873

Royal Souvenirs

Commemorative Collectors Society
25 Farndale Close
Long Eaton, NG10 3PA, United Kingdom

Roycrofters

Roycrofters at Large Association
Erie City
East Aurora, NY 14052

Salt Dishes

New England Society of Open Salts Collectors
c/o Otto W. Olson, Jr.
Olson's Way
East Greenwich, RI 02818

Society of Open Salt Collectors
P. O. Box 553
Marietta, OH 45750

Scales

International Society, Antique Scale Collectors
25W620 Indian Hill Woods
Naperville, IL 60540

Scientific Instrument Society
National Maritime Museum
Greenwich, England

Seats

Cast Iron Seat Collectors
P. O. Box 14
Ionia, MO 65335

Sebastian Porcelain

Sebastian Collectors Society
321 Central
Hudson, MA 01749

Shaving Mugs

National Association of Shaving Mug Collectors
c/o Deryl Clark
Rt. 6, Box 176
Bedford, PA 15522

Sheet Music
National Sheet Music Society
1597 Fair Park Avenue
Los Angeles, CA 90041

Signs, Porcelain
Porcelain Advertising Collectors Club
P. O. Box 381
Marshfield Hills, MA 02051

Snuff Bottles
International Chinese Snuff Bottle Society
2601 N. Charles Street
Baltimore, MD 21218

Spark Plugs
Spark Plug Collectors of America
P. O. Box 2229
Ann Arbor, MI 48106

Spoons
American Spoon Collectors
P. O. Box 260
Warrensburg, MO 64093

Souvenir Spoon Collectors of America
P. O. Box 814
Temple City, CA 91780

The Scoop Club
84 Oak Avenue
Shelton, CT 06484

The Spooner
Route 1, Box 61
Shullsburg, WI 53586

Stained Glass
Stained Glass Association of America
1125 Wilmington Avenue
St. Louis, MO 63111

Stamps
American Philatelic Society
P. O. Box 800
State College, PA 16801

The Collectors Club
22 East 35th Street
New York, NY 10016

International Stamp Collectors
P. O. Box 854
Van Nuys, CA 91408

The Philaletic Foundation
270 Madison Avenue
New York, NY 10016

Society of Philatelic Americans
P. O. Box 9041
Wilmington, DE 19809

Steamships
Steamship Historical Society of America
414 Pelton Avenue
Staten Island, NY 10310

Titanic Historical Society
P. O. Box 53
Indian Orchard, MA 01151

World Ocean and Cruise Liner Society
P. O. Box 92
Stamford, CT 06904

Steins
Stein Collectors International
P. O. Box 463
Kingston, NJ 08528

Stereoscopics
National Stereoscopic Association
1345 Tiverton Square, N.
Columbus, OH 43229

Stevengraphs
Stevengraph Collector's Association
Daisy Lane
Irvington-on-Hudson, NY 10533

Sugar Packets
Sugar Packet Collectors Club
6033 105th Street
Kansas City, MO 64131

Swords
Association of American Sword Collectors
P. O. Box 341
Delmar, DE 19940

Tea Leaf (Ironstone)
Tea Leaf Club International
10747 Riverview
Kansas City, KS 66111

Telephones/Telegraphs
Antique Telephone Collectors Association
614 Main
LaCrosse, KS 67548

Morse Telegraph Club, Inc.
712 S. 49th Street
Lincoln, NE 68510

Shirley Temple
Shirley Temple Collectors' Club
P. O. Box 524
Anchorage, AK 99510

Thimbles
Collector Circle
1313 S. Killian Drive
Lake Park, FL 33403

Thimble Collectors International
P. O. Box 143
Intervale, NH 03845

Timepieces
National Association of Watch & Clock Collectors
Columbia, PA 17512

Timetables
National Association of Timetable Collectors
21 E. Robin Road
Holland, PA 18966

Tin Containers
Tin Container Collectors Association
P. O. Box 4555
Denver, CO 80204

Titanic
Titanic Historical Society
P. O. Box 53
Indian Orchard, MA 01151

Tobacco
Tobacco Collectors
713 Parrott Avenue
Kinston, NC 28501

Tokens/Medals
American Tax Token Society
P. O. Box 26523
Lakewood, CO 80226

American Vecturist Association
P. O. Box 1204
Boston, MA 02104

Society of Ration Token Collectors
P. O. Box 1
Tecumseh, MI 49286

Token and Medal Society
P. O. Box 127
Scandinavia, WI 54977

Tools
Early American Industries Association
P. O. Box 2128, Empire State Plaza Station
Albany, NY 12220

Toothpick Holders
National Toothpick Holder Collectors' Society
Red Arrow Highway
Saywer, MI 49125

Toy Trains
Lionel Collectors Club of America
814 26th Street
Peru, IL 61354

The Toy Train Operating Society
25 W. Walnut Street, Room 306
Pasadena, CA 91103

Train Collectors Association
P. O. Box 248
Strasburg, PA 17579

Toys
Antique Toy Collectors of America
Route 2, Box 5A
Parkton, MD 21120

International Toy Buffs Association
25 W. Walnut Street, Room 306
Pasadena, CA 91103

Matchbox Collectors Club
P. O. Box 119
Wood Ridge, NJ 07075

Trades/Crafts
Trades & Crafts Society
605 Heathcliff Drive
Seaford, NY 11783

Trucks
American Truck Historical Society
201 Office Park Drive
Birmingham, AL 35223

Typewriters
The Typewriter Exchange
Box 150
Arcadia, CA 91006

Unique/Unusual
The Trivials
603 E. 105th Street
Kansas City, MO 64131

Valentines
Antique Valentine Association
P. O. Box 178
Marlboro, NJ 07746

National Valentine Collectors Association
P. O. Box 1404
Santa Ana, CA 92702

Wallace Nutting
Wallace Nutting Collectors Club
Kampfe Lake, East Shore Drive
Bloomingdale, NJ 07403

Watch Fobs
International Watch Fob Association
5892 Stow Road
Hudson, OH 44236

Watches
American Watch Association
39 Broadway
New York, NY 10016

National Association of Watch and Clock Collectors
Columbia, PA 17512

Wedgwood
Wedgwood International Seminar
New York, NY 10003

Wedgwood Society of Philadelphia
246 N. Bowman Avenue
Merion, PA 19066

Whistles
Whistle Collectors
c/o Carlin N. Morton
121 Sea Horse Lane
Fort Myers Beach, FL 33931

Wild Turkey Whiskey
Wild Turkey Ceramic Society
P. O. Box 353
Lawrenceberg, KY 40342

Wine, French
Vin Mariani Wine Collectors
1724 20th Street, NW
Washington, DC 20009

Wizard of Oz
International Wizard of Oz Club
220 N. 11th Street
Escanaba, MI 49829

Woodcarvers
National Woodcarvers Association
718 Fitzwatertown Road
Willow Grove, PA 19099

Wooden Money
American Wooden Money Guild
P. O. Box 3445
Tuscon, AZ 85722

Dedicated Wooden Money Collectors
5575 State Route 257
Radnor, OH 43066

New York State Wooden Money Society
25 N. Wayne Avenue
West Haverstraw, NY 10993

Pioneer Wooden Money Society
787 Null Road
New Cumberland, PA 17070

Wooten Desks
Wooten Desk Owners Society
9-20 166th Street
Whitestone, NY 11357

World's Fair
World's Fair Collectors Society
148 Poplar Street
Garden City, NY 11530

Publications

Antiques/Collectibles, General
American Art & Antiques
1515 Broadway
New York, NY 10036

Antique Monthly
Tuscaloosa, AL 35401

Antiques and the Arts Weekly
Bee Publishing Co.
Newtown, CT 06470

Collectors News
Grundy Center, IA 50638

Hobbies
1006 S. Michigan Avenue
Chicago, IL 60605

The Magazine Antiques
551 Fifth Avenue
New York, NY 10017

Joel Sater's Antique News
Marietta, PA 17547

The Southeast Trader
Lexington, SC 29072

Spinning Wheel
Hanover, PA 17331

Tri-State Trader
Knightstown, IN 46148

Avon Bottles
The Avon Times
P. O. Box 12088
Overland Park, KS 66212

Western World Avon Collectors Newsletter
P. O. Box 27587
San Francisco, CA 94127

Baseball
Baseball Card News
P. O. Box 2510
Del Mar, CA 92014

Bears

Bear Tracks — see Good Bears of the World (club)

Teddy Bear Newsletter
254 W. Sidney Street
St. Paul, MN 55107

The Teddy Tribune
254 W. Sidney Street
St. Paul, MN 55107

Beer Cans

WWBCC Newsletter
P. O. Box 1852
Independence, MO 64055

Black Memorabilia

Black Memorabilia Collectors Monthly Newsletter
156 Schmitz Place
Mt. Arlington, NJ 07865

Blue Ridge Pottery

National Blue Ridge Newsletter
Route # 5, Box 298
Blountsville, TN 37617

Books

AB Bookman's Weekly
P. O. Box AB
Clifton, NJ 07015

Bottles

Bottle News
Kermit, TX 79745

Bottle World
5003 W. Berwyn
Chicago, IL 60630

Old Bottle Magazine
P. O. Box 243
Bend, OR 97701

Campbell Kids

Kiddieland Souper Special
11892 Barlett Street
Garden Grove, CA 92645

Chess

The Chess Newsletter
320 W. 86th Street
New York, NY 10024

China/Porcelain

The Dispatch
P. O. Box 106
Buttsville, NJ 07829

Christmas

Spirit of Christmas Past
P. O. Box 1255
Santa Ana, CA 92701

Coin Amusements

The Coin Slot
P. O. Box 612
Wheatridge, CO 80033

Coins

Bowers & Ruddy Galleries
6922 Hollywood Blvd.
Los Angeles, CA 90028

Comics

Collector's Dream Magazine
P. O. Box 127, Station T
Toronto, Ont. M6B 3Z9, Canada

The Comics Journal
P. O. Box 292
Riverdale, MD 10840

Decorations/Medals

Seven Seas Corp.
P. O. Box 920
Williamsburg, VA 23185

Depression Glass

Depression Glass Daze
P. O. Box 57
Otisville, MI 48463

Dolls

Collectors United
P. O. Box 1160
Chatsworth, GA 30705

Doll Castle News
P. O. Box 247
Washington, NJ 07882

Doll Times
P. O. Box 276
Montgomery, IL 60538

Midwest Paper Dolls & Toys Quarterly
P. O. Box 131
Galesburg, KS 66740

Paper Doll Gazette
c/o Shirley Hedge
Route 2
Princeton, IN 47670

Paper Doll Quarterly
3135 Oakcrest Drive
Hollywood, CA 90068

Doulton
Doulton Collectors Newsletter
P. O. Box 2644
Ft. Myers, FL 33902

Fans (the cooling kind)
The Fan Collectors Society
c/o The Fan Man
4606 Travis
Dallas, TX 75205

Fiesta Ware
Fiesta Collectors & Dealers Newsletters
P. O. Box 100582
Nashville, TN 37210

Fiesta Dispatch
P. O. Box 2625
Toledo, OH 43606

Folk Art
The Clarion Museum of American Folk Art
49 W. 53rd Street
New York, NY 10019

Glass
Glass Review Magazine
P. O. Box 542
Marietta, OH 45750

Houses, Old
The Old-House Journal
69A 7th Avenue
Brooklyn, NY 11217

Indians
American Indian Art Magazine
7333 E. Monterey Way, #5
Scottsdale, AZ 85251

American Indian Basketry Magazine
P. O. Box 66124
Portland, OR 97266

The Indian Trader
P. O. Box 31235
Billings, MT 59107

Jukeboxes
Jukebox Collector
2545 SE 60th Court
Des Moines, IA 50317

Nickel A Tune
9514-9 Reseda Boulevard #613
Northridge, CA 91324

Kitchen Collectibles
Kitchen Collectible News
P. O. Box 383
Murray Hill
New York, NY 10016

Knives
Knife World
P. O. Box 3395
Knoxville, TN 37917

The American Blade
13222 Saticoy Street
N. Hollywood, CA 91605

Lace/Linen
Lace & Linen Newsletter
P. O. Box 7572
Dallas, TX 75209

McCoy Pottery
McCoy Collectors Newsletter
6270 Rogers Park Place
Cincinnati, OH 45213

Military/Nautical
N. Flayderman & Co.
P. O. Box 1000
New Milford, CT 06776

The House of Swords & Militaria
2804 Hawthorne
Independence, MO 64052

MCN Press
P. O. Box 7582
Tulsa, OK 74105

Military Medals
P. O. Box 387
Baldwin, NY 11510

Seven Seas Corp.
P. O. Box 920
Williamsburg, VA 23185

The Soldier Shop
1013 Madison Avenue
New York, NY 10021

Milk
The Milk Route
4 Ox Bow Road
Westport, CT 06880

Movies
The Big Reel
Summerfield, NC 27358

Classic Film/Video Images
Muscatine, IA 52761

Music
Jean Musical News
Box 366
Mason, MI 48854

Jerry's Musical News
4624 Woodland Road
Edina, MN 55424

Music Machines, Mechanical
The Vestal Press
P. O. Box 97, 230 N. Jensen Blvd.
Vestal, NY 13850

Music Rolls
Automatic Music Roll Co.
P. O. Box 3194
Seattle, WA 98114

Musical Instruments
Mugwumps
1600 Billman's Lane
Silver Spring, MD 20902

Owls
The Owl's Nest
P. O. Box 5491
Fresno, CA 93755

Nippon
Nippon Notebook
P. O. Box 102
Rexford, NY 12148

Paper Money
Bank Note Reporter
Krause Publications
Iola, WI 54945

Pens
Fountain Pen Exchange
P. O. Box 22
Oradell, NJ 07649

Phonographs
Phonograph Monthly
502 E. 17th Street
Brooklyn, NY 11226

Talking Machine Review
19 Glendale Road
Bournemouth, England BH6 4SA

Photographic
The Photographic Collector
P. O. Box B
Granby, MA 01033

Pinball
Pinball Collectors Quarterly
P. O. Box 137-0
Lagrangeville, NY 12540

Postcards
American Post Card Journal
P. O. Box 20
Syracuse, NY 13201

Post Card Collectors Gazette
P. O. Box 46
Ames, IA 50010

Postcard Collector
700 E. State Street
Iola, WI 54990

Postcard World Newsletter
P. O. Box 654
Cazenovia, NY 13035

Pottery
American Clay Exchange
800 Murray Drive
El Cajon, CA 92020

The Glaze
P. O. Box 4929 G.S.
Springfield, MO 65808

National Blue Ridge Newsletter
c/o Norma Lilly
Route 5, Box 298
Blountville, TN 37617

Pottery Collectors Newsletter
P. O. Box 446
Asheville, NC 28802

Prints
American Print Review
P. O. Box 6909
Chicago, IL 60680

Print Collectors Newsletter
205 E. 78th Street
New York, NY 10021

Quilts
The Quilter's Newsletter
P. O. Box 394
Wheat Ridge, CO 80033

Radios/Phonographs
Radio Age
1220 Meigs Street
Augusta, GA 30904

The Antique Phonograph Monthly
650 Ocean Avenue
Brooklyn, NY 11226

Edison Phonograph Monthly
44 Arctic Springs
Jefferson, IN 47130

Schoenhut Toys
Schoenhut Newsletter
c/o Robert W. Zimmerman
45 Louis Avenue
West Seneca, NY 14224

Scouts
Scout Memorabilia Magazine
7305 Bounty Drive
Sarasota, FL 33581

Shaker
The Shaker Messenger
P. O. Box 45
Holland, MI 49423

Sheet Music
Sheet Music Exchange
P. O. Box 2136
Winchester, VA 22601

Silver
The Magazine SILVER
P. O. Box 22217
Milwaukie, OR 97222

Slot Machines
Amusement Review Magazine
1853 Ashby
Berkeley, CA 94703

Loose Change Magazine
21176 S. Alameda Street
Long Beach, CA 90810

Stamps
Mekeel's Weekly Stamp News
P. O. Box 1660
Portland, Maine 04104

Minkus Stamp Journal
Minkus Publications, Inc.
New York, NY 10001

Scott's Monthly Stamp Journal
Scott's Publishing Co.
New York, NY 10022

Stamp Collector Newspaper
P. O. Box 10
Albany, OR 97321

Stamps Magazine
c/o H. L. Lindquist Publications, Inc.
New York, NY 10014

Steins
Glentiques, Ltd.
P. O. Box 337
Glenford, NY 12433

Thimbles
The Thimble Guild
315 Park End Drive
Dayton, OH 45415

Thimbletter
93 Walnut Hill Road
Newton Highlands, MA 02161

Tools
Antique Tools Newsletter
c/o Iron Horse Antiques
Route 2
Poultney, VT 05764

Toy Soldiers
Old Toy Soldier Newsletter
209 N. Lombard
Oak Park, IL 60302

Toys
Antique Toy World
3941 Belle Plaine
Chicago, IL 60618

Midwest Paper Dolls & Toys Quarterly
P. O. Box 131
Galesburg, KS 66740

Collectibles from A to Z

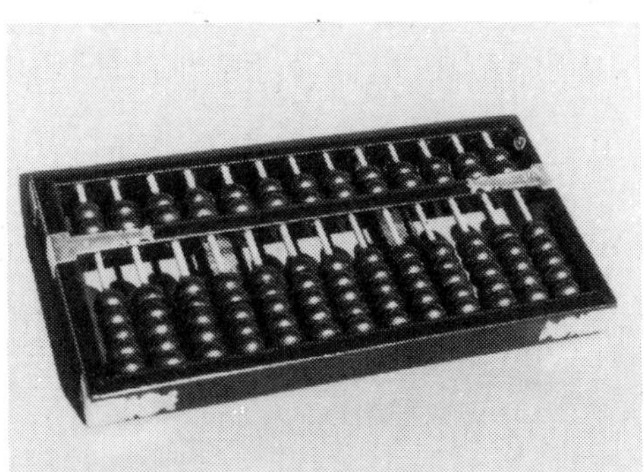

Abacus

Abacus

These Oriental "computers," a counting frame with movable wooden beads, have been around for centuries. All are collectible, and the older the better.

Teakwood frame and beads, brass rods, new	**$32-41**
Ornate teakwood frame inlaid with mother-of-pearl, old	**55-63**
Ebony frame and beads, early 1900's	**40-49**
Mahogany frame and beads, mass-produced, new	**22-29**

Advertising Items

Offset lithography, a method of printing on tin, was discovered in 1875; trade cards originated in the 1870's; postcards could be sent through the mail in the 1870's; celluloid opened an entirely new field in the late 1890's.

All these, and more, created a new field for advertisers at the turn of the century. Most items listed here were given away

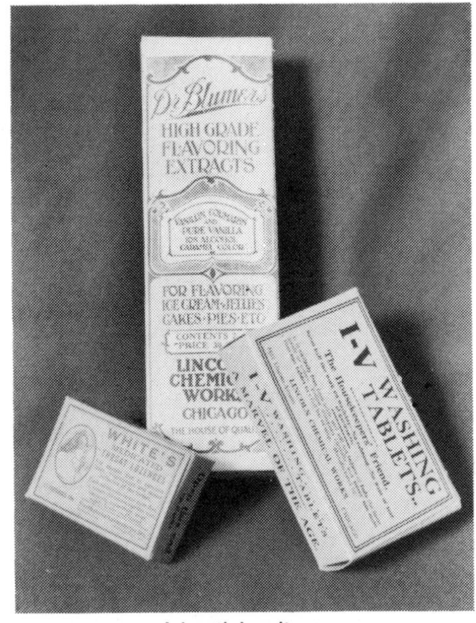

Advertising items

free to customers. Today, all are collectible. Prices given are for items in good to fine condition, with small chips, dents, scratches, or tears taken into consideration. See **Clubs and Publications,** this Price Guide. There are many organizations to do with advertising items, such as **Bottle Openers, Breweriana, Knives, Paper/Advertising, Planters Peanuts, Tin Containers, Watch Fobs,** and many more.

Advertising items

Cartridges and Primed Shells for Ballard Rifles.
RIM FIRE.
CENTER FIRE.

Ammunition

Ammunition/Gun Catalogs

It's fun to collect the catalogs, but NEVER purchase old ammunition or old guns unless you know what you're doing. Old ammo can explode **any** time and old guns that haven't been "head-spaced" by an expert are DANGEROUS!

This editor will not attempt to tell Flea Market operators what they should or should not allow to be sold, BUT this editor will tell the general buying public to be **very** cautious around guns and ammunition. The UNLOADED gun is the one that puts you in the cemetery!

Ballard Rifles $5- 8
Sharps' Rifle Manufacturing Co., Hartford, Conn. 5- 7
The Massachusetts Arms Co. (The Maynard), Chicopee Falls, Mass. 5- 7
The Marlin Firearms Co., New Haven, Conn. 5- 7
Ideal Reloading Implements, Ideal Mfg. Co., New Haven, Conn. 5- 7
J. Stevens Arms and Tool Co., Chicopee Falls, Mass. 5- 7
Colt's Revolving and Breech-Loading Firearms and Co. 6-11

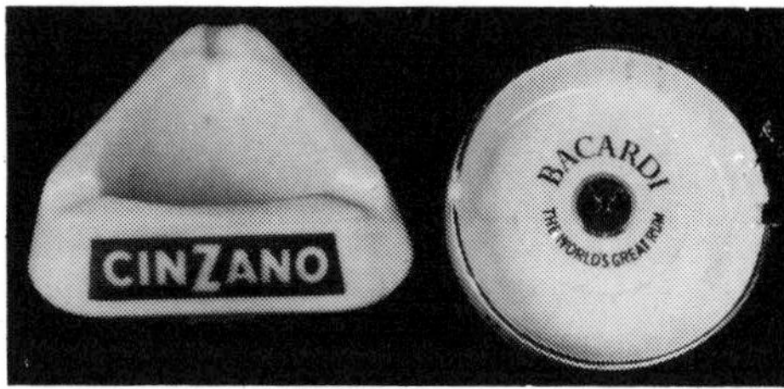

Ashtrays

Ashtrays

Every restaurant, hotel, motel, etc., has them. If you get caught, don't blame me. Lots of firms used them as advertisements; some still do. The older the better.

Boston Red Sox, plaster, 1930's $8-10
Bacardi Rum, porcelain, made in Ireland, 1960's (illus.) 3- 5
CinZano Vermouth, glass, Italian, 1950's (illus.) 3- 5
Firestone Rubber Co., rubber/ glass insert, 1930's 7- 9
Hotel Astor, New York, porcelain, 1920's 7-10
Travel Lodge, glass, 1960's 1- 2
Waldorf-Astoria Hotel, New York, glass, 1930's 5- 6
Looking for a "new" hobby? Here it is!

Breweriana

Beer bottle labels, before 1950, each	75¢- 1
Cardboard coasters, most brands, pre-World War II era, each	50¢- 1
Paper sign, Krantz Brewing Co., 25½″ × 37″	54- 62
Paper sign, Old Dutch Beer, 16¼″ × 22″	85- 92
Paper sign, Pabst Brewing Co., 28″ × 36½″	850-925
Paper sign, Rettig Brewing Co., 15″ × 18″	245-255
Tin sign, Burger Brewing Co., 15″ × 17″	70- 80
Tin sign, Falstaff Brewing Co., 24″ dia. (being reproduced)	240-250
Tin sign, Felsenbrau Beer, 11½″ × 17½″	45- 52
Tray, Anheuser Busch, oval, 15½″ wide	420-440
Tray, Elk Run Brewing Co., 12″ dia.	125-135
Tray, Iroquois Brewery, 12″ dia.	150-160
Tray, Rubsam & Horrmann, c. 1911, 12½″ dia.	347-360

Brochures

Brochures

Booklets, pamphlets, fold-ups; anything that described the product in detail.

Vulcan Plow Co. brochure, paper, 1900's	$3-4
Ford Motor Co. pamphlet, paper. Describes Model A, 1929	4-5
WM Deering & Co. Catalog, 1900's (illus.)	3-4

Keep in mind that age and condition dictate the value.

Buttons

Buttons

Countless thousands were made, advertising almost every product in the world.

Caps

Caps

For some reason we enjoy advertising a company's product. At last count there were more than 1,500 different caps on the market.

Some are giveaways; average price	$4-7

Cigar Box Labels

See **Tobacco.**

Cigarette Cards

Between the Acts, theater personalities, each	$ 5- 6
Gypsy Queen, 1887, each	80- 90
Helmar Turkish Cigarettes, 1916, each	2.50-3
Old Judge, 1887, each	21- 27
Strollers, 1913, each	2.50-3

Glass

Glass

For over 200 years companies have used glass to advertise their products. Some were used as containers, other as "give aways" to promote the product. The earlier the better. Recently, a glass flask sold for over $21,000 in New England.

- Bitters bottle, advertising "Goff's Herbal," embossed, aqua $23-30
- Bitters bottle, advertising "Prickly Ash," quart, amber ... 42-50
- Lincoln bust, used as bank, 7½" high, clear, 1900's 18-25
- Moxie drinking mug, 1900's 6- 9
- Magnifying glass, insurance advertisement, ¼" diameter, 1920's 5- 9
- Paperweight, Bunker Hill Insurance Co., 3" high, 1920's 12-22
- Whiskey flask, Springfield Bottle Works, 7" high, amber, mid-1800's (Illus.) 80-90
- Whiskey flask, "Ain't What It Used To Be," 6" high, amber, mid-1800's 70-80

In less than twenty years, glass will be a thing of the past. Start collecting it now!

Pepsi-Cola

- Button, celluloid, "Drink Pepsi Today" .... $ 2.50-3
- Button, celluloid, Bigger, Better Pepsi-Cola 2.50-3
- Key chain, c. 1940 .... 13- 16
- Sign, wall, "Pepsi-Cola, 12 oz., 5¢" 37- 42
- Tray, 1906 175-184
- Tray, 1925 .... 47- 56
- Watch fob, Jamestown Exposition, 1907 .... 61- 69

Posters

- Cardboard, wall, Clyde Beatty Circus, standard size .... $ 3.50-4
- Cardboard, wall, Golden Crescent Oranges, 14" x 28" 18- 25
- Cardboard, wall, Herkimer's Shoe Polish, 18" x 37" 21- 27
- Paper, billboard size, Frank Buck Circus 175-183

Trade Cards

These were small, thin pieces of cardboard that advertised a manufacturer's product. From the late 1880's until the 1920's, about every company gave them away with every purchase. Those made in sets are harder to find than the individual cards. Few are dated. They come in all sizes and shapes. Prices given are for those in good condition.

Baking

- Babbitt's Baking Powder, girl with kitten $1-1.50
- Czar Baking Powder, black lady cook in kitchen 1.50-2
- Gold Mine Flour, miners panning for gold 1.50-2

Clothing

- Boston & Meriden Clothing Co., small girl wearing glasses $1.50-2
- Gerber Hats, man playing accordion 1.50-2

Hucklemyer Clothiers, man wearing top hat 1.50-2
Myers-Cohen Haberdashers, goat wearing brown derby 1.50-2
Orr's Pantaloon Overalls, men, tug-of-war 1.50-2
Rhostberg & Kline Men's Suits, 3 men on bicycles 1.50-2
Union Clothing Co., young lovers on bridge 1.50-2

Coffee

Arbuckle Bros., girl riding goat $1.50-2
Englehard Coffee, "The Name Means Good Coffee" 1.50-2
Sarica Coffee, maid delivering note on tray 1.50-2

Farm

Ayreshires Milk, "You Can't Go Wrong," cow $1.50-2
Huber Tractors, "Economy, Durability, Safety," tractor 1.50-2
McCormick Harvesting Machine Co., farm scenes 1- 2
Princess Plow Co., "Queen of the Turf" 1.50-2
Vitality Feeds, rooster 1.50-2

Food

Dunham's Cocoanut, black cook with cake $1.50-2
Excelsior Cracker Works, dancing couple 1.50-2
Holmes & Coutts, fruit cake 1- 2
Woolson Spice Co., hunter shooting bird 1.50-2

Medical

Brown's Iron Bitters, farm girl with bucket $1.50-2
Perry Davis Pain Killer, professor at blackboard 1.50-2
Hunt's Remedy, boy in sailor suit 1.50-2
Kluckmyer's Soothing Syrup, girl on swing 1.50-2
Lash's Bitters, man on horseback 1.50-2

Miscellaneous

Blue Ribbon Meat Meal, hog wearing nightcap $1.50-2
Coney Island Amusement Park, roller coaster ride 1.50-2
Heinz, girl in shape of pickle 1.50-2
Keystone Jewelers, pocket watch in keystone 1.50-2
Soapine, the Dirt Killer, whale on beach 1.50-2
White Sewing Machines, kitten making dress 1.50-2

Shoes

Drown Boots & Shoes, girl with crow pie $1-1.50
Chas. D. Griffith Shoe Co., shoe inside letter "G" 1.50-2
Star Brand Shoes, firm's initials in large star 1-1.50
Tess and Ted School Shoes, girl and boy dancing 1.50-2

Stoves

Andes Stoves & Ranges, firm's name in shield $1-1.50
Chicago Stove Works, naked boy by fire in woods 1.50-2
Dixon's Stove Polish, black man by stove, with black kids 1.50-2
New Tariff Ranges, smelters in factory 1.50-2

Tobacco

Camel Cigars, Arab riding camel $1.50-2
Fast Mail Tobacco, railroad engine pulling cars 1.50-2
His Master's Choice Cigar, dog looking at box of cigars 1.50-2
Ojibwa Chewing Tobacco, Indian with tobacco leaf 1- 2

Trays

Change, Bromo-Seltzer, "Cures all Headaches" . . . . . $ 39- 46
Change, El Verso Havana Cigars 31- 40
Change, Moxie, "Eat, Sleep, Feel Better" 23- 28
Serving, Acadia Tea, "Yes, It Is Excellent Tea" 61- 74
Serving, Elk Run Brewing, large elk in field 142-152
Serving, Hampden Brewing Co., "The Handsome Waiter" 59- 68
Serving, Moxie, girl with drink, c. 1905 . . . . 83- 91

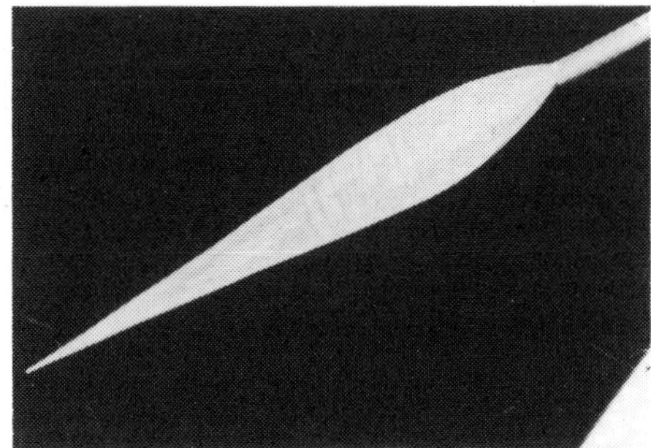

Africana

Africana

Too many collectible items in this category to list. Look for old spears, carved statuettes of animals, animal hides such as zebras and gazelles.

Indicative prices on a few items:

Wooden-carved spear (Illus.)	$ 19- 28
Wooden-carved statuette of antelope, 10″ high	13- 21
Zebra hide, properly cured, with felt backing	220-250
Shield, four feet long, covered with animal hide	178-210
Waste basket made from elephant's foot, brass liner	210-230

Good hunting!

Air Collectibles

Emblems

Each airline has a different logo. The flying goose shown here rides the tail of a neat airline that flies me home to Panama City, Florida. Don't hijack the plane but do look for schedules, tickets, baggage tags, etc.

I.D.'s

You'll find these in your seat compartment. They tell you all about the plane you're flying on.

Air Collectibles

Publications

All major airlines publish a slick magazine once a month. Free to passengers. They contain articles of interest to everyone.

Delta Airline's Sky magazine (Illus.)	25¢-50¢

Schedules

Wander through any airport and you'll find them at any ticket counter. Who knows when you'll want to fly to Yanam for the weekend.

Tickets

Everything to do with flying is sending the price in the same direction!

Akro Agate Glass

Akro Agate Glass

The Akro Agate Glass Co. originally was jobber for a marble company in Ohio, in 1911. In 1914, it moved to Clarksburg, West Va., where it made its own marbles. In 1932, it produced an opalescent type glass, various colors. Its trademark was a crow flying through the letter A. It shut down in the early 1950's.

Ashtrays

Bridge suits (hearts, clubs, spades, diamonds), set of 4 . . . $53-60
Leaf-shaped, green 12-15
Square, blue and white 16-20

Baskets

Basket weave, high arch handle (rare) $75-83
Opaque red 42-47
Orange and white 15-20

Bowls

Blue, children's . . . . $ 7-10
Green slag 14-19
Marbleized orange 14-19

Children's Line

Lemonade set, clear green, 7 pcs., all . . . . $ 28- 35
"Little Miss America," complete set, tea, applied decals, all 9 pcs., original box 114-122
"Playtime," complete set, tea service, green and white, all 50- 56

Garden Line

Opaque yellow $43-48
Planter, Pattern No. 296, opaque orange 36-44
Planter, Pattern No. 307, green and white 28-34

Miscellaneous

Marbles, set of 10, original box $16-24
Match holder, green and white, opalescent 22-27
Toothpick holder, blue and white 39-44

Powder Jars

Colonial lady, white or blue, each $38-44
Dog, white 34-42
"Mexicali," made for Pickwick Cosmetics 38-44
Scotty, green 34-42

Vases

Blue, 6″ high, (Illus.) $15-23
Floral, embossed, white, 4¼″ high 10-15
Being reproduced without "Made In USA," mold number and crow, letter A, on base.

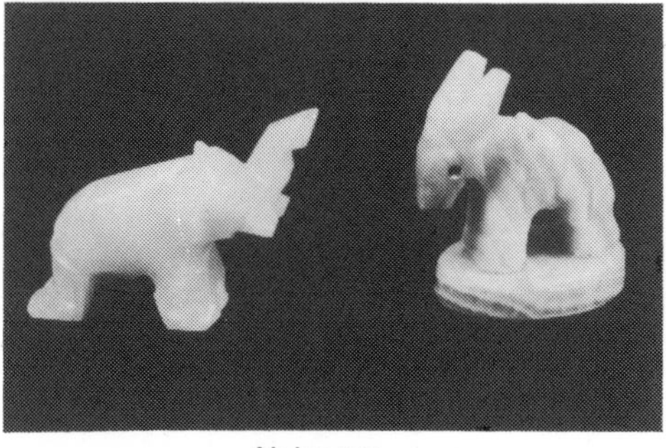

Alabaster

Alabaster

This is a translucent, whitish variety of gypsum, fine-grained. Hundreds of items were made from this material, including clock cases, figurines, eggs, statues, etc. Too many people confuse it with marble.

Chess pieces, 24 in set $16-22
Donkey (Illus.) 2- 3
Elephant (Illus.) 2- 3
Figure, man on horse 8-10

Aladdin Lamps

This is one of the most popular lamps ever made. The Mantle Lamp Company of America, Inc., was founded in Chicago in 1908. These lamps are still being made in Nashville, Tenn. All lamps are priced with complete burners and shades. See **Clubs and Publications,** this Price Guide.

Practicus table lamp $292- 320
Model No. 1 table lamp 190- 210
Model No. 1 parlor lamp 308- 325
Model No. 2 table lamp 261- 272
Model No. 2 parlor lamp 288- 310
Model No. 3 table lamp 200- 222
Model No. 3 parlor lamp 295- 310
Model No. 4 table lamp 210- 240
Model No. 5 table lamp 191- 210
Model No. 10 table lamp 350- 362
Model 1233 blue Venetian Art-Craft crystal vase lamp, 10¼″ tall 171- 188
Model No. 1241 variegated (two-tone) tan crystal vase lamp, 12″ tall 155- 164
Model No. 1242 Bengal red crystal vase lamp, 12″ tall 291- 310
Model 1247 red Venetian Art-Craft crystal vase lamp, 10¼″ tall 274- 292
Style 99, Venetian, clear, Model A table lamp, 1932 . 370- 380
Style 101, Venetian, green, Model A table lamp, 1932 . 199- 219
Style B-25, Victoria, decorated china, Model B table lamp 418- 435
Style B-39, Washington Drape (round base), clear crystal, Model B 125- 140
Style B-62, Short Lincoln Drape, ruby crystal, Model B table lamp 540- 560
Style B-76, Tall Lincoln Drape, cobalt crystal, Model B table lamp (lamps with scallop design on the foot are worth much more) 570- 581
Style B-82, Beehive, amber crystal, light, Model B table lamp 128- 135
Style B-82, Beehive, amber crystal, dark, Model B table lamp 192- 199
Style B-86, Quilt, green moonstone, Model B table lamp 195- 220
Style B-100, Corinthian, clear crystal, Model B table lamp 110- 118
Style B-110, Cathedral, white moonstone, Model B table lamp 268- 290
Caboose lamp, Model B w/shade 193- 240
Caboose wall bracket lamp, alacite font 163- 180
Floor lamp, Model No. 12, w/shade, 1254 series 170- 180
Floor lamp, Model B, brass, w/shade 292- 308
Hanging lamp, Model No. 2 w/shade 341- 365
Hanging lamp, Model No. 3, double chandelier 1,250-1,310
Hanging lamp, Practicus, w/shade 290- 320

Suggested reading: *Aladdin: The Magic Name in Lamps with Price Guide*, J. W. Courter, Wallace-Homestead Book Company.

Albums

Albums

Back in the days when it was expensive to take a photograph, folks preserved them in beautiful albums — velvet-covered, leather, etc. Brass corners and a locking hinge were common in those days. Much sought after today!

Green velvet cover, gold lettering on front, brass corners, 1880's $46-55
Leather cover, contains daguerreotypes, 1860's 57-66
Red velvet cover, usual brass ornamentation, late 1800's 39-45
Red velvet cover, contains photos of Spanish-American War 49-60
Tooled leather cover, usual brass, hinge locks, photos, 1890's 45-53

Also, look for the albums with cardboard covers. Some contain valuable postcards, souvenir items, the like.

Alcohol

Bar Tokens

Napkins, coasters, swizzle sticks—usually free!

Shaker, sterling silver, 1920's $140-150
Whiskey labels, average price . 10¢-25¢

Whiskey Bottles, Miniature

More than 1,500 to choose from. They're still used on most airlines.

Empty	25¢-50¢
Full	2-4

Whiskey Jugs/Flasks

Flask, leather covered, ½ pint	$25-33
Flask, sterling silver, initialed	45-53
Jug, Doulton, late 1800's	85-94
Jug, earthenware, small	5- 8
Jug, Meredith's whiskey	19-25

Whiskey Sample Glasses

Given away free when the salesman visited the local saloons.

Big 6 gin, 1 oz.	$16-20
Habanero "Piza" tobasco, ½ oz.	11-14
Hanover rye, 2 oz.	21-25

Almanacs

Photo Courtesy of
Hake's Americana & Collectibles

Almanacs

Folks consulted their almanacs almost as religiously as the Bible during the 18th and 19th centuries. They're still being published by several companies. The most famous was, and still is, The (Old) Farmer's Almanac.

Bickerstaff's New England Almanac, Norwich, Conn., 1785	$25-33
Centaur Almanac (advertisement for bitters), 1874, New York	11-14
Hagerstown Town & Country Almanac, J. Gruber, 1850	9-12
Lum and Abner's 1936 Family Almanac (Illus.)	8-12
New England Almanac, Nathan Daboll, New London, Conn., 1801	26-35
The Gardener's Almanac, Comstock, Ferre & Co., 1852	9-12

Many published by motor companies, seed firms, etc.

Aluminum, Handwrought

A lightweight, silvery metal that doesn't corrode. The handwrought pieces are collectible today.

Ashtray, tulip design, 5½″ dia., marked Rodney Kent Silver Co.	$ 6- 9
Bowl, curvilinear design, 11″ dia., marked Canterbury Arts	16- 19
Bowl, zodiac signs, 11½″ dia., marked Arthur Armour	47- 56
Butter dish, glass insert, Buenilum's Castle mark	29- 34
Candelabrum, 13½″ high, Buenilum's Castle mark	36- 42
Candy dish, covered, apple blossoms, 7″ dia., marked Wendell August Forge	33- 40
Casserole, covered, 10″ dia., marked Buenilum's Castle mark	16- 22
Cocktail shaker, 12″ high, marked Continental Hand Wrought No. 530	37- 46
Coffee service, chrysanthemum pattern, covered sugar and creamer, coffee server, 8¾″ high, tray, 14¾″ wide, all	115-133

Crumb tray and scraper, dogwood pattern, marked Wendell August Forge, both pcs. . . . 27- 35
Gravy boat, chrysanthemum pattern, marked Continental Hand Wrought Silverlook No. 610 . . . 29- 35
Hurricane lamp, etched crystal globe, No. 1003 . . . 29- 35
Ice bucket holder, glass liner, cut-out leaves, marked Continental Silverlook No. 716 . . . 27- 34
Nut bowl, Wild Rose pattern, 11″ dia., marked Continental Silverlook Brillantone Wild Rose No. 1011 . . . 19- 25
Pie plate holder, incised buttercups, holds 9½″ pie plate, open mark No. 1124 . . . 16- 19
Pitcher, 2 qt., hammer marks . . . 26- 31
Trays
  Bread, Wheat pattern . . . 9- 12
  Bar, pinecone design, 20″ wide . . . 26- 32
  Serving, Rose and Forget-Me-Not pattern, 12″ × 14″, No. 468 . . . 24- 31
Tumbler, hammer marks, No. 987 . . . 5- 6
Vase, weighted base, 12″ high, dogwood design, Arthur Armour . . . 47- 56

American Dinnerware

There are countless thousands of pieces around today. If you're collecting, you'd be wise to buy Jo Cunningham's fine book, *The Collector's Encyclopedia of American Dinnerware.* Value Guide No. AD882 comes with the book. A few of the many ceramic dinnerware manufacturers are listed below.

Blair Ceramics, Inc., was founded in Ozark, Missouri, in 1946. They closed in the 1950's. Most pieces are signed. Their backstamp is "Blair" in script.

Bamboo Pattern

Cup/saucer set . . . $ 9-11
Dinner plate, square or rectangular . . . 7-12
Soup bowl . . . 13-17
Sugar bowl, covered . . . 9-12

Gay Plaid (or Plaid) Pattern

Casserole, handled . . . $16-20
Cup/saucer set . . . 9-12
Dinner plate . . . 5- 7
Mug, handled . . . 13-17
Salt/pepper set . . . 11-14
Tumbler . . . 9-12
Water pitcher w/ice lip . . . 21-28

Primitive Bird (or Bird) Pattern

Celery dish . . . $16-20
Dinner plate . . . 13-17
Plate, 6″ . . . 9-12
Salt/pepper set . . . 13-17
Vegetable plate, square . . . 13-17
Vinegar bottle w/stopper . . . 19-24

Crooksville China Co., Crooksville, Ohio, founded in 1902. Out of business in 1959. "Crooksville" backstamp on all pieces.

Silhouette Pattern

Creamer . . . $11-15
Dinner plate . . . 9-11
Pie baker . . . 16-20
Plate . . . 7- 9
Platter . . . 13-17
Tumbler . . . 11-16

Spring Blossom Pattern

Creamer . . . $13-17
Cup/saucer set . . . 9-12
Gravy boat . . . 16-20
Salad plate . . . 5- 7
Serving bowl . . . 13-17
Sugar, covered . . . 13-17

Apple Blossom, Rose Garland, Country Home and Fruits—just a few of the many patterns made. Usually, comparable prices. French-Saxon China Co., Sebring, Ohio, founded in the 1930's. Out of business in 1964. "F. S." or "French Saxon China" are the backstamps used.

Granada Pattern

Creamer . . . $ 9-11
Cup/saucer set . . . 9-12
Dessert plate . . . 3- 4
Luncheon plate . . . 5- 7
Shaker . . . 7- 9
Sugar, covered . . . 11-14

Zephyr was another popular line. Comparable prices. W. S. George Co., East

Palestine, Ohio, founded around 1904. Out of business in the late 1950's. "W. S. George" was the backstamp used.

Blossoms Pattern

Creamer	$ 7- 9
Cup/saucer set	5- 8
Dinner plate, 10"	4- 6
Soup, 8"	4- 6

Petalware Pattern

Cup, light blue	$ 5- 7
Plate, 9", dark green, maroon, pink	5- 8
Saucer, light green	3- 4
Sugar, covered	7-10

Breakfast Nook (also called Springtime) was another popular pattern. The Hall China Co., East Liverpool, Ohio, founded in 1903. Still in operation. Also a plant in Gilmer, Texas. "Hall," "Hall's China" were the backstamps used.

Cameo Rose Pattern

Made exclusively for the Jewel Tea Co.

Creamer	$ 9-12
Cup/saucer set	7-10
Dinner plate, 10"	6- 8
Salt/pepper set, table size	13-17
Sugar, covered	9-12
Tidbit server, 3-tier	32-38
Vegetable dish, 8¾"	37-44

Crocus Pattern

Beverage mug	$26-33
Casserole	26-33
Creamer	7-10
Drippings jar	16-20
Jug	21-28
Pretzel jar	57-64
Teapot	37-44
Vegetable bowl	21-25

Monticello Pattern

Cup/saucer set	$ 5- 8
Dinner plate, 10"	4- 6
Sugar, covered	7-10
Vegetable dish	27-33

Orange Poppy Pattern

Ball jug	$13-18
Casserole, 8"	19-23
Marmalade jar, complete	24-30
Plate, 7"	4- 7
Teapot, donut-shaped	43-49

Harker Pottery, established in 1940, East Liverpool, Ohio. Didn't get into the whiteware business until the early 1920's. "H Co." and "Harker" are two of several backstamps.

Amy Pattern (Bakerite Oven-Tested)

Bean pot, individual	$ 5- 7
Casserole, individual	4- 5
Creamer	5- 7
Fork	16-23
Teapot	22-28
Utility bowl	13-17

Cameo Shellware/Cameo Rose Patterns

Cup/saucer set	$ 7-10
Jug, small, covered	5- 8
Jug, large, covered	9-12
Jug, medium, covered	5-10
Pepper shaker	5- 7
Plate, 9"	5- 7

Petit Point Rose I Pattern

Pie baker	$ 9- 12
Plate	4- 5
Rolling pin	83-108

Petit Point Rose II Pattern

Cake server	$9-13
Casserole, individual	10-12
Custard, individual	4- 5
Utility bowl, 6"	9-11
Utility bowl, 11½"	13-17

Red Apple I (small decal) Pattern

Pitcher, covered	$22-28
Teapot	16-20
Tray, serving	13-17

Red Apple II (large decal) Pattern

Bowl, red trim	$13-17
Creamer	5- 8
Custard, individual	5- 8
Hot plate	13-18

Rose Spray Pattern

Creamer	$9-12
Cup/saucer set	7- 9
Dessert plate, 6"	3- 5
Dinner plate, square	7-10
Salad plate	3- 4
Serving bowl	9-11

Jackson China Co., 1923 to 1946. "Royal Jackson" backstamp used until the company was purchased by a British attorney in 1976. Now known as Jackson China, Inc. Comparable prices.

Edwin M. Knowles Co. established in 1900. Out of business around 1962. Backstamps were "Knowles Utility Ware" and "Edwin M. Knowles China Co." Dinnerware made for Ben Franklin Stores was marked as such. Comparable prices.

Homer Laughlin Co. products have been around for years. They're most famous for their Fiesta Ware. Backstamps are "Homer Laughlin" (Illus.), "Eggshell Nautilus," "Priscilla Ovenware," "KitchenKraft," "Shenandoah," "Jubilee," "HL," "HLC," and "Wells."

Amberstone Pattern

Butter dish, ¼ lb.	$26-34
Cup	5- 7
Dessert dish	3- 4
Dinner plate	5- 7
Platter	9-12
Salt/pepper set	9-12
Sauce boat	11-14
Tray, handled	13-17

Priscilla Pattern

Coffee server	$13-18
Creamer	5- 8
Pie baker	13-19
Plate, 9″	5- 7
Sugar, covered	7- 9
Teapot	19-25

Virginia Rose Plank

Butter dish, covered	$46-55
Creamer	9-11
Cup/saucer set	11-14
Gravy boat	13-16
Pie baker	13-17

Limoges China Co., founded around 1901, Sebring, Ohio. Around 1946 the word "American" was added to the backstamp to overcome possible lawsuits by Haviland in Limoges, France. Backstamps used are "Limoges," "American Limoges," and "Peachblo." Probably others.

Old Mexico Pattern

Bowl	$ 6- 9
Cup	5- 7
Plate	7- 9
Vegetable bowl	19-24

Petit Point Rose Pattern

Creamer	$5-7
Cup	4-5
Plate	4-5
Sugar	5-7

The Paden City Pottery Co. was founded in 1907 at Paden City, West Virginia. The factory shut down in the 1950's. "Paboco" and "Paden City" are backstamps.

Caliente Pattern

Candleholder	$ 9-12
Cream soup	11-16
Creamer	9-12
Cup/saucer set	9-11
Dessert plate	5- 7
Dinner plate	7- 9
Shaker	7- 9
Sugar, covered	11-14
Teapot	32-40

Far East Pattern

Creamer	$5-7
Plate, 9″	4-6
Sugar, covered	5-7

Nasturtium, Posies, Shenandoah, Yellow Rose, Duchess and Floral patterns, comparable prices.

Purinton Pottery, 1936, Wellsville, Ohio. Factory closed in 1958. Hand painting only; no decals. Backstamps were "Purinton" and "Rubel," the latter pieces in solid color shapes for Rubel, a New York sales organization.

Apple Pattern

Cookie jar	$22-27
Cup/saucer set	9-12
Drippings jar, covered	13-17
Salad plate	4- 7
Tumbler, 6 oz.	13-17
Tumbler, 12 oz.	13-17

Salem China Co. was founded in 1898 in Salem, Ohio. It's still in operation. Backstamp is "Salem." Some of the patterns made were Colonial, Bluebird, Mapleleaf, Tulip, Mandarin Red, Sailing, and Petit Point. Comparable prices.

Sebring Potteries. This family was involved with many pottery firms. Founding city, Sebring, Ohio. Backstamp is "Sebring." Generally, comparable prices.

The Steubenville Pottery Co., founded in 1879, went out of business in 1959. Canonsburg Pottery purchased the molds. Monticello, Steubenville, and American Modern are their nationally advertised lines. Backstamp is "Steubenville" (Illus.). Comparable prices, generally.

Taylor, Smith & Taylor was founded in 1899; in 1973 the facilities were purchased by Anchor Hocking Corp. Backstamps were "Taylor, Smith and Taylor," and "T. S. & T." Lu Ray was one of their most popular lines. It came in five colors: Windsor Blue, Persian Cream, Sharon Pink, Surf Green, and Chatham Gray.

Lu Ray Line

Butter dish, covered, ¼ lb., Sharon Pink	$16-20
Cake plate, Sharon Pink	13-18
Egg cup, Persian Cream	11-14
Gravy boat, Chatham Gray	28-35
Plate, 7″, Windsor Blue	5- 8
Teapot, Surf Green	21-27

Leaf, Sweet Pea, Green Dots, Floral Bouquet, and Morningside are other lines. Comparable prices, generally.

Vistosa Line

Creamer, mango red	$ 5- 8
Egg cup, green	13-18
Plate, 9″, cobalt	7-10
Teapot, mango red	32-39

Universal Potteries was formed in 1934 at Cambridge, Ohio. They shut down in 1960. Backstamps are "Universal. Cambridge, O," "Harmony House Oven Proof," "Cat-Tail" (made for Sears), "Old Holland," "Wheelock Peoria," and another Sears product, "Sweet William."

Cat-Tail Pattern

Batter jug	$52-58
Cake (pie) server	11-14
Iced tea tumbler	13-16
Salad bowl	13-16
Salad servers, fork and spoon, both	27-34
Tumbler	26-34

Rambler Rose (or Iris) Pattern

Canteen refrigerator jug	$13-18
Dinner plate	4- 5
Gravy boat	5- 7
Pie baker	7- 9
Plate, 9″	5- 7

Red Poppy, Windmill, Woodvine, and Calico were other popular patterns. Comparable prices, generally.

Andirons

"Dogs," as they were called in the olden days, are making a comeback. Brass andirons were known in the colonies as early as 1740.

Brass, ball-top, 20th century	$75-90
Wrought iron, hand-forged, 20th century, 16″ high	55-65

Animal Dishes, Covered

Animal Dishes, Covered

The hen on nest is the most common, and reproductions of this collectible are found in almost every form. Careful!

If old:

Cat, white milk glass, 5¼″ ....$ 43- 50
Hen, colored glass, 5″ and 6″ long, amber, each ... 105-115
Hen on sleigh, blue milk glass . 54- 62
Hen, Staffordshire, new, 6″ (Illus.) 45- 52
Rabbit, mule-eared, white milk glass, 5½″ 95-115
Rooster, blue head, white milk glass body............ 79- 85
Squirrel, white milk glass, McKee 157-164
Swans, 5″, 6″, and 7″ long, Staffordshire, each 285-335
Turkey, white milk glass, 5¼″ high, McKee 181-190

Animals/Birds

Little girls love to collect horses. Little boys? Anything that wiggles! Literally thousands of animals and birds around in every type of material—ceramic, blown glass, cast iron, carved wood, glass, etc.

Cat candy container $18-24
Cat figure, Japan 14-19
Horses
Clydesdale, porcelain, 4″ high 22-27
Galloping pony, carved wood, 3½″ high 23-28
Shetland pony, porcelain, 3″ high 22-26
Tennessee walking horse, ceramic, 4½″ high 10-15
Owl, brown and white caramel glass 4- 7
Taxidermy
Deer's head................. 40-50
Fox, 30″ long 45-54
Woodpecker, 9″ high 19-26

Appliances

You'll find all sorts at most Flea Markets and garage sales. You'll do yourself a favor if you have a qualified electrician

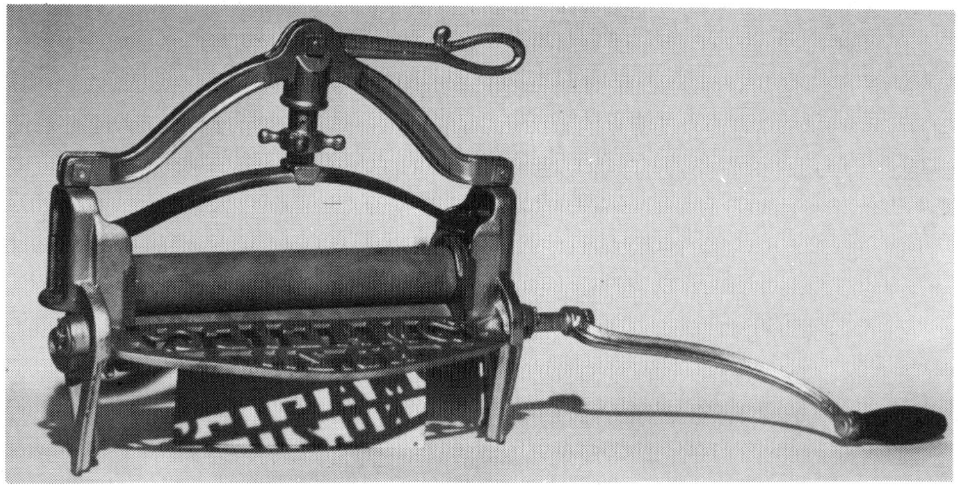

Appliances

check out your purchase **before** you use it. Or, if you prefer, have the local fire department standing by.

- Clothes wringer, cast iron, Magic No. 20, 1920's (Illus.) ... $23-31
- Electric iron, 1930's ... 20-26
- Hair curler, 1950's ... 8-11
- Hair dryer, 1960's ... 6- 9
- Mixer, complete with bowls, 1950's ... 18-26
- Toasters, various models and years, each ... 8-12
- Vacuum cleaner, Bissell, 1930's ... 15-20
- Vacuum cleaner, Hoover, 1930's ... 10-14
- Washing machine, Maytag, has butter churner attachment, 1930's, electrified ... 40-48
- Washing machine, table model, 1930's, electrified ... 26-33

Art Deco

Art Deco

Art Deco or Art Moderne was a style beginning after the Paris Exposition of 1925. It was the first modern design, Lincoln's Zephyr being a classic example. With its contrasting colors and wild lines, it was popular until World War II and is now back in vogue.

- Cocktail shaker, alumimum ... $ 35- 45
- Compote, metal/glass, 19″ high 152-162
- Cup, handled, green/blue, 3½″ high ... 46- 56
- Desk clock, marble and cloisonne, luminous hands .. 72- 80
- Dressing table set, cameo glass, inlaid silver, nudes, 1931 ... 122-140
- Elephant head incense burner . 41- 50
- Figurine, ape in "thinking" pose, bronze, 12″ high ... 161-170
- Figurine, dancing girl, partially nude, bronze, 10″ high ... 155-165
- Figurine, lovers, bronze on marble pedestal, French ... 104-115
- Flower holder, nude, porcelain, 7″ high (Illus.) ... 52- 62
- Lamp, Dutch silver (pot metal), kneeling black dancer, glass shade ... 120-131
- Lamp, naked man holding nude woman overhead, bronze, glass ball shade ... 184-193
- Mirror, hand, 11″ long, nude figure in relief on back ... 59- 69
- Statuette, tubular metals, cubism design, dated 1934 on bottom ... 77- 87
- Vase, black glass, silver holder, Italian, 14″ high ... 163-173
- Vase, blue, geometric design, 16½″ high, French ... 125-140
- Vase, frosted lion over dead lamb, marble and glass, French, 1930's ... 125-150
- Wall plaque, glass and cloisonne, nude figures, 8″ × 15″ ... 128-155

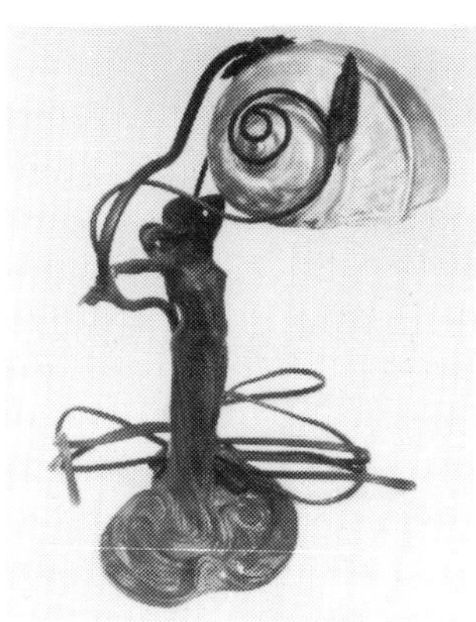

Art Nouveau

Art Nouveau

Rebelling against the accepted forms of art, Art Nouveau was in vogue in the late 1800's, then until just before World War I. Tiffany collectors revived it and today it's highly collectible, in metal, wood, glass. Surface decoration is one of its identifying marks.

- Bookends, nudes, sterling silver, pr. ... $129-144
- Bookmark, 2″ high ... 55- 66
- Bowl, flower, Galle style, deep cut ... 165-194

Box, jewelry, footed, sterling silver, 4½" square 95-108
Brush, sterling silver 128-141
Buckle (also brooch), woman's profile, silver 54- 63
Buttonhook, silver, entwining snake, 8" long...... 47- 57
Buttonhook, sterling silver 69- 84
Cigarette case, chased copper, birds in relief, enamel-lined 125-140
Clock, desk type, nude nymph, in metal case....... 74- 83
Figurine, dancing figure, bronze, 11" high, marble pedestal.................. 164-173
Figurine, nude male, Dresden porcelain, 14" high..... 210-235
Flask, sterling silver, nude lovers on beach 340-360
Inkwell, devil's tail as penholder, bronze, 2½" square . 79- 89
Lamp, lady holding seashell shade, electrified, 14" high (Illus.) 670-685
Lamp, nudes holding 2 glass shades, 14" high, electrified 340-355
Lamp, young girl holding cigarette, cast iron base, 12" high 134-146
Match holder 54- 63
Pin, angel, brass 29- 37
Pin, girl on horseback, brass 32- 41
Pin, profile of lovers, copper-on-brass 42- 55
Spoons, sterling silver, embossed figures, each..... 135-144

Artificial

Artificial

Flowers made of silk or paper, fruit made of plastic, 25¢ to $2 depending on the item.

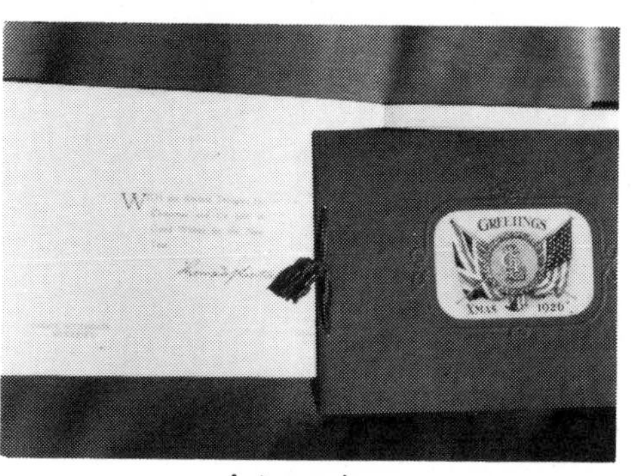

Autographs

Autographs

The signature of any "known" person is collectible, whether they're living or dead. "Holographs" — letters written by hand — highly collectible. After 1839, American presidents had secretaries to sign their documents. Keep that in mind.

Arnold, Edward (1890-1956), popular movie star ....$ 67- 73
Baxter, Ann, movie publicity shot 13- 16
Berlin, Irving, songwriter and composer............. 48- 54
Borge, Victor, pianist, comedian................. 16- 22
Burns, Bob (1895-1956), comedian, "bazooka" player 49- 54
Byrd, Richard (1888-1957), Arctic explorer 67- 74
Caldwell, Erskine, author of *Tobacco Road*............ 44- 51
Carter, Jimmy, American president who liked rose gardens 128-135
Clark, Mark, WW II general 27- 33
Dee, Sandra, actress, married to Bobby Darin 19- 25
Ford II, Henry, his family made a few cars........... 9- 12
Henry of Orleans, Prince, you remember him! 36- 42
Jones, Grandpa, country-western singer 7- 9
Lemmon, "Meadowlark," Harlem Globe Trotter 9- 12
Lipton, Thomas, of tea fame (Illus.)............... 42- 50
Monroe, Marilyn, actress, "cheese cake" pose, 1955 .. 550-575
Morrow, Jeff, TV actor 16- 20
O'Brien, Hugh, actor, played Wyatt Earp on TV.......... 8- 11
Rockwell, Norman (1896-1978), on movie lobby card 250-260

Sinatra, Frank, singer, etc. 98-107
Truman, Bess, wife of America's greatest president 70- 77
Suggested reading: *American Autographs*, Charles Hamilton, University of Oklahoma Press.

Automobiles

Generally, those cars from 1930 until 1948 are considered classics. But, there is a renewed interest in a lot of "hot rods" made during the 1950's and 1960's.

Buick
- **1955 66C convertible .. $ 5,200- 5,800**
- **1962 Electra 225 convertible 4,600- 5,400**

Cadillac
- **1953 6267S Eldorado convertible 13,000-14,000**
- **1956 6267 convertible coupe 9,500-10,300**
- **1963 Eldorado Biarritz convertible 5,800- 6,300**

Chevrolet
- **1955 2434 convertible coupe 8,700- 9,300**
- **1960 El Camino pickup V-8 .... 4,800- 5,300**
- **1969 Camaro convertible 4,300- 4,900**

Chrysler
- **1949 C45 station wagon (Woody) 8,200- 8,800**
- **1957 566 2-door hardtop 6,800- 7,200**
- **1962 845 2-door convertible 5,300- 5,800**
- **1964 Ghia 23,500-24,700**

De Soto
- **1957 153 convertible .. 5,700- 6,200**
- **1961 612 2-door hardtop 4,100- 4,600**

Dodge
- **1957 D67-2 2-door convertible V-8 .... 5,800- 6,300**
- **1960 521 2-door club sedan 1,400- 1,700**

Ford
- **1949 76 convertible coupe V-8 .... 6,900- 7,600**
- **1955 64A Crown Victoria hardtop 5,900- 6,600**
- **1957 Thunderbird convertible 22,500-24,000**
- **1962 Thunderbird convertible Roadster 12,400-13,000**
- **1965 Mustang hardtop coupe, V-8 .... 7,200- 7,900**
- **1969 Mustang Grand V-8 G.T. 500 .... 7,900- 8,600**

Hudson, 1953 7C Hollywood 6,200- 6,700

Jeepster 1951 6-cyl Phaeton 5,600- 6,200

Mercury
- **1955 76B convertible coupe 7,100- 7,600**
- **1962 Monterey convertible 4,700- 5,200**

Nash, 1951 Rambler convertible 4,300- 4,800

Plymouth, 1948 P15 convertible coupe 12,300-12,700

Willys 1955 2-door hardtop 3,900- 4,300

Automobiliana

Photo Courtesy of
Hake's Americana & Collectibles

Automobiliana

From 1900 until 1930 over 1,500 different makes of automobiles were manufactured in the United States. Practically every part of the car is collectible today, especially items such as radiator caps and emblems, dashboard clocks, brass headlamps, hubcaps.

Advertisement, Aerocar Motor Co., "There's No Getting Away," 1908 .... $ 44- 51
Advertisement, Dragon Touring Car, "The motor that motes," 1907 .... 52- 60
Advertisement, Goodrich Safety Tread tires, 1914 .... 31- 39
Advertisement, Metz 22, $475, The Gearless Car, 1913 ..... 39- 45
Advertisement, Midland Motor Co., Moline, Ill., 1910 .... 39- 46
Advertisement, Murine (A tonic for the auto eye), 1907 ..... 39- 50
Auto Blue Books, 1909 through 1919, each 38- 44
Auto Green Books, 1915 through 1926, each 29- 38

Auto Wiring Manual, Abbot-Detroit cars, 1910-1914	58- 68
Book, *Get Out and Get Under,* 1913, illustrated	52- 62
Book, *Salesman's Cadillac,* 1913	61- 70
Book, *The Open Road,* 1914	51- 60
Book, *The Easy Route to California*, 1911	100-111
Bumper sign, "V" (Illus.)	16- 24
Carbide tank for 1909 Ford Model-T	188-195
Carbide tank for 1912 Cadillac	240-260
Dashboard clock for 1914 Pierce Arrow	107-117
Dashboard clock for 1916 Packard	103-112
Emblems: average price, each	38- 47

Buick	Cadillac	McFarlan	Stutz
Oakland	Kleiber	DaVis	Overland
Franklin	Essex	DeLage	

Bail handle light, brass, 1909 Hupmobile	385-420
Hood ornament, 1930's	29- 37
Horn, double twist, brass, bulb-type, 1908 Maxwell	152-160
License plates, enamel-over-metal, 1909-1916, average price	47- 60
Magazine *Car Life,* 1916, 12 issues, all	184-193
Motor meter (forerunner of the speedometer), 1912 Marmon	114-132
Motor meter, 1913 Mercer	152-168
Motor meter, 1914 Columbia	89- 99
Owner's manual, 1908 Rolls Royce	250-270
Owner's manual, 1914 Stutz Bearcat	184-195
Poster, 1913 Auto Show, Chicago, 15″×20″, paper	185-192
Radiator cap ornament, knight with lance	94-103
Radiator cap ornament, Lady Ascot, Rolls Royce, silver, 1911	410-433
Road map showing routes to Chicago from New York City, 1909	84- 93
Sales catalogs, General Motors cars, 1916-1925, all	342-397
Signature of Ramsey E. Olds, creator of the Reo and the Oldsmobile, 1909	47- 57
Spark coil for 1910 Model-T, still works	94-108
Spark plug for 1909 Saxon	29- 39
Vases, cut glass, used in back seat of 1912 Locomobile limo	118-132
Vases, used in back seat of 1913 Cadillac limousine, cut glass, pr.	119-127

Autumn Leaf

Autumn Leaf

The Autumn Leaf line in early years was referred to only as Hall, Jewel, or Autumnal design. It wasn't until the 1940's that the pattern was given the name Autumn. In 1960 it became Autumn Leaf. Designed by Arden Richards of the Hall China Company in East Liverpool, Ohio, for the Jewel Tea Company in 1933, it quickly became a collectible. At least three other firms used the Autumnal design, but Hall's was then and still is the most famous and most sought. All pieces listed were made by Hall for the Jewel Tea Company.

Bowls, 6″, 6½″, 8½″, 9″	$ 11- 14
Butter dish, ¼ lb.	34- 42
Butter dish, 1 lb.	77- 84
Cake plate, footed, metal base	14- 19
Cake safe	24- 30
Cake server, metal	33- 40
Canister, plastic cover	11- 15
Casserole (top is small pie plate)	26- 34
Clock, electric, 9½″ dia.	217-226
Coffee dispenser, 10½″ high	37- 45
Coffeepot, 8 cup	37- 44
Cookie jar, covered, tab handles, early	73- 80
Cookie jar, covered, tab handles, late	46- 52
Creamer and sugar, early	32- 37
Creamer and sugar, late	11- 15
Cup and saucer	7- 9
Custard cup	8- 11
Gravy boat with underplate	24- 29
Marmalade jar with underplate	47- 53
Pitcher, milk, small	14- 19
Pitcher, water, w/ice lip	22- 27
Plates, 7¼″, 10″	7- 10
Platters, 11″, 11½″, 13″, 13½″	13- 19
Salt/pepper set (Illus.)	15- 23
Tablecloth, 54″×54″, 54″×72″	57- 64

Toaster cover, plastic 8- 12
Trivet (hot plate), metal....... 9- 12
Tumbler, 14 oz., frosted 14- 19
Vegetable dish, oval 23- 30

Suggested reading: *The Autumn Leaf Story,* Jo Cunningham, Wallace Homestead Book Company.

Avon Bottles

Avon Bottles

Started in 1886 (as the California Perfume Co.), Avon today has 14 manufacturing laboratories and 25 distribution branches. Its main office is in Rockefeller Plaza, New York City, with branch offices around the world. "Avon calling!" Who hasn't heard that once or twice? Anyway, hundreds of Avon bottles are found at flea markets.

Aladdin's lamp, 1971 ....$ 7-11
Alaskan moose, amber, 8 oz. 6- 9
American eagle, 1971 .... 4- 7
American eagle pipe, amber, 5 oz. 3- 5
Avon Triumph TR 3, 2 oz., aqua, 1955 .... 3- 6
Barber pole, milk glass, 3 oz..... 3- 6
Bay Rum jug w/handle, 1962 6-12
Big Mack (Mack truck), 1973..... 4- 7
Bird of Paradise Cologne, 1970 .. 4- 7
Blue Volkswagen decanter, 1973 . 3- 7
Boxing gloves, 1960, plastic..... 9-12
Bucking bronco, 1971, cowboy on horse 4- 7
Butterfly, 1972, clear glass wings 3- 5
Canadian goose decanter, amber, 5 oz., 1973 .... 3- 7
Casey's lantern, green, bottle in shape of railroad lantern, 1966 9-19
Charlie Brown, plastic, 1968 ..... 3- 5
Christmas tree, cone-shaped, 1968 .... 4- 6
Classics, 4 book-shaped bottles, 1969 9-20
Colt revolver, 1851, amber, etc., 3 oz. 5- 9
Country charm, butter churn, 1973 .... 3- 5
Country kitchen, milk glass chicken, 1973 .... 3- 7
Covered wagon, wagon-shaped bottle, 1970 .... 3- 5
Crystal chandelier, 1969 .... 4- 7
Dachshund, long glass "hot dog," 1973 .... 3- 5
Daylight saving time, bottle in form of watch, 1968 .... 3- 7
Defender, cannon bottle, 6 oz., 1966 7-16
Dollars 'n Scents, roll of bills, 1969 9-22
Dolphin, 1968 .... 5- 9
Dune buggy, car-shaped, 1971-1973 .... 3- 4
Dutch girl, 1973 .... 5- 9
Eiffel Tower, 9″ high, 1970...... 3- 6
Fair lady, 4-bottle set, 1940 75-90
Ferrari, 1953, dark amber, 2 oz., 1975 9-12
Fielder's choice, baseball and glove bottle, 1971 .... 3- 4
First-class mail, mailbox shaped, 1970................ 3- 5
Flying Ace, "Snoopy" bottle, 1969 .... 3- 5
Freddy the frog mug, milk glass, 4½″ high 5- 7
French telephone, 6 oz., 1971 ... 9-26
George Washington, gold eagle cap, 1970.................. 3- 5
Greek warrior, 1967 7-14
Hawaiian White Ginger, hour-glass shape, 1957............ 3- 5
Hunter's stein, 1972 .... 5- 8
Indian chieftain, 1972 .... 3- 7
Jaguar sports car, 1973 5-12
King pin, bowling pin bottle, milk glass, 6 oz., 1969 .... 4- 9
Kittle Little, milk glass cat, 1972 .... 4- 7
Little doll, 1954 30-55
Mallard in flight, amber, 5 oz. ... 3- 7
Mini-bike, 1972 .... 3- 9
Model-A car, 1972 .... 4- 9
Noble prince decanter, amber, 4 oz. 4- 7
Old Faithful, St. Bernard, 1972... 5-11
Opening play, football helmet, 1968 7-12
Packard roadster, 1970 .... 3- 5
Parlor lamp, 1971 .... 3- 5
Pheasant bottle, 1972 .... 6- 9
Piano, 1972.................. 5- 9
Porsche decanter, amber, 2 oz. .. 3- 5
Puffer chugger, toy train set, 1972 .... 5- 9
Red depot wagon, amber, 5 oz. .. 5- 8
Rolls Royce Silver Cloud, 1920's, 1972 (Illus.) 7-11

Banks, Mechanical

Banks, Mechanical

Sure, you're going to find a lot of reproductions, but every once in a while you're going to "luck up" on a genuine article. Banks that do something when you insert a coin are called mechanical. More than 300 kinds were made in this country from the 1870's until the early 1900's. Many reproductions are on the market, some so good it's difficult to tell the old from the new, especially when the new bank has been aged by chipping its paint or fading it with an infrared lamp. Rare banks are expensive, so know your item before you buy. The asterisk (*) indicates it's being reproduced.

*Acrobats	$ 775- 800
*American Sewing Machine	1,300-1,400
*Bad accident	550- 610
*Billy goat	1,200-1,300
Bull tosses boy in well	275- 300
*Butting buffalo	755- 785
Chandlers	235- 255
Clown and dog	735- 765
*Clown on globe	485- 535
Darky bust	475- 520
*Dentist	1,600-1,675
Eagle and eaglets (Illus.)	365- 400
*Elephant, "Light of Asia"	875- 920
*Feed the kitty	245- 265
Flip the Frog	745- 765
*Forty-niner	235- 260
Harold Lloyd	1,350-1,450
*Humpty Dumpty	210- 240
*Initiating first degree	2,175-2,250
*Jolly nigger	120- 135
Leap frog	480- 515
*Lighthouse	335- 375
*Magic safe	200- 235
*Mason	575- 615
Mikado	3,700-3,875
*Monkey and coconut	515- 550
Mosque	165- 180
*Novelty	200- 230
*Paddy and pig	370- 410
*Pelican with rabbit	485- 515
Pig in high chair	275- 310
*Punch and Judy	435- 470
*Red Riding Hood	4,200-4,375
*Tammany	140- 155
*Tank and cannon	230- 255
*Trick dog	115- 135
*Trick pony	310- 330
Wimbledon	1,900-2,100
*Zoo	625- 665

Banks, Still

Banks, Still

They come in all sizes and metals. Pottery, too. Also glass. Not as many repros as the Mechanicals but, still, be careful! Items with an asterisk (*) are being reproduced.

Bear, sitting	$ 60- 68
*Buffalo, standing	95-110
*Cat with ball	245-260
Clown (Illus.)	78- 86
Dog with pack, 6½" high (Illus.)	86- 94
*Elephant, standing	98-110
Horse, prancing	84- 92
Independence Hall, glass, 7½" high	94-103
Lincoln (glass), tin top	19- 26
Lion on tub	75- 83
Log Cabin Syrup (glass)	17- 24
Radio (glass)	16- 23
*Rooster, standing	84- 93
Rooster, standing (pottery)	46- 53
State bank (Illus.)	87- 95
Teddy bear	71- 80
U. S. mail (Illus.)	45- 53

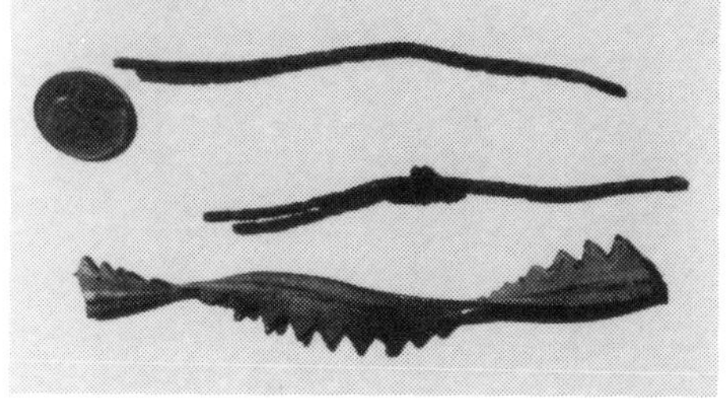

Barbed Wire

Barbed Wire

First patented in the late 1800's, there were more than 600 kinds. It had a great effect on the cattle business in the West. It's very collectible today. Rare, one-of-a-kind pieces bring upwards of $100 for 18″. Also called devil's rope. See **Clubs and Publications,** this Price Guide.

Common variety, 18″ $1-2
Up to $350 for rare pieces.

Barbershop Collectibles

Shaving mugs are a "hot" item. Razor strops, shaving mug cabinets, chairs, even the old striped poles. All being collected.

Chair, metal, leatherette seats, 1930's	**$175-230**
Pole, electrified, 1930's	**200-240**
Razor strop	**1.50- 2**
Razors, commercial type, average price	**17- 24**
Shaving Mugs	
Bakery wagon	**175-190**
B.P.O.E. (Elks)	**65- 75**
Carpenter	**125-135**
Dairy wagon	**155-170**
Floral (Illus.)	**45- 53**
Grocery wagon	**162-171**
K.O.C. (Knights of Columbus)	**55- 63**
Miner	**165-175**
Mortician	**515-560**
Painter	**133-142**
Photographer	**183-191**
Railroad, locomotive	**145-155**
Shrine	**86- 94**
W.O.W. (Woodmen of the World)	**43- 50**

Many, many more and many, many repros. Look for worn places on front and bottom. Still, watch it!

Baseball Cards

Competing cigarette companies in the late 1800's first used world flags, then famous actresses, then baseball players. Gypsy Queen and Old Judge cigarettes led the way. These cards are hard to come by today. There are countless thousands of baseball cards. Obviously, condition plays a big role. Very good to excellent is what you're looking for if you're a serious collector. Whatever took place before, when Topps entered the field in the early 1950's, it was a whole new ballgame. Certainly, look for Goudey Gum cards, 1933 until just before World War II; also, Gum, Inc. and Bowman. Topps purchased Bowman in 1956 and had a lock on the entire market until 1981. Now, Fleer and another company, Donruss, compete with Topps. There are lots of collector clubs, lots of price guides and, unfortunately, lots of repros appearing daily.

Also keep in mind that Sunbeam Bread printed cards in 1947, 1949, and 1950, featuring California minor league baseball teams. And, Remar Bread also printed cards in 1946, 1947, 1948, 1949 and 1950. You can go crazy looking for those baking company cards, but keep looking for companies such as H. Weil Baking Company (1917), Standard Baking (1915-1920's), Morehouse Baking (1916), and Johnston's Cookies (1952-1955). Mother's Cookies, Drake, Clement Bros., Clark's Bread, Tarzan Thoro Bread, and Hostess Foods all "contributed" to the mass hysteria now known as "collecting baseball cards." Have fun!

Baseball Cards

Bowman Gum

1948, 48 cards issued, black/white. Complete set, $225-240. Average price, each, $2-4. Stan Musial, $27-32; Yogi Berra, $11-14; Phil Rizzuto, $17-20; Warren Spahn, $8-10.

1949, 36 cards, color. Supposedly rare, depends on who you talk to. Some say $4,000+ for the set; others, $1,500+.

1950, 252 cards, color. Complete set, $575-625. The first 72 numbers are harder to find, $3-4 each, average price. 73 through 252, $1.50-1.75 each, average price. #22, J. Robinson (Jackie), $30-35, #46, Yogi Berra, $18-22; T. Williams (Ted), $33-36. DiMaggio (#2), J. Vander Meer (#79), Roy Campanella (#75), and Casey Stengel (#217) also highly collectible, $13-24 each, average price.

1951, 324 cards, color. Complete set, $875-925. The first 252 cards, $1.50-1.75 each; 253 through 324, $4.50-5.50 each. #253, Mickey Mantle, $250-265; #304, Willie Mays, $195-218. #1 (Whitey Ford) and #2 (Yogi Berra), $19-24 each.

1952, 252 cards, color. Complete set, $515-540. The first 216 numbers, $1.50-2 each; 217 through 252, $4.50-6 each. Mickey Mantle ($115-125), Willie Mays ($227-235), and Stan Musial ($33-37) are high-demand cards in this series.

1953, 160 cards, color. Complete set, $875-925. The first 112 numbers, $2.50-3 each; #113 through 160, $4.75-7 each. Mickey Mantle ($110-114), Duke Snider ($88-96), Stan Musial (#41-48), and Yogi Berra ($59-63) are high-demand cards.

1953, 64 cards, black/white. Complete set, $540-560. Average price, common players, $5.50-6.50. Casey Stengel ($65-69), Lew Burdette ($54-59), and Bob Lemon ($18-22) are high-demand cards.

1954, 224 cards, color. Complete set, $325-340. 75¢-$1, common players. There are two #66's: Jim Piersall and Ted Williams. Williams is the rarest card, from 1948 to date, $383-393. Piersall, $29-32. He also appears in the series as #210. Mantle and Willie Mays, $39-45 each.

1955, 320 cards, color. Complete set, $265-285. The first 224 numbers, 40¢-55¢ each; 225 through 320, $1.35-1.75 each. Hank Aaron, Willie Mays, Mickey Mantle, $18-20 each. Ernie Banks, $24-29.

Topps Gum

1951, 2 sets, 52 cards, red backs and blue backs. Blue backs, complete set, $218-224. $4-4.75 each, common players. Enos Slaughter, Johnny Mize, and Richie Ashburn, $7-11 each. Red backs, complete set, $122-128. $150-1.75 each, common players. Gil Hodges ($12-14). Yogi Berra and Duke Snider ($8-10 each).

1952, 407 cards, color. Complete set, $3,950-4,150. The first 80 numbers, $2.35-2.55 each; 81 through 250, $1.75-2.10 each; 251 through 310, $4.50-5.10 each; 311 through 407, $19.50-22 each. Mickey Mantle ($330-340), Willie Mays and Eddie Mathews, ($130-144 each), Roy Campanella ($170-177), Pee Wee Reese ($79-83), Gil McDougald, Billy Herman, and Dick Groat ($38-40 each).

1953, 280 cards, color. Complete set, $755-770. Six numbers (253, 261, 267, 268, 271, and 275) were never issued. The first 220 numbers, 90¢-$1.15; 221 through 280, $4.45-4.70 each. Willie Mays ($174-182), Mickey Mantle ($75-80), Satchell Paige and Jim Gilliam ($13-15 each), Preacher Roe, Jackie Jensen, and Milt Bolling ($6.50-7.50 each).

1954, 250 cards, color. Complete set, $380-390. 70¢-90¢ each, common players. #1 and #250 are both Ted Williams ($19-21). Hank Aaron ($54-58), Jackie Robinson ($14-16), Al Kaline ($29-32), Whitey Ford, Duke Snider, and Yogi Berra ($6-10 each).

1955, 210 cards, color. Complete set, $320-335. The first 160 numbers, 65¢-80¢ each; 161 through 210, $1.45-1.60 each. Duke Snider and Willie Mays ($54-58 each), Jackie Robinson and Ted Williams ($22-25 each), Gil Hodges, Yogi Berra, and Sandy Koufax ($15-18 each).

1955, doubleheaders (2 players on each card), 66 cards. Complete set $725-765. Complete set without perforations, $850-900.

1956, 342 cards issued (2 cards had no numbers). Complete set, $280-305, 45¢-55¢ each. Mickey Mantle ($30-33), Hank Aaron, Willie Mays, Ted Williams ($16-18 each). Roberto Clemente and Roy Campanella ($9-11 each).

1957, 411 cards issued (4 cards had no numbers). Complete set, $390-415. The first 264 numbers, 45¢-55¢ each; 265 through 352, $1.45-1.60 each; 353 through 407, 40¢-48¢ each. Sandy Koufax and Brooks Robinson ($37-43 each). Frank Robinson, Hank Aaron, Willie Mays, and Mickey Mantle ($19-22 each).

1958, 494 cards, color. Complete set, $218-235. #145 (gray), not issued. 30¢-38¢ each, common players. Hank Aaron ($27-29), Mickey Mantle and Roberto Clemente ($17-19 each). Ted Williams and Willie Mays ($11-13 each).

1959, 572 cards, color. Complete set, $220-236. The first 506 numbers, 19¢-23¢ each; 507 through 572, 88¢-94¢ each. Mickey Mantle ($14.50-16). Roy

Campanella, Willie Mays, and Hank Aaron ($9.50-11 each).

1960, 572 cards, color. Complete set, $198-218. The first 506 numbers, 25¢-33¢ each; 507 through 572, 69¢-75¢ each. Thronberry, Hadley, and Cimoli are considered high-demand cards, $95-145 each. Mickey Mantle and Willie McCovey ($12-14 each). Willie Mays and Hank Aaron (All Star game or regular), $7-9 each.

1961, 589 cards, color. Complete set, $395-415. Numbers 426, 587, and 588 never issued. The first 522 numbers, 20¢-25¢ each; 523 through 589, $3.25-3.55 each. Mickey Mantle (All Star game), $34-37. Hank Aaron and Willie Mays (All Star game), $22-25 each. Carl Yastrzemski ($15-18).

1962, 598 cards, color. Complete set, $216-224. The first 522 numbers, 18¢-22¢ each; 523 through 598, 83¢-90¢ each. Numbers 135 through 144 feature "Babe" Ruth ($2.25-2.80 each). The first 522 numbers, 18¢-22¢ each; 523 through 589, 82¢-90¢ each. Mickey Mantle ($16-19), Carl Yastrzemski ($17-20), Lou Brock, Bob Gibson, and Willie McCovey ($11-13 each). Gaylord Perry ($8-10).

1963, 576 cards, color. Complete set, $435-448. The first 295 numbers, 19¢-24¢ each; 296 through 446, $3-4 each; 447 through 576, 68¢-77¢ each. Pete Rose ($155-163), Mays, Mantle, Koufax ($13-15 each), Clemente, McCovey, Yastrzemski ($11-14 each).

1964, 587 cards, color. Complete set, $165-177. The first 524 numbers, 19¢-24¢ each; 525 through 587, 34¢-39¢ each. Pete Rose ($36-39), Mickey Mantle and Carl Yastrzemski ($11-13 each).

1965, 598 cards, color. Complete set, $190-209. The first 522 numbers, 17¢-22¢ each; 523 through 598, 29¢-33¢ each. Steve Carlton ($28-30).

1966, 598 cards, color. Complete set, $265-274. The first 522 numbers, 17¢-23¢ each; 523 through 598, $1.60-1.73 each. Gaylord Perry ($24-25), Pete Rose, Willie Mays, and Jim Palmer ($11-14 each).

1967, 609 cards, color. Complete set, $344-365. The first 530 numbers, 16¢-20¢ each; 531 through 609, 81¢-87¢ each. Brooks Robinson ($36-39), Rod Carew ($16-18), Aaron and Mays ($8-9 each). Tom Seaver ($38-42).

1968, 598 cards, colors. Complete set, $144-155. 14¢-19¢ each, common players. Tom Seaver, Willie Mays, Hank Aaron, Yastrzemski ($7-9 each).

1969, 664 cards, color. Complete set, $180-190. 14¢-19¢ each, common players. Reggie Jackson ($19-22), Pete Rose and Mickey Mantle ($11-13 each), Johnny Bench and Steve Carlton ($5-7 each).

1970, 720 cards, color. Complete set, $168-177. The first 633 numbers, 13¢-19¢ each; 634 through 720, 35¢-39¢ each. Johnny Bench ($24-26), Nolan Ryan ($9-12), Frank Robinson ($8-11), Carew, Seaver, Clemente ($3.75-4.25 each).

1971, 752 cards, color. Complete set, $182-190. The first 633 numbers, 14¢-18¢ each; 634 through 752, 34¢-39¢ each. Thurmon Munson, Reggie Jackson, Steve Garvey ($4-6 each).

1972, 787 cards, color. Complete set, $190-215. This is the largest set ever produced by Topps. The first 656 numbers, 13¢-17¢ each; 657 through 787, 35¢-41¢ each. Rose, Garvey, Carew ($16-18 each)

1973, 684 cards (661 through 684, not numbered), color. Complete set, $114-122. Aaron, Rose, "Goose" Gossage, Jackson ($3-4 each).

1974, 660 cards, color. Complete set, $95-104. 25 cards have no numbers. 10¢-14¢ each, average price. Dave Parker and Mike Schmidt ($4-5 each). Pete Rose ($5-6).

1974, 72 cards, black/white, a test set in limited areas. Complete set, $565-615.

1975, 660 cards, color. Complete set, $99-114. 7¢-10¢ each, common players. George Brett ($8-11), Robin Yount ($6-7).

1976, 660 cards, color. Complete set, $59-68. 6¢-10¢ each, common players. Ron Guidry, Jackson, Schmidt, Rose, Yastrzemski ($3-4 each).

1977, 660 cards, colors. Complete set, $48-57. 6¢-9¢ each, common players. Steve Carlton, Gary Carter, Steve Garvey ($1.50-2 each).

1978-1983. Average price per card, 4¢-7¢.

Baskets

Baskets

They've been around for centuries. The

American Indians used many different types of material to make beautiful baskets. During the 1800's strips of oak peeled from the tree were soaked in water so they could be woven more easily. Look for baskets in all sizes and shapes.

Apple gathering (Illus.) $115-128
Berry, oak splint............. 86- 94
Cheese, handled, 26″ dia., 8″ deep 455-480
Clothes, 2 handles, 1920's 60- 68
Egg, 1900's................. 70- 80
Egg, melon-shaped, 1900's.... 88- 95
Gathering, splint 165-180
Gizzard, oak splint 95-110
Harvesting, splint............ 68- 75
Herb drying................. 125-140
Market, wide splint 48- 52
Melon, late 1800's 98-110
Potato, ash, ½ bushel 92-107
Sewing, Chinese coins, beads 40-47
Suggested reading: *The Basket Collectors Book*, Lew Larason, Scorpio Publications.

Bauer Pottery

John "Andy" Bauer founded this company in Los Angeles in 1909. Dinnerware lines introduced after the Depression. Ringware — it looks like crudely thrown pottery — was their most popular line. From the 1930's until the late 1950's it was produced in solid colors such as royal blue, Chinese yellow, and jade green. More than one hundred shapes were available. Moderne and Speckware were also popular lines.

Bowls, #6, #7, #8, Bauer mark, in mold, each .... $ 3- 7
Butter dish, covered, Bauer mark, in mold 43-48
Coffee server, wooden handle, blue 17-23
Coffeepot, rust color, Bauer mark, in mold 53-60
Creamer, all colors, each 5-10
Cup/saucer set, orange 6- 8
Gravy boat, Ringware, royal blue 21-27
Pitcher, 2 qt., blue............ 16-22
Plate, chop, 13″, all colors, each 15-20
Plate, 6″, all colors, each 3- 7
Salad bowl, 9″, Ringware, jade green 23-28
Sugar bowl, Plainware, covered .. 9-14
Teapot, Ringware, Chinese yellow 23-30
Tumbler, 8 oz., Moderne 13-17
Vase, blue, 5½″ 34-38

Beatlemania

Beatlemania

These four young men changed music styles, worldwide.

"The Beatles Story," complete set, gum cards, 102 in all $43-48
Beer cans, pictures sealed in plastic, each 2- 3
Coin purse, red vinyl, squeeze-type 4- 6
Dolls, nodders, 4 in set (Illus.), all 34-40
Jigsaw puzzle, issued by fan club, unopened 10-13
Key chain, record-shaped, Shea Stadium concert, 1965 .... 2- 3
Key ring, Lennon promotional photo, 1972 .... 2- 3
Medallion, brass, 4 Beatles in relief 3- 5
Megaphone, large, yellow/white, sketches of all 4 11-15
Paperback, *Cellarful of Noise* by Brian Epstein, 1965 .... 6- 8
Paperweight, rectangular, glass 10-14
Pocket mirror, 1960's photos 2- 3
Pocketknife, John Lennon 3- 5
Poetry book, *Grapefruit* by Yoko Ono, 1970 16-20
Postcards, English, set of 6, all 7- 9
Tie tacs, set of 4, pewter, 1964, all.................. 11-14
Wig, original, in package, 1964 .. 35-40
Lots more around. Watch out for counterfeit records!

Bed/Foot Warmers

Bed

Hot coals were placed in these lidded brass pans attached to long wooden handles. Lots of repros. A block of

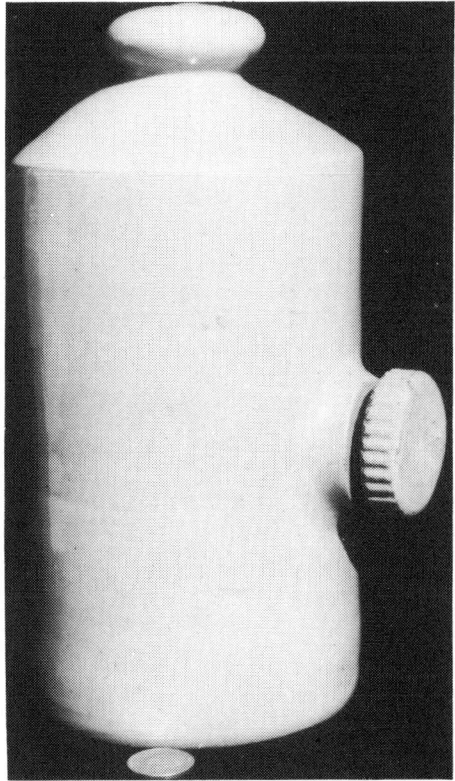

Bed/Foot Warmers

soapstone with wire handle. Also, a husband or wife.

Brass/wood, new .... $ 43- 52
Brass/wood, old 180-215
Soapstone, handled, old 27- 32

Foot

These were used in sleighs and autos.

Metal, carpet-covered, held charcoal, for use in car, 1920's $34- 41
Pottery, cork-lined stopper, held hot water, late 1800's (Illus.) 43- 50
Soapstone, wire handle heated in the oven then put under robe 27- 33

Bells

Used for all purposes, from calling to worship to alerting the town before an Indian raid; they come in brass, glass, iron, and wood. The East Hampton (Conn.) Bell Factory has made them for years.

Bells

Amber, glass, clear handle, 5½" high .... $ 24- 30
Brass, "figure" handle, 8" high 10- 16
Brass, sleigh, 24 on strap 240-250
Cow, sheet iron, 4" high 34- 38
Dinner, stering silver, 2½" high, 1920's 42- 50
Farm, cast iron, #6 yoke 145-160
Locomotive, brass 490-550
School teacher's, turned wooden handle, 6½" high (Illus.) 47- 54
Ship's, brass, 9" high 180-190
Store, w/coiled spring, late 1800's 34- 42
Trolley, East Hampton Bell Works 94-102
Windmill, figural 47- 54

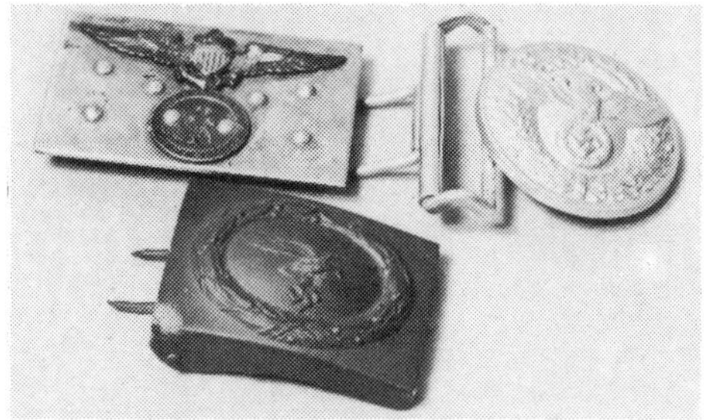

Belt Buckles

Belt Buckles

Gold, ornate, inscribed "Lightweight Champion, 1915," 14K $800-875
Gold-plated, rodeo type (hundreds around) 38- 47
Nazi, World War II, white metal (Illus.) 45- 55
Nazi, World War II, black metal (Illus.) 46- 54

Sterling silver, U.S. Navy wings, St. Christopher medal attached (Illus.) 91-122
Turquoise/silver, Zunl Indians, early 1900's 430-485

Bibles

Bibles

Don't worry too much about finding a King James version or a 15th century Gutenberg printed before 1456. On the other hand, there are many family Bibles turning up in shops today. Many have their backs broken, as this was where money and valuable papers were stored. Did you know the Old Testament contains 39 books, 929 chapters, 23,214 verses, 592,439 words, 2,738,100 letters? The New Testament contains 27 books, 260 chapters, 7,950 verses, 182,253 words and 933,380 letters. Also, the name of Jehovah or Lord occurs 6,855 times in the Old Testament and the word "and" occurs in the Old Testament 35,643 times. See **Clubs and Publications,** this Price Guide.

Embossed leatherbound, brass hinge, c. early 1800's (Illus.) . $120-130
Large, leatherbound, brass hinges, good condition, mid-1800's 98-107
Miniature, 150 pages, microscopic print 82- 91
Small, carrying size, good condition, mid-1800's....... 38- 46

Bicentennial

Actually it should be "BUYcentennial," because by the end of 1976 more than two million items were sold to commemorate our 200th birthday as a nation.

What you pay for an item depends on how badly you want it. Every material from gold, silver, pewter, porcelain, tin, paper — you name it— all were used to make a "Bicentennial" item. Just watch those "genuines" and those "guarantees." Most Flea Market items are "as is, where is" and rightfully so. Don't demand the return of your money if you find you've "been had." You're out to make your best deal and **so** is the seller.

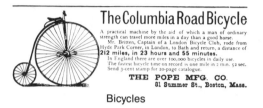

Bicycles

Bicycles

A Frenchman named de Sivrac called it a celerifere as early as 1690; in 1779, Blanchard and Magurier called theirs a velocipede. Later, around 1815, a German baron improved it, calling his a draisine; curricle, boneshakers, and finally the change from iron to rubber-rimmed wheels. In 1877, the famous English bicycle, Ordinary, showed up in America. Then a man named Pope changed it all with this Columbia high wheeler. When John Dunlap invented the pneumatic tire in 1889, bikers worldwide were off and pedaling. See **Clubs and Publications,** this Price Guide.

Accessories
Advertising charm, brass, Corbin Brake .... $ 22- 30
Advertising mirror, National Bicycles 48- 54
Advertising mirror, Zimmy Bicycles 44- 53
Advertising pin, metal, Spalding 29- 38
Catalogue, Stearns Bicycle, c. 1900 .... 54- 62

Lapel stud, enamel, League of American Wheelmen (L.A.W.), 1898 . . . . 11- 16
Lapel stud, enamel, Crown Cycles, La Porte, Inc. 15- 21
Lapel stud, enamel, Alpha Cycle Co., Philadelphia . . . 15- 21
Lapel stud, enamel, L.A.W., Mass. Div., Spring Meet, Boston 1896 . . . . 15- 21
Lapel stud, enamel, Laclede Mfg. Co. (LaTour), St. Louis 15- 21
Ribbons, each 18- 23
Stickpin, Corbin Brake 19- 24
Stickpin, New Departure Coaster Brake 21- 28
Tray, brass and porcelain, Columbia Bicycles 28- 34

Bicycles
Iver Johnson, sprocket-type, 1915, still works 178-192
Schwinn, after World War II . 40- 50

Big Little Books

Photo Courtesy of
Hake's Americana & Collectibles

Big Little Books

Although the Whitman Publishing Company published most of them, there were other companies competing for the reader market in the 1930's and 1940's. Most authorities agree that the modern comic book evolved from these chunky readables.

Prices are for good to mint condition.

Ace Drummond $10- 15
Alice in Wonderland 19- 28
Alley Oop
Alley Oop and Dinny 17- 28
Alley Oop in the Invasion of Moo 19- 30
Alley Oop in the Jungles of Moo 13- 20
Andy Panda and Tiny Tom 10- 14
Bandits at Bay 9- 11
Betty Boop in "Miss Gulliver's Travels" 15- 25
Betty Boop in "Snow White" . . . 15- 25
Bible Stories
Whitman Publishing Co. printed a lot of these books in the 1930's and they're collectible now (Illus.), each 3- 4
Billy the Kid's Pledge 11- 15
Black Beauty 14- 20
Blondie
Blondie and Baby Dumpling, 1937 . . . . 18- 30
Blondie and Bouncing Baby Dumpling 17- 31
Blondie and Dagwood, Some Fun 18- 29
Blondie, No Dull Moments 17- 26
Boss of the Chisholm Trail 12- 19
Br'er Rabbit, 1945 . . . . 34- 42
Bringing Up Father 35- 43
Buck Jones
Buck Jones in Night Riders . . . 23- 31
Buck Jones in Ride 'em Cowboy 22- 32
Buck Jones in the Fighting Code 22- 32
Buck Jones in the Roaring West 21- 31
Buck Rogers
Buck Rogers and the Doomed Comet 34- 41
Buck Rogers and the Overturned World 34- 44
Buck Rogers in the 25th Century A.D., 1933 . . . . 33- 41
Buck Rogers on the Moon of Saturn 44- 56
Bugs Bunny and the Pirate Loot 16- 26
Call of the Wild 25- 33
Captain Easy Hunting for Whales 18- 27
Chandu the Magician 32- 41
Charlie Chan Solves a New Mystery 21- 29
Chester Gump and His Friends . 18- 26
Clyde Beatty in the Steel Arena . 19- 27
Cowboy Lingo 17- 26
Dan Dunn and the Dope Ring . . . 17- 27
Dick Tracy
Dick Tracy and the Mad Killer . 31- 39

Dick Tracy and the Spider Gang 23- 32
Dick Tracy, Detective 11- 16
Dick Tracy Returns 27- 38
Daniel Boone 18- 27
Desert Justice 12- 17
Dixie Dugan Among the Cowboys 14- 22
Don Winslow and the Giant Spy . 14- 27
Donald Duck—more than 25, average price 17- 58
Elmer and His Dog Spot 18- 32
Felix the Cat, 1935, 1943, 1945 . 15- 23
Fighting President 32- 40
Flash Gordon
Flash Gordon and the Ice World of Mongo 71-100
Flash Gordon and the Power Men of Mongo 61- 71
Flash Gordon and the Water World of Mongo 62- 70
Frank Merriwell at Yale 18- 27
Freckles and His Friends 15- 23
G-Man
G-Man and the Missing Clues . 12- 18
G-Man Foils the Kidnappers . . 17- 27
G-Man in Action 21- 28
Gene Autry in Hawk of the Hills . 22- 32
Ghost Avenger 22- 32
Gun Justice 18- 27
Huckleberry Finn 15- 26
Jack Armstrong and the Ivory Treasure 22- 29
Joe Palooka, Gentleman 24- 34
Jungle Jim 41- 47
Katzenjammer Kids 35- 46
Kelly King at Yale Hall (dubious title) 18- 27
Ken Maynard
Ken Maynard in Gun Justice . . 25- 33
Ken Maynard in Western Justice 21- 29
Ken Maynard and the Strawberry Roan 24- 35
Kit Carson 22- 33
Li'l Abner in New York 37- 45
Little Orphan Annie, more than 30, average price 26- 35
Little Women 62- 73
Lone Ranger
Lone Ranger and the Lost Valley 30- 37
Lone Ranger and the Secret Killer 24- 31
Lone Ranger and the Silver Bullets 27- 32
Mandrake the Magician 57- 66
Mickey Finn 19- 26
Mickey Mouse, more than 35, some rare, average price . . . 31- 44
Moby Dick 19- 32
Oswald the Rabbit 22- 31
Phantom and the Sky Pirates . . . 32- 43
Plainsman 24- 33
Popeye, average price 34- 43
Red Berry, Hero of the Hour 19- 29
Red Ryder
Red Ryder and the Code of the West 24- 33
Red Ryder and the Rimrock Killer 26- 36
Robin Hood 9- 14
Roy Rogers, average price 18- 26
Secret Agent X-7 . . . . 15- 23
Secret Agent X-9 . . . . 29- 39
Silly Symphonies 45- 61
Skeezix Goes to War 19- 32
Smilin' Jack and the Jungle Pipeline 26- 34
Smokey Stover, the False Alarm Fireman 22- 31
Stan Kent, Freshman Fullback . . 16- 27
Tailspin Tommy, Air Racer 18- 29
Tiny Tim
Tiny Tim and the Mechanical Man 19- 28
Tiny Tim in the Big Bad World 18- 27
Tom Mix
Tom Mix and the Riding Avenger 38- 47
Tom Mix and the Stranger from the South 34- 42
Tom Mix, Chief of the Rangers 34- 43
Tom Mix Plays a Lone Hand . . 34- 42
Treasure Island 35- 45
Union Pacific 21- 30
Westward Ho 25- 31
Will Rogers 12- 18
Winning of the Old Northwest . . 12- 18

Suggested reading: *The Big Little Book Price Guide,* James Stuart Thomas, Wallace-Homestead Book Company.

Bill Holders

These hung on the kitchen wall in the days when groceries were delivered to the home. Usually painted cast iron, they're collectible.

Average price, good shape $8-16

Bing

Mr. Crosby will always be remembered for his songs and sense of humor. Thousands of items to do with Bing are floating around at Flea Markets and garage sales.

Camera case and camera . . $ 70- 80
Desk, authenticated 1,800-1,900
Humidor, "B. C." initials . . 550- 575
Movie poster, *High Society,* unframed, signed, 14" × 36" 275- 290

Movie poster, *Road to Rio,* unframed, 26″×40″ 255- 270
Record, 78 RPM, "Boise, Idaho," with Peggy Lee, 12/12/47 .... 45- 50
Wastepaper basket, initialed 350- 365
Wool blankets from Pebble Beach home, pr., "Bing Crosby" 185- 195
Wristwatch, Gruen Curvex, "Appreciation, U.S.O." .. 260- 370

Binoculars (Field Glasses)

Binoculars (Field Glasses)

When we went to war in 1941, the U.S. Navy desperately needed binoculars or what were commonly called "field glasses." Thousands of patriotic citizens responded with Bausch and Lombs, etc. Few, if any, that survived were ever returned to their original owners. Today you find them in second-hand stores, pawn shops, etc. Now they're really showing up at Flea Markets as dad empties his closet of all that then-precious junk he lugged home from the war.

The buying price is dependent on the condition of the binocular, especially the lenses. And does it still have the original case?

Bisque

Look for the "flat" finish that distinguishes these unglazed china items. Figurines, slippers, toothpick holders — just a few of the many things made of

Bisque

bisque. Price depends on type, size, and condition. Lots of "Occupied Japan" stuff out there, but it's marked, so look for it.

Box, chick on lid, 2½″×2½″ $22-25
Bust, little boy, 3½″ high 25-33
Bust, Victorian man in big hat, 5½″ high 60-69
Figurine, boy w/shovel, 11″ high (Illus.) 55-63
Figurine, girl w/flowers, 4″ high, Germany 30-38
Figurine, girl w/kitten, 14″ high, Japan 63-71
Figurine, Indian bow, 3″ high, Japan 31-40
Figurine, man w/hoe, 3½″ high, Germany 30-38
Match holder, boy w/dog, 4″ high 40-47
Match holder, girl w/doll, 4½″ high 43-52
Shoe, floral decor, 2½″ long 21-28
Toby jug, 3½″ high, Japan 24-31
Toothpick holder, boy w/dog, 3″ high, Japan 29-35
Toothpick holder, kitten w/ball, Germany, 2½″ high 26-33
Vase, apples and leaves, 6½″ high 37-44
Vase, dragon's head, 4½″ high, Japan 34-41

Vase, leaves and blossoms, 5¼" high 36-44
Vase, yellow/blue daisies, 4" high, Japan 24-29

Black Amethyst Glass

Black Amethyst Glass

When held to a light, the glass looks deep purple. Lots of old and lots of new on the market. Made in every size and shape.

Ashtray, dog's head in relief $14-19
Ashtray, heart-shaped 7-10
Bowl, covered, "crown" finial ... 35-44
Candleholder, 3-light, 5" high ... 19-26
Compote, gold trim on lid, 6" high 45-54
Cookie jar, painted face of woman, 7" high 44-54
Dish, powder, zipper design 24-32
Flower frog, 6½" x 3½" 6- 9
Planter, dancing nudes 44-52
Plate, kittens in relief, 6" dia. ... 24-32
Plate, 7¼" dia. 20-27
Sugar bowl, open 15-22
Toothpick holder, 2" high 19-25
Tray, handled, 10" long 19-25
Tray, pin 16-22
Vase, bud, 7½" high 21-28
Vase, fluted lip, 8" high 28-33
Vase, handled (Illus.) 35-40

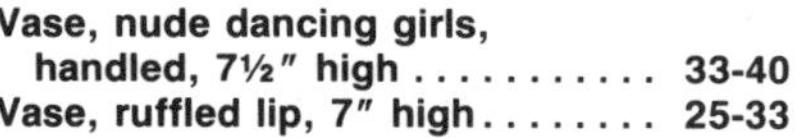
Vase, nude dancing girls, handled, 7½" high 33-40
Vase, ruffled lip, 7" high 25-33

Black Collectibles

Black Collectibles

"Roots" and the late Martin Luther King are but two of the reasons people are collecting this delightful subject. A great people, a great collectible.

Ashtray, boy on potty, ceramic $ 7- 11
Ashtray, Sunshine Sam, plaster 40- 45
Bell, mammy and chef, ceramic, Japan, 3" 18- 23
Bottle opener, boy and alligator, cast iron 80- 89
Candles, Uncle Bub and Mammy, 12 in original box, all 182-190
Clock, peanut vendor, Lux 285-307
Cookie jar, Aunt Jemima, celluloid 99-109
Creamer, Aunt Jemima and Uncle Mose, molded yellow plastic, 3½" 19- 24
Dartboard, tin/cork, Sambo, 14" x 23", by Wyandotte Toys 53- 60
Doll, Aunt Jemima, plastic, 11½", c. 1948 .... 39- 44
Doorstop, mammy, cast iron, 8¼" 130-137

Figurine, boy w/watermelon, bisque, 4″ 22- 30
Incense burner, boy on potty, pot metal, 3″ (Illus.)........ 16- 22
Perfume bottle, golliwog, 3″ high 72- 80
Piebird, chef, 3½″ 19- 25
Pincushion, mammy, chalkware 25- 30
Pipe, man's full face, meerschaum, in original case 250-260
Pot holder hanger, Sambo 12- 16
Print, lithograph, American Beauty, boy smelling roses .. 45- 53
Punchboard, Darky's Prayer, never used 130-140
Salt/pepper set, mammy and chef 32- 39
Spoon, boy eating watermelon, sterling silver 60- 68
Sugar bowl w/lid, Aunt Jemima and Uncle Mose, molded yellow plastic 19- 24
Tape measure, mammy, celluloid, 2″ 77- 82
Tin can, pickaninny, peanut butter, 1 lb................ 98-106
Wall plaque, boy/girl eating watermelon, ceramic 18- 25
Watch fob, 3 smiling children, gold-filled 115-125

Blown Glass Animals/Birds

Blown Glass Animals/Birds

They've been around for years.

Average price ....50¢-$1

Blue Bird China

Around 1910 until around 1933 or 1934. It's decorated with blue birds flying among pink flowering branches. Inexpensive when made, today it brings fairly high prices, considering the quality. Look for makers such as Carrolton, Homer Laughlin, Limoges China, and W. S. George on the backstamps. Probably other manufacturers.

Creamer $13-15
Cup/saucer set 16-20
Dessert plate, 6½″ 4- 6
Luncheon plate 8-11
Platter, 16″ long 19-24
Soup 11-15
Sugar, covered 13-15
Teapot 18-24
Tumbler 7- 9
Waste bowl, 5¼″ dia. 11-14

Blue Ridge Pottery

Blue Ridge Pottery

In 1910 E. J. Owen founded Clinchfield Pottery in Irwin, Tennessee. In 1917 or 1918 the name was changed to Southern Potteries, Inc. During the 1930's and until January of 1957 the firm made commercial dinnerware. In the 1940's and 1950's Sears and Montgomery Ward sold a great deal of Southern's products.

Ashtray, Autumn Apple ....$ 6- 8
Butter dish w/lid, Mountain Daisy 13-17
Coffeepot, Ridge Daisy 16-23
Cup/saucer, demitasse, Ridge Daisy 14-18
Cup/saucer, Mountain Ivy 11-15
Plate, Mountain Ivy, dinner...... 5- 8
Plate, Poinsettia, dinner 5- 8
Platter, Ridge Daisy 8-11
Vegetable bowl, Mountain Ivy ... 9-13

Bohemian Glass

Bohemian Glass

Bohemia is now part of Czechoslovakia. This glass is ruby-colored, flashed, stained, blue, yellow, green AND being heavily reproduced. Buy it if the price is right, but few amateurs can tell the genuine from the "skinned again!"

Caster sets, compotes, decanters, goblets, lustres, pitchers, vases, etc. — all made in this glass.

Bell, blue/clear, 5½" high $34-40
Bell, deer/forest, 5" high 44-51
Candlestick, ruby/clear, 10" high, pr. 65-74
Decanter, red/clear, 11" high 55-64
Decanter w/tumble-up glass, 10½" high (Illus.) 58-65
Goblet, yellow/clear, deer, 4½" high 24-33
Plate, ruby/clear, etched deer, 8" dia. 65-73
Plate, yellow/clear, church in valley, 7½" dia. 60-68
Tumbler, ruby/clear, coin spots, 5" high 42-51
Vase, amber/clear, deer and castle, 8¼" high 67-74
Vase, blue/clear, vine decor, 7" high 44-52
Vase, ruby/clear, castle scene, 9" high 55-64
Wine, ruby/clear, floral decor 23-30

Bone Dishes

When people ate with their fingers years ago, these dishes were used to spit the

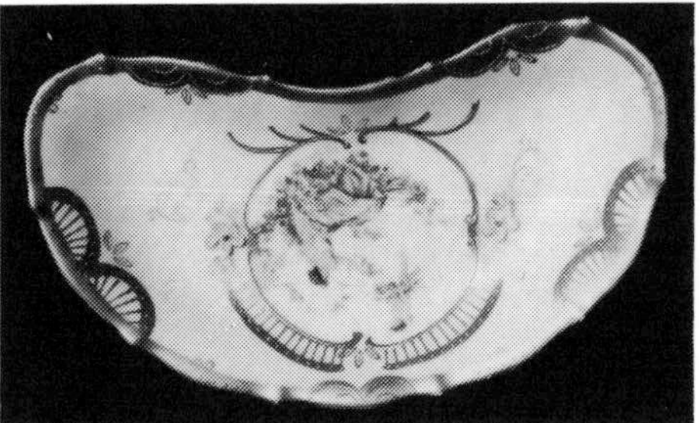

Bone Dishes

bones into, the curved edge fitting around the neck. Today, they make great ashtrays or candy dishes. Average prices depend on maker and age. Obviously, one by Haviland would cost more than a run-of-the-mill Ironstone. Lots of "new" around.

Book Matches

In the 1850's sheets of thin wooden matches appeared on the market. In 1897, the Diamond Match company produced them in folder form with advertisements on the outside. Today, millions of advertisers use them to sell their products. Countless thousands of collectors are saving them. Any and all are collectible. If you begin a collection, it's a good idea to remove the matches before putting them in an album.

Common, usually purchased in bulk (per thousand) $17-28
Early 1900's, usually purchased in bulk (per hundred) 31-38

Bookends

Bookends

These were made of brass, cast iron, copper, glass, even silver.

Art Deco decor, extension type, bronze, pr.	$ 70- 78
Bison, brass, pr.	175-185
Cats, cast iron, pr.	40- 50
Dog heads, plaster, 1930's (Illus.)	12- 18
Elephants, brass, pr.	95-110
German Shepherd, cast iron, pr.	40- 47
Horse rearing, bronze, pr.	95-112
Lions, cast iron, pr.	40- 47
Pirate ship, cast iron, painted, pr.	54- 62
Tiger, bronze, pr.	165-180

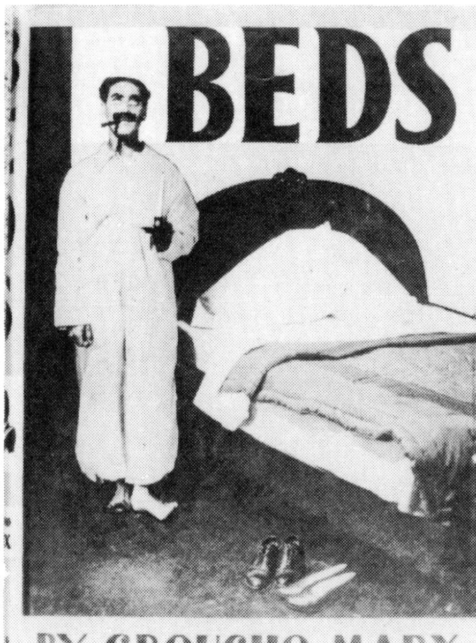

Books

Books

There are millions in every category. Keep in mind that age doesn't necessarily make a book valuable. Two things do: Is it a **first** edition? Is it **author-signed?** Also, condition. Does it have its original dust jacket? Is it leatherbound? Many authors in the 1930's used an autopen to "sign" their books; 90 percent of what you'll find today is in the 50¢-$1.50 range.

Beds by Groucho Marx (Illus.) (One of G's best jokes: "I shot an alligator in my pajamas—how he got in my pajamas I'll never know!")	$14-17
Chester Gump at Silver Creek Ranch by Whitman	7-10
Chester Gump Finds the Hidden Treasure by Whitman	7-10
Smilin' Jack, Freckles, Smokey Stover all by Whitman	5- 8
Tom Corbett Push-Out Book, front and back covers	9-12
Souvenir book, Coronation of Queen Elizabeth II	6-10

Thousands of books at every Flea Market.

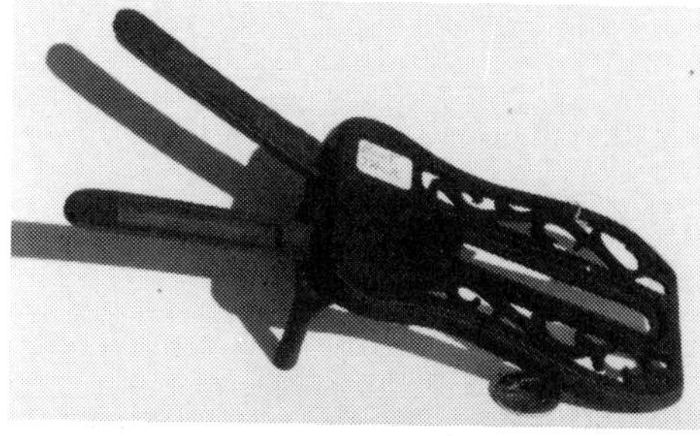
Bootjacks

Bootjacks

"Naughty Nellie" and the "Beetle" are two famous "jacks" and both are now being reproduced.

Heel rods push back into base, old (Illus.)	$34-43
Beetle, old, cast iron	35-42
Cricket, cast iron, old	34-38
"Naughty Nellie," old, cast iron, 11½" long	44-52
Wooden, hand-carved, cherry, mid-1800's	28-33

Boot Scrapers

Boot Scrapers

Fastened to the front porch stoop, they were used to scrape the mud from one's boots, early 1800's to mid-1900's.

Cast iron, bristle brush, 1920's	$18-23
Scottie dog, cast iron, 1930's (Illus.)	24-33
Whale's belly, cast iron (rare)	48-63

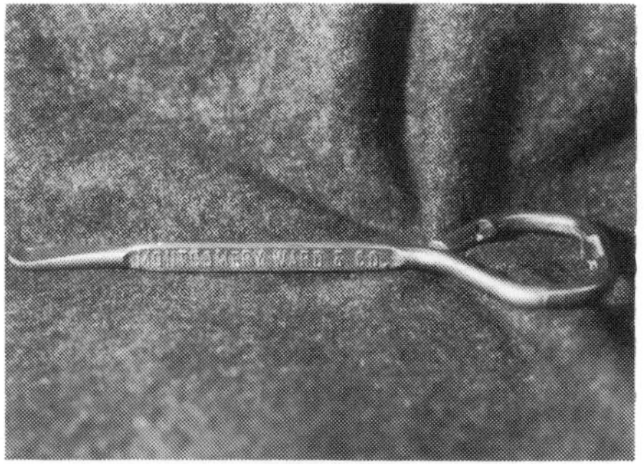

Bottle Openers/Stoppers

Bottle Openers/Stoppers

They're made of brass, iron, aluminum, cork, and wood. They all do the same thing — remove a cap or "stop" a bottle. See **Clubs and Publications,** this Price Guide.

Bottle Openers

Alligator, cast iron, 6½"	$47-52
Baseball cap, Reingold Beer, cast iron	33-38
Black face, brass	38-52
Chicken, aluminum	3- 4
Cowboy, brass	34-38
Donkey, original paint, cast iron	51-58
Dragon, green, cast iron	44-49
Drunk, 4-eyed	23-28
Drunk, high hat	14-19
Elephant, brass	39-45
False teeth, wall mount	14-19
Hammer, brass	18-24
Iroquois (Ale) Indian, aluminum, Montgomery Ward and Co. (Illus.)	75¢- 1
Nude, brass	39-44
Nude, chrome-plated	28-33
Pabst Blue Ribbon, bottle-shaped	14-19
Parrot, cast iron	31-38
Shovel	18-22
Swordfish, cast iron	68-73
Tennis racket	13-18
Trout, cast iron	24-29
Waiter, wood	31-35
Whale, brass	14-19

Bottle Stoppers

Bing Crosby/Bob Hope, wood/cork, (Illus.), each	$7-10
Plastic measure-a-drink type	1.50-2

Apothecary Bottle

Beer Bottle

Bottles

See **Clubs and Publications,** this Price Guide.

Apothecary

Blown, Masson's Guaranteed on label, 14″ high	$34- 40
Blown, Self Cure on label, 15″ high	32- 40
Blown, squat green, 5″ high (Illus.)	31- 37
Brown, Extr. Strict on label, ground stopper, 15¼″ high	32- 40
Brown, blown, gold label, 8½″ high	31- 36
Brown porcelain, label, 7″ high	31- 35
Bulbous, salesman's sample, fancy base, 11″ high	31- 37
Capsicum on porcelain label, blown, 10½″ high	29- 38
Clear, blown, stopper, 8″ high	31- 40
Clear, blown, Tinc, Orsc on label, 12″ high	29- 36

Ardos

Clock	$ 45- 52
Green Duck	45- 52
Rocker	27- 37

Ballantine (Whiskey)

Duck	$ 27- 36
Fisherman	27- 35
Golf bag	18- 27
Knight, silver	24- 33

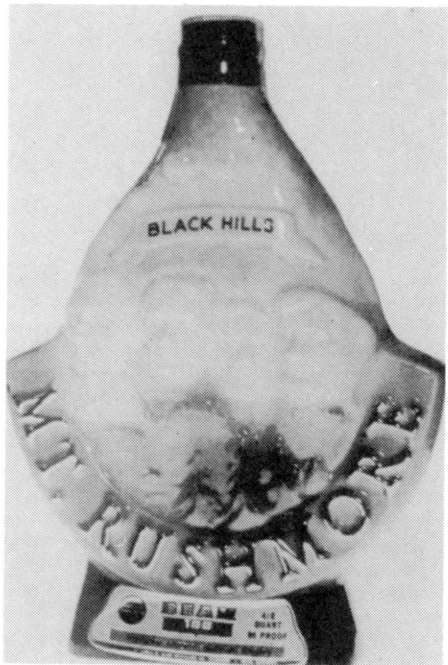

Jim Beam

Jim Beam

Jim Beam bottles created quite a sensation in the bottle field. Several books are now available on these bottles. The Jim Beams listed here are for identification purposes.

Centennial Series

Alaska Purchase (1966)	$ 30- 34
Baseball	18- 23
Civil War: North, South, each	30- 37
Laramie	14- 24
Preakness	12- 18
St. Louis Arch, 1964	20- 27

Customer Specialties

Cal-Neva	$ 17- 24
Foremost, black and gold, gray and gold	130-140
Foremost, pink speckled beauty	300-350
Harold's Club: 12 bottles made so far, more to come, each	22- 27
Harold's Club, blue slot machine	20- 26
Harold's Club, man in a barrel, No. 1, 1957	320-340
Harold's Club, VIP Executive, 1967, 1968, 1969, 1970, 1971	38- 50

Executive Series

Royal porcelain, 1955	$140-160
Royal di Monte, 1957	60- 70
Blue cherub, 1960	60- 70
Royal rose, 1963	50- 58
Marbled fantasy, 1965	60- 65
Prestige, 1967	30- 37
Presidential, 1968	14- 19

Political Series

Ashtrays, elephant and donkey, all years, pr.	$ 20- 24
Boxers, pr.	30- 33
Clowns, pr.	14- 19

Regal China Series

Arizona tombstone	$ 18- 22
Black canasta, 1956	16- 22
Broadmoor Hotel	15- 19
Cable car, 1968	14- 20
Grand Canyon, 1969	18- 23
Kentucky Cardinal, 1973 trophy	22- 29
Oatmeal jug	32- 37
Pony Express	10- 13
Scotch bell ringer	14- 20
Thailand	8- 10
Yosemite	8- 10

State Series

Alaska Star, 1958, 1964, 1965	$ 45- 53
Hawaii, 1959, 1967	47- 57

Kentucky Derby, black head, 1967 .... 12- 20
Nebraska 16- 23
North Dakota 72- 82
West Virginia Centennial 82- 92

Trophy Series

Dog, 1959 .... $ 60- 70
Doe, 1963, 1967 .... 22- 29
Fish, 1965 .... 23- 31
Horses, three colors, each 27- 36
Ram 110-118
Woodpecker 10- 14

Glass Specialties

Cannon .... $ 10- 12
Cleopatra, rust, 1962 .... 18- 22
Dancing Scot, short, 1963 .... 20- 27
Dancing Scot, tall, 1963 .... 14- 19
Delft blue, Delft rose 14- 18
Mark Antony, 1962 .... 13- 18
Pin: gold top, white top, wooden top 10- 14
Pyrex coffee warmers, 1954, four colors 12- 16
Royal Emperor 14- 19
Royal Reserve 18- 22
Smoked Crystal, 1964 .... 14- 20

Beer (also see Breweriana)

Cobalt, 9¾" high (Illus.) .... $ 12- 18
Milk glass, 9" high 21- 27
Olive green, qt. 12- 18
Red, qt. 22- 29
Schmidt, original label, qt. 23- 33

Bischoff

Bell tower, 1959 .... $ 53- 61
Boy, Chinese, Spanish 42- 52
Egyptian vase: single, double 44- 54
Fish bottle ashtray 28- 34
Grecian vase, decanter 21- 29
Nigerian mask 27- 38
Red clown 22- 34
Senorita 23- 33

Bols

Ballerina .... $ 28- 34
Cream de menthe, Delft 36- 47
Dutch: boy, girl 44- 52

Borghini

Dog .... $ 37- 46
Ford car, recent, old 25- 35
Horse's head 28- 37
Nubian girl 19- 23
Santa Maria 14- 22

Ezra Brooks

Antique cannon .... $ 35- 42
Bucket of blood 38- 44
Cable cars, 3 colors, each 26- 36
Churchill bust 27- 38
Clown on drum, short, tall 88- 94
Dueling pistol 27- 37
Grizzly bear 22- 31
Gun series (4) 38- 46
Harold's Club dice 28- 40
Kentucky gentleman 35- 44
Mr. Foremost 33- 40
Oil derrick (gusher) 30- 39
Potbelly stove 20- 26
Queen of hearts 27- 36
Reno arch 21- 31
Trout and fly 27- 36
Wheat shocker, Kansas 33- 41

J. W. Dant

Alamo (black) .... $ 28- 33
Bobwhite 39- 47
Crossing the Delaware 27- 35
Field birds (chukar partridge, etc.), each 28- 38
Indianapolis 500 .... 40- 44
Patrick Henry 28- 37

George Dickel

Golf club, large .... $ 35- 40
Golf club, miniature 14- 23
Powderhorn 25- 33

Figurals

Figurals

Black bear, Smirnoff vodka .... $ 28- 36
Brown owl 24- 35
Christmas tree, star stopper .... 155+
Crying baby, clear, 6½" high 58- 64
Elephant (used as bank) 19- 24
Face, 12" high (Illus.) 61- 67
Fish, ashtray 38- 47
Guitar, brown 19- 26
Hunter, lady, pr. 51- 61
Lincoln (used as bank) 22- 32
Queen Elizabeth II 27- 38
River Queen boat 27- 38
Violin, blue 66- 75
George Washington bust, miniature 35- 44
Watchtower bell 38- 46

Garnier

Bellows	$ 34- 42
Bullfighter	38- 47
Cardinal	40- 48
Duck	27- 36
Indian	31- 40
Locomotive	36- 46
New Mexico road runner	27- 37
Parrot	42- 50
Pheasant	28- 35
Quail	26- 35
Ship scene	27- 37

Grenadier (Soldiers)

Colonial series, 5 so far, military in nature	$ 34- 42

House of Koshu

Daughter	$ 27- 31
Golden pagoda	24- 31
Pink geisha	73- 78
Princess	24- 30
Two lovers	22- 32
White pagoda	32- 40

Luxardo

Bacchus	$ 22- 32
Clock	30- 38
Dolphin	71- 78
Gondola	22- 31
Miss Luxardo	31- 40
Santa Maria	33- 42
Tapa Print	24- 33
Zodiac	44- 54

Medicine

Bird's lung cure, aqua	$ 30- 37
Davis vegetable compound	38- 45
Hall's catarrh cure, aqua	23- 34
Lydia Pinkham (most famous)	24- 33
Moxie Nerve, aqua	34- 41
River Swamp chill and fever cure	94-103
Shiloh's consumption cure, aqua	22- 29

Mineral Waters

Buffalo Lithia water, green, qt.	$ 28- 35
Clark and White, olive green, qt.	49- 54
Congress and Empire 'E', pt.	38- 44
Empire water, qt.	51- 60
Gettysburg, green, qt.	68- 78
Hathorn Spring, qt.	38- 45
John Ryan, cobalt, pt.	38- 45
Mississquoi Springs, brown, pt., qt.	50- 58
Saratoga Red Spring, pt.	63- 70

Miniatures

Ardo Paestum	$ 20- 30
Borghini black cat	24- 30
Borghini candleholder	28- 38
Borghini candlelamp	24- 32
Borghini redbird	19- 28
Drioli cat	28- 34
Drioli dog	31- 40
Drioli duck	28- 38
Irish Mist soldier	19- 22
Larson's Viking ship, china	31- 40
Larson's Viking ship, glass	27- 38
Ryenbende: churn, cruet, oil lamp, shoe	18- 27

Old Fitzgerald Cabin Still

Candlelight, pr.	$ 37- 44
California	23- 32
Fish	19- 24
Florentine	27- 34
Gold coaster	34- 40
Hillbilly, pt., fifth, 1969 (Illus.)	25- 33
Lexington	21- 31
Quail	19- 27
Sons of Erin, 1969	28- 37
Tournament, 1963	32- 44
Tree of Life	24- 33
Venetian	18- 28
Weller masterpiece	64- 72

Perfume

Black amethyst, marked Guerlain France	$ 29- 36
Bulbous, sterling silver overlay, 7″ high	101-110
Crystal, silver overlay, floral, birds	91-108
Cut glass, Harvard cut, silver cap	55- 63
Diamonds, sunbursts, cut glass	62- 70
Hobnail pattern, clear	24- 31
Lalique, rectangular	61- 70
Pelican, Germany, porcelain	30- 37
Silver overlay, leaf decor, ball stopper	31- 40
Thousand-eye, bulbous	40- 48

Poison

Amber, 3-sided, riffled, marked Poison	$ 29- 37
Cobalt, 3-sided, riffled, marked Poison	32- 40
Skull and Crossbones, embossed Poison on all sides	34- 41

Soda and Sarsaparilla

Ayers compound extract sarsaparilla, aqua	$ 18- 23
Babcock's sarsaparilla, aqua	72- 80
Bull's sarsaparilla, plain, aqua	100-109
Coca-Cola, dated 1909, Knoxville, brown	28- 37
Dana's sarsaparilla, Bangor, Me., aqua	38- 43
DeWitt's sarsaparilla, aqua	38- 45
Dr. Green's sarsaparilla, clear	28- 37
Joy's sarsaparilla, aqua	41- 50
Rodway's sarsaparilla, aqua	41- 53

Scoville's unembossed, aqua .. 28- 38
Verner's ginger ale, embossed seal 27- 33

Boxes

Boxes

Every material known has been used to make boxes.

Cigarette, silver-plated, 1950's (Illus.) $10-16
Cigarette, tin, Lucky Strike "flat fifties" 3- 4
Deed, tin, has key 25-33
Hat, cardboard, round, "Saks Fifth Avenue" 18-24
Jewelry, gold-plated, late 1800's 24-28
Jewelry, quadruple plate, late 1800's 23-32
Knife, wood, 2 compartments ... 25-32
Sewing, leather, brass feet, 1930's 45-52
Stamp, copper, 1930's 12-18
Tool, compartments, handled, wood 30-37

Boyd's Crystal Art Glass

Bernard C. Boyd and son purchased the Degenhart Glass Factory (see Degenhart Glass) in 1978. Some fifty of Elizabeth Degenhart's molds, with the familiar "D in heart" trademark removed, are used by Boyd. Boyd also makes Zack the Elephant, Joey the Pony, and Louise the Doll.

Chicks, 1", ice blue, chocolate, robin's egg blue, each $11-14
Debbie Duck, cobalt, milk glass, each 4- 7

Elephant-head toothpicks

Apricot $26-30
Chocolate 14-17
Lemon ice 32-37

Joey the Pony

Chocolate $32-36
Crown tuscan 12-15
Golden delight 12-15
Willow blue 23-27

Louise the Doll

Candy swirl $26-31
Dawn 21-25
Firefly 21-25
Heather 21-25
Old ivory 13-17

Owls

Candy swirl $27-31
Magic marble 37-41

Skippy

English yew .... $ 9-12
Golden delight 9-12

Zack the Elephant

Delphinium $16-21
Flame 47-51
Lavender 16-19
Old ivory slag 16-22
Snow 16-21

Breweriana

Anything to do with "suds" is collectible. Also see **Clubs and Publications,** this Price Guide.

Beer Bottles

These will become more collectible, especially those made in the 1950's and 1960's IF they have their original labels.

Average price .... 50¢-75¢

Beer Cans

A few years ago everyone was collecting them. And no! Your Billy Beer cans are NOT worth a king's ransom.

Average price .... 50¢-75¢

Glasses/Mugs

Blatz mug, 1 gal., advertising novelty $35-42
Heineken stein, fairly new 2- 3
Large "growler" from old Parker House, Boston 15-19
Schlitz Beer glasses, set of 6 11-14

Miscellaneous

Blatz Beer change tray .... $ 7-10
Falstaff Beer plaque, tin, 1970's 49-57
Reingold Beer tray 14-20
Ruppert's Beer calendar, 1931 .. 5- 8

Sheet Music

"Under the Anheuser Bush" ... $4-6

Bridge Scorecards

Photo Courtesy of
Hake's Americana & Collectibles

Bridge Scorecards

Eli Culbertson was one of the world's best players. Some of the scorecards from bridge clubs are worthy of framing.

Betty Boop and Bimbo scorecards (Illus.) $11-14
Average price for other scorecards, each .... 75¢-$1

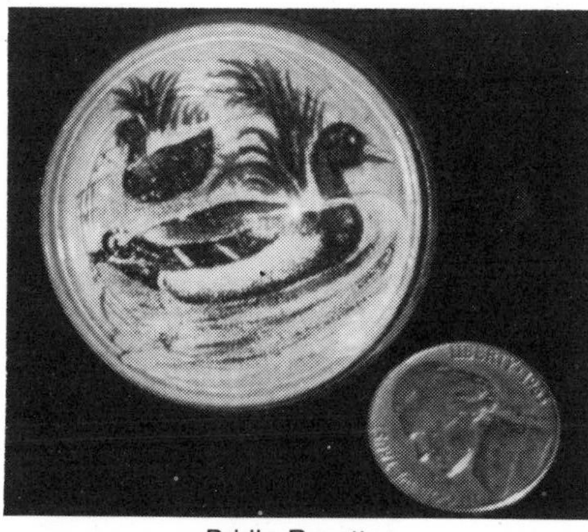

Bridle Rosettes

Bridle Rosettes

They were used to decorate the horse's bridle. Made of glass, women wear them today as pins on a lapel.

Double heart, brass background $19-26
Eagle and flag, blue background, brass 24-33
Shield and thirteen stars, brass background 35-44
Yoked oxen, brass background .. 22-29

British Royalty Collectibles

Every time there's a coronation or a wedding, interest surges in these items. Some are quite good, some are quite bad. All are being sought by collectors who continually seek the older and rarer pieces.

King Edward VII/Queen Alexandra

Mug, porcelain, coronation, color photos, Foley China, 3¼" high .... $ 55- 59
Mugs, porcelain, lithopane, c. 1902, 3" high, pr. 230-240
Plate, porcelain, coronation, color portraits, gold rim, 7¼" dia. 69- 75
Teapot, porcelain, coronation, color portraits, gold trim, 4" high 68- 74

King Edward VIII

Bowl, abdication, sepia portrait, Sovereign Potters, Canada, 7¼" dia. $100-108
Bowl, coronation, arms, porcelain, shields around outside, Keith Murray, Wedgwood, 10" dia. 210-220
Bust, "E. R." on base, porcelain, signed Donald Hastings, 4½" high 38- 45
Dish, brass, 1936, raised profile, 4" dia. 27- 34
Egg cup, porcelain, coronation, sepia portrait, gold rim, 2" high 35- 40
Mug, memorial, porcelain, black/white portrait (Duchess of Windsor on reverse), gold trim, 4¼" high 85- 91
Plaque, tin, color portrait, signed "Hancor," Mitcham, England, 17½" × 14½" 109-116
Plate, coronation, porcelain, color portrait, red/blue border, John Maddock & Sons, 9" dia. 59- 67
Print, color, 8¼" × 6½", Photochrom Co., Ltd., London 32- 39
Shoehorn, brass, 7½" long ... 32- 38

George V/Queen Mary

Candy box, porcelain Princess Mary, Christmas, 1914, hinged .... $ 54- 60

Dish, porcelain, coronation, Queen Mary, color portrait, Royal Doulton, 5¾" dia. 59- 65
Egg cup, porcelain, coronation, color portraits, gold rim, 2½" high 48- 54
Glass, marriage, "Joy to HSH Pr. Mary of Teck & HRH Duke of York," etched, flowers, feathers, 4¾" high . 64- 70
Money box, tin, color portraits, hinged, coronation dates, 3" high 62- 70
Plate, porcelain, silver jubilee, sepia portraits, silver rim, 5¾" dia. 56- 60
Tin, coronation, color portraits, hinged, 4½" high 47- 53

King George VI/Queen Elizabeth

Bowl, coronation, amber glass, ruffled edge, 9" dia. ..$ 44- 50
Bowl, coronation, porcelain, sepia portraits, gold rim, 5" dia. 60- 68
Cup/saucer, porcelain, sepia portraits, bone china 53- 60
Dish, coronation, porcelain, color decorated, gold rim, 4" dia., Paragon China 44- 50
Teapot, porcelain, color portraits, Paragon China, 7" high, gold lion finial handle 483-490
Tin, coronation, color portraits, Huntley Palmer, 4" high 49- 53

Prince and Princess of Wales

Busts, white glaze porcelain, 4½" high, pr. ....$ 70- 77
Figurine, Prince of Wales, color decorated, limited edition (1,000), 8¾" high ... 235-242
Ginger jar, royal wedding, sepia portrait, Mason's Ironstone, 5" high 48- 54
Matchbox, tin, royal wedding, "St. Paul's," doors open, 4¾" long 18- 24
Money box, porcelain, royal wedding, pastel rose, green decorated, 3¾" high 24- 28
Playing cards, royal wedding, color portraits 6- 8
Tray, tin, royal wedding, color portrait, Woodgrange Products, 12" dia. 11- 14

Prince William of Wales

Beaker, porcelain, gold lion handles, color/gold decorated, limited edition (1,000), Caverswall, 4½" high ....$ 53- 59
Bell, porcelain, Windsor Castle, portraits, gold trim, 3" high 26- 33
Cup plate, glass, name, date, feathers, R. Wetzel, limited edition (3,000), 2¼" dia., boxed 8- 11
Egg cup, color portraits, 2½" high, porcelain 16- 22
Mug, porcelain, Guyatte design, limited edition (1,000), Wedgwood, 4" high . 56- 60
Plate, christening, color, gold decorated, limited edition (500) 193-200

Princess Margaret

Cup/saucer, porcelain, birth, parakeets, rose, thistle, Paragon China $118-124
Plate, porcelain, birth, same as above, 7" dia. 80- 88
Teapot, porcelain, same design as above, Paragon China 189-194

Queen Elizabeth/Prince Philip

Box, Wedgwood, coronation, covered, white on royal blue, 1½" high ....$ 52- 57
Bust, parian, coronation, Queen Elizabeth II, maroon glazed base, Foley China, 5½" high 64- 70
Film, black/white, 8mm, wedding, 1947 .... 52- 57
Film, black/white, 8mm, coronation, 1953 .... 44- 49
Jam pot, porcelain, red/gold decorated, crown finial on lid, 4" high 53- 58
Pitcher, coronation, brown portrait of Queen Elizabeth II/background, Royal Doulton, 6¼" high 195-204
Playing cards, jubilee, color portraits 26- 30
Teapot, porcelain, coronation, sepia portrait of Queen Elizabeth II, gold background, 5½" high.......... 84- 99

Queen Victoria/Prince Albert

Bowl, glass, coronation, death dates, crown center, 10" dia. ....$ 84- 89
Bowl, pressed glass, jubilee, gold backing portrait, 8¾" dia. 89- 94
Cup/saucer, porcelain, royal family, pink lustre.......... 158-166
Double dish, pressed glass, jubilee, 6¾" long 63- 69
Jug, pressed glass, jubilee, dates, crown in base, 3¾" high 58- 64

Milk jug, porcelain, Dominion of Canada, color portrait of Victoria, gold trim, 3¾" high 48- 53
Mug, porcelain, Victoria, 1837-1887, brown/white, 4" high (Illus.) 49- 54
Plaque, brass, Prince Albert, 7½" high 24- 28
Plate, porcelain, jubilee, blue decorated, "Compliments of A. Stowell & Co.," 10½" dia. 118-124
Saucer, porcelain, 1897 jubilee, green portrait of Victoria, Windsor, Balmoral, 5½" dia. 28- 34
Teapot, porcelain, jubilee, gold trim, Aynsley China, 6" high 226-233

Brownie Collectibles

Palmer Cox, an artist-author, created these creatures of fantasy in 1888. During the 1900's they were copied by other artists.

Book, *The Brownies* by Cox $42-52
Book, *The Brownies, More Nights* by Cox 40-55
Candlestick, Brownie, German, 7½" high (Illus.) 46-54
Cup/saucer, American Belleek china, 1900's................ 48-58
Mug, silver plate, enameled Brownie figures, 5" high 33-43
Soda bottle, embossed, patented by Cox, early 1900's 27-37
Tile, 4" square, German-made ... 36-46

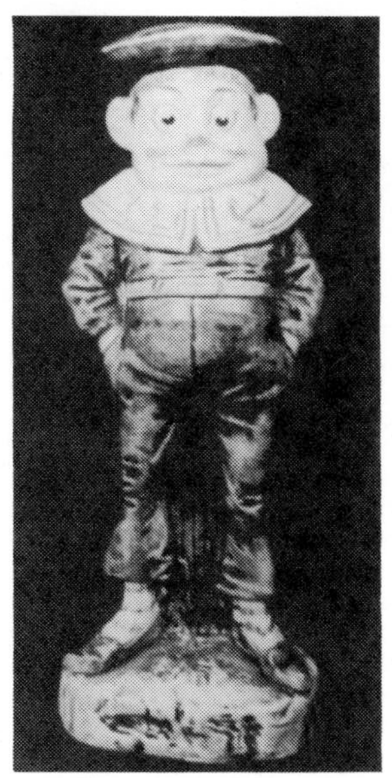

Brownie Collectibles

Photo Courtesy of Hake's Americana & Collectibles

Printed fabric showing Brownies at work and play............. 48-58

Bubblegum Cards

Photo Courtesy of Hake's Americana & Collectibles

Bubblegum Cards

Usually called "trading cards," they were all the rage in the 1880's until the early 1890's. More than 500 sets were issued. When World War I ended they fell out of favor with collectors. Early cards put out by National Chicle, Goudey Gum, and Gum, Inc. are much sought after today. Bowman and Topps made most of what the general collector finds today, c. 1948 until the early 1960's. Donruss

Chewing Gum and the Frank Fleer Company control the field today. Try to collect in sets, but don't overlook the "hot" singles.

Addams Family, Donruss, 1964, 66 cards	$ 33- 40
Batman, Topps, 1966, 55 cards	33- 40
Beverly Hillbillies, Topps, 1963, 66 cards	36- 44
Bionic Woman, Donruss, 1976, 44 cards	10- 13
Dallas, Fleer, 55 cards	7- 11
Dukes of Hazzard, Donruss, 1980, Series 1, 66 cards	7- 10
Elvis, Donruss, 1978, 66 cards	8- 11
Gomer Pyle, Fleer, 1965, 66 cards	12- 16
Gong Show, Fleer, 1979, 66 cards, 10 stickers	7- 10
Hogan's Heroes, Fleer, 1960's, 66 cards	123-130
James Bond, Philadephia Chewing Gum, 1965, 66 cards	38- 45
McHale's Navy, Fleer, 66 cards	12- 15
Monkees, Donruss, 1967, Series A, B, or C, 44 cards, each series	24- 30
Saturday Night Fever, Donruss, 1978, 66 cards	5- 8
Six Million Dollar Man, Donruss, 1975, 66 cards	8- 11
Star Trek, Topps, 1976, 88 cards, 22 stickers	18- 22
Star Wars, Topps, 1977, Series 1, 66 cards, 11 stickers	11- 15
Tarzan, Philadelphia Chewing Gum, 1966, 66 cards	33- 40
Welcome Back Kotter, Topps, 1976, 54 cards	7- 10

Buffalo Pottery

This firm was established in 1901, Buffalo, N.Y. Its best-known pattern is "Deldare" — English tavern scenes.

Cinderella pitcher, Deldare	$ 83- 92
Creamer, village scene, Deldare	45- 56
Cup/saucer, Ye Olden Days, Deldare, 1908	109-122
Plate, Willow, blue, 1915 (Illus.)	20- 30

Buffalo Pottery

Burnt Wood Items

Just that — a scene was burned into the wood with a hot nail or a soldering iron. Sometimes a branding iron-type stamp was used for mass-produced items.

Burnt Wood Items

Swiss Village (Illus.) $11-15
Average price, about the same. The older pieces will probably cost more.

Buster Brown Collectibles

Buster Brown Collectibles

Dick Outcault created a comic strip in 1902 that was eventually syndicated. Buster Brown and his dog, Tige, appeared on the American market in the form of dolls and other objects. The most famous, of course, were shoes, which are still sold under the Buster Brown name.

Buster and Tige bank, cast iron, 5″ high	$172-188
Buster "to call dog" whistle	26- 34
Button, brass	15- 25
Button pin, Buster and Tige	29- 37
Camera, Ansco, in original box	47- 56
Cards, playing, c. 1907	48- 52
Clicker, advertising shoes	19- 27
Comb, brass	19- 28
Cup/saucer, Buster and girl	32- 41
Dish, Buster and girl	31- 41
Fork and spoon, silver metal, both	40- 50
Knife, pocket	92-101
Game, At the Zoo, deck of comic cards	27- 37
Hand puppet, Buster holding Tige, 1906	92-107
Mirror, advertising	19- 24
Mug, china, gold trim, 3″ high	69- 78
Pencil, advertising shoes	15- 22
Plaque, advertising	101-111
Plate, 5″ dia.	58- 61
Postcard, Buster at zoo with Tige and girl	11- 19
Scissors	44- 51
Shoe horn, advertising shoes	16- 22
Sign, Buster and Tige, advertising shoes, 21″ × 25″, tin	158-162
Toy, Buster and Tige cart	162-171
Whistle, advertising shoes	18- 27
Wrapping paper, Buster and girl, poems, complete roll	19- 28

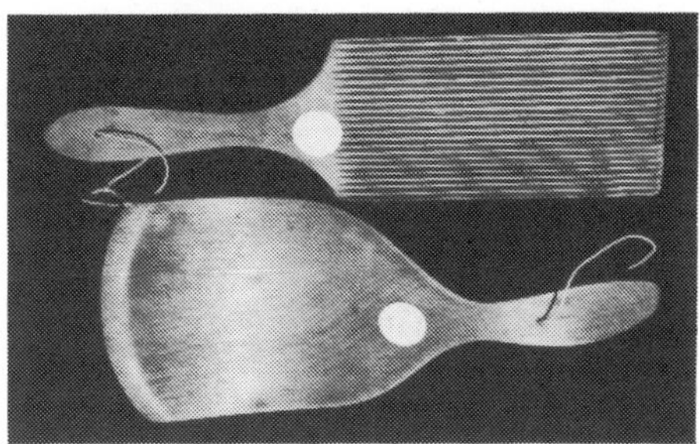

Butter Paddles/Spades

Butter Paddles/Spades

They were used to scoop butter from the tub and to "roll" a chunk of butter into a ball. Usually hand-carved. Maple was a favorite wood. $9-15 pair.

Butter Pats

Butter Pats

These were used in railroad dining cars, in restaurants, diners; still being used on the airlines but they're plastic. Lots of them around.

Porcelain, c. 1880 (Illus.)	$6-9
Pewter, c. 1880	5-8
Porcelain, with railroad insignia	5-7
Porcelain, with hotel/restaurant insignia	5-7
Plastic, American Airlines (or other carriers)	free to 25¢

Buttonhooks

No greater invention, especially before the days of shoelaces, when you had 18 or 24 persnickety buttons to fasten. Hundreds around today.

Abalone handle	$16-20
Agate handle	26-30
Antler handle	11-14
Bone handle, average price	3- 9

Brass handle, average price 3- 8
Copper enameled 53-61
Hard rubber 4- 6
Horn 6- 8
Ivory, average price 11-18
Leather 13-16
Metal, "Walk-Over" (Illus.) 9-15
Mother-of-pearl handle, average price 9-20
Pewter handle 31-36
Plastic, average price 3- 5
Plastic, celluloid (also called French Ivory), average price . . . 4-10
Porcelain handle 16-19
Silver plated, average price 9-17
Steel, average price 3- 5
Sterling silver, average price 18-28
Tortoiseshell handle 23-29
Wooden handle, average price . . . 3-7
Suggested reading: *Buttonhooks,* Cynthia L. Compton, Interstate Publishing.

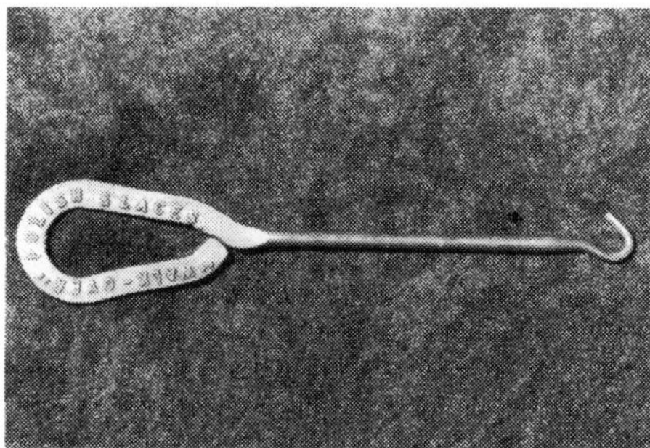

Buttonhooks

Buttons (Pin Backs)

The first year celluloid pin back buttons were made was 1896. The Whitehead & Hoag Company, Newark, New Jersey, filed the first patents around 1893. Major producers in the early days were Bastian Bros., St. Louis Button Co., American Art Works, and Torsh and Franz. By 1920 lithographed tin buttons were being mass-produced for every occasion. The Green Duck Company of Chicago was the largest producer of this type button. Reproduced political buttons are called *brummagems.* A jugate is a button with side-by-side pictures of the presidential and vice-presidential candidates. A law passed in 1973 (The Hobby Protection Act) supposedly protects the collector from imitation hobby items. Like most laws passed by the residents of Foggy Bottom (Washington, D.C.), this one doesn't work either. Just know with whom you're doing business. Prices given are for buttons in fine condition.

Buttons (Pin Backs)

Cause: "Stop the poll tax!," "Keep out of war," etc., average price . . . . 85¢-3
City: Chicago, Pasadena, New Orleans, etc., average price . 60¢-2.50
Famous people: Lincoln, Washington, Teddy Roosevelt, etc., average price 1.75-2.75

Labor: John L. Lewis, C.I.O., etc., average price .... 90¢-1.75

Military: U. S. Battleship Iowa, War Before Dishonor, etc., average price 1-1.75

N.R.A. (National Recovery Act): "We do our part," "Member," etc., average price .... 75¢-2.50

Spanish American War: "Remember the Maine," "Teddy's Rough Riders," etc., average price 1.75-2.50

Sports: Babe Ruth, Lou Gehrig, etc., age and popularity are big factors here, average price 1-3.75

Union and Confederate, average price 1.50-6

World War I: "Welcome Home, 77th Div.," "Welcome Home Rainbow," etc., average price 1.25-3

World War II: "I'll meet you in Tokyo," "Remember Pearl Harbor," "To hell with Hitler," etc.. average price . 1-2.50

Cabbage Patch Kids

Cabbage Patch Kids

These dolls were originated by Xavier Roberts of Cleveland, Georgia. His originals sell for $100 to $1,000. Coleco Industries mass-produces them in the Orient. The dolls come with adoption papers, birth certificates, and a first year birthday card.

Doll, various hair colors (Illus.) . . $17-25
Rocker and carrier (Illus.) 16-20
Stroller (Illus.). 14-19

Calculators

Some work, some don't. Hundreds around.

Average price, if working $4-7
Average price, not working . . . . . 75¢-$1

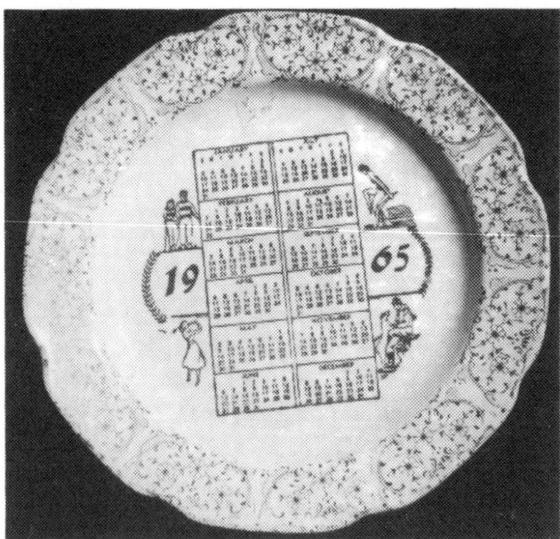

Calendar Plates

Calendar Plates

These plates were used as premiums or giveaways by many merchants in the early twentieth century until just after World War I. Look for the company's name on the front of the plate. They originated in England in the 1880's. Usually decorated with transfer prints, they featured pretty ladies, animals, flowers, patriotic scenes, automobiles, and city scenes.

1908, Santa and Holly, 7″ $36-42
1909, floral decor, California, 6¼″ 34-40
1912, Heavy Brobst, Nuremburg, Pennsylvania, 7″ (Illus.) 32-38
1913, Cadillac, Detroit, 7½″ 42-50
1916, Battleship, Iowa, 6½″ 35-42
1918, Dough Boys, WW I, Pennsylvania, 6¼″ 34-40
1920, Peace, Illinois, 8″ 24-29
1922, Betsy Ross w/flag, 6¼″ . . . 27-33
1925, Horse Race, Kentucky, 7¼″ 33-40
1930, Grant's Tomb, New York, 6½″ 25-31
1935, God Bless Our Home, 7¼″ 22-28
1940, Auto Race, Indy, 7″. 32-39
1950, Windmill, Holland, Michigan, 6½″ 18-26
1955, Zodiac signs, 7″ 19-26
1960, Baby w/bottle, 7¼″ 17-24
1965 to present, average price . . . 13-19

Calendars

Calendars

In the 1920's and 1930's, scantily clad ladies adorned the walls of every garage and gas station in America. The pretty girls are well-known, as are the girls in the Esquire and Playboy magazine calendars. Travelers Insurance of Hartford,

Connecticut, sent Currier & Ives calendars to their clients for years. Prices are for those in fine to very fine condition.

- 1900, American Seal Paint, Uncle Sam $135-145
- 1901, Austin Powder Co., hunting scene .... 400+
- 1907, Harrington & Richardson Arms Co., Indian guide ..... 350+
- 1909, Peters Cartridge Co., hunting scene .... 325+
- 1928, Remington Fire Arms, hunting cabin scene .... 275+
- 1930-1940, "girlie" garage type, various firms, each 20- 28
- 1940-1950, Petty Girls, Esquire, each 24- 33
- 1954, Marilyn Monroe, nude pose 140-150
- 1958, Playboy Playmate, 1st issue, wall type 69- 77
- 1959, Playboy Playmate, 2nd issue, wall type 48- 55
- 1962, Playboy Playmate, 1st issue, desk type 35- 42
- 1962, Playboy Playmate, 5th issue, wall type 29- 35
- 1964, Playboy Playmate, 7th issue, wall type 19- 25
- 1965, Playboy Playmate, 4th issue, desk type 19- 25

Cambridge Glass

Cambridge Glass

Made in Cambridge, Ohio, by the Cambridge Glass Company, c. 1902, this pressed glass was usually marked with a C in a triangle; after 1906, the words NEAR CUT were used. See **Clubs and Publications,** this Price Guide.

Amber (true amber brown)

- Basket, footed, Jenny Lind pattern, 9″ .... $ 52- 58
- Beverage set, 9-pc., ebony foot and base, all 230-240
- Bonbon, 2-handled, gold-encrusted, "C" mark 41- 50
- Bowl, apple or fruit, Ivy Cut pattern, 11″ 120-132
- Bowl, etched, w/figure flower holder, 11½″ 153-162
- Bowl, ram's head, Gadroon pattern, 9″ 260-270
- Bowl, rose, footed, Jenny Lind pattern 54- 61
- Candlesticks, 9½″, pr. 226-240
- Cologne, engraved, Tempo pattern 32- 40
- Colognes, etched American Beauty Rose pattern, gold encrusted, pr. 58- 64
- Cream and sugar w/tray, 3-pc., all 144-155
- Ink bottle 38- 44
- Letter holder 49- 52
- Pen point holder 25- 34
- Plate, tomato, Decagon pattern, "C" mark, 8″ 166-172
- Sweetmeat w/cover, 5″ 42- 48
- Tumbler, Georgian, 8 oz. 21- 34

Azurite (or azure blue—dark opaque blue)

- Bowl, ebony foot, 6″ .... $ 50- 58
- Bowl, gold, encrusted etching, 6″ 60- 68
- Bowl, rolled edge, gold-encrusted, 10″ 74- 84
- Candlesticks, Hexagon pattern, 7″, pr. 82- 90
- Dish, candy, w/cover, gold-encrusted etching, 3-compartment, 6½″ 77- 84
- Mayonnaise set, 2 pc., both ... 77- 86
- Tray, sandwich, handled, 10″ .. 70- 80
- Vase, crimped top, bud, 12″ .. 60- 70
- Vase, sweet pea, etched gold-encrusted band, 7″ 119-127

Carmen (clear, brilliant ruby red)

- Bowl, ram's head, Gadroon pattern, 9″ $453-474
- Box, candy, w/cover, blown, crystal foot, 5⅜″ 79- 83
- Box, cigarette, w/cover, crystal foot, 3″ × 3½″ 64- 72
- Cocktail, etched Portia pattern, gold-encrusted, 3 oz. 28- 38
- Cup, sherbet, Wild Rose pattern, handled 35- 45
- Flower center, w/crystal foot, Seashell pattern, 8″ 150-160
- Ivy ball, w/crystal foot, 8½″ ... 57- 67
- Ivy ball, w/crystal foot, 7″ 56- 66

Salt/pepper set, w/crystal holder, 3 pc., all 48- 58
Sugar, Nautilus design, crystal handles 68- 78
Wine set, 7 pc., all 128-137

Crown Tuscan (fleshlike opaque)

Ashtray, nude statue, 6½″ $117-126
Ashtray, Seashell pattern, "C" mark, 3-toed 35- 44
Bowl, Pristine pattern, 10″ 75- 83
Bowl, salad, Seashell pattern, 11″ 115-121
Butter shell (or ice cream), 3-toed, 5″ 47- 56
Candlesticks, nude statues, 9″, pr. 220-230
Candlesticks, ram's head, each side of top, 4″, pr. 127-140
Candlesticks, 3-lite, 5″, pr. 160-170
Celery/relish, Gadroon pattern, 3-compartment, 3-toed, 10″ . 75- 84
Cocktail, nude statue, Gold Krystol bowl, 3 oz. 80- 84
Cocktail, seafood, Seashell pattern, 4½″ oz. 56- 64
Compote, nude statue, flared, 7″ 147-159
Cornucopia, miniature, 3″, pr. . 57- 66
Dish, nut, w/place card holder, 3-toed, 3″ 33- 40
Flower block, turtle, 3½″ 93-107
Ivy ball, footed, 7½″ 66- 73
Jug, Doulton, 76 oz., 9¼″ 240-247
Plate, Evergreen pattern, 8½″ . 63- 73
Plate, Gadroon pattern, 2-handled, round, 13″ 63- 72
Plate, salad, Seashell pattern, 7″ 57- 65
Relish, Seashell pattern, 3-compartment, 3-toed, 9″ . .
Slipper, 5″ 64- 74
Swan, 3″ 55- 65
Swan, 6″ 93-101
Vase, etched Portia pattern, footed, 11″ 147-153
Vase, Chintz pattern, black enamel etching, globe shape, 6½″ 296-310
Vase, footed, etched Rose Point pattern, 11″ 267-273
Vases, cornucopia, etched Portia pattern, gold-encrusted, 9½″, pr. 349-360

Ebony (black opaque)

Basket, handled, 11″ $88- 94
Bowl, needle-etched peacocks, gold-encrusted, 12″ 248-260
Bowl, punch, w/foot, Marjorie pattern, early, 10½″ 283-294
Candlesticks, Hexagon pattern, 8½″, pr. 58- 66
Console set; candlesticks, 7½″, pr.; bowl, footed, 7″, all 133-140
Ewer and basin set, Community pattern, 1-gal. ewer, 15½″ basin, both 410-430
Vase, urn, etched Rose Point pattern, gold-encrusted, 10″ . 255-263
Vases, footed, etched Classic pattern, gold-encrusted, 10″, pr. 218-233

Helio (purple opaque)

Bowl, ebony foot, gold-encrusted etching, 10″ . . . . . $ 74- 83
Candlesticks, 8″, pr. 134-142
Cheese and cracker set, 10″, both 120-130
Cigarette box w/cover, 6″ 67- 77
Cologne, gold-encrusted, etched band, 7″ 75- 85
Compote, 9″ 83- 92
Console set, 3 pc.: candlesticks, 10″, pr.; bowl, footed, 10″, all 187-195
Vase, blown, footed, gold-encrusted band, 9½″ 98-108

Ivory (light cream opaque)

Atomizer, floral decorated, hand enameled, 8″ $127-140
Bottles, cologne, Iris pattern, enamel decorated, pr. 135-142
Bowl, ebony foot, figure flower holder 246-260
Candlesticks, 9″, pr. 108-117
Compote, 6″ 84- 92
Jar, candy, w/cover, 8″ 89- 99
Mayonnaise set, 3 pc., all 94-102
Plate, etched border, 10″ 74- 83
Tray, sandwich, handled, 10″ . . 73- 83
Vase, 10″ 77- 86

Jade (blue-green opaque)

Bowl, gold-encrusted etching, 9″ $189-206
Candlesticks, Hexagon pattern, 7½″, pr. 87- 96
Compote, gold-encrusted etching, 7″ 124-133
Vase, blown, footed, 12″ 88- 94
Vase, blown, 10″ 87- 96

Milk Glass (white opaque)

Ashtray, Seashell pattern, 3-toed, 4″ . . . . $ 34- 39
Ashtray, w/card holder, Seashell pattern, gold decorated, 3-toed, 3″ 35- 46
Bowl, Seashell pattern, 3-toed, 9″ 88- 94
Box, puff, w/cover, Community pattern, 4½″ 47- 54
Bucket, ice, w/tongs, Mt. Vernon pattern 83- 93
Compote, footed, Mt. Vernon, 6″ 42- 51
Cordial, footed, Mt. Vernon pattern, 1 oz. 21- 30

Cornucopia, miniature, Seashell pattern, 3″ 29- 38
Figure, Dresden 77- 87
Hat, match or toothpick holder, Saratoga pattern 39- 47
Mug, Everglade pattern, 12 oz. 50- 54
Salt, individual, oval, 2-handled, Mt. Vernon pattern 37- 46
Tumbler, footed, Mt. Vernon pattern, 3 oz. 27- 36
Urn, covered, footed, Mt. Vernon pattern 74- 83

Primrose (yellow opaque, green cast)

Bonbon, gold-encrusted, "C" mark, 6″ $127-136
Bowl, ebony foot, black/gold-encrusted band, 10″ 123-132
Box, pomade, w/cover, 3″ 52- 62
Box, puff, w/cover, 4¼″ 70- 78
Candlesticks, black/gold-encrusted, 9¼″, pr. 124-132
Candlesticks, 6¼″, pr. 73- 82
Compote, footed, 6″ 74- 85
Vase, gold band, 10¼″ 74- 83
Vase, gold-encrusted, iridescent, 12½″ 122-132

Royal Blue (dark blue)

Bowl, flared, etched Portia pattern, 4-toed, 12″ $101-111
Candlestick, crystal foot, crystal bobeche and prisms, Martha Washington pattern, 10″ 84- 93
Candlesticks, 8½″, pr. 108-116
Cigarette holder, Mt. Vernon pattern 34- 39
Cordial set, w/chrome holders; marked "Farber Bros. N.Y.C.," 9-pc., all 247-259
Eye cup 22- 30
Goblet, crystal foot, 9 oz. 35- 44
Goblet, Mt. Vernon pattern, 9 oz. 38- 48
Mustard w/cover, holder marked "Farber" 54- 64
Oil, glass stopper, chrome holder marked "Farber" 55- 65
Sherbet, crystal foot, 6 oz. 33- 39
Sherry set, 5-pc., decanter in chrome holder, marked "Farber" 169-177
Vase, 5″ 48- 58

Rubina (ruby top blending to blue, then to green)

Bowl, Honeycomb pattern, 9½″ $221-230
Bowl, ram's head, Gadroon pattern, 8½″ .... 910+
Bowl, ribbed optic, 11″ 238-248
Box, candy, w/cover, Honeycomb pattern, "C" mark 281-292
Candlesticks, Dolphin pattern, 9½″, pr. .... 950+
Candlesticks, 8½″, pr. 178-186
Compote, low, footed, 7½″ ... 201-211
Lemonades, handled, ribbed optic, "C" mark, set of 6, all .... 900+
Tumblers, blown, ribbed optic, set of 4, all 294-310

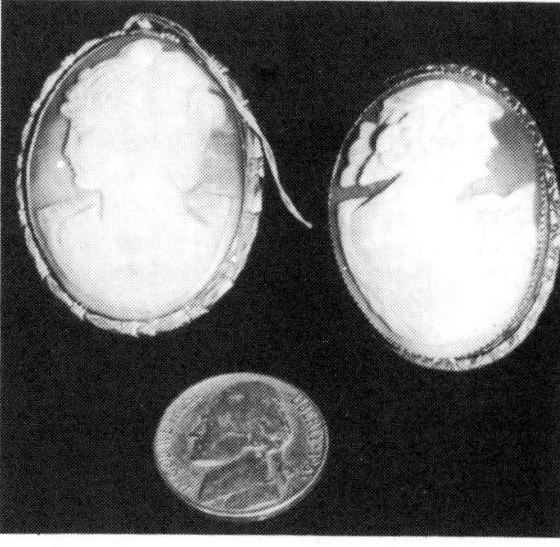

Cameos

Cameos

Once popular between 1840 and 1875, they're now "back!" Only trouble is, thousands of plastic repros around and, unless you know how to identify a genuine cameo carved from the conch shell or in rarer cases, glass, lava, or stone, **you** are going to be burned. Don't pay too much. Then, if you're cheated, it doesn't hurt as much.

Bracelet, six cameos, ladies' faces, silver links, 1890 .... $55-65
Brooch, brown/white, ladies' faces, mounted in 14-K gold ring (illus.) 75-85
Earrings, brown/white faces, 10-K gold mountings, pr. 30-40
Necklace, matches above, on 10-K chain 45-53
"New" cameos: pins, brooches, bracelets, etc., average price .. 8-10

Campaign Items

Any time someone runs for a political office someone is going to print a program, make a badge, produce a plate or, as is generally the case, manufacture a product that the buying public "just has to have!" The older the better, obviously. Today's collectible has to do with those politicans after World War II. Don't worry about finding the stuff made before 1900. Or before World War I. But there are countless thousands of "collectibles" out there. Just keep in mind that, like so many others, there are a lot of repros!

Carter peanut holder, plaster, 8¾" high $24-31
Carter souvenir plate, 10¼" dia. . . 12-17
LBJ ashtray, in shape of his hat, 6" long 14-18
LBJ belt buckle, 2" × 3¼" 9-11
Nixon/Agnew jug, 4¾" high 19-25
Nixon toothpick holder, 2½" high 21-27
Reagan/Bush plate, star-trimmed, 10¼" dia. 54-61
Reagan *First Family* paper doll cutout book 6- 9
Reagan glass, Kansas City Convention, 1976, 3¼" high 9-13
No! We haven't forgotten JFK. Just too many to mention. Pay what you like, make your own deals, and go from there.

Suggested reading: *Presidential and Campaign Memorabilia with Prices,* Stan Gores, Wallace-Homestead Book Company.

Candlewick Crystal

This glass was introduced in 1936 by the Imperial Glass Corporation, Bellaire, Ohio. Paper labels were used, but the stems, handles, and crystal rims, said to have been inspired by the tufted needlework done by our great grandmothers, make this glass easy to identify. Most of the more than 740 items produced were in the 400 series. 3400, 3800, and 4000 are other series numbers found. Also see **Clubs and Publications,** this Price Guide.

Bowls, 7", various styles, each . . $16-22
Bowls, 8", 8½", various styles, each 12-18
Bowls, 10", various styles, each . 14-24
Bowls, 10½", various styles, each 24-29
Bowls, 11", various styles, each . 13-24
Butter dish, covered, round, 5½" 19-24
Cake stand, footed, 3-bead stem, 11" high 55-63
Candle holder, floral, 5" high 16-20
Compote, fruit, 10" high 24-30
Cup/saucer set 14-19
Egg cup, beaded foot 16-19
Goblet, 3800 series, 1 oz. 22-27
Pitchers, 16 oz., 20 oz., each 23-29
Plate, dinner, 10" 14-18
Plates, 13", 14", 17", each 23-28
Salt/pepper set, chrome caps 7-10
Sugar, bead handle, 6 oz. 6- 9
Tray, 400 series, 5½" long 19-23
Tumblers, juice, tea, 400 series, each 11-16
Vase, beaded handle, fluted rim, 8" high 24-29
Suggested reading: *Candlewick, The Jewel of Imperial,* Mary M. Wetzel, Taylor Publishing Company.

Candy Containers

Candy Containers

These have been around for years and are being reproduced in many forms. Original paint? Is the candy original? Is the closure original? All important, pricewise. The earlier ones are in private collections, but a lot from the 1930's are still being found. See **Clubs and Publications,** this Price Guide.

Bear, c. 1940's (Illus.) ....$ 16- 23
Bulldog, 2⅛" high, screw-on closure, Victory Glass Co., c. 1930 .... 43- 51
Chicken on nest, 5¼" long, J. H. Millstein Co., 1940's 9- 15
Fire Department No. 99, 5³⁄₁₆" long, Victory Glass Co., c. early 1940's 41- 50
Kiddies' breakfast bell, 3⅛" high, packed by T. H. Stough Co., Jeanette, Pa., c. 1955 .. 23- 31
Locomotive, 5" long, "888" embossed under double windows, Jenet Glass Co. 26- 33
Rabbit, basket on arm, 4½" high, screw-type closure, c. 1920's 76- 83
Rabbit (gilded), pushing cart, 4" long, Victory Glass Co., Jeanette, Pa. 230-240
Santa Claus, 8¾" high, styrofoam head, made for Sears, c. 1960's 11- 17
Santa Claus with double cuffs, 4½" high, screw-cap closure, c. mid-1920's.............. 230-240
Scotty dog, 3¼" long, packed by T. H. Stough, made by J. C. Crosetti, Jeanette, Pa. . 18- 26
Tank, 2 guns, 4⅛" long, Victory Glass Co., c. mid-1940's 24- 32
Turkey, 3⅝" high, slide-on closure, Victory Glass Co., c. 1924-1930 .... 86- 94
Wheelbarrow, 6" long, Victory Glass Co., Jeanette, Pa., red tin wheel 44- 51

Cap Pistols

Not as many found today in shops and at Flea Markets as there were five years ago. Most of what you find today are the cast iron models from the 1930's until the late 1940's, and the die cast material and plastic types, these coming into use around 1950. How bad do you want it? What's its condition? The toy guns listed here are in good to very good condition.

Ace, cast iron, 5" long, c. 1936 ..$15-20
American, cast iron, Kilgore, 9½" long, c. 1939 29-37
Bang, cast iron, Kilgore, "Made in U.S.A.," 6" long 15-22
Biff, cast iron, automatic, Kenton, 4½" long, c. 1936 12-17
Big Horn, cast iron, revolving cylinder, Kilgore, 8¼" long 20-29
Boy's Police Automatic, cardboard pop-type, 8" long, c. 1944 .... 3- 5
Bull dog, cast iron, Hubley, Pat. 1,489,046, c. 1935, 6" long 8-14
Clip Jr., cast iron, Stevens, 5¼" long, c. 1936 12-17
Cowboy, cast iron, Hubley, "Made in U.S.A.," 8¼" long, c. 1940 13-18
Dick, cast iron, automatic, Hubley, 4¼" long, c. 1940 .... 4- 7
Dragnet detective special, repeating revolver, c. 1955 13-18
G-Man, bakelite frame, automatic, 6" long, c. 1940 12-18
Hero, cast iron, Stevens, 5¼" long, c. 1938 6-10
Jr. police chief, cast iron, automatic, Kenton, c. 1938 12-18
Lone Ranger, cast iron, Kilgore, 8½" long, c. 1940 25-35
Mascot, cast iron, automatic, 4" long, c. 1936 13-21
Pono, cast iron, Kenton, 5" long, c. 1937 11-15
Roy Rogers, cast iron, 11" long.. 29-38
Texan, cast iron, Hubley, "Made in U.S.A.," 9½" long, c. 1939.. 13-19
Western, cast iron, Kenton, 7½" long, c. 1939 11-16

Caramel Slag Animals

Birds, horses, dogs — these "purty beasts" are showing up more often than not at Flea Markets, Swap Meets, the like. $5-8 each.

Carnival Glass (New)

Around 1960 the Imperial Glass Corporation, Bellaire, Ohio, reproduced some sixty-one pieces of "old" Carnival glass, marking most with the familiar IG (IG) trademark. An 8" compote in the Octagon pattern and a 13" tall punch bowl in the Whirling Star pattern have been found without the familiar trademark. The two colors produced were Rubigold (golden rust highlighted with iridescent) and Peacock (deep purple blue highlighted with iridescent). At least twenty items were made in Crystal only. One dealer in Chattanooga, Tennessee, sold more than 50,000 pieces as "genuine." Dishonest people have ground off the IG mark and sold the pieces as genuine. This "new" Carnival is showing up at shows and creating confusion among beginning collectors of Carnival glass. If you haven't heard, Imperial is no longer in business. Prices shown are original 1960 prices. Add 15 to 20 percent for today's value. See **Clubs and Publications,** this Price Guide. Descriptions are from the original catalog.

- **Basket, 9½″ tall, #40, Rubigold $ 3.50**
- **Bowl, 4½″, Grape, #49, Peacock 1.50**
- **"Lion" box and cover, #159, Peacock 7.50**
- **Cake stand, 8″, #98, Crystal ... 6**
- **Cake stand, 10″, #98, Crystal .. 7**
- **Cake stand, 12″, #98, Crystal .. 8**
- **Coaster, #160/76, Crystal...... 85¢**
- **Cream pitcher, #301, Rubigold . 2.50**
- **Cruet, 4 oz., #160/119, Crystal . 2.75**
- **Cup and saucer, Grape, #4737, Peacock, each 3**
- **Decanter and stopper, Grape, #163, Rubigold............. 7**
- **Juice, 6 oz., footed, Grape, #307, Peacock 2**
- **Pitcher/vase, 3 pt., Rose, #24, Rubigold 6**
- **Plate, 7½″, Grape, #3D, Peacock 2.50**
- **Punch ladle, #91, Crystal...... 3.50**
- **Salt dip, individual, #400/61, Crystal .... 50¢**
- **Salt dip spoon, #400/616, Crystal .... 25¢**
- **Salt/pepper set, Grape, #96, Peacock, each 4**
- **"Spoonholder" sugar/cover, #304, Rubigold............. 4**
- **Tumbler, 10 oz., Grape, #473, Peacock 2**
- **Vase, 10″, Loganberry, #356, Peacock 6**
- **Wine, 3 oz., Grape, #473, Rubigold 2.50**

Water Set

- **Pitcher, 3 pt., Rose, #24, Rubigold ....$ 6**
- **Tumblers, 9 oz., Rose, set of 6, #489, Rubigold, each 2**

Punch Set

- **Bowl, #500, Peacock ....$ 8**
- **Base, #500, Peacock 4.50**
- **Cups, set of 12, #500, Peacock, each .... 75¢**
- **Ladle, #91, Crystal 3.50**

Tea Tumbler Set

- **Set of 6, Grape, in gift-shipper carton, #4736, rubigold, set . . $12**

Note: If an item comes in Peacock, it also comes in Rubigold.

Carnival Glass (Taffeta)

Carnival Glass (Taffeta) 

This originally low priced, iridized glass was made to compete with the expensive Art Glass (Tiffany, Steuben, Durand, Kew Blas, Quezal, etc.) of the early 1900's. It was originally called Taffeta glass and got its present name during the 1920's when circuses and carnivals gave it away as prizes. Grocery stores also gave it away with food purchases. Color of individual pieces determines value. Prices range upward from peach (lowest), to marigold to blue, green, or purple, to pastels (any color), to genuine *old* Red Carnival, the most valuable. Being reproduced. See **Clubs and Publications,** this Price Guide.

Banana Boat

- **Floral ....$ 61- 68**
- **Grape and Cable, green 194-202**
- **Grape and Cable, marigold 177-183**
- **Peach and Pear, marigold..... 82- 88**
- **Thistle 103-109**
- **Wreathed Cherry, purple...... 158-167**
- **Wreathed Cherry, red 360-372**
- **Wreathed Cherry, white....... 202-211**

Bank

Bell, marigold .... $ 46- 54
Owl, marigold 71- 80

Basket

Basketweave, marigold .... $ 67- 80
Stippled Rays, 2 handles, purple 53- 59
Tree of Life, marigold 51- 57

Berry Set

Beaded Shell, 6 pcs., purple .. $283-288
Imperial's Grape, 7 pcs., green 163-169
Three Fruits, N mark, 6 pcs., purple 221-230

Bonbon

Persian Medallion, blue .... $ 91-106
Pond Lily, blue 88- 96
Three Fruits, basketweave, marigold 71- 77

Bottle

Barber, marigold .... $ 69- 75
Horn of Plenty 70- 77
Toilet Water, marigold 74- 82
Whiskey, Golden Wedding, marigold 68- 74
Wine, New England Wine Co., marigold 66- 70

Bowl

Acorn pattern, marigold ...... $ 74- 80
Apple Blossoms, 5½" dia., purple 82- 90
Berry, Acorn pattern, 7½" dia., blue 63- 70
Berry, Butterfly and Berry, marigold 74- 81
Berry, Peacock at the Fountain, amethyst 166-174
Berry, Vintage Grape, 5½" dia., purple 67- 75
Berry, Water Lily and Cattails, marigold 67- 77
Blackberry Wreath, 9" dia. 80- 86
Bouquet and Lattice, 6½" dia., cereal 55- 62
Candy, Fine Cut and Roses, N mark, purple 83- 90
Captive Rose, 8¾" dia., green . 82- 92
Chrysanthemum, footed, 10" dia., blue 91-102
Dogwood Sprays, marigold 81- 90
Dragon and Lotus, 8" dia. 81- 89
Embossed Grapes, 9½" dia., marigold 74- 80
Embossed Scroll, 8" dia., green 82- 91
Grape and Cable, green 114-119
Grape and Cable, 6½" dia., marigold 66- 73
Grape and Cable, 7½" dia., purple 86- 94
Grape and Gothic Arches, marigold 59- 64
Heart and Vine, blue 85- 90
Heart and Vine, 8" dia., green . 85- 91
Holly, 9" dia., blue 84- 92
Horse's Head Medallion, 6½" dia., marigold 88- 98
Imperial's Cherries, footed, 10" dia., marigold 84- 90
Imperial's Grape, 8¾" dia. 77- 81
Leaf pattern, 5½" dia., marigold 68- 77
Little Flowers, 10½" dia. 93-102
Louisa, 8¼" dia., amethyst ... 71- 80
Millersburg's Cherry, marigold . 84- 92
Millersburg's Cherry, 7" dia., green 78- 81
Millersburg's Primrose, 9¼" dia. 95-108
Millersburg's Whirling Leaves, 9½" dia. 107-115
Pansy Spray, amber 77- 86
Peacock and Dahlia, 7½" dia., marigold 75- 85
Peacock and Grape, 7½" dia., 3" high 77- 86
Peacock and Grape, 9" dia. ... 183-190
Peacock at the Fountain, 8" dia. 150-160
Persian Medallions, 9" dia., marigold 78- 88
Roses and Ruffles, 8" dia., marigold 74- 83
Stag and Holly, 10" dia., blue . 152-161
Stag and Holly, 10" dia., marigold 123-132
Star and File, 6½" dia., marigold 49- 56
Stork and Rushes, 10" dia., marigold 87- 95
Thistle, footed, 8" dia., marigold 68- 78
Thunderbird, 5½" dia., marigold 118-126
Wild Daisy and Lotus, footed .. 69- 78
Wild Rose, 6" dia., green 77- 85

Bowl, Centerpiece

Double Scroll and Oval $102-111

Bowl, Fruit

Butterfly and Tulip, marigold .. $308-318
Fenton's Grape 196-205
Imperial Jewels, red 178-184
Ski Star, 5½" dia., peach 84- 93

Bowl, Nut

Grape, 6-footed, purple .... $ 99-107
Louisa, footed, purple 89- 97
Louisa, footed, red 94-103
Vintage, red, 7" 230-240

Bowl, Punch

Grape and Cable, 2 pcs., 6 cups, purple $778-786
Imperial's Hobstar, 2 pcs., 12 cups 297-308
Memphis, green 342-350
Orange Tree, purple 330-340

Bowl, Rose

Butterscotch, blue-green ...... $ 97-105
Daisy and Plume, footed 103-112
Fine Cut and Roses, marigold . 92-101
Grape and Leaf, 6-footed 114-121
Grape, purple 109-118
Leaf and Beads, footed, green . 121-130
Leaf and Beads, footed, marigold 94-103
Leaf and Beads, footed, white . 158-166
Louisa, green 83- 92
Star and File, marigold 81- 90
Vintage, purple 108-116
Wreath of Roses, marigold 242-251

Bowl, Sugar

Peacock at the Fountain, cover, marigold .... $ 84- 93
Stippled Rays, footed, marigold 35- 41
Strutting Peacock, cover, marigold 69- 76

Butter Dish

Arabic, 2 handles, 8″ dia., blue $ 69- 78
Basketweave 68- 75
Butterflies, marigold 108-116
Cable and Thumbprint, N mark, blue 235-244
Flute, N mark, blue 174-184
Gold/green, signed Northwood 108-117
Grape and Cable, N mark, purple 303-316
Grape and Cable, Thumbprint, green 274-282
Maple Leaf, purple 185-194
Question Mark, 2 handles 88- 98
Water Lily and Cattails, marigold 177-186
Wide Panel, marigold 84- 93

Cake Stand

Butterfly and Berry, marigold .. $133-142

Candlestick

Cornucopia, white, pr. $183-192
Double Scroll, 8½″ high, marigold, pr. 88- 97
Grape, N mark, 5½″ high, purple, pr. 274-282
White, domed foot, 7¾″ high, pr. 78- 86
Wide panel, 6½″ high, marigold, pr. 86- 94

Carafe

Grape, purple $173-182

Champagne

Masonic, white, 1912 .... $101-110

Cologne

Grape and Cable, stopper, marigold $173-183

Compote

Basketweave, N mark, 7″ dia., purple .... $ 87- 96
Beaded Panel, marigold 59- 68
Blackberry Spray, 6½″ high, green 65- 75
Cathedral, marigold 115-121
Fenton's Peacock and Urn, marigold 93-102
Imperial Arcs, 4″ high, marigold 58- 68
Imperial Jewels, green 84- 93
Octagon, 7¾″ dia., marigold .. 84- 93
Propellor, marigold 88- 93
Scotch Thistle, blue 106-112
Smooth Rays, clear stem, marigold 66- 73
Thumbprint, 5″ high, purple ... 73- 83
Wreath of Roses, 6″ dia., purple 89- 99

Creamer and Sugar

Pansy Spray, marigold .... $ 79- 88
Peacock at the Fountain, amethyst 179-188
Pineapple, dome foot, marigold 158-168
Singing Birds, marigold 168-177
Strippled Rays, green 85- 93

Cup and Saucer

Bouquet and Lattice, marigold . $ 54- 63
Many Carnival glass patterns, average price 53- 63

Cup, Punch

Acorn Burrs, N mark .... $ 65- 75
Buzz Star, marigold 54- 64
Grape and Cable, blue 72- 82
Grape and Cable, N mark, purple 63- 72
Imperial's Grape, set of 6, marigold 92-101
Memphis, amethyst 77- 86
Vintage, marigold 55- 65

Cuspidor

Orange Tree .... $ 88- 96

Decanter

Golden Harvest, marigold $124-133
Grape Clusters, stopper, marigold 115-123
Imperial's Grape, green 187-196
Imperial's Grape, marigold 117-126
Octagon, stopper, marigold ... 125-134

Dish

Berry, Grape and Cable, N mark .... $ 68- 77
Berry, Octagon, marigold 84- 92
Berry, Peacock and Urn, purple 83- 92
Berry, Three Fruits, N mark, amethyst 77- 86
Candy, Blackberry, 6″ dia., red 174-183
Candy, Fine Cut and Roses, 8″ dia. 102-110

Candy, Lacy Rim, blue 69- 78
Candy, Millersburg's Holly, green 102-110
Candy, Persian Medallion, marigold 68- 78
Candy, Stippled Rays, marigold 65- 73
Candy, Wreath of Roses, green 75- 82
Celery, Grape and Cable, purple 124-132
Celery, Pansy Spray, amber ... 107-115
Dessert, Fluted Paneled Rays, N mark 74- 83
Ice Cream, Beaded Cable, footed, 7½" dia. 77- 85
Ice Cream, Peacock and Urn, N mark, blue 142-150
Pickle, Beaded Cable, fluted, footed, 7¾" dia. 77- 82
Pickle, Imperial's Pansy, marigold 68- 75
Pickle, Windmills, green 79- 84
Relish, Grape and Cable, purple 107-115
Relish, Pansy, marigold 77- 85
Sauce, Acorn Burrs, N mark, marigold 60- 70
Sauce, Acorn Burrs, purple ... 75- 84
Sauce, Butterfly and Berry, marigold 60- 67
Sauce, Fenton's Cherry 74- 82
Sauce, Grape and Gothic Arches, blue 73- 83
Sauce, Grape and Thumbprint, N mark, purple 74- 83
Sauce, Lustre Rose, marigold . 62- 72
Sauce, Northwood Flute, purple 77- 85
Sauce, Panther, ball and claw, marigold 84- 90
Sauce, Panther, footed, 6" dia., purple 92-100
Sauce, Peacock at the Fountain 66- 73
Sauce, Star Medallion 58- 68
Sauce, Stippled Rays, purple .. 74- 82
Sauce, Thistle and Thorn, marigold 58- 68
Sundae, Northwood's clear stem, marigold 71- 80
Vegetable, Bouquet and Lattice, marigold 43- 50

Doughnut Stand

Question Mark, white $101-110

Epergne

Grape pattern, purple $177-186
Vintage, purple 183-190

Fernery

Grape Variant, footed, green ..$ 87- 96
Lustre Rose, green 95-104
Vintage Grape, footed green .. 84- 93

Goblet

Imperial Grape, 6" high, marigold ....$ 95-103
Wine, Flute, blue 88- 98
Wine, Orange Tree, blue 88- 99

Hat

Blackberry, banded ....$ 74- 83
Blackberry, blue 69- 76
Blackberry, 5", red 185-194
French Knots 81- 90

Hatpin

Bumblebee, purple ....$ 79- 87
Butterfly 96-105
Flying Bat 79- 88
Plum and Stem 75- 80

Hatpin Holder

Grape and Cable, N mark $174-184
Grape, purple 114-125
Orange Tree, marigold 121-130

Insulator

Corning Pyrex, marigold ......$ 75- 83
Marigold 74- 84
Marigold, large 124-130

Jar

Candy, cover, 8" high, marigold ....$ 69- 76
Candy, crinkled lid, marigold .. 78- 85
Cookie, Hourglass and Daisy, cover, marigold 94-103
Pickle, Golden Flowers, marigold 67- 74
Powder, Bambi, marigold 57- 64
Powder, Orange Tree, cover, marigold 103-114
Powder, Vintage, cover, marigold 94-102
Powder, Wreathed Cherries, blue 110-115
Tobacco, Illinois Daisy, marigold 118-125

Lamp

Metal holder, marigold ....$ 94-102
Zipper and Loop, 2-burner, 7" high, marigold 265-274

Mug

Orange Tree, blue ....$ 87- 93
Robin Red Breast, marigold ... 85- 94
Singing Birds, marigold 94-103
Singing Birds, N mark, marigold 96-105
Singing Birds, purple 98-106
Stork and Rushes, marigold ... 75- 83
Vintage, marigold 87- 97

Nappie

Leaf Rays, marigold ....$ 84- 93
Northwood's Butterfly 84- 92
Question Mark, marigold 66- 74
Stippled Rays, N mark 73- 82

Pitcher

Butterfly and Berry, marigold ..$168-178

Diamond Lace, 6 tumblers, purple, all 554-564
Floral and Grape, 6 tumblers, marigold, all 297-310
Grape and Gothic Arches, marigold 166-177
Imperial's Grape, blue 230-240
Imperial's Grape, 6 tumblers, purple, all 294-299
Millersburg's Diamond, green . . 184-193
Nesting Peacock 175-183
Northwood's Maple Leaf, 6 tumblers, marigold, all 332-341
Poinsettia, marigold 100-110
Rose pattern, 8 tumblers, all . . 163-172
Star Medallion, small, marigold 83- 92

Plate

Grape and Cable, footed, green $184-193
Honeycomb, purple 91-100
Imperial Jewels, white 93-100
Peacock and Urn, white 261-271
Peacock on the Fence, green . . 238-248
Strawberry, N mark, green 190-199
Three Fruits, marigold 119-121
Three Fruits, white 215-221
Vintage, green 130-140
Wild Strawberry, N mark, green 140-148

Sauceboat

Fan pattern, purple $123-130

Shade

Gas, Mayflower, marigold, pr. . $ 93-101
Light, signed Nu Art, marigold, pr. 100-109
Light, quilted, white, pr. 80- 90
Light, white 60- 70

Sherbet

Bouquet and Lattice, pedestal, set of 6, marigold . . . . $ 84- 92
Flute, N mark, green 71- 81
Iris and Herringbone, marigold . 70- 80
Orange Tree, stemmed, marigold 70- 77

Spoonholder

Butterfly and Berry, marigold . . $ 80- 90
Hobstar, marigold 70- 78
Kittens, small, marigold 112-121
Lustre Rose, green 83- 90

Sugar

Grape and Cable, cover, purple $124-133
Lustre Flute, handle 88- 96
Lustre Flute, N mark, purple . . 79- 89
Millersburg's Cherry 105-114
Star and File 90- 99

Swan

Millersburg, purple $218-227
Pastel blue 91-100
Pastel green 90- 98

Tray

Butterfly, footed, white $169-177
Grape, center handles, marigold 101-110

Tumbler

Apple Tree, marigold . . . . $ 74- 82
Blackberry/checkerboard 81- 90
Blueberry, white 88- 95
Butterfly, purple 76- 84
Dandelion, N mark, green . . 88- 95
Enameled Cherry, blue 67- 75
Grape and Cable, purple . . . 85- 94
Grape and Lattice, white . . . 85- 94
Grapes, Maple Leaves, N mark, marigold 79- 89
Lattice and Grape, blue 70- 80
Maple Leaf, set of 6, purple . 262-271
Millersburg's Diamond Band, marigold 60- 70
Oriental Poppy, white 170-180
Peacock at the Fountain, blue 84- 94
Peacock, N mark, purple . . . 89- 95
Rambler Rose, marigold 60- 68
Singing Birds, N mark, green 85- 94
Stork and Rushes, blue 86- 94
Vineyard, set of 6, marigold . 170-177
Water Lily and Cattails, N mark 85- 95

Vase

Beaded Bull's Eye, 11″ high, marigold . . . . $ 88- 98
Corn, N mark, green 274-283
Corn, N mark, marigold 365-374
Cornucopia, marigold 92-100
Diamond Point, N mark, 8″ high, purple 94-103
Feather, green 71- 81
Fine Rib, N mark, marigold . 88- 98
Grape, N mark, 16″ high, blue 95-104
Knotted Beads, 11″ high, red 176-184
Northwood's Drapery, 8¼″ high, amethyst 88- 98
Ripple, 17″ high, marigold . . 79- 89

Wine

Grape, marigold . . . . $ 65- 75
Iris, set of 6, marigold 77- 86
Orange Tree, green 96-105
Sailboats, frosted stem, marigold 75- 86

Suggested reading: *Carnival Glass Tumblers,* by Richard E. Owens, Wallace-Homestead Book Company.

Cartoon Books

The first popular cartoon books were merely reprints of old comic strips from

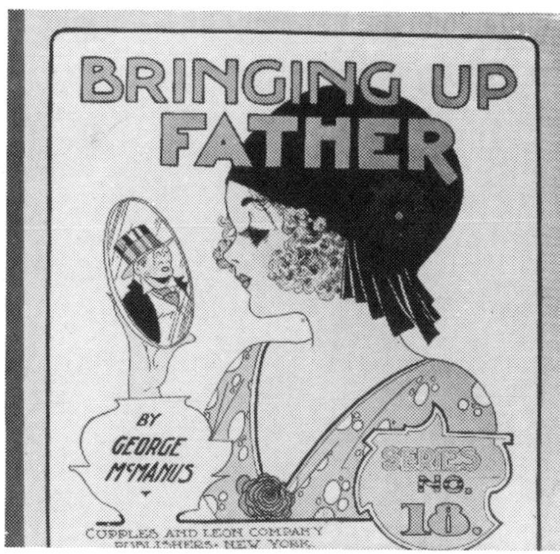

Cartoon Books

Photo Courtesy of
Hake's Americana & Collectibles

newspapers, in color or black/white, popular in the mid-1930's until World War II. Cupples and Leon Company, New York, published more than a hundred different titles.

Bringing Up Father, #9	**$33-40**
Bringing Up Father, #17	**43-49**
Bringing Up Father, #18 (Illus.)	**45-51**
Mutt and Jeff, Book 5	**69-74**
Mutt and Jeff, Book 6	**66-74**
Mutt and Jeff, Book 7	**45-51**

Cash Registers

Cash Registers

Don't worry too much about finding pre-World War I types. Lots of the type illustrated here still showing up at sales, everywhere.

No. 307 (Illus.) $210-235

Cassette Tapes

Cassette Tapes

Some work and some don't. A former president I know wishes he'd never heard of them. Why not; you're collecting everything else!

Average price .... 50¢-$1

Cast Iron Collectibles

Cast Iron Collectibles

Objects such as kettles, old skillets, you-name-it, all are available at your neighborhood Flea Market. Sometimes sold by the pound. Otherwise, argue a lot.

Kettle, 1920's (Illus.)	**$ 28- 37**
Skillets, all sizes	**8- 23**
School bell, 1900's	**158-190**
Train bell, 1930's	**250-270**

Caster Sets

Caster Sets

Usually four or five bottles in a metal, handled rack. It sat on the table — vinegar, oil, spices, peppers, etc. Popular in the mid-to-late Victorian period.

4-bottle set, quadruple plate rack (Illus.) $177-186
6-bottle set, sterling silver rack 350-385
The bottles are being reproduced in many glass patterns.

Ceiling Fans

Ceiling Fans

Used in homes and stores after introduction of electricity. Being collected today by decorators and others. See **Clubs and Publications**, this Price Guide.

Average price, good condition $195-260
Reproductions available — higher priced.

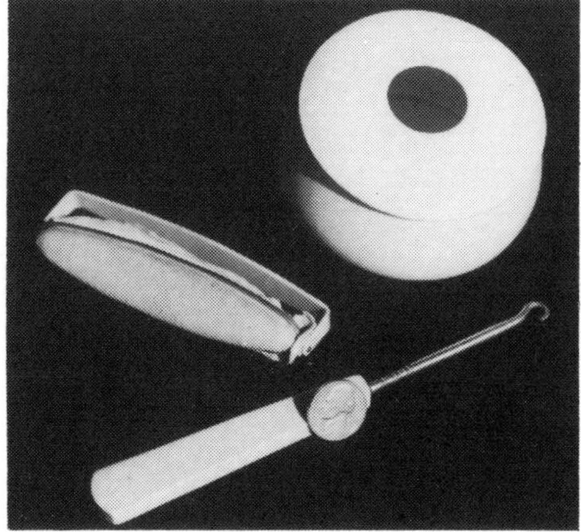
Celluloid

Celluloid

Also called French Ivory. Celluloid was the trademark for a product invented by John W. Hyatt in 1868. A pyroxlin plastic, he patented it a year later, although the material had been used for many years before. It's become collectible in the past few years, but it's still affordable and there's lots of it around.

Buttonhook (Illus.) . . . . $ 3- 4
Collar box, square shape, tinted, "Collars and Cuffs" on lid 55-63
Cream jar w/cover, glass liner . . . 25-31
Dresser set: tray, comb, mirror, hair holder, powder box, all . . . 78-85
Dresser tray, 11½" long 17-23
Glove box, "woman" on lid 39-44
Hair holder (Illus.) 13-19
Lady's travel kit 39-43
Manicure set, pink velvet lined . . 39-44
Nail buffer, 2-pc. (Illus.) 14-18
Napkin ring, initialed 12-16
Necktie case, sateen lining, 11½"long 35-42
Opener, letter 17-23
Pansy vase, 4" high 24-28
Rattle, baby's 16-22
Shoehorn 10-14

Centennial Plates

Centennial Plates

When a city or a state celebrates its 100th anniversary, it usually issues a commemorative plate to celebrate the occasion. These plates have now become collectible.

Ringgold County, Iowa, 1855-1955 (Illus.), average price $15-21

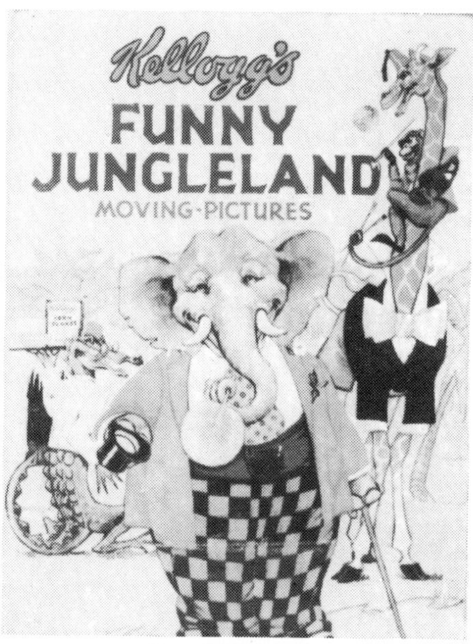

Cereal Premiums

Photo Courtesy of
Hake's Americana & Collectibles

Cereal/Radio Premiums

If you can remember when a boxtop and a dime brought all kinds of goodies in the mail, well, then you're about my age. Whatever, all those wonderful toys and gadgets are highly collectible today.

Cereal

Bobby Benson, H-O Oats, H-BAR-O ranger club button . . . $ 4- 8
Buck Rogers, Cream of Wheat, flight commander whistle badge 48-57
Buck Rogers, Cream of Wheat, solar scout manual 65-80
Buck Rogers, Kellogg's, origin story book 67-79
Chandu the Magician, Beechnut, photo of Chandu 15-22
Cisco Kid, Butter-Nut Bread, metal tab of Cisco 4- 7
Cisco Kid, Tip-Top Bread, giveaway photo postcards 5- 8
Don Winslow of the Navy, Kellogg's, good luck coin 19-25
Gabby Hayes, Quaker Cereals, shooting cannon ring 30-39
Jack Armstrong, Wheaties, "Champs of the USA" stamps, each 8-10
Lone Ranger, Butter-Nut Bread, Lone Ranger safety club badge 13-18
Lone Ranger, Silvercup Bread, safety scout membership badge 13-18
Melvin Purvis, Post Cereals, Junior G-man corps ID card . . . 8-12
Renfrew of the Mounted, map of Wonder Valley 36-43
Renfrew of the Mounted, Wonder Bread, photo of Renfrew 8-11
Roy Rogers, Post Cereals, pop-out cards, each 2- 4
Roy Rogers, Quaker Oats, contest postcard 6- 9
Sgt. Preston of the Yukon, Quaker Puffed Wheat, pedometer 21-29
The Singing Lady, Kellogg's, Old King Cole booklet 9-13
Superman, Kellogg's Corn Flakes, F-87 black plastic airplane ring . 32-41
Superman, Kellogg's Pep, balsa wood airplane 6-10
Superman, Kellogg's Pep, silver metal airplane ring 25-33
Terry and the Pirates, Quaker Oats, pocket-size comics, each 7-11
Tom Mix, Ralston Purina, bandana 36-43
Tom Mix, Ralston Purina, cowboy hat 53-62
Tom Mix, Ralston Purina, spurs with leather strap 47-55

Tom Mix, Ralston Purina, western lariat 42-50
Countless thousands of objects were made!

Radio

Amos 'n Andy, map of Weber City, complete . . . . . . $ 27- 34
Amos 'n Andy puzzle 22- 28
Buck Jones, horseshoe pin . . . 8- 11
Captain Hawks, newsletter (bike contest winner) 6- 9
Captain Hawks, sky patrol ring . 27- 34
Captain Midnight, mystery dial code-o-graph 26- 33
Captain Midnight, Ringo Jumpo Jumping Bean game 26- 34
Captain Midnight, trick & riddle book 22- 30
Captain Tim's Ivory Stamp Club, membership pin, red or blue 8- 11
Captain Tim's Ivory Stamp Club, stamp album, 1935 . . . . 10- 14
Charlie McCarthy, see Character Collectibles
Counterspy, match book 4- 7
Counterspy, membership certificate 16- 22
Death Valley Days, 1931, *Story of Death Valley* 6- 9
Death Valley Days, *Cowboy Songs in Death Valley*, 1934 . 5- 8
Dick Tracy, air detective cap . . 26- 33
Dick Tracy, enameled hat ring . 26- 33
Dick Tracy, inspector-general badge 53- 60
Dick Tracy, pocket flashlight . . 27- 32
Don McNeill's Breakfast Club, *Breakfast Club Yearbook*, 1948 . . . . 5- 9
Don McNeill's Breakfast Club, *Don's Other Life*, 1944 . . . . . . 6- 10
Eddie Cantor, Magic Club pin . . 5- 8
Eddie Cantor, photo albums, 1933, 1934, 1935, each 5- 8
Ed Wynn, face mask 26- 32
Fibber McGee and Molly, advertising spinner 13- 20
Fibber McGee and Molly, Wistful Vista game 11- 18
Frank Buck, *Adventure Club Handbook*, 1934 . . . . 43- 50
Frank Buck, ivory knife, 1939 . . 26- 33
Fred Allen, *Collection of Funniest Donut Cartoons* 10- 18
Gangbusters, Phillip H. Lord badge 14- 20
Green Hornet, glow-in-the-dark seal ring, secret compartment 115-125
Hop Harrigan, flight wings 16- 23
Hop Harrigan, para-plane kit . . . 24- 31
Jack Benny, Jell-o recipe book 5- 9
Jimmi Allen, Flying Cadet flight wings, Skelly type I or II 9- 14
Jimmie Allen, Flying Lesson 1, 2, 3, 4, or 5, each 9- 14
Joe E. Brown Club, membership pin 7- 10
Joe E. Brown Club, membership ring 22- 28
Lum and Abner, family almanac, 1936, 1937, 1938, each 9- 14
Mandrake the Magician, Magic Club pin, 1934 . . . . 47- 54
One Man's Family, Jack Barbour's Scrapbook 10- 14
One Man's Family, *20th Anniversary Souvenir Cookbook* 13- 19
Red Ryder, pony contest pin back 11- 15
The Shadow, Blue Coal ink blotter, 4-color 13- 19
The Shadow, Blue Coal match book 26- 32
Skippy, ceramic cereal bowl . . . 21- 28
Skippy, Racer Club 9- 14
Sky King, Aztec Indian ring . . . 43- 50
Sky King, electronic television ring 42- 50
Sky King, mystery picture ring . 36- 43
Space Patrol, chart of the universe 36- 42
Space Patrol, cosmic smoke gun 31- 40
Straight Arrow, puzzles, 12 different, each 10- 13
Straight Arrow, Rite-A-Lite arrowhead 36- 43
Tarzan, Radio Club badge, Drink More Milk 53- 60
Tarzan, statue set, Numa (lion), Kala (ape mother), each 6- 10
Tom Corbett, Space Cadet, belt buckle decoder 57- 65
Tom Corbett, Space Cadet, insignia ring 36- 42
Wizard of Oz, condensed story, *Ozma and the Little Wizard* . . 26- 33
Wizard of Oz, condensed story, *The Scarecrow and the Tin Woodman* (remember Ray Bolger and Jack Haley?) 26- 33

Chafing Dishes

Beautiful copper, and most of them are complete with the Sterno burner. Can still be used and are great shelf decorators. $35-50. The usual "age and condition" bit.

Chalkware

Contrary to popular belief, this was not made by the Dutch Germans in Pennsylvania in the mid-1800's. Italian im-

Chalkware

migrants in this country, 1820's to the Civil War, made the best — simply, plaster of paris decorated with water colors.

Bank, dog, black, glass eyes . . $ 54- 63
Bank, rearing horse 31- 38
Bank, turkey, natural colors . . . 59- 64
Betty Boop, 14½″ high 194-202
Bookends, boy and girl reading, pr. 58- 68
Bookends, pirates, painted, pr. 59- 69
Cat (Illus.) 64- 73
Dog, 11½″ high, early 83- 93
Dove, green/blue wings 208-217
Figurine, bust of Indian 105-114
Figurine, cat sleeping 74- 80
Owl, 12″ high 191-199
Pigeon, green leaves, red berries 160-170
Sailor boy, 9″ high 28- 36
Snow White, 12½″ high 51- 61
Squirrel 180-190
Stag, on rectangular plinth 244-252

Character Collectibles

Though not antiques in the true sense of the word, there are many comic strip, movie, and television character items being collected today.

Amos 'n Andy

Exhibit card (Illus.), each . . . . . $ 2- 3
Map of Weber City in original envelope 14- 19
Toy windup "Fresh Air" taxi (rare), tin, 1930's 540-630

Character Collectibles

Madame Queen doll, plastic, 1930's 56- 65

Andy Gump

Doll, chalkware . . . . $ 20- 26

Betty Boop

Doll, celluloid windup, 7″ high . $ 51- 60
Playing cards 57- 64
Tambourine, 6¼″ 52- 61
Soap figure, in original box . . . 81- 90

Buck Rogers

Disintegrator gun, 10″ . . $227-236
Flash blast attack ship 60- 68
Liquid helium water pistol, red/yellow 77- 86
Puzzle, 1950's 48- 58
Pocket watch, by Ingraham . . . 232-240

Charlie Chaplin

Glove box, wooden . . . . $ 57- 65

Charlie McCarthy

Large cardboard figure, mouth and eyes move (Illus.) . . . . . . $ 19- 27
Hand puppet 29- 38
Radio 106-115

Donald Duck (see also Disneyana)

Card game, 1950 . . . . $ 21- 29
Cookie jar 46- 55
Doll, bisque, 3″ high 40- 41
Doll, celluloid, wearing Santa Claus suit 110-116
Doll, chalkware, 3½″ high 27- 36
Wristwatch 78- 85

Flash Gordon

Compass . . . . $ 50- 60
Compass, wrist 30- 37
Radio repeater space gun 170-180
Rocket fighter ship 64- 72
Signal pistol space gun 390-410
Space outfit: belt, glasses, watch, all 43- 52

Hopalong Cassidy

Belt and spurs, both . . . . $ 41- 50

Bowl, cup, and plate, all	44- 53
Field glasses, in original box	50- 60
Lunch pail and thermos, both	29- 37
Pennant, circus	16- 25
Radio, Arvin, black/silver	92-103
Tumbler, 5″ high	20- 28

Howdy Doody

Beanie kit, leather	$ 26- 34
Earmuffs	23- 32
Handkerchief	18- 27
Teaspoon, silver-plated	27- 33

Mickey Mouse (see also Disneyana)

Bubble gum cards, 12, all	$ 49- 57
Camera	35- 44
Charm, celluloid	22- 31
Crayon box, tin	22- 30
Doll, rubber, 5¼″ high	15- 23
Paint set	35- 44
Phonograph	58- 68
Salt/pepper shakers (Minnie, too)	23- 31
Tea set, china, 15 pcs., all	88- 97
Wristwatch, 1939	115-126

Popeye

Bank, dime register, 1950's	$ 23- 31
Game, Pipe Toss, in original box	60- 70
Harmonica, 1920's	77- 86
Pencil box, 1930	37- 45
Wallet, 1950's	33- 43

Roy Rogers

Boot tops, leatherette, pr.	$ 22- 32
Cap gun, cast iron	29- 39
Clicker, tin	19- 27
Mug, plastic	15- 25
Wristwatch	54- 63

Shirley Temple

Book, *Rebecca of Sunnybrook Farm*	$ 25- 33
Cereal set: bowl, creamer, mug, all (creamers)	110-118
Doll, soap	52- 61
Salt, 3″ high	25- 33
School bag	64- 73
Teapot, 2 cups, pink plastic, both	71- 80

Snow White

Wristwatch	$ 40- 48

Superman

Brush, early	$ 21- 30
Card game, by Ideal	22- 31
Club button, 3¼″	7- 11
Club member's certificate	38- 46
Game, in original box, early	109-118
Mug, 1960's	15- 24
Water gun	15- 24

Tarzan

Cardboard sign, advertising movie	$ 33- 42

Tom Mix

Belt buckle	$ 42- 51
Handkerchief	9- 12
Periscope ring	58- 68
Ralston ring, Straight Shooters	19- 27
Telescope, tin	61- 70

Children's Collectibles

Children's Collectibles

Books

These have been around for centuries. Usually what you find today at Flea Markets and garage sales were published after World War II.

Average price	75¢-3
Slow and Sure by Horatio Alger (Illus.)	6-20

Furniture

Chair, oak (Illus.)	$ 65-75
Desk, oak (Illus.)	95-115
Easel, alphabet on roller above board	40- 49
High chair, walnut	120-130
Poster bed w/canopy, half-size	165-180
Storage chest, toys, painted	40- 50

Molding/Coloring Sets

Average price	$ 1- 3

Nursery

Cereal dish, Bunnykins, porcelain (Illus.)	$ 15- 23
Drinking mug, sterling silver	35- 43
Drinking mug, silver plate	11- 16
Teething ring, sterling silver	24- 30

Tea Sets/Dishes

Aluminum

Bread, cake pans, each .... $ 1-1.25
Colander, muffin tin, each .. 1.75-2.25
Measuring cup, plate, scoop, each .... 75¢-1

China

Bluebirds, "Made in Japan," 4-place set .... $ 46- 54
Cameoware, Harker China Co., 4-place set 287-310
Dutch figures, Edwin M. Knowles China Co., 4-place set 77- 85
Floral, Edwin M. Knowles China Co., 4-place set ... 55- 63
Floral medallion, "Made in Japan," 4-place set...... 44- 52
Godey prints, Salem China Co., 4-place set 82- 90
Kate Greenaway, Cleve-ron China, USA, 4-place set .. 290-318
Little Bo Peep (Victory), Salem China Co., 4-place set ... 93-108

Glass

Cherry Blossom, Jeanette Glass Co., 1932-1938. All pieces being reproduced.

	Pink	Delphite
Creamer, 2¾"	$ 26-29	23-27
Cup, 1½"	21-23.50	21-23.50
Plate, 5⅞"	8-9	6-7
Saucer, 4½"	5-6	5-6
Sugar bowl, 2⅝" ...	23.50-27	21-23

Homespun, Jeannette Glass Co., c. 1939-1940.

	Pink	Crystal
Boxed set, 12 pcs. .	$	73-87
Boxed set, 14 pcs. .	195-216	
Cup, 1⅝"	28-30	13-15
Plate, 4½"	6-7	4-5
Saucer, 3¼"	4-5	3-4.50
Teapot w/lid, 3¾" ..	48-54	

Laurel, McKee Glass Co., c. early 1930's. French Ivory, decorated trim, add 25 percent.

	French Ivory	Jade Green	Scottie Decal
Boxed set, 14 pcs. ..	$170-190	189-209	255-282
Creamer, 2⅝"	21- 24	23- 26	33- 36
Cup, 1½" .	21- 23	23- 26	29- 32
Plate, 5⅞" .	8- 9	9.50-10	13- 15
Saucer, 4⅜"	5- 6	5-6.50	5-6.50
Sugar bowl, 2⅜"	19- 22	21- 24	34- 37

Moderntone, Hazel Atlas Co., c. 1940's — early 1950's. White, add 20 percent.

	Pastel Colors	Dark Colors
Boxed set, 16 pcs.	$	28-33
Creamer, 1¾"	3.50-4.50	3.75-4.25
Cup, 1¾"	3-3.50	3-3.50
Plate, 5¼"	2.50-3	3-3.75
Saucer, 3⅞"	1.50-2	2.50-3.25
Sugar bowl, 1¾" ..	3.50-4	3.75-4.25
Teapot w/lid, 3½" .		28-33

Miscellaneous

Beater (Glasbake), 6⅜" .....$ 24-27
Bowl (Glasbake), 3⅝" 1.50-2
Lemonade server set, "Little Deb" 22-27
Mixer (Delta Detroit), 5" 20-23
Pitcher, 3⅞" 4.25-4.75
Tumbler, 2⅛" 2.50-3

Pattern Glass

Arched Panel, Westmoreland Glass Co.

	Crystal	Amber	Cobalt
Pitcher	$ 20-23	76-80	76-80
Tumbler	7.50-9	20-23	21-24
Water set, 7 pcs. (being reproduced)	57-70	188-200	210-220

Bead and Scroll, maker unknown

Butter dish w/lid, 4" $152-160
Creamer, 3" 57- 67
Spoonholder, 2¾" 55- 68
Sugar bowl w/lid, 4"........ 76- 97
Table set" 335-380

Buzz Saw

Butter w/lid, 2⅜" ....$ 30- 34
Creamer, 2⅜" 22- 24
Spoonholder, 2⅛" 22- 24
Sugar bowl w/lid, 2⅞" 30- 34
Table set 98-116

Cloud Band, Gillinder and Sons.

	Crystal	White Milk Glass
Butter dish w/lid, 3¾"	$108-116	154-163
Creamer, 2½" ...	34- 39	44- 51
Spoonholder, 2⅜"	34- 39	44-50
Sugar bowl w/lid, 4"............	66- 75	95-102
Table set	230-260	328-348

Drum, Bryce, Higbee & Co., c. 1880's.

Butter dish w/lid, 2¼" ......$ 99-108
Creamer, 2¾" 66- 74
Mug, 2", 2½", each 31- 38
Mug, 2 3/16" (being reproduced) 20- 24
Spoonholder, 2⅝" 71- 78
Sugar bowl w/lid, 3½" 96-105

Flute

	Crystal	Crystal with Gold
Berry set, 5 pcs. .	$ 56-61	174-184
Master berry	22-25	51- 56
Small berry	6.50-8	23- 29

Liberty Bell, Gillinder and Sons. Prices are for crystal. White milk glass, 100 percent higher.

Butter dish w/lid, 2¼" $177-186
Creamer, 2½" 74- 82
Mug, 2" 115-130
Spoonholder, 2⅜" 97-106

Sugar bowl w/lid, 3⅝" 133-143
Table set 475-500

Pattee Cross, U.S. Glass Co. Prices are for crystal. Crystal with gold, add 30 percent.

Master berry, 1¾" ....$ 39- 44
Pitcher, 4½" 44- 48
Punch bowl 78- 85
Punch cup, 1⅛" 22- 24
Small berry, 1" 11- 13
Tumbler, 1¾" 13- 15

Pert (Ribbed Forget-Me-Not), Bryce Bros., c. 1880.

Butter dish w/lid, 2¾" $125-132
Creamer, 3¼" 84- 90
Spoonholder, 3" 123-128
Sugar bowl w/lid, 5⅛" 140-148

Two Band

Butter dish w/lid, 2" ....$ 59- 66
Creamer, 2¾" 28- 36
Spoonholder, 2⅞" 34- 39
Sugar bowl w/lid, 3¾" 49- 54

Wooden Pail (Bucket), Bryce Bros.

Butter dish w/lid, 2¼" ......$ 68- 77
Creamer, 2½" 55- 64
Spoonholder, 2½" 35- 44
Sugar bowl w/lid, 3¾" 54- 62

Pewter

Creamer, 3¼" ....$ 24- 29
Cup, 1⅜" 18- 23
Spoon, 3¼" 4- 6
Spoonholder, 2⅝" 35- 40
Sugar bowl w/lid, 3½" 35- 40
Teapot w/lid, 4½" 43- 48

Suggested reading: *Children's Dishes*, Margaret and Kenn Whitmyer, Collector Books.

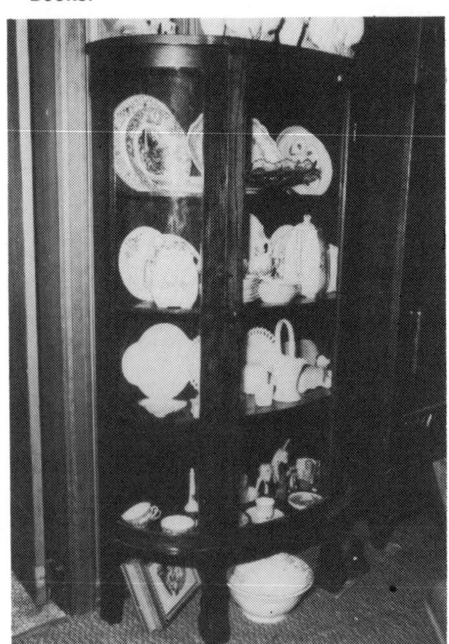

China Cabinets

China Cabinets

There are china cabinets and there are china cabinets. Oak can be ornate or plain; curved glass or plain; with or without lots of carving and scrolls. They range from $150 to $800, so do know what you're buying. The illustrated cabinet is in the $185-240 range.

Christmas Cards

Photo Courtesy of
Hake's Americana & Collectibles

Christmas Cards

Average price, depending on age and condition .... 50¢-$2

Christmas Easter Seals

Christmas/Easter Seals

Almost as much fun as collecting postage stamps. Whole sheets, 75¢-$1.50. Singles, 5¢ to 10¢ each.

Christmas Plates

Bing & Grondahl and the Royal Copenhagen factories in Copenhagen, Denmark, made and still make the most famous plates. B & G started making them

Christmas Plates

Christmas Ornaments

in 1895; RC in 1908. You'll just have to study up on this one as prices range from $25 for the newer ones to over $1,800 for the older, more rare plates. Look out for repros, please!

Christmas Ornaments

Old-fashioned Christmases are a thing of the past in this country. No stringing of popcorn to drape on the tree, no hiking through the snow to cut down a favorite tree. Older Christmas items are popular collectibles, but if you find old electric Christmas tree lights, be careful. Old wire can cause a fire in a matter of seconds.

Bulbs, Electric

Basket of fruit, green/red $10-14
Bell 19-21
Bluebird, milk glass 12-15
Clock 16-19
Donald Duck 26-30
Flower, rose 15-19
Gingerbread man, brown 13-17
House, Santa on roof 14-18
Humpty Dumpty 34-41
Kayo (comic strip character) 41-50
Lantern, Japanese 10-14
Mickey Mouse 16-22
Minnie Mouse 12-20
Parrot, milk glass 13-18
Pinocchio 27-32
Santa, 5″, 6″, 6½″, 7″ 13-20
Santa, 8″, 8½″, 9″ 54-61
Snowman, 5½″, 6″, 7″ 13-22
Star, various sizes, 3″ to 6″ 11-21

Ornaments

Angel, carved wood, c. 1880's . . . $47-54
Angel, spun glass wings 12-16
Basket of flowers 15-18
Basket, pressed paper (holds candy) 27-33
Beetle 15-19
Bell, clip-on 11-15
Bell, pressed paper 18-23
Bell, red mercury glass 12-22
Bird, cotton, clip-on 11-16
Bird, spun glass tail 13-18
Bugle, clip on 10-14
Bugs Bunny 27-35
Church, clip-on 15-21
Church, mercury glass 11-16
Clown head 10-15
Crane, clip-on 9-17
Fish, mercury glass 10-16
Heart, red glass 11-16
Horse, 5½″, 6½″, 8″ 12-18
Lion's head, pressed paper (holds candy) 29-33
Owl, pressed paper 13-17
Peacock, clip-on 14-21
Pear, green glass 12-20
Pipe, carved wood, painted, c. 1880's 47-54
Pipe, painted glass 14-18
Santa, basket on back (holds candy) 49-54
Santa, mercury glass 16-20
Santa, open bag, pressed paper (Illus.) 43-50
Santa, pressed paper (Illus.) 47-55
Snowman, mercury glass 14-19

Suggested reading: *The Glass Christmas Ornament Old and New,* Revised, Maggie Rogers and Judith Hawkins, Timber Press.

Churns, Crocks, and Jugs

Always check for cracks, especially if you want to use it to hold a liquid.

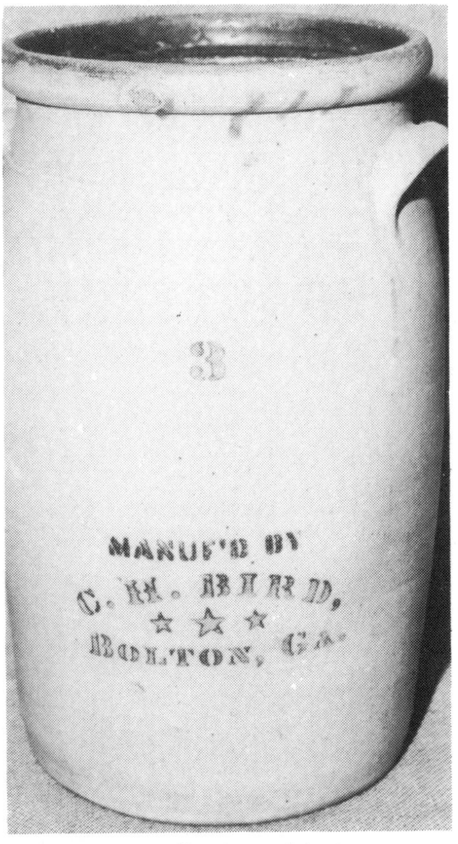

Churns, Crocks, and Jugs

#3 crock, "C. H. Bird, Bolton, Ga.," good condition (Illus.)	$39-47
2-handled jug, brown/white, early, good condition	24-32
1-handled jug, clay-colored, not cracked	22-28

The number on a jug usually denotes how many gallons it holds.

Circusiana

"Hey, Rube!" Ringling Bros. and Barnum and Bailey brought the circus to its peak during the 1920's in America. After World War II, expenses for travel, salaries, food, etc. and the advent of television wrote the circus' demise. No longer do you hear expressions such as "It's a straw house" or "cherry pie" or "windjammer." Today's broadway production at a convention center is a far cry from the open fields in every hamlet

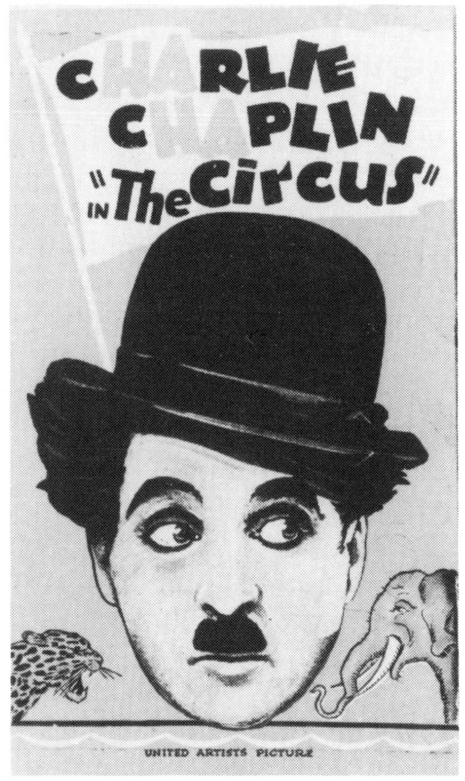

Circusiana

in America. See **Clubs and Publications,** this Price Guide.

Annie Oakley, free pass, signed by John Ringling	$ 9-15
Books	
Barnum, by R. M. Werner	25-31
The Big Top, by Fred Bradna	25-30
Jack of the Circus, by Madeleine Brandeis	14-19
Life of P. T. Barnum, by P. T. himself	29-34
On the Road with the Circus, by W. C. Thompson	27-33
The Ringlings—Wizard of the Circus, by Alvin Harlow	23-38
Struggles and Triumphs, by P. T. Barnum	32-37
This Way to the Big Show—The Life of Dexter Fellows (circus press agent), by Fellows and Andrew A. Freeman	18-25
Christmas cards depicting various circus scenes, average price, each	2- 6
Doll, celluloid, lady performer w/real feathers, 4½″ high	26-32
"Gargantua" photograph, 1938	6- 9

Giustino Loyal, bareback rider, photograph 8-11
Handbill, Barnum and Bailey, 1922 7-11
"Jumbo" photograph 9-14
Letterheads
A. G. Allen's Big Minstrel Show, photos of Allen and G. W. Quine 2- 3
Barnum & Bailey, photos of owners, clown head 1- 2
Big John Strong & Son Circus 2- 3
Christy Bros., The Wonder Show, various performers .. 1- 2
Cole Bros. Circus, photo of brothers w/tiger 1- 2
Gentry Bros. Circus, lions, tigers, etc. 1- 2
Hagenbeck Wallace Circus, giraffes, clowns, photo of owners 1- 2
Hunt Bros. Circus 1- 2
John Robinson's Circus, photo of J. R. w/performers 1- 2
Miller Brothers, rearing horse 1- 2
M. L. Clark & Sons, lions, tigers, photo of brothers 1- 2
Ringling Bros. and Barnum & Bailey, tents, clown head .. 1.50-2
Sells Floto Circus, clown head, two show rings 1- 2
Sparks Circus, tiger's head, clown 1- 2
World at Home and Polack Bros., globe, Atlas (?) 1- 2
Little Orphan Annie punch-out circus 40-50
Lobby card, Charlie Chaplin (Illus.) 26-32
Mills Bros. circus band w/Joseph Rossi, photograph . 9-15
Pennant, felt, Cole Bros., 1930's 8-11
Postcards depicting various scenes of circus life, average price, each ....50¢-3.50
Posters, 1930's, one sheet, 28″ x 41″, average price, each 48-65
Ring, made of lead, sold by circus giant, 1¼″ dia. 18-23
Sideshow "freak" cards, each . 2-3.50
Souvenir program, Ringling Bros., Barnum & Bailey, 1939, Madison Square Garden 5- 8
Window cards, quarter sheets, cardboard, 1920's to 1930's, each 8-15

Clickers

Buster Brown Hosiery ....$ 5-6
"Cricket" on back, 4″ long 3-4
Quaker State Motor Oil 1-2
"Health Shoes" (Illus.)..........1-1.50
Little Sergeant shoes 1-2

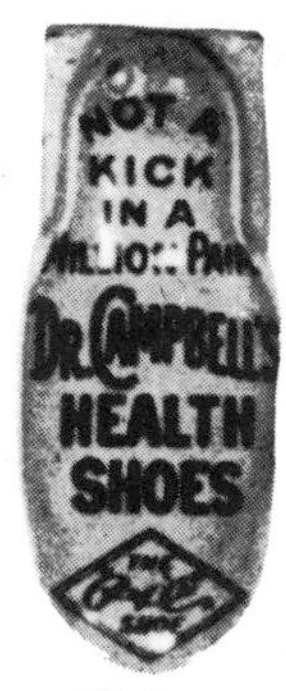

Clickers

Phoenix socks 1-2
"Smile" soft drink 2-3
Bonnie Laddie shoes 1-1.50

Clocks

Clocks

If you're collecting the Victorian style clocks, read Wallace-Homestead's *Clock Guide Identification with Prices, No. 1, Revised Edition.* So far no one has published a price guide that deals with 20th-century style clocks, other than those made until World War I. There were some very good clocks made in the 1930's. Look for the German Junghaus; oak case, brass works, and still rather inexpensive and available. Ya Masu Vonole and Company in Japan made some excellent clocks. Look for the Dutch clocks with porcelain faces, made in the 1920's and 1930's.

And don't forget those cuckoos, made in the Black Forest in Germany after World

War I. The Eikosha (Japan) clock is beginning to show up in shops and at shows. The Japanese wall Regulator "Sato" is another to look for. There are hundreds of mantel clocks, oak or mahogany cases, that were made in the 1920's and 1930's. If you're serious about collecting clocks, think about joining the National Association of Watch and Clock Collectors, P. O. Box 33, Columbia, PA 17512. Write for particulars.

Cloisonné

Cloisonné

Developed during the 19th century, glass enamel was applied between small ribbon-like pieces of metal on a metal base. Supposedly from Japan, it was and is still being made all through the Orient, France, and Italy. It's being heavily reproduced.

Item	Price
Cigarette box, green with flowers, late 1900's (Illus.)	$30-37
Desk blotter, blue/green, roll type, 1900's	22-29
Napkin ring, blue/green birds, late 1900's	8-12
Matchbox holder, goes with cigarette box above	12-18
Vase, beige ground, turquoise, gold trim, pair, 20th century	45-53

Clothing

Clothing

Capes

Item	Price
Opera, black, red silk lined, tassels, c. 1920's	$ 115- 130
Sealskin, c. 1930's	49- 58

Coats

Item	Price
Army, WWI, olive drab, brass buttons, full length	$ 78- 85
Calfskin, half length, c. 1930's	80- 90
Lady's long (or automobile), c. 1915, all wool jersey	103- 113
Man's moleskin, full length, c. 1920's	80- 90
Raccoon, man's, full length	1,200-1,300

Collars

Item	Price
Mink, 8″ wide, c. 1930's	$ 48- 54
Rabbit, c. 1940's	32- 40

Dresses

Item	Price
Lady's black silk peau de soie, c. 1915	$ 70- 77
Lady's evening, blue silk, full bustle, c. WWI	140- 150
Lady's taffeta, silk, c. WWI	55- 65

Handbags

Item	Price
Alligator, chatelaine, chain and belt attachment	$ 65- 75
Beaded, cut steel, steel bead fringe, chamois back, silver-plated frame, chain, hook	39- 47
Beaded, red/black, tasseled bottom, purse string top	32- 38
Leather, nickel-rivoted frame, leather straps, belt hook	37- 42
Metal, chatelaine, nickel, chain and belt hook	32- 38

Opera shopping bag, black moiré silk, silk cord handles	28-	37
Silk, embroidered head initials, silver frame and chain	49-	59

Hats

Lady's Italian leghorn, pink/white Japanese silk, c. 1920's	$ 53-	63
Lady's jaunty turban, silk finished black mull, c. WWI	57-	64
Lady's mushroom brim, c. WWI	44-	53
Man's derby (or stiff), c. 1920's	32-	39
Man's fedora, nutria fur, c. 1915	41-	51
Man's Stetson, Dakota style, c. 1910	50-	60
Man's top hat, black silk, collapsible type, c. 1920's	52-	60

Jackets

Lady's muskrat, half length, c. 1920's	$ 47-	56
Lady's sheared lamb, full length, c. 1930's	90-	100
Man's buckskin, c. 1930's	78-	88
Man's cardigan, double breasted, c. WWI	45-	54

Parasols/Umbrellas

Lady's all-silk, colored serge, c. 1920's	$ 42-	50
Lady's tight roll taffeta silk, c. 1920's	44-	53
Lady's twilled silk, white pearl handle, c. WWI	44-	53
Man's taffeta silk, weichsel wood hook handle, c. WWI	52-	60
Man's twilled silk, Prince of Wales hook handle, c. 1915	51-	60

Petticoats

Fast-colored striped gingham, c. WWI	$ 27-	32
Mercerized percaline, black/white stripes, c. 1915	31-	40
Sateen, flounce around bottom, lined with black glazed cloth	33-	42

Shawls

Lady's all wool split zephyr, c. 1915	$ 41-	50
Lady's Shetland wool, 36" dia., c. WWI	48-	54

Shoes

Lady's black cloth top, c. 1908	$ 41-	50
Lady's patent leather, c. WWI (Illus.)	56-	63
Lady's velour calf, Goodyear welt, c. 1915	44-	52
Man's box calf, c. WWI	43-	50
Man's coin toe stain calf, c. 1915	44-	51
Man's leather oxford, c. 1915	39-	48

Spats

Man's, pearl gray, M-O-P buttons, c. WWI	$ 32-	41

Suits

Man's long roll frock, c. WWI	$ 45-	53
Man's square cut single breasted sack, c. 1915	49-	57
Man's three button cutaway sack, c. WWI	48-	56

Suggested reading: *Collectible Clothing with Prices,* Sheila Malouff, Wallace-Homestead Book Company.

Coal Buckets

Another "newie" but purty. Brass w/a copper handle; copper w/a brass handle. Usually called a hod.

Brass w/copper handle, old	$160-	170
Brass w/copper handle, new	58-	67

Coca-Cola Collectibles

Anything with "Coke" or Coca-Cola on it is highly sought after today. The prices are high, too. See **Clubs and Publications,** this Price Guide.

Bingo board, 1930's	$ 32-	37
Binoculars, 1910	195-	218
Blotter, 1930	28-	34
Blotters, 1900's-1920's, each	94-	102
Book, *Know Your War Planes,* 1943	59-	66
Book, *Pause for Living,* 1960's	32-	39
Bottle openers, 1910-20's, each	61-	69
Buddy Lee doll, deliveryman, 1928, 12½" high	215-	225
Calendar, 1975	9-	15

Coca-Cola Collectibles

Item	Price
Calendars, 1900-08, complete	750- 825
Calendars, 1909-15, complete	600- 660
Carrying tray, 1915	122- 131
Case, miniature, 28 bottles, gold finish	64- 72
Case, wooden, 24 bottles, c. 1920	28- 35
Cigarette case, 50th anniversary, 1936	195- 211
"Coke Can" radio, 1971	77- 85
Comb, "Drink Coca-Cola 5¢"	45- 55
Coupons, good for one free bottle of Coca-Cola, 1900	160- 170
Coupons, same deal, 1920's	73- 84
Cribbage board, 1930	61- 70
Dominoes, 1940	56- 66
Glass, drinking, 1900	228- 237
Glass, drinking, 1921	52- 60
Glass, drinking, 1930's, pewter	70- 78
Key fob, bulldogs, 1½" × 1", metal, 1925	130- 140
Key fob, 1½" dia., celluloid, 1900	355- 365
Key fob, oval, 1¾" × 1¼", 1906	310- 320
Knife, switchblade type, 1909	121- 130
Landmarks of the U.S.A. (Illus.)	9- 14
Leaded glass globe, hanging type, late 1920's	5,000 +
Mechanical pencil, 1930	54- 62
Menus, 1900-05, "Hilda Clark," each	188- 197
Milk glass shade, dome light, 10" dia., 1920's	610- 645
Miniature plastic bottle and case, 1970	26- 34
Mirror, "Girl in bonnet," 1914	177- 186
Needle cases (held sewing needles), 1920s, each	74- 83
Night light, "Courtesy of your C-C Bottler," 1945	34- 39
Pencil sharpeners, 1930's-60's, each	49- 57
Playing cards, 1909-27, each deck	88- 97
Playing cards, 1930-40's, each deck	44- 54
Postcard, "Coca-Cola Delivery Truck," 1915	114- 121
Pretzel dish, "Coke" bottles for legs, 1936	77- 87
Radio, shaped like drink box, 1949	190- 210
Radio, shaped like "Coke" bottle, 24" high, 1930	320- 340
Seltzer bottles, 1900-20's, each	86- 93
Sheet music, "Old Folks at Home," "The Palms," "Rock Me to Sleep, Mother," "Juanita" "My Old Kentucky Home," each	152- 160
Sign, 8" dia., glass, 1915	135- 143
Sign, 30" × 7¾", tin, in shape of arrow, 1927	137- 145
Sign, tin, 15" × 18½", "Hilda Clark," 1904	2,400 +
Syrup bottles, 1910-20's, each	190- 210
Take home carton, late 1930's	57- 67
Toy drink dispenser, 1960	140- 150
Toy stove, electrified, 1938	244- 252
Thermometers, 1930-50's, each	61- 70
Thimble, aluminum, 1920	55- 65
Tray, "bottle," 9¾" dia., 1900	1,400 +
Tray, girl in yellow bathing suit, 1937	66- 74
Tray, 8½" × 19½", "Elaine," 1917	154- 163
Tray, oval, "Hilda Clark," 18½" × 15", 1904	1,700 +
Tray, 10" dia., "Vienna Art," 1905	190- 210
Tray, 10½" × 13¼", farm boy w/dog, 1931	97- 106

Suggested reading: ***Wallace-Homestead Price Guide to Coca-Cola Collectibles,*** **Deborah Goldstein Hill, Wallace-Homestead Book Company.**

Coin-Operated Machines

Coin-Operated Machines

Music, games of skill and chance — all are collectible. The penny and five-cent machines are a thing of the past and a part of the nostalgia boom sweeping America today. See **Clubs and Publications,** this Price Guide.

Candy/Gum

Item	Low	High
Advance, candy bars, 5¢	$ 132-	142
Advance, packaged gum, 5¢	140-	150
Columbus, gum balls, 1¢	155-	165
Flatbush, gum balls, 1¢	210-	230
Hershey, chocolate bars, 1¢	185-	198
Imp, gum balls/game, 1¢	258-	268
National, gum/mint, 5¢	172-	181
Star, candy, 1¢	152-	162
Wrigley, gum, 5¢	140-	150

Games

Item	Low	High
Bowling, metal puck, 10¢	$ 550-	570
Charger target game, 1¢	275-	285
Genco, hand squeezer, strength, 5¢	178-	188
Kicker-Katcher, 1¢	335-	350
Smiley counter game, 1¢	290-	325
Steeple Chase, 1¢	545-	610
Target Pistol, counter game, 5¢	385-	410

Jukeboxes

Item	Low	High
AMI Model A, c. 1946, 40 tunes, lots of plastic and lights	$ 2,400-	2,700
AMI Model FR, c. 1930's, 20 tunes, Art Deco style	675-	770
Capehart Deluxe, 1930's, horizontal record racks	1,100-	1,350
Mills Empress Model 910, c. 1939, 20 tunes	1,875-	1,990
Mills Throne of Music, 20 tunes, gawdy	1,750-	1,900
Rock-Ola Comet, c. 1950, 120 tunes	1,700-	1,990
Rock-Ola Model 1422	1,600-	1,800
Rock-Ola Monarch, c. 1939, 20 tunes, wood case, metal grill	1,150-	1,350
Seeburg Audiophone, c. 1929, 8 tunes	1,375-	1,500
Seeburg Commander, c. 1940, 20 tunes, lots of plastic	1,395-	1,550
Seeburg Symphonola Regal, c. 1940, 20 tunes	1,700-	1,900
Wurlitzer Model 24, c. late 1930's, 24 tunes, floor model	700-	800
Wurlitzer Model 71, c. early 1940's 12 tunes	875-	1,100
Wurlitzer 616A, c. late 1930's, 16 tunes	600-	700
Wurlitzer Model 1015 (Illus.)	3,100-	3,300

Slot Machines

Item	Low	High
Caille Four Reel Superior, 10¢	$ 3,700-	3,900
Caille nude front, 10¢	3,600-	3,800
Caille Superior Jackpot, 10¢	2,900-	3,000
Caille Victory Bell, 25¢	10,500-	10,700
Groetchen Columbia Deluxe, 5¢	1,875-	2,000
Groetchen Columbia, 5¢	950-	1,100
Mills Q.T., 10¢	2,000-	2,200
Mills Thunderbird Q.T., 1¢	3,200-	3,400
Pace Bantam, 1¢	2,600-	2,800
Vendet Midget, 5¢	3,700-	3,900
Watling bubble gum front, 1¢	3,800-	4,000

Coins, American

You've got to be an expert to buy and sell intelligently, and no single book can accomplish that for you. But, there are more than 28 million coin collectors in the United States, so some of you must know what you're doing.

Coins, American

The American Numismatic Association has established these standards for grading coins.

Proof-70 Perfect Proof
Proof-65 Choice Proof
Proof-60 Proof
MS-70 Perfect Uncirculated
MS-65 Choice Uncirculated
MS-60 Uncirculated
AU-55 Choice About Uncirculated
AU-50 About Uncirculated
EF-45 Choice Extremely Fine
EF-40 Extremely Fine
VF-30 Choice Very Fine
VF-20 Very Fine
F-12 Fine
VG-8 Very Good
G-4 Good
AG-3 About Good

If you learn these codes, you'll be ahead of the game — more so than those collectors who simply take the seller's word.

Coins, Foreign

Coins, Foreign

Generally, copper coins from a foreign country have little or no value. Obviously, there are silver coins and there are gold coins. Did you know there are foreign coins made of aluminum, acmonital, billon, brass, bronze, copper, iron, magnesium, nickel, steel, tin, and zinc? A.D. means *anno Domini* . . . in the year of our Lord. Don't pay the price for a genuine silver or gold coin ***unless*** you know the seller's reputation.

Collectors' Plates

Photo Courtesy of
Hake's Americana & Collectibles

Collectors' Plates

How many were made? Who decorated/painted the plate? Year made? There are countless thousands on the market today and with a few exceptions, they're not worth what you paid for them. See **Clubs and Publications,** this Price Guide.

Combs

Dating back to the 16th century, they had one purpose — keep m'lady's hair in place. Quite popular during the Victorian period, they went out of style during the Depression. Now back in vogue, the older ones are being collected.

Baretta, black celluloid, white rhinestones, c. 1930's . . . $16-20
Baretta, carved tortoiseshell, c. 1915 (Illus.) 18-23

Combs

Chignon pin, clear celluloid, blue rhinestones, c. late 1920's 14-19
Pompadour, red enamel on clear celluloid, pink rhinestones, c. 1920's 36-42
Sterling silver, ornately carved, c. 1920's 34-40
Toilet w/handle, satin finish aluminum, coarse teeth 13-18
Tortoiseshell, carved (Illus.) 22-27

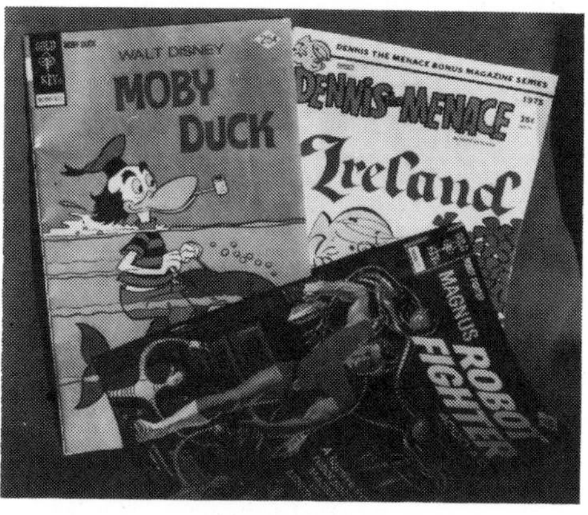

Comic Books

Comic Books

There are countless thousands involved in this category. Prices given are for books in mint condition. See **Clubs and Publications,** this Price Guide.

A-1 Comics (Compix Magazine Enterprises), 139 Issue #s, 1944-1955
#18, Jimmy Durante $29- 37
#41, Cowboys/Indians 7- 9
#62, Starr Flag Undercover Girl #5 .... 53- 60

Ace Comics (David McKay Publications), 151 Issue #s, 1937-1950
#2 .... 84- 93
#6-10 .... 47- 56
#26, Prince Valiant 127-137
#135, The Lone Ranger 8- 11

Action Comics (National Periodical Publications), more than 400 Issue #s, 1938-present
#1, Superman (1st appearance) .... 7,000+
#4, Superman .... 1,500+
#252, Supergirl (1st appearance) 150-160

Adventures of Bob Hope (National Periodical Publications), 109 Issue #s, 1950-1968
#1 .... 39- 46
#36-60 .... 5- 7
#91-105 .... 4- 5

Adventures of Pinky Lee (Atlas Comics), 5 Issue #s, 1955
#1 .... 22- 28
#4-5 .... 10- 14

Al Capp's Shmoo (Toby Press), 5 Issue #s, 1949
#1 .... 34- 40
#4-5 .... 12- 18

Boots and Her Buddies (Standard Comics/Sisual/Argo Publishers), 9 Issue #s
#1-3 (reprints) 6- 8
#9 .... 29- 37

Boy Explorers Comics (Harvey Publications)
#1, 1946 110-130

Butch Cassidy (Skywald Comics), 3 Issue #s, 1971
#1-3 .... 2- 3

Captain Tootsie and the Secret Legion (Toby Press), 2 Issue #s
#1...................... 22- 30
#2...................... 15- 18

Chamber of Darkness (Marvel Comics Group), 8 Issue #s, 1969-70
#1-3 .... 4- 6
#5-6 .... 3- 4

Comics Revue (St. John Publishing Co.), 5 Issue #s, 1947-1948
#1, Ella Cinders and Blackie . 15- 19
#4, Ella Cinders 8- 10

Daredevil Comics (Lev Gleason Publications), 134 Issue #s, 1941-1956
#1, Daredevil Battles, Hitler Silver Streak 700-800
#12, Claw 140-152

Diary of Horror (Avon Periodicals)
#1, 1952 .... 22- 30

Fight (Fiction House Magazines), 86 Issue #s, 1940-1954
#1, Spy Fighter............ 123-135
#31-50 .... 18- 22
#80-86, Tiger Man 10- 12

Funny Pages (Centaur Publications), 45 Issue #s, 1936-1942
#6, The Clock 39- 44
#7-20 .... 29- 39

Green Giant Comics (Harvey Publications) #1 Issue, 1940 720-800

Human Torch (Marvel Comics Group), 8 Issue #s 1974-1975
#1 .... 3- 4
#2-8 .... 2-2.50

Monsters Unleashed (Marvel Group), 11 Issue #s, 1973-1975
#1 .... 4- 6
#5, Man-Thing 5- 7
#10 .... 4- 5

My Friend Irma (Marvel Comics Group/Atlas Comics), 46 Issue #s, 1950-1955
#4 .... 32- 40
#6-10 .... 7- 13

Namora (Marvel Comics Group), 3 Issue #s, 1948
#1 121-130
#2-3 91-101

Not Brand Echh (Marvel Comics Group), 13 Issue #s, 1967-1969
#1 .... 6- 8
#6-13 .... 2- 3

Our Gang Comics (Dell Publishing Co.), 59 Issue #s, 1942-1949
#1 330-345
#8-11 119-147
#37-55 .... 8- 12

Silly Tunes (Timely Comics), 7 Issue #s, 1945-1947
#1 .... 10- 12
#2-7 .... 7- 13

Speed Carter, Spaceman (Atlas Comics), 8 Issue #s, 1953-1954
#1-8 .... 14- 19

Spy Smasher (Fawcett Publications), 11 Issue #s, 1941-1943
#1 250-260
#3-11 .... 67- 76

Teen Confessions (Charlton Comics), 90 Issue #s, 1959-1976
#1 .... 13- 21
#11-30 .... 4- 6
#32-90 ....1.50-2.50

Tim Holt (Magazine Enterprises), 41 Issue #s, 1948-1954
#2-3 .... 45- 50
#17 .... 62- 70

Tom Mix Western (Fawcett Publications), 61 Issues #s, 1948-1953
#1 .... 71- 80
#11-25 .... 32- 40
#26-61 .... 17- 26

Vacation Parade (Dell Publishing Co.), 5 Issue #s, 1950-1954
#1 270-285
#3-5 .... 23- 32

Venus (Marvel Comics Group/Atlas Comics), 19 Issue #s, 1948-1952
#1 .... 64- 73
#2-19 .... 35- 44

Where Creatures Roam (Marvel Comics Group), 8 Issue #s, 1970-1971
#1 .... 4- 5
#2-8 .... 1.50- 2

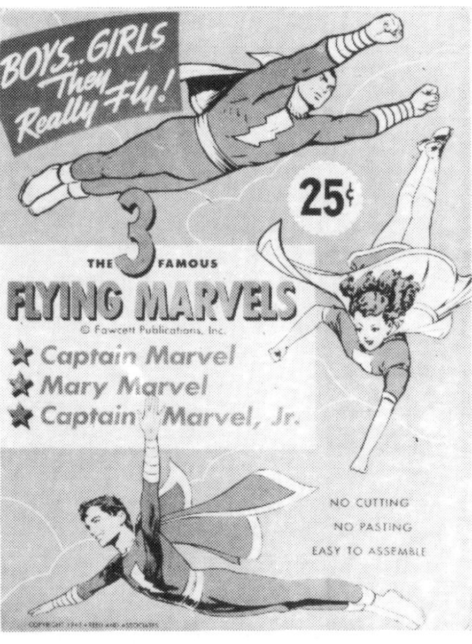

Comic Strip Characters

Photo Courtesy of
Hake's Americana & Collectibles

Comic Strip Characters

Who knows when you'll find one **personally** autographed? Keep lookin'!

Autographed copy, Gospel According to PEANUTS (Illus.) ...$16-21
Dick Tracy Secret Service Patrol Certificate 11-14

Commemorative Glasses

The same "rule of thumb" applies here as with beer cans and bottles. Fragility enters into the picture. The glass shown is one of a set of eight issued to honor the Winchester Rifle. Many companies did this on a grand scale in the mid-1900's and if the glasses still survive, they're certainly worth collecting.

Commemorative Glasses

Winchester-Western glass, set of 8 (Illus.) **$19-25**
Philadelphia Centennial mug, 1876, 4″ high **13-19**
World's Fair, New York, mug, 5½″ high **9-13**

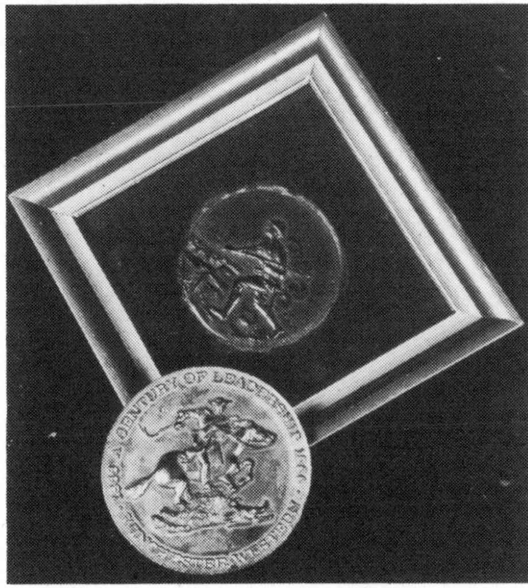

Commemorative Medals

Commemorative Medals

Do you know how many "special" days we have in America? "National Cheese Week"; "National Cat Week." Americans like to "strike" medals for just about any occasion. The two shown are to honor those fighting men who went to Europe with "Black Jack" Pershing during World War I and to "commemorate" the Winchester Rifle. Dependent on the metal, silver, lead-plated gold, 10 karat, 14 karat, or other materials — this decides the cost to you, the buyer. Also, how badly do you want it?

Prices for the illustrated:
"Dough Boy, 1919" **$42-50**
"Winchester Rifle" **17-24**

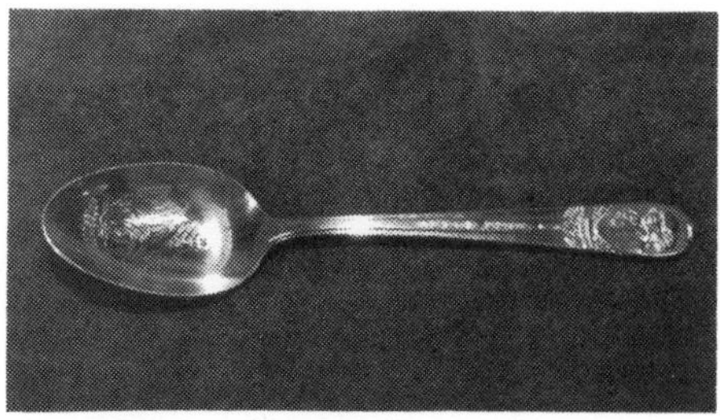

Commemorative/Souvenir Spoons

Commemorative/Souvenir Spoons

Another "people, places, and things" category. Memento spoons have come back into popularity. During the 1880's and 1890's countless thousands were made, both here and abroad. Differences in patents, copyrights, and trademarks cause a lot of confusion in this field of collecting. Rarity and type of metal dictate the price. The spoons listed here are .800 to .900 fine silver.

John Adams (Illus.) **$25-34**
Battle of Plattsburg **27-35**
James G. Blaine **39-44**
Boston Tea Party **27-35**
Brooklyn Heights **27-35**
Commodore Perry **27-35**
Confederate Monument **31-40**
Devil **34-40**
Easter Chick **22-27**
Easter Lily **24-28**
El Camino Real **22-28**
Fort Dearborn **29-35**
Fort Pitt **30-38**
General Sherman **38-42**
German coats-of-arms **14-19**
Grant's Tomb **27-35**
Lexington Minuteman **27-36**
Massachusetts, sterling **38-41**
Memphis, sterling **37-44**

Merry Christmas 24-28
Miner 24-33
Minneapolis, Minnesota 25-29
Nantucket Old Mill 38-44
Pan-American Exposition 23-29
William Penn, 2 styles 39-95
Philadelphia 30-35
Priscilla and John 29-36
Rip Van Winkle 28-38
Betsy Ross 41-50
St. Augustine, designs 1 through 4 27-45
Springfield Rifle 39-45
Miles Standish 35-45
Harriet Beecher Stowe 34-44
Thanksgiving 32-40
Uncle Sam, 3 sizes, each 41-50
Washington, D.C. 44-50
White House 19-25
Yuletide 29-36

Cookbooks

Cookbooks

These cookbooks, especially those printed in the early 1900's, are collectible. Condition and age establish the price.

Agate Iron Ware, c. 1890's . . . . . . $ 9-12
Arm & Hammer Valuable Recipes, c. 1921 8-12
Baker's Chocolate *Best Chocolate Recipes*, c. 1934 . . . . 6- 8
Cutco Cookbook, c. 1960 . . . . 5- 7
Denver Post Prize Recipes, c. 1932 8-10
Fannie Farmer's *Boston Cooking-School Cook Book*, c. 1920 (Illus.) 8-12
Fleischmann Yeast Recipe Booklet, c. 1900's 7- 9
Granite Iron Ware, c. 1800's 8-10
Hamilton Beach Blender Recipes, c. 1949 . . . . 4- 5
Jell-O Recipe Booklet, Jack Benny promotion, c. 1930's . . . 12-15
Kate Smith's Favorite Recipes, c. 1940's 10-13
Kellogg's *Keep on the Sunny Side of Life*, c. 1933 . . . . 3- 6
Maxwell House Coffee Cookbook, c. 1960's 7- 9
National Biscuit's *Biscuits for Salads*, c. 1920's 3- 4
Pepsi-Cola Recipe Book, c. 1940 . 12-16
Purefoy (Alabama) Cookbook, c. 1930's 5- 7
Royal Baking Powder's Baker and Pastry Book 6- 8
SnowDrift Secrets, c. 1913 . . . . . . 5- 7
Wesson Oil Recipes, c. 1913 . . . . 5- 8
Wine in Cooking, France, c. 1920 10-13

Cookie Molds

Cookie Molds

Hand-carved molds have been around for years. Made of wood, they come from Holland, Austria, France, etc. You can still use most of them; if not, hang same on the kitchen wall. Being reproduced.

Average price, if in good condition and old $17-25

Copper

One of the world's most important metals, it's been used for centuries in every shape, size, and object. Wire, cooking utensils, jewelry, weathervanes, you-name-it.

Basket, Art Nouveau, cherubs in relief, 13″ high . . . .$ 92-102

Copper

Basket, double handle, hammered bottom, 1920's, 10″ dia.	**60- 70**
Chafing dish, complete, 1920's	**108-117**
Coachman's horn, 38″ long, pewter mouthpiece, new	**50- 58**
Cover pan, zinc handles, 1900's	**69- 76**
Desk set, 5-pc.—inkwell, blotter holder, letter holder, pen(s) holder, tray, 1920, all	**140-150**
Dippers, many types, all ages, average price	**39-110**
Planters, set of 6, brass handles, pre-WWI, all	**110-120**
Plaque, hand-tooled, Vikings-in-ship, 3″ × 7″, dated 1905	**85- 95**
Samovar, brass-footed, 15″ high	**310-320**
Teapot, 9″ high (Illus.)	**55- 63**
Umbrella stand, brass bottom, tooled scenes of flowers, 1900's	**153-161**
Vase, pewter base, tulip lip, 14″ high, 1900's	**77- 86**
Vase, silver inlay of butterflies, flowers, 9½″ high, 1900's	**130-140**
Wash boiler w/lid, burnished, early 1900's	**125-133**

Copper "Paintings"

Actually, the process is one of stamping, scorping, pressing, onto soft copper. Then the various colors are added. You'll find these in all sizes, every description. Prices vary.

Carp, made in Japan (Illus.) $19-25

Copper "Paintings"

Cordey China

Cordey China

The Cordey China Company was founded in 1942 by Boleslaw Cybis in Trenton, New Jersey. Gift shop items and lamps were produced. Cybis' figurines and busts featured floral appliqués, ruffles, and lace. He called his porcelain formula "Papka" and each piece was given its own number imprinted or impressed in the base. Cybis Porcelains was founded in 1950.

Ashtray, gold/cream/roses, 6¼″	**$ 27- 34**
Box, #8021, scrolls/roses	**58- 64**
Bust, #5009, lady, blue hat/flowers, 5½″	**48- 55**
Bust, #5038, Napoleon, 7½″	**79- 87**
Bust, #5053, lady w/cape, 7″	**74- 82**
Figurine, #302, lady in red hat	**230-240**
Figurine, #304, fruit girl, 10″	**158-165**
Figurine, #4074, man in frock	**168-176**
Lamp, bird in flowers, 14½″ (Illus.)	**125-133**

Lamp, #5041, gentleman 110-118
Vase, bird in tree, 8¼″ 59- 66
Vase, oriental lady, 9″ 46- 53

Corkscrews

Corkscrews

They've been around since the first cork had to be removed from a jug or bottle.

Anheuser Busch, Pat. 1897, brass $32-40
Figural, bottle shape, "Drink Blatz" 19-25
Figural, "naughty boy," steel shaft, wooden handle 38-44
Goat's head, brass 45-52
Metal shaft, wooden handle (Illus.) 14-19
Naughty nude, brass 54-62
Sterling silver head, steel shaft . . 44-51
T handle, double, metal shaft (Illus.) 14-20

Corn Husk Dolls

The pioneers made dolls for their children from corn husks. Sometimes the head was a shriveled apple. Fun to collect and showing up at Flea Markets around the U.S.

Average cost $5-8

Coronation Collectibles

Coronation Collectibles

After a coronation, items in china and glass appear on the English market. Tin candy and cracker boxes are especially collectible. Elizabeth II paperweights are considered prizes by those who seek out coronation items.

Beaker, Edward VII, 1902, Royal Doulton . . . . $ 59- 67
Brandy snifter, King Edward VIII, coat of arms 47- 55
Cup, Garter emblem, 5″ high . . 51- 61
Cup, King Edward VII 44- 52
Cup/saucer, Mary/George V . . . 42- 49
Globe, Edward VIII, porcelain . . 46- 53
Handkerchief, Elizabeth II, 1953 18- 21
Humidor, Queen Elizabeth II, 1953, silver plate 51- 60
Mug, George V and Mary, 1911, portraits, 3″ high 60- 70
Paperweight, Queen Elizabeth II, 1953, St. Louis . 355-370
Pitcher, Victoria, 6″ high (Illus.) 42- 51
Plaque, Edward VII, Alexandra, 1902, Royal Doulton 100-112
Plate, bread, George VI, 1937 . 47- 56
Plate, Edward VII, 1902 . . . . 54- 64
Spoon, George VI, 1911, demitasse 38- 47

Country Store

Before World War II lots of folks had to shop at the country store for just about everything or rely on the Sears or Montgomery Ward catalogs.

Bill holders, average price . . . . . . $ 9-17
Carpet beaters, average price . . . 16-23
String holders
Glass, beehive type (rare) 68-78
Cast iron, beehive, counter type (illus.) 33-40

Country/Western Memorabilia

Country/Western Memorabilia

Early examples are very scarce, those items that date 50 to 60 years ago. But, happily, there are countless thousands of items just waiting to be discovered. Careful of those printed signatures on photographs of semi-modern and modern stars such as Roy Acuff, Roy Rogers, Johnny Cash, Gene Autry, etc. Collect, but don't pay too much.

Photos

Acuff, Roy, song folio (Illus.) . . . . $ 7-11
Allen, Rex, photo, signed 8-11
Arnold, Eddy, photo, signed 11-14
Atkins, Chet, typewritten letter, signed, 1963 . . . . 7- 9
Autry, Gene, photo, signed, 1950 11-15
Britt, Elton, snapshot, signed 6- 9
Carlisle, Cliff, photo, signed 9-13
Dalhart, Vernon, photo, signed, 1925 30-37
Davis, Jimmie, photo, signed 8-10
Dexter, Al, photo, signed 7- 9
Jones, Grandpa, photo, signed . . 7- 9
Kincaid, Bradley, photo, signed . . 12-15
Macon, "Uncle" Dave, photo, signed, 1937 26-32
Monroe, Bill, LP record album, cover only 26-33
Poole, Charlie, photo, signed 18-24
Ritter, Tex, 78 rpm record of "High Noon," signed on label . 42-50
Robertson, Texas Jim, photo, signed 5- 8
Rodgers, Jimmie, postcard photo, facsimile signature 23-30
Rogers, Roy, photo, signed, 1960 (see also Cereal/ Radio Premiums) 7- 9
Snow, Hank, 78 rpm record, signed on label 17-23
Tanner, Gid, photo, signed 32-40
Tubb, Ernest, photo, signed 6- 9
Williams, Hank, postcard photo, signed 13-17

45 rpm Records

Campbell, Glen. Glen recorded for Ceneco, Crest, and Capitol. $3-5 will get you most, but expect to pay $9-17 for "Guess I'm Dumb/That's All Right."

Cash, Johnny. Most of Johnny's Sun labels can be found for $2-5.

Everly Brothers. Their Columbia label "Keep A-Loving Me/The Sun Keeps Shining" brings $23-33. Most of their other songs, done for Cadence, bring $1.75-4.

Lee, Brenda. $2.50-5 will get you most of this pretty lady's songs.

Lewis, Jerry Lee. $2-4.50 hacks it here.

Twitty, Conway. Love that name! $6.50-11 on the Mercury label; $2-4 on the MGM label.

78 rpm Records

Acuff, Roy. Ninety percent of Roy's records sell for $4-7 each. Songs such as "Gonna Have a Big Time Tonight/Yes Sir, That's My Baby," and "Great Speckled Bird #2/Tell Mother I'll Be There" sell for $17-30.

Arnold, Eddy. Most of Eddy's records are in the $20-35 range though one or two such as "You Must Walk the Line/Many Years Ago" and "Mommy, Please Stay Home With Me/Mother's Prayer" sell as high as $37-53.

Autrey, Gene. Early records are in the $45-65 range. Columbia labels bring $9-12, generally. All are collectible.

Davis, Jimmie. His "Bear Cat Mama from Horners Corners/She's a Hum Dinger" goes for $70-80, while most of his other Bluebird labels can be found for $27-55. Also his Decca labels.

Jones, Grandpa. This star of Hee Haw recorded on the King Label. His 78's go for $11-17.

Rodgers, Jimmie. Very few, if any, of Jimmie's records sell for less than $60-100 and a whole lot bring a whole lot more!

Rogers, Roy. $5-8 will buy most of Roy's great stuff.

Tanner, Gid. Gid and his Skillet Lickers cut for Bluebird, and most of his records go for $35-48. A few in the $50-70 range.

Williams, Hank. $400-475 will buy a copy of "Calling You/Never Again," if you're lucky enough to find a copy! His MGM records are in the $11-17 neighborhood.

Cowan Pottery COWAN Pottery

Founded by R. Guy Cowan, Cleveland, Ohio, in 1913, it was called the Cleveland Pottery and Tile Company. Wayland

Gregory was one of Cowan's leading artists. Lusterware and crackleware in a wide variety of colors were offered. Redware of the 1913-1917 period was incised with "Cowan Pottery." On later work the stylized semicircular Cowan mark was used. In 1931 Cowan closed his shops and moved to Syracuse, New York. He died in 1957.

Bowl, blue luster, footed, 12¼″ high . . . . $ 52- 61
Bowl, green luster, 7″ high . . . 50- 60
Candlesticks, blue luster, Art Deco, 6″ high, pr. 50- 60
Candlesticks, pink/white, 6″ high, pr. 41- 60
Flower frog, nude dancers, ivory glaze, 9½″ dia. 41- 52
Vase, blue luster, 9″ high 32- 52
Vase, orange luster, 5½″ high . 17- 21
Vase, redware, black glaze over orange ground, 12″ high 178-188
Vase, yellow luster, marine decor, 6½″ high 47- 53

Cowboy Heroes

Cowboy Heroes

The real cowboys lasted about forty years, from the Civil War until the beginning of the 20th century. The movie/radio/television version stuck around a lot longer. Since John (Duke) Wayne's death, the perennial kids (of all ages) who worshipped the riders of the purple sage have had slim pickings. Hopalong Cassidy (William Boyd) took over from Tom Mix, opening the door to movie/radio cowboys such as Bob Baker, Andy Devine, Buck Jones, Tom Tyler, Lane Chandler, "Sunset" Carson, Gabby Hayes, Dick Foran, Tex Ritter, Monte Hale, Don "Red" Barry, Smiley Burnette, George Montgomery and a lot more including, of course, Gene Autry, the Lone Ranger, Roy Rogers, Randolph Scott, and Gary Cooper. Today, anything to do with these stalwart heroes of the saddle is highly collectible.

Buck Jones, Dell Comic Book #1, 1951 . . . . $ 6- 8
The Cisco Kid, Dell Comic Book #5 . . . . 4- 6
Gene Autry
Badge, Flying A Brand 7- 10
Cap pistol, Kenton, red grips, cast iron 40- 48
Charm w/Champion, sterling silver, 1946 . . . . . . 52- 60
Coloring Book, 1950 . . . . 6- 9
Holster, cuffs and spurs, mint, in box 38- 46
Horseshoe ring, on card 8- 10
Lunch box w/thermos bottle 36- 43
Rain boots, mint, in box 45- 55
Ranch outfit, complete 55- 64
Wallet 9- 13
Wristwatch, mint, in box 148-160
Hopalong Cassidy
Banner, felt 5- 8
Bedspread, twin size 185-194
Belt and spurs, mint, in box 34- 42
Billfold, mint, in box 24- 30
Button, Pan-O-Gold Bread . . . 7- 9
Camera, box type 42- 50
Chinese Checkers 15- 20
Clock, alarm type 47- 55
Cookie jar, 1950 . . . . 64- 70
Field glasses, mint, in box . . 44- 50
Flashlight 16- 22
Game, Hopalong Cassidy (Illus.) 9- 14
Hat rack 52- 60
Knife, pen 29- 34
Leather cuffs, mint, in box . . 33- 40
Mug, milk glass 18- 25
Place mat, celluloid 6- 9
Puzzle, Milton Bradley 7- 11
Radio, Arvin 58- 66
Ring, radio premium 24- 28
Roller skates 94- 99
Salt/pepper set 9- 14
Tumbler, juice 16- 20
Wristwatch, Good Luck Hoppy 48- 58
Lone Ranger
Badge, Deputy, numbered . . . 15- 19
Badge, Safety Club 14- 18
Belt, glows in dark, secret codes 69- 77
Box, first aid kit, tin 29- 33
Bullet, silver metal 9- 14
Flashlight, mint, in box 22- 28
Guitar . . . . 145+
Horseshoe, Silver's, Lucky . . 17- 23
Necktie 8- 12
Paperweight, snow type 23- 31

Ring, filmstrip 32- 39
Ring, six gun 39- 46
Scarf, used as mask 35- 42
Statue, w/Silver, early 55- 63
Wristwatch, mint, in box, 1939 300-325

Randolph Scott, pencil tablet . . 8- 11

Red Ryder, cloth/imitation leather gloves 12- 16

Rocky Lane Western, Fawcett Comic #41, 1952 . . . . 5- 8

Roy Rogers
Badge, Deputy 14- 18
Bag, school, pictures of Roy . 13- 19
Bank, cast iron 24- 32
Camera 20- 28
Clock, animated 62- 70
Crayon/pencil set 9- 15
Creamer, figural, plastic 21- 28
Gloves, leather 14- 19
Guitar, wooden, 1956 . . . . 78- 85
Horseshoe, Lucky 23- 29
Lantern, ranch type, mint, in box 39- 46
Lunch box w/thermos 14- 21
Mug, figural, plastic 12- 17
Necktie, early 14- 19
Pencil box 13- 18
Plate, Roy and Trigger, ceramic, 9¼″ 22- 27
Ranchhouse, tin, Marx 33- 41
Ring, branding iron 25- 32
Toy, wagon train, Marx 78- 84
Wristwatch, Dale Evans 49- 56

Tim Holt, "Western Heritage," RKO Radio one-sheet poster, 1948 . . . . 13- 19

Tom Mix
Book, coloring, Whitman, 1935 144-152
Buckle, belt 39- 46
Compass/magnifier, glows in the dark 39- 45
Earphone 28- 35
Handkerchief 7- 12
Knife, Straight Shooter, Ralston 42- 50
Poster, circus, 1936 . . . . 70- 79
Ring, periscope 53- 60
Spinner, good luck 32- 40
Telescope, metal 54- 60

Cracker Jack Collectibles

Caramel covered popcorn and a prize to boot! Did we buy the box for the popcorn or to see what the prize was? Anyway, this product's prizes and advertisements are now collectible, so look away, Dixieland!

1907 advertisement, "Bears" (Illus.) . . . .$ 4- 7

Cracker Jack Collectibles

Photo Courtesy of Hake's Americana & Collectibles

Bookmark, dog's head 3- 5
Cart, 2 wheels 4- 6
Delivery truck, early 14-18
Early pot metal prizes, before World War I, each 1- 2
Modern prizes, plastic punchouts . . . . 5¢-10¢
Plate, tin 18-22
Wheelbarrow, tin, wheels turn . . . 16-20
Whistle, signed 16-20

Cruets

Made of blown or pattern glass, they held vinegar and/or oil for salad making at the table.

Cobalt overlay, cut-to-clear, rose pattern $99-107
Frosted glass, green enamel decor, 7½″ high 65- 73
Clear glass, painted rose (Illus.) 11- 15
Clear glass, pattern glass 10- 13

Cruets

Cuspidors (Spittoons)

Cuspidors (Spittoons)

The world's record is something like 18′ — tobacco spitting, that is. In hotels and bars years ago, these were convenient for the guy who had worked up a cud. Being reproduced because they're so, so popular for flower plants.

Average price, brass, old	$89-106
Average price, brass, new	29- 36
Porcelainized metal, cheapie	12- 18

Cut Glass

It's sharper to the touch than pattern glass. It rings if it has a high lead oxide content, and so does a church bell. If you don't know cut glass, read a book or leave it alone. So much junk coming in from Europe, and a rub on the bottom with sandpaper makes it "old." Watch out!

Cut Glass

Cybis Porcelain

Boleslaw Cybis painted the murals in the Polish Pavilion's Hall of Honor at the New York World's Fair in 1939. When World War II began, he and his family were stranded in the United States. He founded Cordey China Company in 1942. In 1950 he founded Cybis Porcelain. The firm is still operating. When found, his work is expensive.

Bunny (Illus.)	$ 69- 75
Dormouse	210-218
Edith	235-244
Emily Ann	145-153
George Washington	230-244
Holiday child	183-192
Little owl	69- 75
Marigold	208-216
Pandora	210-218
Rebecca	212-323
Tiffin	210-217
Windflower	309-318
Yellow pansies	260-270

Cybis Porcelain

Czechoslovakian Collectibles

Czechoslovakian Collectibles

The Czechs and Slovaks settled in Bohemia hundreds of years ago. Because of their assistance to the Allies in World War I, in 1918 they were granted a country of their own called Czechoslovakia. They're well-known for their glass in many colorful designs, using flowers, birds, beads, and dancing girls in the Art Deco motif. Many, many pieces were marked with ink stamp, paper label, acid etched, or a small metal plate. All are collectible today. Pottery and porcelain were also made.

Candy baskets, blown cased art glass

- Black w/silver mica, blue lining, jet handle, 8″ .... $ 70- 77
- Light green, varicolored, matching handle, 8″ 83- 92
- Mottled colors, crystal twisted handle, 7″ 105-115
- Pink, varicolored, matching handle, 8″ 83- 92
- Solid color, jet rim, crystal handle, 6½″ 62- 70
- Candy jar, green, applied apricot pedestal base, 6″ 75- 83
- Decanter, green bubbly glass, hand-painted decoration, 9½″ 103-110

Jewelry, glass

- Cameo pin, 1¾″ .... $ 28- 34
- Cut crystal beads, 7½″ 23- 30
- Green beads, green bead clasp, 7½″ 19- 26

Lamps, glass

- Basket, crystal beaded, fruit, 10″ $390-410
- Dancing elf, crystal bubbly glass paperweight, Art Deco, 9″ 325-345
- Mottled shade and base, 12½″ 125-140
- Peacock, beaded tail, solid brass bird, onyx base, 12¼″. 370-385

Perfume bottles, cut glass

- Amber, 6⅛″ .... $ 77- 85
- Amethyst, jeweled ornamentation, 5⅜″ 133-144
- Pink, 6⅛″ 75- 83
- Topaz, 6⅛″ 78- 85

Thousands of pieces were made. Look for the "Czechoslovakia" mark.

Porcelain and semi-porcelain pieces

- Covered sauce, lobster, 3½″ .. $ 19- 25
- Creamer, flowers (Illus.) 10- 12
- Creamer, moose, 4¾″ 30- 38
- Cup/saucer set, child's 52- 58
- Flower holder, bird, 5½″ 19- 24
- Jardiniere, Amphora, 6½″ 160-170
- Lamp, world globe, Amphora, 8½″ 265-274
- Planter, Amphora, 7″ 184-193
- Vase, Amphora, 7″ 134-142
- Vase, Egyptian decor, 9¼″ 184-193
- Wall pocket, bird/birdhouse, 5½″ 15- 22
- Wall pocket, bird/pineapple, 7″ 22- 29

Thousands of pieces in shops, at shows, garage sales, etc. All marked "Czechoslovakia" in one form or another.

Puff boxes, cut glass

- Clear, 3″ .... $ 82- 90
- Light blue, 4″ 87- 95
- Pink, 4⅜″ 88- 95

Vases, glass

- Applied serpentine decorations, 8½″ .... $ 52- 60
- Black painted decoration, 8½″. 53- 61
- Jack-in-the-Pulpit, mottled colors, 7½″ 38- 44

Decoys

Decoys

This field of collecting has exploded, pricewise. There probably are a lot still to be "discovered" but what you're finding today in shops and at swapmeets are the common, run-of-the-mill type, mixed in with a lot of fakes. Hopefully, you'll "luck up" on an Elmer Crowell, a Shang Wheeler, or a Ward Bros. Meanwhile, the illustrated is what you're apt to find.

Average price (Illus.) $35-50
Canvasback drake, 1950's 30-38
Coot, glass eyes, 1950's 34-39
Goldeneye hen, 1940's 35-42
Mallard drake, glass eyes, 1950's 34-40
Redhead hen, tack eyes, 1960's . 26-33
Scoter, white wings, 1950's 36-44

Suggested reading: *Collecting Antique American Bird Decoys, an Identification and Value Guide*, Carl F. Luckey, Books Americana.

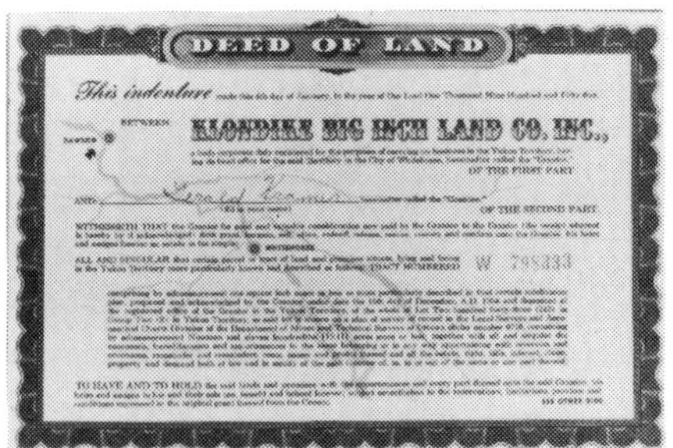
DEED OF LAND

This indenture

KLONDIKE BIG INCH LAND CO., INC.,

OF THE FIRST PART

OF THE SECOND PART

Deeds

Photo Courtesy of
Hake's Americana & Collectibles

Deeds

Some were serious, others supposed to be funny. Either way, if you like to collect something "different," look no further.

Klondike Big Inch Land Co., Inc., deed to 1″ of Yukon Territory (Illus.) $11-14
Old land deeds 5- 7

Degenhart Glass

Mentioned here because so much new Degenhart glass is surfacing at Flea Markets and garage sales. Crystal Art Glass was founded at Cambridge, Ohio, in 1947 by John and Elizabeth Degenhart. When Island Mold Company purchased the molds in 1978 they removed the familiar trademark. Currently they are reproducing the original Degenhart glass without the "D" within the heart mark. A few molds were left intact to produce glass for a proposed Degenhart museum. The museum will emphasize that these pieces are current, not old. More than 200 colors were produced in numerous variations. John Degenhart was world famous for his paperweights. Bernard Boyd purchased the plant. His mark is a "B" inside a diamond. See **Boyd's Crystal Art Glass** and **Clubs and Publications,** this Price Guide.

Animal Dishes, Covered

Amberina hen, 5″ $360-370
Amethyst hen, 5″ 188-197
Peachblow turkey, 5″ 120-124

Bicentennial Bells

Ivorine . . . . $ 47- 56
Pearl gray 51- 60
Vaseline 31- 39

Candleholders, Bird

Basic colors, crystal . . . . $ 27- 38
Opaques 71- 80

Creamer and Sugar

Crystal Daisy and Button . . . . . $ 88- 96
Crystal Texas 92-107
Opaque Texas 140-150

Drawer Pulls, Sandwich-type

Crystal . . . . $ 18- 27
Milk blue 51- 60
Opalescent 68- 74

Owls

Champagne, 3″ high	$190-198
Crystal, 3″ high	27- 31
Lemonade, 3″ high	37- 44

Paperweights

Bubbles with miniature bird or other animal	$250-260
Name	138-145
Novelty	137-142
Rose, footed, most colors	121-130

Pooch Dogs

Amber, 2½″ high	$ 50- 60
April green, 2½″ high	37- 46
Blue, 2½″ high	110-120
Snow white, 2½″ high	55- 63

Portrait Plate (Elizabeth Degenhart)

Amberina crystal	$ 87- 94
Canary crystal	57- 63
Smoky	114-121

Shoes

Crystal	$ 28- 36
Opaque	42- 51

Slippers, Cat and Bow

Crystal	$ 27- 35
Opaque	41- 50

Depression Glass

Depression Glass

The glass is confusing because collectors and those compiling books about it have given names to patterns unnamed by the makers. It was made during the Depression (late 1920's and early 1930's) and was considered inexpensive tableware. Hocking, Westmoreland Glass Company, and the Indiana Glass Company were three of many firms making it. Pink, green, milk white, and amber were a few of the colors. Reproduced in a number of different patterns.

Adam or Adams

Jeannette Glass Co., Jeannette, Pa., 1930-1934. Crystal, green, pink. Prices are for all colors.

Ashtray, 4½″	$10-14
Bowl, casserole, covered, 9″	21-30
Bowl, salad, 7⅞″	13-19
Bowl, vegetable, 9¾″	14-20
Candlestick, 3⅞″	29-35
Plate, dinner, 8⅞″	9-16
Plate, salad, 7¾″	6-10
Pitcher, footed, square base, 8″ high	23-31
Tumblers, 7 oz., 9 oz., each	13-21
Vase, flange rim, 7½″	27-35

Alternating Flue and Panel

Imperial Glass Co., Bellaire, Ohio, 1931. Crystal, ebony, green, rose.

	Cry'l Gr'n Rose	Eb'y
Bowls, 8″ berry, 9″ fruit, each	$10-17	14-20
Bowls, shallow, deep, 9″, each	8-14	13-19
Creamer, footed	6-10	13-19
Sugar, footed, cone shape	6-10	13-19

American Sweetheart

MacBeth-Evans Division, Corning Glass Co., Corning, N.Y., 1930-1936. Cherry red, monax, pink, ritz blue, smoke.

	Pink	M'x	Red Blue	Smoke
Bowl, soup	$10-18	24-30		
Bowl, vegetable, 11″	19-26	37-46		
Creamer, footed, oval	9-13	10-14	130-143	34-40
Pitcher, ice guard, 60 oz.	74-81			
Plate, chop, 11″	10-13	12-17	154-162	
Plate, luncheon, 9″	10-12	10-14		11-17
Tumbler, juice, 3½″	19-22			

Anniversary

Jeannette Glass Co., late 1940's. Pink. Sprayed-on iridescent-type sold in 1969-1970.

Bowl, fruit, 9″	$ 9-13
Bowl, soup (or cereal), 7⅜″	6-10
Cake plate, 12½″	10-14
Pickle dish, 9″	9-13
Plate, sandwich server, 12½″	10-14
Sherbet, footed stem	6-10
Vases, wall pin-up, 6½″ each	12-18

Bee Hive (Prisma Line)

Hazel Atlas Glass Co., factories in Ohio, Pennsylvania, and West Virginia, 1939. Crystal, pink.

	Cry'l	Pink
Bowl, berry, tab handles	$ 4- 8	5- 9
Bowl, fruit, tab handles	7-12	8-13
Butter dish, covered	12-16	16-22
Creamer	6-11	7-12
Plate, cake, covered	19-28	
Sugar, flat, covered	7-11	7-12

Blossoms and Bands

Jenkins Glass Co., Kokomo, Ind., 1927-1928. Crystal, clear green, clear pink, iridescent, marigold.

	Cry'l	Pink Gr'n	M'gd Irid't
Bowl, berry or salad, 7¼″	$ 8-13	12-18	16- 25
Bowl, individual berry	6-10	11-17	12- 16
Lamp, sewing	40-46	70-81	173-198

Cameo

Anchor-Hocking Glass Co., Lancaster, Ohio, 1930-1934. Crystal, green, topaz, with or without platinum trim; pink.

	Gr'n Topaz Cry'l Plat. Trim	Pink
Bowl, console, 3 legs, 11″	$44-56	51-58
Bowl, master berry, 8¼″	13-21	
Bowl, salad, 7¼″	11-19	
Candlestick, 3¾″	23-32	
Cookie jar w/cover	27-32	
Creamer, footed, cone, 4¼″	10-15	35-43
Creamer, footed, round bowl, 3¼″	11-16	
Plate, dinner, 9½″	10-17	25-34
Plate, serving, 10″	16-23	
Sherbet, footed, 3⅛″	10-13	
Tumbler, juice, 5″	15-19	27-37
Tumbler, table, 9 oz.	15-21	35-45
Vase, swelled shape, 8″	21-25	

Vinegar bottle (Illus.)	27-31
Water bottle, cork stopper	23-29

Cherry Blossom

Jeannette Glass Co., 1930-1939. Crystal, delphite, green, jadeite, pink, rose.

	Pink Rose	Gr'n	Delphite
Bowl, cereal, 5¾″	$ 9-15	8- 15	16- 26
Bowl, salad, handled, 9″	17-27	19- 29	31- 34
Bowl, 3 legs, 10½″ (If jadeite, $230+; crystal $14-22)	29-40	127-146	125-147
Creamer, 3¼″	9-16	10- 20	22- 32
Plate, cake, legs, 10¼″	14-22	20- 31	30- 42
Plate, dinner, 9″	9-14	10- 19	19- 27
Plate, oval, 11″	16-22	20- 27	
Plate, sherbet, 6″	7-12	8- 13	13- 22
Sherbet, round foot	9-13	10- 15	17- 27
Tumbler, cone, round foot, 9 oz.	18-24	19- 28	30- 40
Tumbler, flat, banded, 5 oz. (Crystal $6-9)	11-16	13- 20	

Cloverleaf

Hazel Atlas Glass Co., 1930-1936. Black, crystal, green, topaz.

	Topaz	Black	Pink Gr'n Cry'l
Ashtray, 5¾″	$	72-78	
Bowl, cereal, 5″	9-12		9-12
Bowl, dessert (or berry), 4″	9-12		19-26
Candy dish, covered	54-62		44-53
Creamer, footed, 3⅝″	8-12	11-19	8-13
Plate, grill, 10¼″			9-16
Plate, salad or luncheon, 8″	7-13	14-19	7-12
Salt/pepper shakers, pr.	71-79	53-62	28-38
Sherbet, footed stem, 3 oz.	8-13	18-25	6-11
Tumbler, flat, table, 8½ oz.	14-22		14-22
Tumbler, footed cone, 13 oz.	14-23		13-20

Colonial Petals

U.S. Glass Co., 1928-1931. Green, salmon pink. Prices are for both colors.

Creamer, 4½″	$10-16

Salt/pepper shakers, silver-plated cone lids, 3¾″, pr.	14-21
Sugar, 3½″	10-17
Tumbler, footed	15-20

Cube (Cubist)

Jeannette Glass Co., 1929-1933. Crystal, green, pink.

	Pink Cry'l	Gr'n
Bowl, salad, 6½″	$ 9-15	10-16
Bowl, serving, 4½″	6-10	9-13
Butter dish, w/lid	44-53	55-63
Candy jar w/cover	17-24	17-26
Creamer, 3″	8-14	8-14
Cup	5- 8	7-10
Plate, dessert or sherbet, 6″	4- 7	17-23
Plate, salad, 8″	7-11	8-12
Salt/pepper shakers, pr.	24-33	32-38
Sherbet, stemmed, footed, 5 oz.	5-10	6-10
Tumbler, table, 4 oz., 9 oz., each	12-17	15-24

Diamond Point Columns

Hazel Atlas Glass Co. (?), 1920-1930's. Crystal, clear green, clear pink; also iridescent — listed in Carnival books.

	Gr'n Pink	Cry'l
Bowl, master berry, 7¼″	$12-20	8-12
Bowl, salad, 6¼″	10-13	8-13
Butter dish w/cover, table, 6¾″	33-44	18-26
Creamer, 4″	10-13	7-12
Plate, sherbet liner, 5⅞″	6- 8	4- 8
Sherbet, footed stem	6- 9	5- 9
Sugar, cylinder	10-13	6-12
Tumbler, table, 9 oz.	10-14	7-14

Diana (Swirled Sharp Rib)

Federal Glass Co., Columbus, Ohio, 1937-1941. Crystal, golden glow, pink. Prices are for all colors.

Ashtray	$ 7-11
Bowl, cream soup, handled	10-17
Bowl, salad, 9″	9-17
Child's set: rack w/6 each cups, saucers, plates (also called demitasse set), all	76-84
Plate, bread and butter, 6⅛″	7-10
Plate, dinner, 9⅜″	7-14
Plate, sandwich, 11¾″	9-15
Salt/pepper shakers, pr.	31-37
Tumbler, table, 9 oz.	11-19

Floral

Jeannette Glass Co., 1931-1935. Crystal, emerald green, jadeite, pink, rose, other colors. Prices are for all colors except jadeite.

Bowl, salad, 7½″	$ 17- 21
Bowl, vegetable, oval, 9″	19- 24
Bowl, vegetable, round, covered, 8″	19- 31
Candy jar, covered	31- 41
Coaster, 3¼″	7- 11
Creamer, flat bottom, cylinder	11- 16
Pitcher, lemonade, 10¼″	168-179
Pitcher, water, 8″	34- 41
Plate, dinner, 8⅞″	9- 14
Plate, salad, 8″	8- 12
Refrigerator box, covered, 4¾″ sq.	18- 27
(Same in jadeite $15-22)	
Salt/pepper shakers, pr.	31- 39
Tumbler, footed cone, 7 oz.	14- 21
Tumbler, footed cone, juice, 4″	12- 20

Heritage

Federal Glass Co., 1940's-1960's. Crystal, Madonna blue, pink, spring green.

	Cry'l	Pink, Spr'g Gr'n	Md'na Blue
Bowl, berry (or salad), 8½″	$10-16	14-19	17-26
Bowl, fruit, 10½″	12-15	14-20	19-21
Bowl, sauce, 5″	9-12	10-14	10-16
Creamer, footed	7-11		
Cup, 3⅝″	7-12		
Plate, bread and butter	4- 9		
Plate, dinner, 9¼″	7-10		
Plate, salad, 8″	4- 8		
Plate, server, 12″	7-14		

Hobstars Intaglio

Imperial Glass Co., late 1920's, early 1930's. Crystal, green, pink. Prices are for all colors.

Bowl, individual berry	$ 8-14
Bowl, master berry	19-29
Creamer, scalloped edge	17-26
Plate, cake (or sandwich)	18-27
Plate, dessert, 7″	9-14
Sugar, scalloped edge	18-27

Lace Edge (Open Lace)

Hocking Glass Co., mid-1930's. Crystal, frosted, pink. Prices are for all colors.

Bowl, cereal, 6⅜″	$10-14
Bowl, flower, ribbed sides	23-32
Bowl, salad, 7¾″	11-17
Butter (or bonbon), covered	21-29
Candy jar, covered, ribbed sides	15-24
Compote, covered, footed	18-28
Compote, open, footed, 7″	29-39
Creamer, ribbed sides	11-19
Plate, dinner, grill, 10½″, each	11-15
Plate, salad, 8⅜″	9-12
Plate, serving, 3-partition, 13″	12-18
Sherbet, footed stem	23-30
Sugar, ribbed sides	12-19
Vase, 7″	23-31

Madrid

Federal Glass Co., 1932-1939. Crystal, golden glow, Madonna blue, rose glow, spring green.

	Cry'l Golden Glow Rose Glow	Spring Green	Madonna Blue
Bowl, individual berry, 5″	$ 7-10	9- 13	11- 16
Bowl, master berry, 8″	13-17	17- 23	19- 29
Bowl, vegetable, oval, 10″	13-19	15- 21	21- 29
Butter dish, covered	73-81	99-108	175-185
Candlesticks, 2¼″, pr.	22-29		
Cracker jar, covered	34-42	61- 70	
Creamer, footed	7-12	9- 12	18- 29
Pitcher, square, 60 oz.	40-50	92-101	170-180
Pitcher, swelled, 80 oz.	59-70	154-163	
Plate, dinner, 10⅝″	15-22	15- 22	21- 31
Plate, grill, 10⅝″	10-14	12- 20	12- 20
Plate, salad, 7½″	7-12	9- 14	11- 18
Salt/pepper shakers, pr.	31-35	42- 51	110-115
Sherbet, cone shape, footed	9-12	10- 14	15- 20
Tumbler, blown, footed cone, 10 oz.	16-23	20- 29	
Tumbler, blown, iced tea, 12 oz.	17-21	19- 24	23- 33
Tumbler, blown, juice, 5 oz.	9-14	11- 15	15- 21

Miss America

Hocking Glass Co., early 1930's-1937. Crystal, apple green, green, honey amber, pink, cerise.

	Cry'l	Pink Cerise	H'y Amber	Gr'n Apple Gr'n
Bowl, cereal, 6¼″	$ 9-14	10- 15		
Bowl, fruit, 7¾″	29-39	39- 47		
Bowl, sauce (or berry), 4½″				9-14
Bowl, vegetable, oval, 10″	16-24	22- 27		
Butter dish, covered	60-68	255-275		
Celery tray, 10½″	14-19	17- 27		
Creamer, footed	13-18	14- 19		
Compote, 5″	12-20	16- 24		
Goblet, 4¾″ high	11-15	14- 18	12-19	
Goblet, 10″ high	14-22	19- 25	19-30	
Pitcher, ice lip, 65 oz.	52-61	62- 69	68-74	
Pitcher, no ice lip, 65 oz.	43-52	47- 56	52-61	
Plate, bread and butter, 6¾″	7-11	8- 12		
Plate, cake, footed, 12″	21-29	23- 29		
Plate, dinner, 10¼″	11-16	14- 20		
Plate, salad, 8½″	10-14	12- 16		
Platter, oval, 12″	14-21	15- 21		
Salt/pepper, shakers, footed, pr.	27-35	26-35		
Sherbet, footed stem, 5 oz.	10-12	11- 14		11-16
Tidbit server, 2-tier	18-24	22- 29		

New Century

Hazel Atlas Glass Co., late 1920's-1935. Amethyst, crystal, cobalt, green, pink.

	Am'st Cobalt	Gr'n Pink Cry'l
Bowl, individual berry, 4½"	$10-14	7-11
Bowl, master berry, 8"	17-23	11-14
Butter dish, covered, 6¾"	62-73	52-61
Creamer, footed, 3¾"	14-19	10-14
Cup, 2¾"	9-14	7-11
Decanter w/stopper	42-51	31-37
Pitcher, 60 oz.	34-41	29-39
Pitcher, ice guard, 80 oz.	45-55	31-40
Plate, dinner, grill, 10" each	10-14	9-13
Plate, salad, 8½"	9-12	9-12
Salt/pepper shakers, pr.	22-25	15-20
Saucer, 5⅜"	6-9	4- 7
Tumbler, highball, 10 oz.	14-19	10-14
Tumbler, iced tea, 12 oz.	17-21	12-19
Tumbler, juice, 5 oz.	12-17	11-15
Tumbler, juice, footed 5 oz.	12-17	9-13
Wine, footed stem	16-21	11-15

No. 600 (Modern Art)

Indiana Glass Co., 1920's-1930's. Crystal, frosted on crystal, green, pink.

	Pink Gr'n Cry'l	Frosted on Cry'l
Banana split, footed, 7½"	$10-14	
Bowl, finger	9-12	
Bowl, oval, 9½"	22-29	
Bowl, master berry, 8½"	12-19	
Candlestick, irregular rim	9-14	
Creamer, berry, large, footed, 4"	10-14	
Ice bucket, metal bail handle	19-30	
Plate, dessert, sundae or sherbet liner	5- 9	5- 8
Plate, salad, 8½"	9-14	9-13
Plate, sandwich tray, 10½"	12-18	
Sandwich server, center glass handle	22-29	
Sundae, low foot, 3¼"	7-10	
Sugar jar, spout, metal cover	15-23	
Tumbler, flat bottom, 12 oz.	9-16	
Tumbler, footed, tapered, milk shake, 12 oz.	14-22	11-20
Tumbler, 6 oz.	6-11	7-11
Vase, bud, slender, 11"	14-21	
Vase, crimped rim, 11"	29-39	

Peacock and Rose

Paden City Glass Co., Paden City, W. Va., 1930's. Emerald green, rosepink. Prices are for both colors.

Bowl, console, 11"	$18-24
Bowl, footed, 8½"	14-21
Bowl, fruit, handles, 8½"	15-21
Candlestick, rolled top, 5"	7-15
Candy dish, covered, footed, 7" high	14-21
Compote, footed, 6"	12-22
Compote, mayonnaise, 3-pc. w/liner plate, ladle	27-36
Creamer, footed, 4"	9-12
Ice tub, tab handles, 5¾"	12-21
Plate, cake, footed, 11"	11-21
Relish dish, 3 compartments, covered, 6¼" dia.	14-22
Sandwich tray, center handle, 10½" dia.	11-20
Sugar, footed, 4"	9-12

Pressed Hobnail and Diamond

Hocking Glass Co., 1930's. Green, rose, topaz.

	Gr'n	Rose	Topaz
Bowl, Hocking handles, 10"	$12-20	10-16	9-13
Bowl, low centerpiece, 11"	13-24	11-21	11-20
Bowl, salad, Hocking side handles, 9"	9-18	8-13	7-12
Plate, cake, 12"	11-19	9-13	9-13
Plate, salad, 8"	6- 9	5- 9	5- 9

Princess

Hocking Glass Co., 1931-1935. Apricots, crystal, green, pink, topaz.

	Topaz Apr't	Gr'n Pink Cry'l
Ashtray, 4½"	$ 8-13	7-12
Bowl, individual berry, 4½"	6- 9	5-10
Bowl, salad, octagon, tab handles, 9"	11-18	9-15
Bowl, vegetable, oval, 10"	12-18	10-17
Butter dish, covered, 7½" dia.		66-75
Cookie jar w/cover, 7" high	21-28	16-23
Creamer, oval, flange rim	9-14	7-12
Pitcher, juice, 37 oz.	34-42	22-30
Pitcher, 60 oz.	52-61	38-48
Plate, cake, 10"	15-19	13-17
Plate, dinner, grill, 9½" each	9-12	7-13
Plate, sandwich, handled, 11½"		10-15
Plate, sherbet liner, 5½"	5- 9	5-10
Relish dish, 4-part, 7½"	14-19	10-14
Salt/pepper shakers, 4½", pr.	42-51	18-26
Salt/pepper shakers, 5½", pr.		27-31
Sherbet, footed, stem, blown	7-11	6-12
Tumbler, iced tea	14-21	13-19
Tumbler, juice, 5 oz.	11-17	11-18

Tumbler, juice, 9 oz.	12-17
Vase, 8"	17-22

Rosemary (Dutch Rose)

Federal Glass Co., 1935-1937. Crystal, golden glow, rose glow, spring green.

	Spr'g Gr'n	Rose Glow G'ldn Glow Cry'l
Bowl, cereal, 6"	$ 9-13	5-10
Bowl, cream soup, 5"	10-15	8-14
Bowl, vegetable, oval	13-21	11-19
Cup	10-16	5-10
Creamer, footed, 4"	12-19	7-12
Plate, dinner, grill, 9½", each	9-13	7-11
Plate, salad (or dessert), 6¾"	7-10	5- 9
Saucer	5- 9	4- 7
Tumbler, table, 9 oz.	19-22	12-19

Royal Lace

Hazel Atlas Glass Co., 1934-1941. Amethyst (special orders only), cobalt, crystal, green, pink.

	C'blt	Gr'n	Cry'l Pink
Ashtray, 3½" ..$		12- 17	10-14
Bowl, fruit, 3 legs, 10"	32- 37	29- 36	17-24
Bowl, individual berry, 5"	12- 17	11- 17	7-11
Bowl, master berry, 10" ...	27- 35	22- 31	13-21
Butter dish and cover	235-250	232-246	75-85
Candlestick, flared edge ..	27- 34	25- 35	16-22
Candlestick, ruffled edge .	25- 35	23- 33	16-21
Cracker jar w/glass cover	73- 79	52- 60	38-44
Cracker jar w/metal cover	76- 85		
(Amethyst 95-108)			
Creamer, footed	25- 32	29- 35	10-15
Pitcher, ice guard, 80 oz..	83- 93	124-135	47-56
Pitcher, no ice lip, 60 oz. ...	74- 84	101-112	44-54
Pitcher, no ice lip, 96 oz. ...	150-165	142-145	48-56
Plate, dinner, 9⅞"	20- 24	13- 18	8-12
Plate, grill, 9¾"	19- 24	14- 18	9-12
Plate, luncheon, 8⅜"	15- 21	9- 12	7-10
Sherbet, all glass, footed .	22- 29	15- 22	11-15
Sherbet, in metal holder	26- 33		
Sugar, footed ..	24- 32	28- 35	9-12
Tumbler, juice, 5 oz.	18- 22	17- 24	11-16
Tumbler, table, 9 oz.	24- 31	21- 28	13-19
Tumbler, either height, 12 oz.	29- 34	22- 31	14-22

Tiered Semi-Optic

Paden Glass Co., 1927-1933. Amber, crystal, green, pink. Prices are for all colors.

Banana split dish, 8½" long	$12-17
Bowl, console, 14"	18-26
Creamer, 6 oz.	7-11
Goblet, footed, 8 oz.	6- 8
Goblet, footed, malted milk, 10 oz.	7-11
Goblet, iced tea, 12 oz.	9-12
Oyster cocktail, footed, 3½ oz. ..	6-10
Parfait glass, 5 oz.	7-12
Pickle (or banana split) dish, 8¼"	8-12
Plate, coaster for tumblers, 6" ...	6- 9
Plate, sandwich (or salad), 8" ...	6-10
Sundae, high footed, 5½ oz.	8-12
Sundae, low footed, 4½ oz.	6-11
Tumbler, cola, cupped rim, 6 oz. .	5- 9
Tumbler, cupped rim, phosphate or water, 8 oz.	7-11
Tumbler, iced tea, 12 oz.	8-14
Water jug, ½ gal.	23-29

Vitrock Kitchen Line

Hocking Glass Co., 1935-1936.

Ashtray, match holder, 2 rests, plain	$ 8-12
Dripping jar w/cover	8-14
Bowls, mixing, 6½", 7½", 8½", each	5-10
Bowls, mixing, 9½", 10½", 11½", each	7-14
Egg cups on standard	7-11
Entire range set, 4 pcs.	28-39
Leftovers jar and cover	8-14
Orange reamer, table	10-16
Orange reamer, utility, for bowl or cup	7-12
Range set, shakers, each	7-12

Waffle (Waterford)

Hocking Glass Division of Anchor Hocking, 1938-1944. Crystal, forest green, pink.

	Cry'l	Pink
Ashtray, 4"	$ 4- 7	4- 6
Bowl, cereal (or sauce), 5½"	4- 7	5-10
Bowl, individual berry, 4¾"	4- 7	4- 8
Bowl, master berry, 8¼" ..	5- 8	6-11
Butter dish with cover	29-42	55-63
Creamer, oval	4- 7	5- 8
Pitcher, ice lip, 80 oz.	24-33	31-38

Pitcher, juice, ice guard, 42 oz.	12-18	
Plate, dinner, 9½″	5- 9	7-11
Plates, salad, 7⅛″; liner, 6″, each	4- 7	5- 9
Salt/pepper shakers, pr.	8-12	
Sherbet, footed stem, scalloped rim	6-10	
Sherbet, footed stem, smooth rim	4- 8	5-11
Tumbler, table, footed, 10 oz.	6-12	9-14
Vase, 6¾″	7-11	9-15
(Forest green $10-15)		

Windsor

Hocking Glass Co., 1930's. Apple green, crystal, pink, ruby.

	Pink Ruby Apple Green	Cry'l
Pitcher, 85 oz.	$31-39	14-22
Pitcher, 64 oz.	17-24	9-16
Tumbler, iced tea, flat bottom, 12 oz.	7-12	5-11
Tumbler, juice, 5 oz.	4- 8	4- 8
Tumbler, juice, 9 oz.	5-10	4- 8

Windsor Diamond

Jeannette Glass Co., 1936-1946. Crystal, green, wild rose.

	Cry'l	Wild Rose	Gr'n
Ashtray	$ 4- 7	5-11	5-12
Bowl, individual berry, 4¾″	4- 8	5- 9	5- 9
Butter dish with cover	31-39		
Compote, covered, tall	12-15		
Pitcher, juice	12-18	11-19	11-21
Pitcher, milk, 16 oz.	7-12	11-21	14-23
Pitcher, table, 52 oz.	14-22	23-34	27-33
Plate, salad, 7″	4- 7	4- 8	4- 8
Plate, sandwich, handles, 10¼″	7-12	7-13	8-15
Plates, chop, 13⅝″; serving, 13½″, each	6-10	7-12	7-13
Tray, 4″ sq.	4- 8	5- 9	8-11
Tray, oblong, 4⅛″×9″	5- 9	8-13	9-14
Tumbler, iced tea, 12 oz.	7-12	9-14	9-13
Tumbler, juice, 3¼″	5- 9	7-13	9-14

Disneyana

Anything to do with Walt Disney is highly sought after today. Some of the Mickey Mouse/Minnie Mouse toys take a bank loan to acquire.

Bank, Donald Duck, ceramic	$ 22- 28
Bank, Mickey Mouse, post office, tin	35- 42
Bank, Snow White, ceramic	17- 24
Book, Bambi, 1949	6- 9
Book, pop-up, Mickey Mouse (also see Big Little Books)	88- 94
Bracelet, 7 dwarfs	12- 17
Bracelet, 12 characters	12- 17
Card game, Donald Duck, 1950	11- 17
Celluloid figure, Cinderella, wedding dress	147-156
Celluloid figure, Mickey Mouse as bandleader	147-155
Clock, alarm, Mickey Mouse, animated	60- 67
Crayon box, Minnie Mouse, tin, 1947	15- 21
Cup, Mickey Mouse, silver plated	39- 44
Dish, Donald Duck, plastic	5- 7
Doll, Mickey Mouse, 12″ high	34- 40
Doll, Pluto, rubber, 7″ high	6- 9
Ears, Mickey Mouse Club	4- 6
Fork, Donald Duck, stainless steel	3- 5
Game, Mickey Mouse Club	10- 15
Hairbrush, Donald Duck, 1930's	27- 34
Knife, Davy Crockett, Barlow	10- 13
Moviejector, Mickey Mouse	108-115
Napkin ring, Pluto, plastic	14- 18
Pail, Donald Duck, tin, 1930's	24- 32
Pencil tablet, Mickey Mouse	12- 20
Planter, Snow White	19- 24
Plate, Pinocchio, tin	8- 10
Umbrella, Pluto, 1947	47- 52
Watch, Mickey Mouse, Ingersoll	175-220
Watch fob, Mickey Mouse	48- 54
Yo-yo, Mickey Mouse	6- 8

Dolls

Photo Courtesy of Hake's Americana & Collectibles

Dolls

The dolls we're listing here are those made in the early 1930's until the late 1950's. If you're interested in antique dolls, please refer to the *Wallace-Homestead Price Guide to Dolls, 1984-1985 Prices.* Generally, prices given are for those dolls in good to very good condition.

Advertising

Aunt Jemima, litho/cloth, 12″ . $ 22- 29
Campbell Kid, compo/cloth, 10½″ 138-146
Gerber Baby, rubber, 11″ 27- 33
Gerber Baby, vinyl, 14″....... 14- 21
Mr. Magoo, vinyl/cloth, 16″ ... 28- 34
Phillip Morris' "Johnny," compo/cloth 108-116
Pillsbury Poppin Fresh Doughboy, rubber 8- 11
Smokey the Bear, cloth, 16″ .. 11- 18

(Madame) Alexander Doll Co.

Usually marked "Alexander" w/doll's name on a cloth label. The earliest dolls, from 1923 until just before World War II, are out of sight, pricewise.

Annabelle, 1952, hard plastic, 14″ $218-240
Cissy, 1955-1959, plastic/vinyl, 21″ 165-240
Edith, 1958-1959, plastic/vinyl, 15″ 168-185
Jenny Lind (Cissette, 1957-1963), plastic, 10″ 435-475
Kathy, 1951, plastic, 14″...... 330-370
Little Genius, 1956-1962, plastic/vinyl, 8″ 128-140
Maggie Face, 1948-1956, plastic, 14″.......... 168-178

American Character Doll Co.

(Various marks)

Happytot, rubber, 10½″ ......$ 83- 92
Tiny Tears, plastic/rubber, 13″ 42- 50
Toodles, vinyl, 21″ 95-130

Arranbee Doll Co.

Marked "Arranbee" or "R & B," 1922 until 1960.

Debu Teen, 1938 on, compo or compo/cloth, 17″ $110-120
Nancy, 1938 on, compo, 12″ .. 85- 94

Cameo Doll Products Co.

Betty Boop, compo/wood, 12″ .$395-425
Champ, compo/wood pulp, 16″ 218-235
Margie, vinyl, 17″.......... 34- 42

Celluloid dolls

Carnival, feathers, Occupied Japan, 6″ ....$ 31- 38
Clown, Japan, 6″ 26- 32
Kewpie, Japan, 2¼″ 32- 38

China Dolls

Powder Puff, 7½″ ....$ 39- 46
Ruth, Germany, 19″.......... 185-205

Comics Dolls

Charlie Brown, vinyl, 7½″ ....$ 9- 14
Dennis the Menace, vinyl/cloth, 13″ 32- 38
Elmer Fudd, vinyl, 8″ 15- 21
Linus, vinyl, 8¼″ 13- 17
Mighty Mouse, vinyl, 9½″..... 14- 19
Porky Pig, vinyl, 7″ 11- 15
Sad Sack, vinyl, 16″ 15- 22

Effanbee Doll Co.

1912 on. Usually marked "EFFanBEE;" also, heart-shaped bracelet; later, gold paper heart label.

Chubby boy, compo, 7¼″.....$ 35- 43
Dy-Dee baby, plastic/rubber, 15½″ 47- 55
Girl Scout, plastic/vinyl, 15¼″ . 36- 44
Lovums, compo/cloth, 18″ 97-105
Patsy Ruth, compo/cloth, 14″ . 97-105

E. I. Horsman Co.

1901 on. Usually, "E.I.H." or "Horsman."

Baby Dimples, compo/cloth, 21½″ ....$ 87- 96
Chubby baby, compo, 17½″... 37- 45
Kewpie Kin, vinyl, 5″......... 15- 20

Ideal Novelty and Toy Co.

1907 on. Various marks, usually includes "Ideal."

Betsy Wetsy, vinyl, 13″.......$ 35- 43
Deanna Durbin, compo, 14″ ... 235-260
Nancy Lee, compo, 13½″ 33- 39
Posie, plastic, 24½″ 38- 46
Shirley Temple, compo, 13½″ (Illus.).......... 795-830

Mattel, Inc.

1959 on. "Mattel" and © year.

Barbie #1, vinyl, 1959, 11½″ ..$265-365
Barbie #2, 1959-1960, vinyl, 11½″ 265-365
Barbie #3, 1960, vinyl, 11½″ .. 125-135
Dancerina, vinyl, 24″......... 38- 48
Dee Dee, vinyl, 15¼″ 30- 38
Ken, 1960, vinyl 23- 30

Raggedy Ann and Andy Dolls

Various makers from 1915 to present.

Early, 15″ to 17″ $107-117
Georgene, 15″ to 18″ 37- 46

Suggested reading: *Herron's Price Guide to Dolls and Paper Dolls,* R. Lane Herron, Wallace-Homestead Book Company.

Collector's Encyclopedia of Cloth Dolls, Joana Gast Auderton, Wallace-Homestead Book Company.

Door Knockers

Door Knockers

These have been around for hundreds of years and are made of wood, metal, even glass. Iron and brass were the most popular in animal heads and other forms.

Brass, American Eagle, 1800's	$340-380
Brass, dog's head, 7″ high, old	78- 88
Brass, fox head, 8″ high, 1920's	50- 55
Brass, hand holding ball	108-113
Brass, jaguar growling, 8″ high	80- 87
Brass, lion with ring in mouth, French, 1800's (Illus.)	210-220
Grecian bust, head only, bronze, 4½″ high, 1930's	40- 48
Iron, cat's head, smiling, 4″ high, 1930's	28- 37
Iron, gloved hand	60- 68
Iron, hammer	52- 60
Iron, hand, fist-shaped, 8″ high, old, 1920's	35- 43
Iron, horseshoe	50- 58
Iron, horseshoe hitting hammer head, 1930's	60- 68
Iron, spur hits metal block on wooden board	55- 63
Pewter (?), hand holding ball, 1920's	50- 55
Spur	60- 67

Doorstops

Made of many materials. Metal stops in the shapes of animals or buildings were used for propping open doors. Particularly popular in the 1920's.

Doorstops

Cottage, iron, 5¾″ high	$44-53
Dogs: Airedale, Bulldog, Chow, German Shepherd, etc.	54-63
Fala, FDR on side, 10″ high	61-70
Flower basket, cast iron, 7″ high (Illus.)	42-50
Flowerpot, cast iron, enameled, 7¼″ high	39-50
Frog, iron, webbed feet, 15″ high	50-55
Horse pulling cart, iron, 6½″ high	44-52
Horse, rearing, lead base, 1930's	49-60
Lady, cast iron, enameled	40-49
Lion, painted, 15″ high	60-61
Parrot, red/yellow/green, 10″ high	55-63
Polo player on horse, 9″ high	48-59
Rabbit, iron, 11″ high	61-68
Ship, Mayflower, cast iron	66-73
Sunbonnet girl, 6½″ high	65-75
Squirrel, iron, 11″ high	63-72
Wagon train, horse, 10″ high	67-76
Wolf, on leash, iron	51-60

Drawing/Coloring/Tracing Books

Every kid "scribbled" his days away, especially when it was raining or he was sick in bed.

Little Orphan Annie's Coloring Book	$15-24
Moon Mullins Drawing and Tracing Book	13-17
Leave it to Beaver Coloring Book	5- 7

Easter Collectibles

Easter Collectibles

Baskets (Illus.), average price, good condition .... $ 3-4
Cards, average price (if a postcard, don't destroy the stamp) 50¢-90¢
Seals, average price per sheet .. 2-5

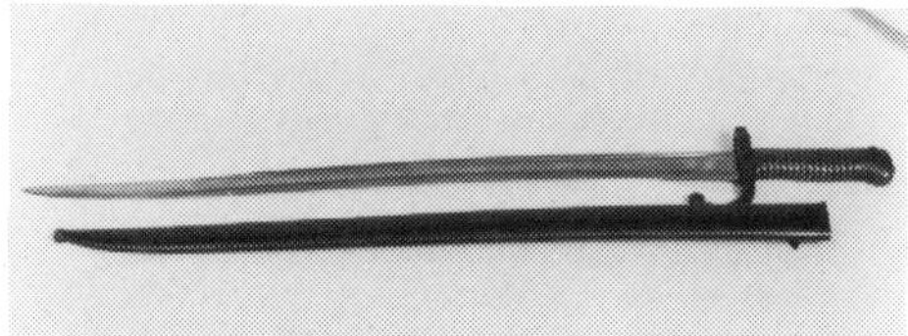

Edged Weapons

Edged Weapons

Bayonets, swords, snees, daggers, dirks — all very collectible. A lot of World War I bayonets have been surfacing of late. See **Military.**

French bayonet, c. 1870 (Illus.) $162-170

Elephants

The elephant has meant a lot of things to a lot of people. Today, there's even a club. See **Clubs and Publications,** this Price Guide.

Bookends, brass, 5½″ $50-58
Cigarette box, "elephant" is inlaid Mother-of-Pearl 35-42

Elephants

Cigarette holder, carved ivory, 2 elephants, 3″ long 45-51
Pipe holder, carved wood 14-18
Pot metal, painted, 4″ high (Illus.) 12-16
Soapstone, 9″ 43-51
Toothpick holder, blue milk glass, 2″ 18-25

Elvis!

Photo Courtesy of
Hake's Americana & Collectibles

Elvis!

The **hottest** collectible in the world today! Anything to do with this nice gentleman is pure gold. If I didn't understand his music, I respected his military service and the way he conducted himself in public. Pillows, key rings, T-shirts, mugs, ashtrays, spoons, buckles, books, pennants, lockets, clocks, money clips, photos, paper weights. Start collecting — today!

Alarm clock, full-color face $22-28
Arcade cards, postcard size, each 75¢-1
"Beer" cans, 12 novelty, all 26-31
Dog tags
Elvis' picture/blood type, metal, 1965 .... 4- 7
"I'm An Elvis Fan!," metal, 1965 .... 4- 7
Dollar bill with Elvis' photo 6- 9
Fan Club pin, blue/gold, 1965 ... 75¢-1
Feather pen, movie promo for *Tickle Me,* 1965 .... 6- 8
Flasher pin, "Love Me Tender," 1965 .... 1- 3
Hat (Illus.) 22-30
Key ring, guitar shaped 2- 4
Photos, various poses (Illus.), each 7-11
Scarf, "Sincerely Elvis" 24-30
Special edition, *Memphis Press Scimitar,* Elvis' death 7-10
Wristwatch, leather strap, young Elvis 29-36

European Souvenirs

European Souvenirs

Everyone brings presents home from Europe. Tons came back during World War II. Lots of it showing up at meets.

"Nest" of 4 wooden dolls, Russia (Illus.) $3- 6
Miniature Eiffel Tower, 10" high, France 5- 9
Native costume dolls, all countries 5-17
Porcelain plate, "Shakespeare," England 7-10

Fairy Tale Collectibles

Photo Courtesy of
Hake's Americana & Collectibles

Fairy Tale Collectibles

"Once upon a time . . ." It was a warm feeling when Mom or Dad tucked you in and read about castles, kings, and princes. Today, it's a different ball game. I'm glad I grew up when I did. Today's kids go from birth to "grown-up" with no stops in between.

Hansel and Gretel tin container, late 1800's (Illus.) $42-51
Lots of "dreamland" stuff at Flea Markets.

Father's/Mother's Day Collectibles

Some smart guy decided these two dates should be as sacred as Lincoln's or Washington's Birthday. Today, look at the stuff foisted off on the American buying public to celebrate (?) these two days.

Father's/Mother's Day Collectibles

Cards, cards, cards, and fifty thousand other items. Mom? Dad? Well, they pay for it. Meanwhile, it's becoming a "collectible," so start looking for it at Swap Meets, etc.

Fenton Art Glass

Founded in 1905 by Frank Fenton, at Martins Ferry, Ohio. Soon afterward the company moved to its present location in Williamstown, West Virginia. Carnival glass, opalescent, custard, stretch, ruby, mandarin, dolphins are a few of the many types made there.

Apple Tree (cobalt)

Pitcher $347-370
Tumbler 64- 72

Buttons and Braids

Pitcher $194-222
Tumbler 42- 52

Celeste Blue (stretch)

Bonbon, covered . . . . $ 53- 64
Bowls
Flared, 7½" dia. 52- 62
Lily, 5" dia. 45- 55

Orange, crimped 109-119
Butter ball, 7″ dia. 57- 67
Candlestick, 6″ high 49- 58
Cologne, w/drip stopper 109-116
Compote, flared 44- 53
Fern dish, footed 44- 54
Night set (carafe and tumbler) . 63- 70

Cherry and Scale (custard)

Butter dish, covered $281-291
Creamer 174-183
Master berry 79- 87
Sauce 94-105
Sugar bowl, covered 198-208

Dolphins

Bonbon, Diamond Optic, crimped, 6″ sq. ....$ 55- 65
Bowls
Cupped, 9″ dia. 88- 98
Oval, 10½″ dia. 163-172
Candlestick 65- 75
Compote, round 163-172
Sandwich tray, Diamond Optic, 10″ dia. 64- 74

Florentine Green (stretch)

Bowl, candy $124-132
Candlestick 66- 76
Cigarette holder 84- 94
Creamer 34- 42
Pitcher 114-118
Plate, salad, 8″ dia. 44- 52
Sugar, open 42- 52
Vase, fan, etched, 5″ 49- 58

Jade Green

Basket, wicker handle, 10½″ dia. ....$ 74- 83
Bowl, flared, 11″ dia. 47- 56
Candlestick 16- 19
Candy jar w/lid 57- 63
Lemon tray 42- 52
Vase, 10″ high 51- 61

Mandarin Red

Ashtray, pipe ....$ 90- 97
Bowl, flared, 11″ dia. 152-162
Cake stand, Mikado .... 385+
Candlestick, 10″ high 112-120
Compote, Mikado .... 365+
Vase, flared, 8″ high 127-136

Marigold

Candlestick, 6″ high ....$ 34- 38
Candy jars, ½ lb. and ¾ lb., each 55- 64
Cigarette holder 65- 73
Cologne 65- 71
Guest set (water glass "stopper" in pitcher) .... 365+

Milady (cobalt)

Pitcher $655-680
Tumbler 82- 91

Rose

Ashtray, cut ....$ 51- 60
Compote, dolphin stem, oval .. 52- 61
Flower pot w/base 51- 61
Goblet, 9 oz. 47- 57
Plate, dolphin handles 56- 66
Sherbet, cut 52- 62

Velva Rose (stretch)

Bowl, crimped, 10″ dia. $154-163
Candlestick, dolphins 55- 63
Candy jar, ½ lb. 54- 63
Cologne 101-112
Guest set 142-150
Vase, bud, 12″ 49- 58
Vase, crimped top, 12″ 72- 82

Water Lily and Cattails (chocolate)

Berry, 4″ dia. ....$ 84- 93
Creamer 375-382
Spooner 452-470
Sugar, covered 580-590
Tumbler 310-315

Fern Stands

Fern Stands

Usually made of oak, poplar, mahogany, they're a popular collectible at many Flea Markets. $22 to $65, depending on type wood, age and condition.

Juan Ferrandiz

Juan Ferrandiz (Castells) is a Spanish artist whose wood carvings have brought him world attention. Most are carved from hard maple using a master carving created by Master Carver Emmerich Mussner. Mussner works for ANRI in St. Christina, Groden, Italy. All figures are signed "Ferrandiz" in script, usually on the lateral edge of the base. There are two organizations for collectors. See **Clubs and Publications**, this Price Guide.

- Adoration, 6″ ... $210-230
- Angel (or Pathfinder), 6″ ... 125-135
- Artist, 3″ ... 75- 84
- Basket of Joy, 3″ ... 92-100
- Blessing, 3″ ... 78- 86
- Bouquet, 6″ ... 245-260
- Catch a falling star, 6″ ... 155-164
- Cherub, 2″ ... 55- 63
- Courting, 6″ ... 218- 226
- Cowboy, limited edition, 6″ ... 525-540
- Donkey, 6″ ... 94-103
- Flight into Egypt, 3″ ... 94-102
- Flower girl, 6″ ... 265-280
- Gardener, 6″ ... 165-175
- Girl with rooster, 6″ ... 165-174
- Happy strummer, 6″ ... 178-186
- Harvest girl, limited edition, 6″ 560-570
- Have you heard?, 6″ ... 175-180
- High riding, 5″ ... 155-163
- Mary, 4″ ... 118-126
- Nature girl, 6″ ... 170-180
- Ox, 5″ ... 92-101
- Peace pipe, 6″ ... 258-266
- Riding through the rain, 10″ ... 575-590
- Sheep (kneeling), 2″ ... 48- 55
- Sheep (lying), 2″ ... 48- 55
- Sheep (standing), 2″ ... 50- 57
- Star struck, 3″ ... 72- 80
- Stitch in time, 6″ ... 162-170
- Tracker, 3″ ... 80- 90
- Trumpeter, 3″ ... 72- 80

Fiesta Ware

Homer and Shakespear Laughlin founded the Homer Laughlin China Company in East Liverpool, Ohio, in 1871. At one time it was the world's largest single pottery plant. In March, 1937, Fiesta Ware was patented in red, blue, yellow, and green. Fiesta was a first in commercial pottery. Red was the most difficult color to control. A redesign took place in 1969 and the ware was discontinued in 1973. Most pieces are incised "FIESTA." Red pieces bring 45 to 80 percent more than other colors.

Fiesta Ware

Ashtrays

- Chartreuse, 1947 ... $30- 35
- Green, 1959 ... 28- 35
- Red, 1959 ... 33- 37
- Turf green, 1972 ... 20- 27

Bowls

- Dessert, old ivory, 1936, 6″dia. $12- 18
- Fruit, turquoise, 1939, 11¾″ dia. ... 34- 39
- Nested, 7 in set, 1943, 5″ to 11½″ dia., all ... 77-220
- Salad, footed, red, 1941, 12″ dia. ... 56- 66
- Salad, individual, green, yellow, 1959, 7⅝″ dia., each ... 9- 15

Candleholders

- Bulb-type, old ivory, turquoise, 1936-1945, each ... $38- 46
- Tripod-type, red, 1936-1943 ... 52- 62

Casseroles

- Covered, turquoise, 1940 ... $55- 65
- French, old ivory, 1939 ... 62- 71

Creamers

- Regular, turquoise, 1938 ... $12- 19
- Stick-handled, green ... 15- 23

Coffeepots

- A.D., green, 1941 ... $38- 45
- Regular, red, 1940 ... 95-106

Cups

- Egg, red, 1941 ... $22- 29
- Cream soup, green, 1945 ... 19- 27
- Onion soup, covered, turquoise, 1938 ... 75- 82
- Jug, red, 1941, 2 pt. ... 26- 35

Marmalades

Regular, yellow, 1943 ....$35- 43
W/metal holder, green, 1943 ... 43- 52

Mug

Tom and Jerry, red, 1941 ......$41- 50

Mustard

Green, 1939 ....$31- 40

Pitchers

Disc, water, rose, 1947, 2 qt. ..$39- 47
Ice, green, 1944, 2 qt. 81- 89
Juice, yellow, 1941, 30 oz. 48- 56
Syrup, red, 1941 96-104

Plates

Chop, turquoise, 1941, 13", 15", each $11- 18
Compartments, various colors, 1937, 10½", 11 ⅝", each 21- 27
Deep, green, 1943, 8" 12- 19
Various colors, 1936-1968, 6", 7", 9", 10" (Illus.), each 9- 19
Platter, oval, yellow, 1941, 12" . 27- 36
Salt/pepper shakers, all colors, 1936-1973, set.............. 11- 22
Sugar, creamer and tray, turquoise, 1941, set 38- 46
Tumblers, green, 1943, 5 oz., 10 oz., each 16- 23

Vases

Bud, yellow, 1939 ....$38- 48
Old ivory, yellow, blue, 1936-1941, 8", 10", 12", each 41- 53

Figurines

Figurines

Some are old and valuable, some aren't. Well, if **you** like it, buy it.

Boy-with-dog, bisque...........$18-22
Dionne Quints, plaster 16-22
Mickey Mouse with saxophone, plaster 28-34
Mickey Mouse in canoe, bisque .. 44-53
"Scrappy" figure, bisque 8-12

Firearms

Photo Courtesy of
Hake's Americana & Collectibles

Firearms

Please read **this** editor's comments about "Ammunition." I just don't think guns should be sold, traded, bartered, etc., unless both the buyer **and** the seller know of what they speak.

Most Flea Markets attract tremendous crowds, which is "the name of the game," but, in all the harried hustle and bustle, guns tend to "quietly disappear" because someone under-or-over-age comes along with the right price. No way! Anyone who doesn't know about firearms and purchases same is a damned fool and there aren't any other words to describe same. Collect the ads having to do with firearms and you'll live to enjoy your collection!

Winchester Arms Co. advertising felt banner (Illus.) $19-27

Fireplace Frames

Fireplace Frames

The illustrated "frame" is made of oak and would enhance any home, new or old. Look for them at Flea Markets; also, where and when an old home is being demolished.

Oak fireplace frame (Illus.) $225-250
Walnut frame, ornately carved, late 1800's 385-435

Fish Sets

Consisting of a large platter and twelve plates, all with a fish motif, these sets were in vogue during the late Victorian era. Haviland, Rosenthal, and lots of other companies made them. It's unusual to find the complete set, but the "fish" plates make neat wall decorations.

A single plate by Haviland or Rosenthal . . . . $ 39- 47

Fish Sets

A single platter, same firms . . . 52- 62
Complete sets, Haviland, Rosenthal, Royal Bayreuth, etc. 285-320

Fishing Collectibles

Fishing Collectibles

The earlier the better! Of course, condition is most important, especially with wooden plugs. Original paint, original hooks. This is a hobby that is beginning to pick up speed, especially after Carl F. Luckey published his fine book, *Identification and Value Guide to Old Fishing Lures and Tackle,* Books Americana, $14.95. Early plugs were made of metal and wood; plastic plugs first appeared in 1922. The first jointed plugs, around 1907. American-built spinning reels, around 1940. Split bamboo rods are highly collectible as are the early reels. This is a "swap" hobby; trading is more important than money.

Lures (Plugs), Plastic

Cool Ripple Frog, c. 1947 . . . . . $	3- 4
Gentleman Jim, c. 1949	3- 5
Hula Popper, c. 1948-1955	2.50-3.50
Jitterbug, early	2.50-4
Killer Diller, c. 1941	4.50-8
Ladybug	2.50-4
Magnetic Weedless	4.50-8
Striper Pikie, c. 1950	2.50-4
Water Scout Streamliner, 800 series	2.50-4
Waterville weedless, c. 1948 . .	5- 8

Lures (Plugs) Wooden

Bass Catcher, c. 1920's . . . . . . $	3.50-6
Creek Chub "jigger," c. 1930's	6-11
Crippled Minnow, c. 1920's . . .	4- 8
Diving Doodle Bug, c. 1960 . . .	2- 4
Jigolet, c. 1941	3- 5
Jitterbug, c. 1940	6-10
Master Biff Plug, c. 1926	6.50-11
Master Dillinger, 300 series, c. 1948	3- 4
Open Mouth Shiner, c. 1920 . . .	12-20
Pike Mauler, c. 1930's	7-12
The Polly Wiggle, c. 1920's . . .	6-11
Sea-bait, c. 1932	12-16

Reels

Arrow, #60 . . . . $	5-11
Atlantic Surf Caster	10-19
Bristol #65	7-11
Bronson Belmont	6-11
Heddon Pal #P-41	8-17
Heddon Winona #105H	7-12
Horrocks-Ibbotson, Commodore #1865	3.50-7
Langley Streamlite #310	8-14
Ocean City #970	3- 6
Ocean City Nile	8-12
Pflueger Capitol #1988	13-19
Pflueger Pastime #1743	10-17
Shakespeare Alamo	9-17
Shakespeare Leader #1731	5-11
Shakespeare Tournament #1922	8-13
South Bend #30 Levelwind Model D	6-11
Southbend No. 666 Free Cast .	7-15
Union Hardware Co. #7255S . . .	6-11
Winchester #4350	7-14

Just keep in mind that there are hundreds and hundreds of different types of plugs, rods, and reels. Read Carl F. Luckey's book. You'll be glad you did, if you're into collecting fishing tackle and lures.

Flue Covers

They look like a pie pan. Used to cover the hole in the wall when the stovepipe was removed. Some are painted and they're attractive wall decorations.

Average price	$2-3

Food, Candy Molds

Food, Candy Molds

Usually made of tin or ironstone pottery — food; usually made of metal — candy.

Tin food mold	$12-15
Aluminum candy molds	3- 4
Average price, good condition . . .	6-10
Ironstone pottery food mold, "rabbitt" design, late 1800's . .	34-44

Football Cards

In 1933 Goudey Gum released its Sports Kings set; two years later National Chicle issued their first full set. Thirteen years later Leaf and Bowman both issued full sets. Topps entered the market in 1950. NFL players were issued from 1956 until 1963; AFL players in 1961. Prices given are for those in very good condition. Common cards, all years, 1948 to 1954, average price, each, 35¢-$1.75. Common cards, all years, 1955 to present, average price, each, 30¢-$1.20.

Bowman, 1950, #s 1-144, color only

#1, Doak Walker, Detroit Lions, back . . . . $	4.50-6

#5, Y. A. Tittle, Baltimore Colts, quarterback 6.60-7.40
#6, Lou Groza, Cleveland Browns, tackle 4.55-5.25
#17, Bob Waterfield, L. A. Rams, quarterback 4.75-5.10
#27, Sid Luckman, Chicago Bears, quarterback 4.60-5
#37, Bobby Layne, Detroit Lions, quarterback 6.95-7.40
#45, Otto Graham, Cleveland Browns, quarterback 1.15-12
#52, Elroy Hirsch, L. A. Rams, end 4.80-5.35
#100, Sammy Baugh, Washington Redskins, quarterback 10.15-10.80

Bowman, 1951, #s 1-144, color only

#4, Norm Van Brocklin, L. A. Rams, quarterback .$ 6.40-6.90
#10, Steve Van Buren, Philadelphia Eagles, back 5.20-5.70
#12, Chuck Bednarik, Philadelphia Eagles, center 5.20-5.60
#20, Tom Landry, NY Giants, back 9.65-10.25
#42, Glenn Davis, L. A. Rams, back 4.80-5.35
#56, Charlie Conerly, NY Giants, back 3.85-4.30
#102, Bobby Layne, Detroit Lions, back 8.35-8.90
#137, Charlie Trippi, Chicago Cardinals, back 3.85-4.25

Bowman, 1952, #s 1-144, color only

#1, Norm Van Brocklin, LA Rams, quarterback ......$ 8.45-8.95
#2, Otto Graham, Cleveland Browns, quarterback 9.55-9.90
#16, Frank Gifford, NY Giants, back 11.50-12.40
#48, George Halas, Chicago Bears, coach 8.75-9.40

Bowman, 1953, #s 1-144, color only (same stars, 1954, #s 1-96, 10 percent less; 1955, #s 1-128, 20 percent less)

#9, Marion Motley, Cleveland Browns, back .$ 3.75-4.30
#15, Dante Lavelli, Cleveland Browns, end .. 3.70-4.15
#26, Otto Graham, Cleveland Browns, quarterback 9.20-9.65
#32, Hugh McElhenny, San Francisco 49ers, back ... 4.85-5.30

Fleer, 1960, #s 1-132, color only

#20, Sammy Baugh, NY Titans, AFL, coach ....$ 4.35-4.70
#58, George Blanda, Houston Oilers, AFL, quarterback kicker 3.55-3.95
#66, Billy Cannon, Houston Oilers, AFL, back/end ... 6.75-7.35
#124, John Kemp, LA Chargers, AFL, quarterback 4.35-4.65

Fleer, 1961, #s 1-220, color only

#11, Jim Brown, Cleveland Browns, back ....$ 16.50-18
#30, John Unitas, Baltimore Colts, quarterback 5.45-5.85
#41, Don Meredith, Dallas Cowboys, quarterback ... 5.50-5.80
#88, Bart Starr, Green Bay Packers, quarterback 4.45-4.75
#117, Bobby Layne, Pittsburgh Steelers, quarterback 4.35-4.70
#155, John Kemp, same team 5.50-5.80

O-Pee-Chee, 1968, Canadian Football League, #s 1-132, color only

Average price .... 80¢-1.50

Topps, 1956, #s 1-120, color only

#6, Norm Van Brocklin, LA Rams, quarterback ......$ 4.20-4.55
#9, Lou Groza, Cleveland Browns, tackle/kicker 2.80-3.25
#11, George Blanda, same team 5.45-5.95
#28, Chuck Bednarik, same team 2.80-3.45
#29, Kyle Rote, NY Giants, end 3.25-3.55
#53, Frank Gifford, same team 6.50-6.90
#60, Lenny Moore, Baltimore Colts............. 2.70-3.15
#86, Y. A. Tittle, San Francisco 49ers, quarterback . 4.40-4.80
#116, Bobby Layne, same team 4.85-5.45

Topps, 1957, #s 1-154, color only

#14, Pat Summerall, Chicago Cardinals, end ....$ 1.95-2.25
#31, George Blanda, same team 6.60-7.10
#71, Andy Robustelli, NY Giants, end 2.15-2.45
#88, Frank Gifford, same team 7.45-7.95
#119, Bart Starr, Green Bay 10.15-10.65
#151, Paul Hornung, Green Bay Packers, back 10.40-10.85

Topps, 1958, #s 1-132, color only

#22, John Unitas, same team ....$ 6.40-6.80
#62, Jim Brown, same team 37-39

#90, Sonny Jurgensen, Philadelphia Eagles, quarterback 6.50-6.95
#93, Joe Perry, San Francisco 49ers, back 2.35-2.60
#129, George Blanda, same team 4.95-5.45

Topps, 1959-1962, #s 1-176; #s 1-132; #s 1-198; #s 1-176, color only

#1, John Unitas ....$ 4.85-5.85
#s 10, 23, 28, Jim Brown, same team 11.75-19.75

Others, 15 to 20 percent less, generally, per year.

Topps, 1964, #s 1-176, color only

#30, Jack Kemp, Buffalo Bills, AFL, quarterback ..$ 5.15-5.35
#68, George Blanda, same team 5.10-5.55
#96, Lenny Dawson, Kansas City Chiefs, AFL, quarterback 3.80-4.40

Topps, 1965, #s 1-176, color only

#122, Joe Namath, NY Jets, AFL, quarterback ....$ 94-100
#161, John Hadl, San Diego Chargers, AFL, quarterback 2.75-3.20

Topps, 1966, #s 1-132, color only

#96, Joe Namath, same team ....$ 8.95-9.75
#119, Lance Alworth, San Diego Chargers, AFL, end 1.90-2.35

Prices fluctuate from 1967 until present. Buy a price guide. From 1973 until 1981, 528 color cards were issued each year by Topps.

Fostoria Glass

Fostoria Glass FOSTORIA

Built in 1887 at Fostoria, Ohio, the plant was moved to its present location in Moundsville, West Virginia, in 1891. Quality glass has always been their trademark, making such patterns as American, Baroque, Beverly, Chintz, Fairfax, and Lafayette, to mention just a few of the many patterns. See **Clubs and Publications,** this Price Guide.

Ashtrays
- American, 5½" ....$ 8- 11
- Fairfax, blue 23- 28

Bowls
- American, 5" 11- 15
- Baroque, flared, 12" 23- 28
- June, pink 16- 20
- Meadow Rose, 11¼" 34- 39
- Pioneer, 10" 9- 13

Butter dishes
- American 23- 27
- Colony 19- 23
- Fairfax, amber 77- 84

Candlesticks
- American, 2-light, 6½" 24- 28
- Baroque, 2-light 24- 28
- Chintz 16- 20
- Colony, pr. 34- 38
- Meadow Rose, 3-branch 24- 28

Compote, American, jelly 32- 37
Cookie jar, American, 9" 78- 84

Creamers
- Beverly, amber 19- 24
- Colony, large 7- 10
- Trojan, topaz 24- 28
- Versailles, topaz 22- 27

Cup/saucer
- Baroque, crystal 17- 21
- Colony 11- 14
- Fairfax, amber 14- 18
- Hermitage, crystal 10- 13
- June, blue 44- 49
- New Garland, pink 18- 22
- Pioneer, green 10- 13
- Vernon, amber 18- 22

Decanter w/stopper, 9¼" ... 89- 94

Goblets
- American, sherbet, 4½" ... 14- 18
- Beverly, claret, amber 24- 28
- Colony, 5¼" 10- 13
- June, blue, 8¼" 37- 41
- Meadow Rose, water 18- 22
- Vesper, water, green 16- 20

Ice bucket w/tongs,
- American 37- 42

Lamp, hurricane, American .. 67- 72

Mustard jars
- American 19- 23
- Baroque, topaz 16- 19
- Fairfax, amber 25- 29
- Hermitage 31- 35

Pitchers
- American, pt., 5¼" 29- 32
- Fairfax, amber 131-140
- Hermitage, topaz, pt. 57- 61
- June, blue 585-600
- Royal, amber 282-291
- Vesper, amber 311-320

Plates
- American, 17¾″ 32- 38
- Chintz, 7″ 7.50-8.50
- Colony, 8″ 5- 7
- Fairfax, amber, 9½″ 14- 17
- June, blue, 6″ 11- 14
- Lafayette, topaz, 9″ 8- 11
- Pioneer, amber, 6″ 3- 6
- Versailles, blue, 10¼″ 44- 48

Sugar bowls
- American 16- 19
- Chintz, individual 6- 8
- Meadow Rose, large 19- 23
- Trojan, topaz 24- 27
- Versailles, green, large 13- 16

Trays
- American, handles, 6″ 16- 19
- Baroque, topaz, for individual sugar and creamer 19- 24

Tumblers
- American, whiskey, 2½″ 9- 12
- Chintz, footed, 5 oz. 9- 13
- Colony, footed, 4¼″ 6- 9
- Fairfax, amber, 9 oz. 10- 13
- Meadow Rose, footed, 4½″ 17- 20
- Versailles, blue, 5¼″ 25- 29

Vases
- American, 10″ 27- 31
- Baroque, crystal, 7¼″ 24- 28
- Hermitage, topaz 16- 19
- Trojan, pink, blown, 8¼″ 78- 83

Frankart

This firm operated during the 1920's in New York City. Their metalware had a greenish finish and most pieces were marked "Frankart" with a patent number and manufacture date.

- Bookends, cowboy on horse, 7½″ $240-250
- Candlesticks, entwined nudes, pr. 255-265
- Figurine, elk, 6½″ 45- 53
- Lamp, child reading book 130-138
- Night-light, sailboat, 10½″ 250-260

Frankoma Pottery

Frankoma Pottery

John Frank began the pottery firm in Sapulpa, Oklahoma, in 1933. Pieces made from 1936 to 1938 are highly collectible today as the factory was destroyed by fire in 1938. A loping leopard was the mark. Today, look for FRANKOMA. In 1965 they began making commemorative Christmas plates.

- Bookends, cowboy boots, pr. $15-22
- Candle holder, black glaze, 5¼″ 8-12
- Christmas card, 1967 39-44
- Christmas card, 1969, 1970, each 23-28
- Cup/saucer set (Illus.) 48-55
- Donkey mug, yellow, pink, moss, or brown, each 7-13
- Donkey mug, 1968 79-84
- Elephant mug, 1968 77-80
- Elephant mug, 1970, 1971, each 64-72
- Elephant mug, 1974, 1975, each 22-29
- Elephant mug, Nixon-Agnew 75-83
- Pitcher, 8″ 19-24
- Pitcher, Aztec design 6-11
- Sculpture, #116, reclining puma 24-31
- Sculpture, #142, Indian chief 18-24
- Trivet, rooster 10-14
- Vase, bulbous, blue/brown, 6″ 11-15
- Vase, ram's head, small, patina 46-52
- Vase, shell form, 6″ 18-25
- Vase, #85, bird handle 46-53

Fraternal Order Collectibles

Fraternal Order Collectibles

Elk, Moose, Lion, Eagle, Mason, Odd Fellow — all are fraternal organizations. What they wore or carried during the 18th and 19th centuries is collectible today.

- A.O.F. parasol, 1908 convention $52-61

BPOE ashtray, Cincinnati, 1904, Rookwood pottery (rare) 69-75
BPOE handled mug, elk and clock 53-60
F.O.E. watch fob 44-54
Knights of Columbus match safe . 51-61
Masonic shaving mug 51-60
Plate, Masonic, 10¼″ dia. 41-49
Ribbon, Modern Woodmen (Illus.) 26-33
Shrine goblet, Washington, D.C., 1902, red flashed glass 51-60
Shrine, Omaha, 1918, mug 49-58

Fresh-Water Pearls

These pearls came from mussels which were "farmed" from the rivers in the South. The shell of the mussel was used for making buttons, etc. These odd-shaped pearls are highly collectible and bring brisk prices when found, some bringing as much as $600 each!

Fruit Crate Art

From their beginnings in the late 1880's, these colorful paper labels have attracted collectors. When cardboard replaced the wooden boxes around World War II, the paper labels were no longer necessary. Prices are for labels in excellent condition. See **Clubs and Publications,** this Price Guide. Key: (A) Apples, (GP) Grapes, (G) Grapefruit, (L) Lemons, (O) Oranges, (P) Pears, (V) Vegetables.

Airship (O), transport plane descending at night (Fillmore) . $16-22
Athlete (L), 3 olympic runners in coliseum (Claremont) 9-13
Bronco (O), cowboy on galloping horse (Redlands) 4- 7
California Dream (O) 2 golden peacocks/castle (Bradford) 19-24
Channel (L), sailing ship/islands (Goleta) 3- 5
Ensign (P), flag on pink background 3- 5
Fido (L), white puppy on black background (Orosi) 14-19
Fli-Hi (O), flying geese (Tustin) . . 19-25
Golden Bosc (P), streamlined train 3- 5
Gulf Brand (V), sailboats near shore (Gulf) (Illus.) 3- 5
Head Man (G), dancing rooster . . 4- 7
Jackie Boy (A), sailor boy w/apple 8-11
Lemonade (L), 3 large lemons (Ivanhoe) 3- 6

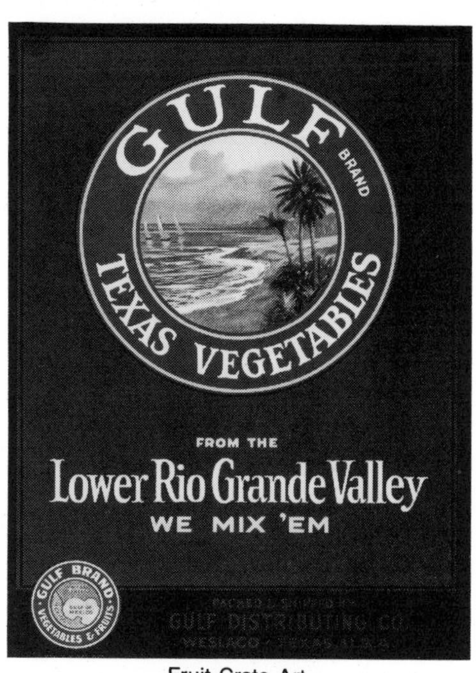

Fruit Crate Art

Navajo (O), full-color Indian bust (Riverside) 11-16
OK Apples (A), red apple on green background 3- 5
Oneonta (P), 2 pears on black background 3- 5
Oxnard (L), ox team/plow near mission (Oxnard) 4- 7
Pacific Maid (L), sailor girl, 1940's (Montalvo) 21-28
Panama (L) green map on blue ocean (Santa Barbara) 5- 8
Pete's Best (A), blonde boy w/apple 4- 7
Polo (O), polo player on horse (East Highlands) 6- 9
Redman (A), fierce-looking warrior, blue background 6- 9
Reindeer (O), stag in orchard (El Cajon) 9-12
Retriever (A), large dog on light blue background 7-10
Rooster (O), crowing cock (Orange) 16-20
Sails (A), sailboat on blue background 7-10
Schooner (L), sailing ship (Santa Barbara) 5- 8
Sea Breeze (L), surf and orchard (Carpenteria) 4- 7
Sea Gull (L), 3 flying gulls (Upland) 5- 8
Shamrock (L), green shamrock over orchard (Placentia) 4- 7
Silver Moon (L), large moon over mission (San Fernando) 5- 9
Silver Tips (O), mama bear and baby bear (Tustin) 24-29

Snow Boy (A), snowman w/earmuffs 5- 9
Stalwart (O), white polar bear (Santa Paula) 16-20
Swan (A), swan on dark background 6- 9
Taylormaid (A), pretty blonde girl 4- 7
Tomcat (L), black cat (Orosi) 33-39
Trojan (O), greek warrior (Olive) . 19-25
Tulip (P), tulips on black background 5- 8
White House (V), picture of the White House w/vegetables 4- 7
Wildflower (L), stone litho of flower bouquet (Randolph Market) 73-80
Wisebird (O), owl and moon (Florida) 4- 7
Yokohl (O), Indian at campsite, red background (Exeter) 4- 7
Yucca (O), large yucca plant, dark background (Mutual Orange) . . . 7-10
Zeus (O), Zeus w/eagle and lightning bolt, yellow background 19-24

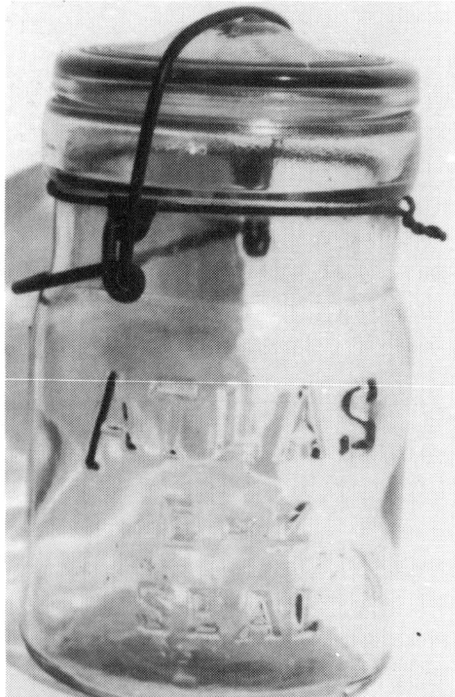

Fruit Jars

Fruit Jars

Color, shape, age, and maker control the price. Mason made the first one that really worked. Hundreds of brands on the market today.

Acme, aqua or light green, each . . . .$ 6- 8
Atlas E-Z Seal, amber, qt. 43- 52
Atlas (4 leaf clover) Good Luck, light green 7- 10
Aylmer Canning Co., clear, 1 pt. 9- 12
Ball Eclipse, clear (Pat. 7-14-08 on base) 3- 5

Keep in mind that Ball made more than 200 different fruit jars!

Ball Improved Mason's Patent 1858, aqua, various sizes . . . 2- 5
Ball Special (wide-mouth jar), blue, ½ pt. 11- 14
Baltimore Glass Works, aqua . . 195-220
Beaver, aqua (beaver gnawing on log) 21- 26
Beaver, midget, amber (beaver, log) . . . . 1,000+
Benton Myers & Co., Cleveland, Ohio, clear 3- 5
Bunte Brothers, Chicago, clear 13- 16
Carroll's True Seal, clear 10- 13
Clarke Fruit Jar Co., Cleveland, Ohio, aqua 47- 52
Cohansey, aqua 18- 22
Dictator D., aqua 81- 90
Eng Hung Chi Bean Cake, 12 oz., net, clear 4- 7
Forster (atlas type), clear 8- 11
Franklin Dexter Fruit Jar, aqua . 29- 35
Hansee's Palace Home Jar, clear 46- 53
E. C. Hazard & Co., New York, clear 11- 15
Kerr "Economy" Trademark, clear, various sizes 3- 6
Kinsella 1874 True Mason, clear 8- 10
Lightning Fruit Jar, clear 11- 14
Mason's (cross) Improved, aqua, various sizes. 3- 6

Mason made more than 500 different designs. There are countless thousands lying around in barns, garages, etc.

Mason's (keystone) Improved, aqua, various sizes 7- 10
Mason's (keystone) Improved, midget pint, aqua 30- 36
Mason's Patent Nov. 30th, 1858, aqua, clear or light green, each 14- 17
Monarch (on shield w/stars and stripes), clear 8- 11
National, Super Mason, clear . . 10- 13
Ottwell's Pickles, aqua 13- 16
Rach Cocoa Co., Waverly, N.Y., aqua 3- 6
Reliable Home Canning Mason, clear 4- 6
Samco Super Mason, clear 2- 4
Sealfast, clear. 3- 5
Smalley Full Measure AGS Quart, clear or aqua, each . . . 10- 14

Sure Seal, blue or light green, each 5- 9
Union No. 1, 2, or 3, aqua, each 39- 45
Weaver Costello & Co., Pittsburgh, clear 2- 4
Whitall Tatum & Co., Philadelphia, New York, clear 35- 42

Fuller Brush Man

Lucille Ball and "Red" Skelton helped immortalize him. Nowadays people are afraid to open their doors to strangers. Anyway, Fuller Brush products, including the salesmen's kits, are collectible.

Funeral Collectibles

Relax, we all have to go sometime. Like it or not, items used in funeral parlors, etc. ARE collectible today.

Bottle, Durfee Embalming Fluid, early 1900's (Illus.) . . . $ 8- 12
Embalming tools, set of twelve, early 1900's 78- 87
Horse-drawn hearse, original condition, 1890's . . . . 4,500 +

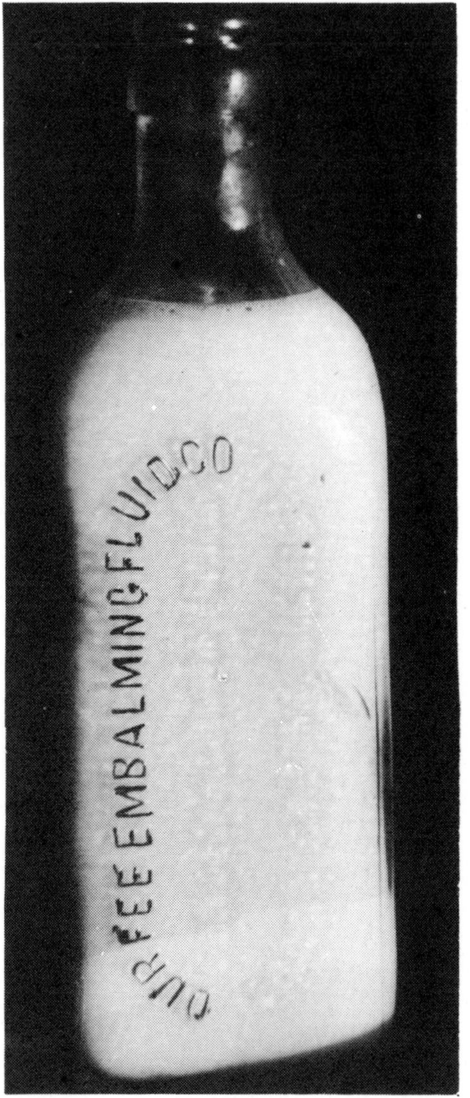

Funeral Collectibles

Gambling Collectibles

Gambling Collectibles

The equipment and cheating devices used by professionals are highly sought after. The "quick buck" syndrome has been around for years and in the late 1700's and on into the early 1800's our beloved leaders used lotteries and other schemes to raise money for schools, roads, libraries, whatever. The lotteries then are no more "fixed" than they are today. Gambling supply houses sold their equipment through catalogs. Just about anything to do with gambling is being collected today. "I have a system!" and "I can beat the house!" are famous last words, uttered by too many who didn't heed the proverb, "A fool and his money are soon parted."

All-in-One game, in original suitcase w/wheel and all paraphernalia. Nine games at one time could be played. . . . $295-355
Baseball dice, pr., ½" square, imitation ivory. 27- 35
Bezique set, 2 complete decks, GOODALL LONDON cards, 2 registers, pamphlet describing game, etc. 170-190
Book, *Bet A Million Gates, the Story of a Plunger,* first edition, 1932, by Irving Warshaw 29- 36
Book, *Card Manipulations,* by Jean Hugard, no date. 10- 17
Book, *How to Figure the Odds,* by Oswald Jacoby, 1950 . . . . 6- 12
Card box, decorated w/king of diamonds, 2 drawers, metal handles 32- 40
Card shuffling machine, metal, wooden carrying handle. 150-159
Card trimmer, made by G. Henry & Co., Chicago, 6" square, brass trimmed shears, etc. . . 920-960
Catalog, "Magical and Amusement Novelties," 1921, 40 pages, illustrated 145-192
Catalog, 1961, K. C. Card Co., 79 pages 60- 68
Cigar tokens, 36 total, ¾" dia., aluminum, all. 29- 37
Dice drop, octagonal, 9" tall, glass sides, green billiard cloth on bottom 178-185
Dice, celluloid, pr., w/weights, ½" dia. 11- 19
Dice cup, carved wood, 3" tall, early 19th century. 82- 90
Door pops, 1 dozen in box, made by ELK BRAND, "7" or "11" only 18- 27
Faro deck, in box, complete, c. 1868, Consolidated Card Co. . 135-143
Faro layout, straight board, suit is clubs, wood trim, early . . . 380-425
Gum vendor, "Daval," works (Illus.) 385-395
Horse race wheel, 5½" dia., 7 horses and riders, German silver spinner, brass hardware 95-114
"Longhop, the Great Game of Chance," boxed set, made by De La Rue, London 81- 90
Lottery flyer, Royal Havana, c. 1886, pink/black 9- 16
"Lotto," game, box, complete, early 1900's 44- 53
Print, colored, "A Winning Hand," by Howard Chandler Christy, 1905 . . . . 60- 68
"Put & Take," brass top, 1¼" tall 32- 39
Roulette wheel, 8" dia., bakelite w/cast aluminum center . 60- 70
Tokens, brass, "Recreation 50," 4 doz., all 31- 39

Games

They've been around for years, parlor and otherwise. Does it have all of its pieces? Is it in its original box? Is it in good to fine condition? All important, if you're a serious collector. J. C. Babcock and Charles Darrow? One invented Mah-

Games

Jongg in 1924; the other invented Monopoly in 1933.

Bet Your Life, Groucho Marx, 1955	$22-27
Checkers, complete, c. 1930's	6-10
Chess, alabaster pieces, Mexico, c. 1950's	35-43
Chinese Checkers, Uncle Wiggilly	14-19
Dick Tracy, playing-card game	11-15
Dominos, complete, in original box	6- 9
Elsie the Borden Cow	19-25
Ferdinand the Bull, Disney (Illus.)	10-14
Fibber McGee and Molly	9-13
Football, Tom Hamilton	8-12
Grab-the-Cat, mint, in box	10-14
Happy Landing, complete	6- 9
Jab-a-Jap, complete w/darts, board	9-14
Lotto	6-10
Monopoly, 1940's, all pieces, original box	14-19
On Your Mark	6-10
Patty Cake	4- 8
Pit, complete	9-13
Rook, Parker Bros.	6- 9
Tiddlywinks, all pieces	4- 8
What's My Line?	6- 9
The Wizard	15-19

Geisha Girl Porcelain

What you'll find is from the late 19th century until the late 1940's. Japanese ladies in kimonos, this souvenir-type ware has suddenly become "collectible," which means the price will shoot up in the next few years. Though much of it is unmarked, "Nippon," "Japan," or "Made in Japan" are marks to be found. Most are hand painted over an overglaze of various colors. Borders of blue, red, green, and brown are to be found. Orange/red is the most common. Look for dresser sets, chocolate sets, tea sets, vases, and bowls. Being reproduced, so know your Geisha, girl!

Geisha Girl Porcelain

Bowl, fruit, green, 8½″	$ 25- 32
Bowl, ladies in garden, 6″	23- 29
Butter dish w/underplate, green border	74- 82
Chocolate cups, ladies in garden, set of 6	44- 52
Chocolate pot, ladies on bridge, 10½″	82- 90
Hair receiver, red border	17- 24
Hatpin holder, garden scene	46- 52
Match holder, 3½″	27- 33
Nut cups, pond scene, set of 6	23- 31
Plates, 5″, 6″, 7″, 7½″, each	14- 27
Salt/pepper set, ladies in garden	18- 24
Sugar shaker, lady in garden (Illus.)	19- 27
Tea set, 12 pieces, all	190-213
Teapot, scenic, 5½″	26- 34
Toothpick holder, blue trim, 2½″	13- 18
Vase, ladies near mountain, blue border, 6″	28- 35

Gentlemen's Charms

Gentlemen wore charms on their watch chains for years. These old charms are collectibles and those stamped 14K on the back spell M-O-N-E-Y!

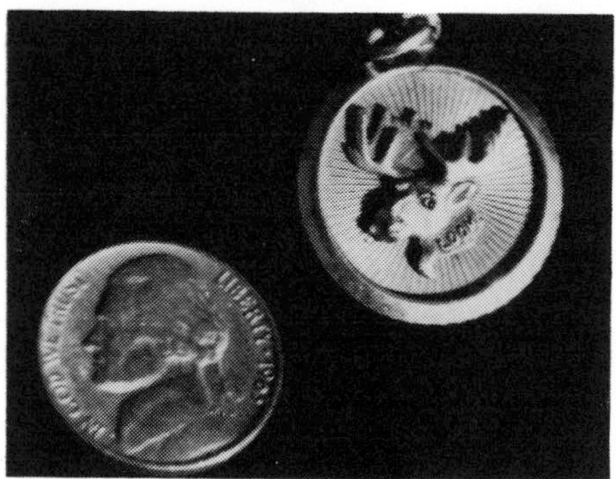

Gentlemen's Charms

"LOOM" (Loyal Order Of Moose) (Illus.) .... $ 6-10
"BPOE" (Benevolent Protective Order of Elks) 6-10
Elk's tooth, genuine. (Imitation teeth become sticky when placed in muriatic acid for a few minutes.) 12-21

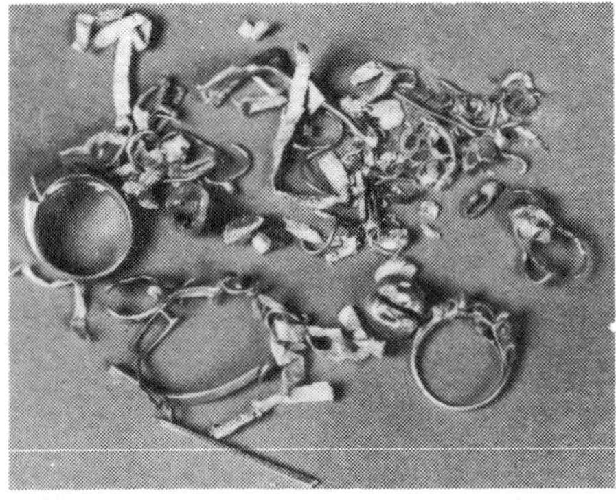

Gold

Gold

Teeth caps, rings, gold dust, watch chains, and watch cases are all made from gold. There is **so** much old gold at Flea Markets, nationwide, it's pathetic that more people don't gobble it up. If marked "14K, 18K," buy it! Gold pieces have gone crazy!

Gonder Pottery

In 1941 Lawton Gonder opened his Gonder Ceramic Arts in Zanesville, Ohio. Flambe, gold crackle, and Chinese crackle were his most popular glazes. His pieces are marked "Gonder" in script. It's a fairly inexpensive collectible, but it'll go up in value as it's a quality commercial ware and sure to be "discovered" soon. See **Clubs and Publications,** this Price Guide.

Basket, blue/pink $17- 23
Bowl, blue/brown, 7¼" dia. 11- 16
Bowl, rose/green, 6½" dia. 11- 16
Cookie jar, snoozing dog 40- 47
Cornucopia, blue/brown 10- 14
Creamer, brown drip glaze 9- 13
Ewer, drip glaze, pink/blue interior, 6" 22- 28
Pitcher, horses 17- 23
Planter, swans 7- 11
Vase, Chinese crackle, blue, 21½" 98-106
Vase, fan form, flambe, 9" 38- 44
Vase, lavender, swans, 8" 26- 33

Goofus Glass

Goofus Glass

The name adequately describes this inexpensive pressed glass. Garishly painted in red/gold, blues, and greens, it's a product of the early 20th century. Northwood, LaBelle, Crescent, and Imperial were a few of the companies guilty of "temporary insanity."

Bowl, carnations, 9¼" $24-29
Bowl, roses, 8½" 23-27
Compote, water lilies, 10" 24-28
Creamer, peach/clear 14-19
Dish, ruffled edge, gold/red, 10" . 24-29
Lamp, kerosene, miniature 39-44
Pickle jar, peacocks 19-24
Plate, fruit center, usual colors, 8" 24-28
Plate, ruffled edges, gold/red, 10" (Illus.) 26-35

Vases

Daisy and Scroll, 9½" $25-31
Green w/red bird 18-24
Roses in relief, 7½" 21-26
Roses w/gold, 7¼" 22-28

Graniteware

Graniteware

This name is given to all the enamelware made after the Civil War until the 1930's. Some called it agateware, others speckleware. Early pieces look like granite, and blue, gray, brown, yellow, and red are favorite colors of collectors. *Graniteware, A Collector's Guide with Prices,* Wallace-Homestead, $12.95, is a beautiful book on the subject. See **Clubs and Publications,** this Price Guide.

Baby Accessories

Bathtub, decorated with nursery rhymes, 24" dia......... $ 77- 86
Food, cup, tin lid, with tray ... 52- 60
Humpty Dumpty dish 30- 38
Mugs, various sizes and colors 25- 32
Plate, ABCs 30- 34

Bath Accessories

Comb case .... $ 23- 30
Basin, 10" dia. 30- 40
Douche pan, strap handle 64- 72
Foot tub 34- 42
Pitcher and wash basin, both .. 52- 60
Potty, child's 30- 35

Breadmaking

Batter bucket, tin lin, handled . $ 50- 60
Biscuit pan, 2 sizes 18- 26
Bread pan 24- 29
Measure, qt. 32- 41
Salt box, wooden lid 50- 60

Coffeepots

Percolator type .... $ 53- 63
Pt. 34- 42
Qt. 40- 45

Cups

Coffee .... $ 17- 25
Demitasse, w/saucer 16- 25
Mexican, fairly new 6- 9
Tea, w/saucer 17- 21

Funnels

Fruit jar (Illus.) .... $ 17- 26
Elliptical 17- 21
Strap-handled 18- 22
Toy 39- 45

Graters

Cheese and vegetables, marked "Ideal" .... $ 40- 43
Table type, w/wooden pusher . 51- 60
Toy, various sizes, each 19- 22

Invalid

Feeder .... $ 17- 26
Medicine cup 11- 17
Urinals, male, female, each ... 14- 24
Utility bucket 31- 39

Milk/Cream Can

Tin lid, ½ gal. .... $ 32- 41
Tin lid, qt. 30- 38
Tin lid, pt. 31- 37

Miscellaneous

Buckets, various sizes, each .. $ 21- 27
Candlesticks, various sizes, each 31- 38
Colanders, various sizes and shapes, each 24- 44
Cuspidors, various sizes and shapes, each 30- 37
Dippers, various sizes, each ... 19- 27
Lid racks, various sizes 18- 26
Measures, various sizes, each . 18- 27
Pitchers, various sizes and shapes, each 29- 34
Skillets, various sizes and shapes, each 12- 27
Teakettles, various sizes, each 29- 40
Teapots, various sizes, each .. 15- 32

Molds

Barley design .... $ 33- 38
Corn design 29- 37
Gelatin 19- 28
Strawberry design 38- 46
Tube 21- 28

Muffin Pans

8-cup .... $ 19- 27
6-cup 33- 40
Turk's Head 37- 40

Picnic Sets

Coffee flask	$ 41- 48
Water carrier	40- 50

Plates

Breakfast, various sizes, each	$ 11- 17
Dinner, various sizes, each	13- 21
Luncheon, various sizes, each	13- 20

Pots/Pans

Double boilers, various sizes	$ 21- 31
Roaster, self-basting, w/cover	27- 33
Vegetable dish, w/cover	32- 41

Scoops

Candy/ice	$ 39- 47
Druggist's	57- 65
Grocer's, covered	29- 35
Utility	32- 40

Stoves

Electric burner	$ 50- 58
Kerosene, 1-burner	199-260
"Mothers Oats Fireless Cooker"	91- 98

Toys

Dustpan	$ 25- 35
Graters, various sizes, each	16- 26
Ladle	23- 32
Mold	17- 26
Pie pan	11- 19
Wash basin	24- 32

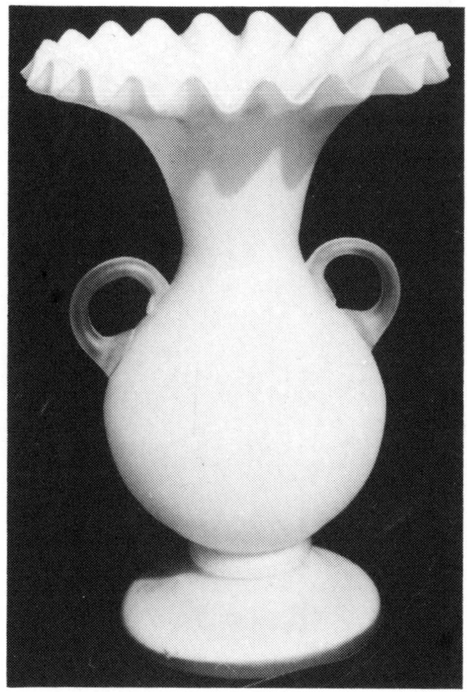

Gunderson Peachblow

Gunderson Peachblow

It looks like Satin glass and it's fairly new — made from 1952 until 1957 in New England.

Cup/saucer, opal handles	$145-165
Goblet, blue, 4½" high	210-230
Toothpick holder, 2" high	137-148
Vase, fluted lip, double-handled (Illus.)	262-272

Hall China

See **American Dinnerware.**

Hardware

Doorknobs

Bennington-type (Illus.) $19-25
Brass 17-24
Cut glass, brass rims 55-63
Porcelain, hand painted 19-26
Porcelain, white (Illus.) 6- 9

Drawer Pulls

Brass, 1920's, set of 8 .... $18-23
Porcelain, set of 12 14-19

Hardy Boys Mystery Books

This is a category all by itself since the popular TV series.

Any volume in good condition ... $3-6

Harker Pottery

See **American Dinnerware.**

Hatbands

Hatbands

No hat should be without one. They come in every variety.

Hand-tooled leather, sterling silver buckle $54-63
Feather with Guatemalan jade (Illus.) 59-67
Handwoven from Peru (Illus.) 7-12
Rattlesnake skin 19-31
Leopard fur 34-42
Zebra skin 28-35

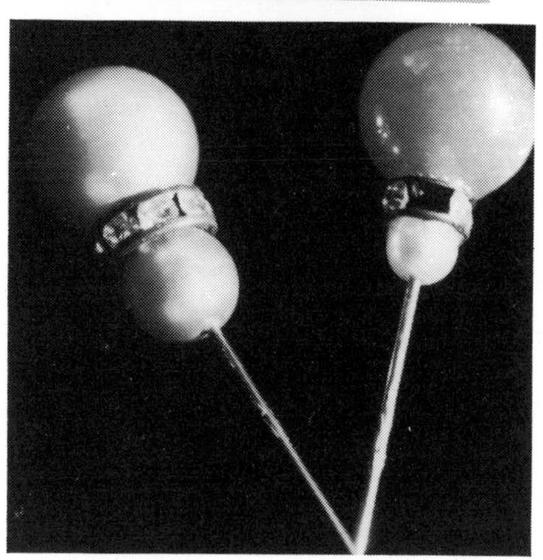

Hatpins and Hatpin Holders

Hatpins and Hatpin Holders

Holders made of every type of material but usually glass, they were plain, decorated, even cut. Popular during the mid-1800's, they make fine flower holders. See **Clubs and Publications,** this Price Guide.

Originally designed to hold m'lady's hat in place, some hatpins had a metal shaft 12 inches long. Usually they had an ornamental "jewel" on the end. They went out of style right after World War I when the gals started wearing smaller hats.

Holders

Blue/gold, birds, flowers, gilt edge, Austria	$ 45- 53
Carnival glass, Marigold, trunk-shaped, N in bottom	63- 73
Fastened to porcelain tray, ring tree each side, Austria	45- 52
Flowers and birds, gilt, Bavaria (Illus.)	32- 37
Sterling silver, initialed, signed Tiffany and Company on side	120-128
Tiffany glass, probably part of dresser set	152-161
White ground, blue/green/purple, Iris decor (Illus.)	45- 55

Pins

Abalone, 10k shaft, 10″ long	$ 19- 27
Blue/white porcelain button, 11″ shaft	26- 35
Butterfly, rhinestones, 11″ shaft	25- 33
14k gold knob, 2 initials, 10½″ shaft	37- 45
Jade button in 14k gold setting, 11″ shaft	42- 51
Kitten, 10k shaft, 11″ long	21- 27
Porcelain, flowers, 11″ shaft	31- 38
Sterling silver flower, 11″ shaft, Tiffany jewelry, flower-shape	110-120

Hats

All shapes and sizes!

Pinocchio felt hat (Illus.)	$ 9-12
Silk top hat, collapses, 1920's	35-42
Felt fedora, wide brim, 1920's	10-13
Lady's, wide brim, ostrich feather, 1920's	19-28

Hats

Photo Courtesy of
Hake's Americana & Collectibles

Haviland China

Haviland China

Don't try to figure out this confusing china. It was made at Limoges, France. Just turn the piece over; **if** it says "Haviland," give it some consideration.

Pitcher, mid-1800's, 7″ high	$67-74
Creamer, white, flower motif, 1900's	29-37
Sugar bowl with lid, late 1800's	37-46

Study up before you tackle this item! Not really a F.M. item, but lots around.

Heisey Glass

Heisey Glass

From 1895 until 1954 some of the finest glass in the world was produced by this firm at Newark, Ohio. It was made in clear and in colors. Imperial Glass Company, Bellaire, Ohio, purchased many of the Heisey molds and is reproducing Heisey today, sometimes without the Heisey trademark — an "H" inside a diamond. Paper labels were also used. See **Clubs and Publications,** this Price Guide.

Ashtrays

Crystolite, 3½″ sq. . . . . $ 13- 17
Old Sandwich, individual 13- 18
Ridgeleigh, bride 11- 13
Ridgeleigh, round or square, each 11- 16
Whirlpool, 3″ sq. 10- 15

Baskets

Cake, Beaded Panel and Sunburst, 9″ $131-139
Double Rib and Panel, Flamingo, 6″ 81- 91
Raised Panel, 9″ 122-132

Bonbons

Crystolite . . . . $ 12- 16
Ridgeleigh, 6″ 13- 18

Bottles

Bitter, Crystolite, 4 oz. . . . . $ 42- 50
Cologne, Crystolite, 4 oz. 41- 47
Oil, Crystolite, 3 oz. 52- 60
Rye, 1 qt. 57- 62

Bowls

Finger, Old Sandwich . . . . $ 22- 27
Floral, Flamingo, 16″ 51- 60
Floral, Moongleam, 16″ 47- 57
Floral, oval, Ridgeleigh, 12″ . . . 37- 45
Floral, Queen Ann, 12½″ 37- 46
Fruit, Fern, 13″ 43- 52
Hollandaise sauce 33- 42
Salad, Tourjours, 10″ 34- 39

Boxes

Cigarette, Colonial . . . . $ 27- 35
Cigarette, Crystolite, footed . . . 30- 37
Cigarette, Crystolite, oval 22- 27
Cigarette, Ridgeleigh, 4″ 28- 31

Candlesticks

Crystolite, 1-light . . . . $ 22- 28
Diamond Optic, Sahara, pr. . . . 101-110
Horn of Plenty, Warwick, individual 27- 33
Queen Ann, 2-handled, pr. 42- 52
Ridgeleigh, 2-light, pr. 57- 63

Champagnes

Coleport, 5½ oz. . . . . $ 17- 22
Ridgeleigh, 5 oz. 18- 27
Saucer, Ipswich, 4 oz. 16- 20
Saucer, Old Sandwich, 5 oz. . . 17- 21
Victorian, 5 oz. 17- 22

Coasters

Crystolite, 4″ . . . . $ 8- 12
Plain bottom 8- 12
Ridgeleigh 8- 13
Star bottom 8- 11

Cocktail Shakers

Coronation, 28 oz. . . . . $ 73- 81
Coronation, martini mixer, 30 oz. 71- 80

Cocktails

Coventry, 3 oz. . . . . $ 17- 21
Duquesene, plain, 3 oz. 16- 25
Kenilworth, 3 oz. 15- 21
Kohinoor, 4½ oz. 17- 26
Monte Cristo, 3½″ oz. 18- 25
Old Glory, plain, 3 oz. 16- 25
Park Lane, 3 oz. 14- 22

Compotes

Monte Cristo, 7″ . . . . $ 55- 65
Old Williamsburg, low-footed, 4½″ 44- 51
Queen Ann, oval, 7″ 56- 63
Spanish, 6″ 52- 61

Cordials

Albemarle, Diamond Optic, 1 oz. . . . . $ 27- 35
Duquesene, plain, 1 oz. 21- 31
Old Glory, plain, 1 oz. 19- 21
Spanish, 1 oz. 31- 34
Wabash, Wide Optic, 1 oz. . . 31- 37

Creamers and Sugars (sets)

Fern . . . . $ 54- 64
Old Sandwich, oval 55- 63
Old Williamsburg, Colonial . . 52- 61
Queen Ann, footed 61- 70

Ridgeleigh, tray included 62- 70
Tourjours, footed 72- 80

Cruets

Queen Ann, pickle and olive, 13″ ....$ 31- 37
Queen Ann, triplex relish, 7″ 31- 36

Cups and Saucers

New Era, after dinner ....$ 32- 37
Queen Ann 27- 31

Decanters

Flamingo, Diamond Optic, cut or pressed stopper ....$ 86- 92
Moongleam, Diamond Optic . 85- 91

Goblets

Ipswich, 10 oz. ....$ 20- 25
Jacobean, low foot, 10 oz. .. 19- 27
Jamestown, 9 oz. 19- 26
Monte Cristo, 9 oz. 21- 27
Old Glory, 9 oz. 18- 26
Old Sandwich, 10 oz. 19- 26
Ridgeleigh, 9 oz. 22- 31
Victorian, 9 oz. 19- 26

Ice Tub

Moongleam, silver-plated handle $105-112

Jars

Candy, Pleat and Panel .....$ 63- 68
Horseradish, Old Williamsburg 31- 37
Jam, Crystolite, 7″ 24- 32
Jelly, Old Williamsburg, 4½″ 31- 37
Mustard, Old Williamsburg ... 31- 36
Mustard, Ridgeleigh 30- 35
Pickle, Colonial 34- 37

Mayonnaise Sets

Crystolite ....$ 31- 37
Moongleam 52- 57

Mugs

Fern ....$ 29- 36
Ipswich 31- 37
Pineapple and Fan 31- 38

Nappies

Crystolite, 4½″ ....$ 17- 24
Old Williamsburg, 4½″, 5½″, each 18- 24
Queen Ann, 4½″ 20- 24
Ridgeleigh, 4½″ 19- 26

Plates

Colonial, 6″ ....$ 34- 37
Crystolite, 7″ 19- 26
Fancy Loop, 8″ 34- 39
Fern, torte, 13″ 27- 31
Greek Key 13- 19
Old Sandwich, 6″ 24- 29
Tourjours, torte, 14″ 26- 32
Victorian, buffet, 21″ 29- 36

Punch Sets

Colonial, 2-pc. w/12 cups, all $446-453
Greek Key, 2-pc. w/12 cups, all 452-470
Priscilla, 2-pc. w/12 cups, all 472-481
Puritan, 2-pc. w/12 cups, all . 451-461

Salts and Peppers (sets)

Colonial ....$ 24- 31
Pineapple and Fan 21- 28
Ridgeleigh 19- 27
Victorian 23- 26
Victorian, No. 2 tops 20- 26

Sherbets

Carcassone, plain or Wide Optic, 6 oz. ....$ 21- 24
Duquesene, plain, 5 oz. 17- 25
Monte Cristo, 6 oz. 21- 27
Wabash, Wide Optic, 6 oz. .. 20- 27

Toothpick Holders

Fancy Loop ....$ 66- 69
Loop 41- 43

Tumblers

Colonial, 6 oz. ....$ 20- 27
Fancy Loop 28- 34
Greek Key, 8 oz. 36- 38
Ipswich, 10 oz. 31- 37
Monte Cristo, 9 oz. 21- 27
Victorian, footed, 10 oz. 27- 31

Vases

Bud, Diamond Optic .... $ 31-38

Suggested reading: *Heisey on Parade*, Sandra Stout, Wallace-Homestead Book Company.

Heisey Glass Animals

Some were made in the 1930's but the most famous were designed by Royal Hickman, who worked for the Haeger Pottery Company. All were pressed in a mold. Some animals were marked with the Diamond H, some were even marked twice, while others weren't marked at all. Most were made in crystal but some were made in deep amber, honey amber, and cobalt (blue). Some were frosted completely, others only partially. In 1962, Imperial Glass Company, which had purchased Heisey's molds in 1958, reproduced certain animals. Not all the reproductions are marked with the Diamond H. Those listed here have never been reproduced. See **Clubs and Publications,** this Price Guide.

Chick, 1″ high ....$ 67- 74
Ducklings, floating or standing, $2\frac{1}{4}$″ and $2\frac{5}{8}$″ high 68- 75
Elephant, $4\frac{1}{2}$″ and $5\frac{7}{8}$″ high .. 92-100
Fish bookend, $6\frac{5}{8}$″ high 124-134
Gazelle, 11″ high 108-116
Giraffe, 11″ high 100-107
Rearing horse bookends, $7\frac{7}{8}$″ high, pr. 210-215
Rooster, $5\frac{5}{8}$″ high 108-116
Rooster vase, $6\frac{1}{2}$″ high 107-117
Tropical fish piece, 12″ high .. 125-134

Others were goose (wings down), Clydesdale horses, filly horse (head forward), same (head backward), show horse, horsehead bookends, piglets, bunnies, rabbit, cygnet, sparrow. Reproduced items, 1962-1968, were bull, hen, fighting rooster, dogs (Airedale, Scotty), donkey, ducks (3 mallards), medium elephant, geese (wings up, wings halfway), horses (flying mare, plug horse, ponies), pheasant, pigeon, rabbit, rabbit paperweight, and swan.

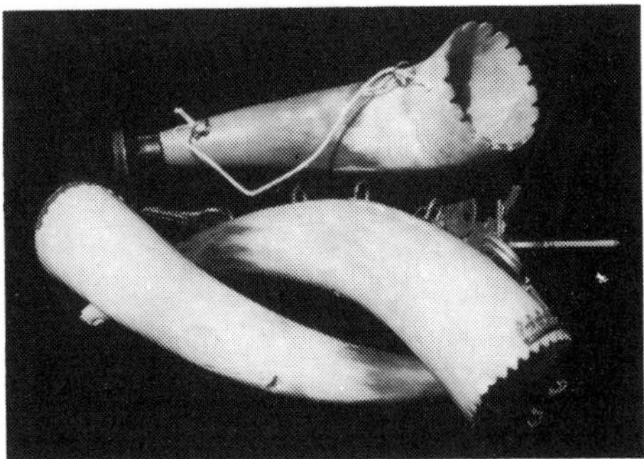

Horn

Horn

Used to hold liquids, gunpowder, and food. They've been around for years.

Calf horns, used to hold car keys, for blowing, each (Illus.) ......$ 9-12
Napkin ring, buffalo horn, 1900's 7- 9
Snuff box, steer horn, late 1800's 27-34
Texas longhorns, ready for mounting, sold by the foot, $60 and up.

Horses

Without a doubt, there are more statues, figures, models, drawings, paintings, photographs, you-name-it of horses. Every child at one time probably collected things to do with horses.

Horses

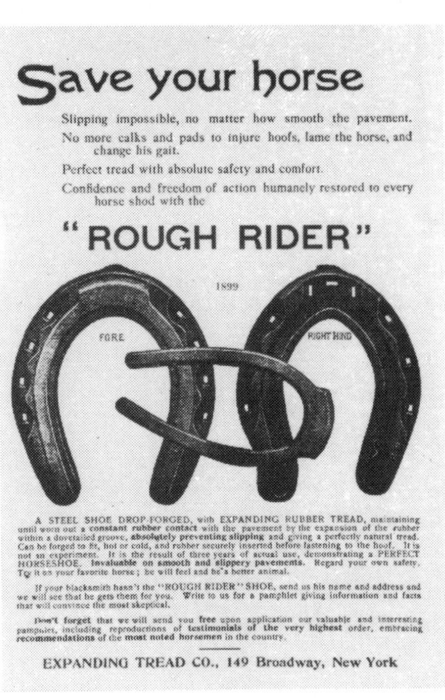

Horsehoes

Horseshoes

Hung over the doorway to bring good luck, thrown by a race horse coming down the home stretch, or just tacked on the wall because the iron looks attractive. These "U" shaped shoes for some reason bring better than average prices at Flea Markets. I have a pony's shoe over my front door. But then I'll settle for just a little bit of luck!

Whether from a Clydesdale or a Shetland, average price $1.50-7

Hull Pottery

hull
Oven Proof
USA

Hull Pottery

The Acme Pottery Co., Crooksville, Ohio, was purchased in 1905 by Addis E. Hull. Around 1917 Hull began producing art pottery for florists and gift shops. Figural kitchenware such as Little Red Riding Hood was made in 1943 and until the 1950's. The factory is still in operation, specializing in dinnerware and florist ware.

Bow Knot design, 1949. Matte finish, marked Hull Art U.S.A. in raised letters. Green/cream/pink/flowers.

Basket, B-12, 10½″	**$ 37- 43**
Bowl, B-18, 5¾″	**26- 32**
Candleholder, B-17, 3½″	**16- 20**
Cornucopia, B-5, 7½″	**26- 33**
Creamer, B-21, 4″	**22- 28**
Jardiniere, B-19, 9⅜″	**71- 78**
Planter, B-6, 6½″	**49- 54**
Sugar bowl w/cover, B-22, 4″	**24- 30**
Teapot w/lid, B-20, 6″	**35- 42**
Vase, B-7, 8½″	**39- 45**
Vase, B-9, 8½″	**39- 45**

Camellia (Open Rose) design. Matte finish, HULL U.S.A. in raised block letters. Cream/light greens/pinks/yellows/flowers.

Candleholders, 117, 6½″, pr.	**$ 29- 35**
Console bowl, 116, 12″, bird candleholders, 117, 6½″, 3 pcs. all	**68- 74**
Cornucopia, 101, 8½″	**43- 48**
Pitcher, 106, 13¼″	**49- 55**
Vase, handled, 102, 8½″	**34- 40**
Vase, 131, 4¾″	**19- 25**

Continental design, 1959. Glossy finish in 3 colors: blue, green, and persimmon. Impressed "Hull (script) U.S.A."

Ashtray, 1, blue	**$ 17- 23**
Basket, 55, persimmon	**42- 49**
Compote, covered, 62, blue	**44- 50**
Console bowl, 51, green	**35- 42**
Planter, 68, green	**35- 42**
Vase, 54, 12½″, persimmon	**37- 44**

Dogwood (Wildrose) design. Matte finish, HULL U.S.A. (impressed, block letters). Dogwood blossoms on cream/pink/green.

Basket, 501, 7½″	**$ 44- 51**
Bowl, 521, 7″	**41- 48**
Candleholder, 512	**19- 25**
Cornucopia, 511, 11½″	**43- 50**
Pitcher, 505, 6½″	**35- 42**
Teapot w/lid, 507, 6½″	**39- 45**
Vase, 502, 6½″	**29- 36**
Vase, 516, 4¾″	**24- 29**

Figural planters. Glossy finish. Most are marked with Hull U.S.A. in script.

Colonial girl, orange/white or blue/white, 954, 1940-1941, each	**$ 32- 38**
Double goose, greens/blues/pinks, 95	**21- 26**
Giraffe, brown/green, 115	**33- 39**
Poodle, yellows/greens, 114	**26- 34**
Rooster, 1951, HULL (impressed) U.S.A.	**32- 40**
Swan, large, 23, white	**31- 38**
Swan, small, no mark	**16- 23**

Little Red Riding Hood design, 1937-1947.

Butter dish w/cover	**$141-150**
Canisters, coffee, tea, salt, cereal, flour, each	**215-245**
Cookie jar	**84- 92**
Creamer	**55- 58**
Jam jar w/lid	**100-112**
Mustard pot w/matching pottery spoon	**146-152**
Salt/pepper set, large	**34- 40**
Salt/pepper set, small	**24- 29**
Sugar bowl, large	**55- 62**
Teapot	**93-102**
Wall plaque	**57- 66**

Magnolia design, 1947. There are 2 types: the matte finish pieces are marked with a number series; the glossy finish pieces are marked with an H and a number series. Marked "Hull Art U.S.A." (raised letters). Light tans/browns/magnolia blossoms.

Candleholders, 27, 4", pr. ....$ 25- 31
Cornucopia, double, H-15, 12". 46- 53
Creamer, 24, 3¾" 13- 18
Pitcher, 5, 7" 28- 33
Sugar bowl, 25, 3¾" 13- 18
Teapot, 23, 6½" 30- 36
Vase, H-9, 8½" 22- 27
Vase, H-18, 12½" 36- 42

Narcissus design. Matte finish, HULL U.S.A. (block letters, impressed). Cream/green/pink/flowers.

Basket, 408, 7" ....$ 34- 40
Hanging basket, 412, 7" 28- 35
Jardiniere, 413, 9" 43- 51
Vase, 404, 8½" 26- 33

Poppy design. Matte finish, HULL U.S.A. (raised mark, block letters). Cream/light green/pink/poppies. Supposedly, hard to find.

Basket, 601, 12" ....$ 55- 65
Bowl, 608, 4¾" 52- 60
Vase, 607, 6½" 37- 44

Rosella design. Glossy finish, Hull Art (raised letters). White (or tan) ground, tan or white flowers, green leaves.

Cornucopia, R1-13, 8½" ......$ 27- 34
Creamer, R-4, 5½" 12- 17
Ewer, R-11, 7" 28- 34
Vase, R-8, 6½" 20- 25
Wall vase, R-10, 6¼" 22- 27

Serenade design, 1957. Textured finish. Hull U.S.A. © 1957. In yellow, pink, or blue. Two birds "serenading" each other.

Ashtray, S-23, yellow ....$ 33- 39
Basket, S-14, pink 26- 33
Creamer, S-18, blue 10- 14
Planter, S-4, pink 17- 23
Sugar bowl w/lid, S-19, blue ... 11- 16
Vase, S-6 .... 17- 22
Vase, S-11, blue 24- 27

Speckled design. Glossy finish, Hull U.S.A. (script, impressed). Pink or green; probably other colors.

Basket, W-9, 8¾" ....$ 27- 34
Compote, 65 .... 24- 28
"Fish" planter, double (E-2 shape) 27- 34
Planter, B-24 .... 26- 33
Urn, 775, 7" 33- 39
Vase, wall type, W-13, 7½" ... 29- 36

Stoneware. Glossy finish. Mark on most pieces, impressed.

Pitcher, 6 mugs, alpine scene, brown/cream, all $235-250
Pretzel jar, alpine scene, brown/cream 55- 65
Vase, pink/blue/cream 42- 49

Water Lily design. Matte finish, Hull Art U.S.A. (raised mark). Usual colors: pinks/greens w/flowers.

Candleholder, L-22 ....$ 13- 17
Console bowl, L-21, 13½" 27- 34
Cornucopia, double, L-27, 12". 35- 42
Jardiniere, L-28, 8½" 26- 33
Pitcher, L-3, 5½" 24- 28
Teapot, L-18, 6" 34- 39
Urn, L-13, 10½" 28- 36
Vase, L-12, 10½" 29- 36

Wild Flower design. Matte finish, Hull Art (raised letters). Warm tans/pink/greens w/various flowers.

Basket, W-16, 10½" ....$ 32- 38
Candleholder, no mark 11- 16
Console bowl, W-21, 12" 19- 26
Cornucopia, W-10, 8½" 34- 39
Pitcher, W-2, 5½" 31- 37
Vase, W-1, 5½" 18- 25
Vase, W-9, 8½" 29- 35
Vase, W-15, 10½" 53- 61

Woodland design. Matte finish, before 1950; glossy glaze, 1952. Both marked Hull U.S.A. (script, raised letters). Cream/yellow/flowers; cream/blue/flowers.

Basket, W-9, 8¾", glossy .....$ 45- 51
Candleholder, W-30, glossy ... 20- 25
Console bowl, W-29 .... 30- 36
Cornucopia, W-5, 6½", matte finish 23- 27
Ewer, W-3, 5½", glossy 16- 24
Planter, W-14, 10", matte finish 20- 25
Vase, W-18,10½", matte finish. 58- 63
Wall vase, W-13, 7½", matte finish 28- 34

Hummel Items

Sister Maria Innocentia, born Berta Hummel in Massing, Germany, loved children, and her sketches, first sold in the 1930's, attracted the attention of the Goebel porcelain factory in Rodental, a small town near Coburg, in Bavaria.

Hummel Items

Authentic pieces bear both M.I. Hummel and the Goebel mark. Look out for Japanese fakes. See **Clubs and Publications,** this Price Guide.

Hummel Trademarks

TMK-1 Crown Mark	TMK-2 Full Bee Mark
1935-1948	1950* -1959
TMK-3 Stylized Bee Mark	**TMK-4** Three Line Mark
1960* -1965	1966* -1971
TMK-5 VEE/G Mark	**TMK-6** G Mark
1972* -1979	1979-

*Dates are approximate — earlier documented examples are known.

Ashtrays

Boy with Bird, Full Bee, #166	$ 198- 220
Happy Pastime, Stylized Bee, #62	124- 130
Joyful, Stylized Bee, #33	98- 127
Let's Sing, VEE/G, #114	59- 68
Singing Lesson, Full Bee, #34	177- 205

Bells

1st Annual, Let's Sing, G, #700	$ 121- 131
2nd Annual, Farewell, G, #701	74- 83
3rd Annual, Thoughtful, G, #702	98- 112

Bookends

Apple Tree Boy and Girl, 3-line, #252/A&B	$ 148- 162
Bookworm, Stylized Bee, #14/A&B	240- 260
Good Friends, She Loves Me, Full Bee, #251/A&B	371- 388
Goose Girl and Farm Boy, Crown, #60/A&B	462- 471
Little Goat Herder and Feeding Time, VEE/G, #250/A&B	148- 158
Playmates and Chick Girl, Stylized Bee, #61/A&B	222- 240

Candleholders

Angel Duet, Full Bee, #193	$ 182- 199
Angel with Accordion, Full Bee, #39	67- 75
Angel with Lute, Full Bee, #38	67- 76
Angel with Trumpet, Full Bee, #40	66- 74
Angelic Sleep, 3-line, #25	89- 107
Boy with Horse, Stylized Bee, #117	48- 58
Candlelight, Stylized Bee, #192	325- 350
Girl with Fir Tree, Stylized Bee, #116	48- 58
Girl with Nosegay, Stylized Bee, #115	47- 58
Herald Angels, 3-line, #37	89- 108
Little Band, VEE/G, #388	120- 128
Lullaby, Crown, 24/III	2,250-2,400
Silent Night, Crown, #54	288- 320

Figurines

Angelic Care, 3-line, #194	$ 129- 170
Apple Tree Boy, Stylized Bee, #143/I	132- 141
Auf Wiedersehen, Crown, #153/I	875- 920
Band Leader, Stylized Bee, #129	108- 122
Barnyard Hero, Full Bee, #195/I	272- 310
Be Patient, Crown, #197/2	172- 182
Big Housecleaning, 3-line, #363	129- 162
Birthday Serenade, VEE/G, #218/O	120- 132
Boots, VEE/G, #143/O	72- 85
Boy with Toothache, Full Bee, #217	172- 192
The Builder, VEE/G, #305	79- 89
Carnival, 3-line, 328	92- 108

Chick Girl, Crown, 57/I 275- 285
Chimney Sweep, Crown, 12/I 242- 252
Cinderella, VEE/G, #337 ... 98- 109
Congratulations, Full Bee, #17 .... 152- 162
Crossroads, 3-line, #331 ... 199- 218
Doctor, Stylized Bee, #127 . 88- 98
Doll Bath, 3-line, #319..... 95- 111
Duet, Crown, #130........ 340- 350
Easter Time, VEE/G, #384.. 102- 109
A Fair Measure, 3-line, #345 121- 152
Farewell, VEE/G, #65...... 92- 107
Favorite Pet, 3-line, #361 .. 110- 120
Feathered Friends, 3-line, #344 .... 118- 129
Feeding Time, Crown, #199/I (Illus.) 282- 321
Festival Harmony (Flute), Crown, #173/II.......... 540- 555
Festival Harmony (Mandolin), Stylized Bee, #172/II. 228- 272
Follow the Leader, 3-line, #369 .... 482- 521
For Mother, 3-line, #257 ... 62- 72
Friends, 3-line, #136/V 453- 462
Going to Grandma's, Crown, #52/O 251- 262
Good Shepherd, Crown, #42/I 2,300-2,500
Guiding Angel, 3-line, #357 47- 57
Happy Birthday, Crown, #176/I 562- 582
Happy Pastime, Stylized Bee, #69 .... 120- 138
Hear Ye, Hear Ye, Crown, #15/I.................. 252- 272
Heavenly Protection, Full Bee, #88/II............. 520- 542
Home From Market, Full Bee, #198/I 171- 182
Just Resting, Full Bee, #112/I................. 174- 190
Latest News, Stylized Bee, #184 .... 132- 148
Letter to Santa Claus, 3-line, #340 .... 152- 182
Little Cellist, Full Bee, #89/II 360- 372
Little Gardener, Stylized Bee, #74 .... 92- 107
Little Guardian, 3-line, #145 72- 102
Little Pharmacist, VEE/G, #322 .... 82- 92
Little Shopper, 3-line, #96 . 61- 71
Little Thrifty, Full Bee, #118 162- 199
The Lost Sheep, Full Bee, #68/O 188- 220
March Winds, Full Bee, #43 161- 172
Meditation, 3-line, #13/V ... 1,720-1,840
Mother's Darling, Full Bee, #175 .... 195- 202
On Secret Path, 3-line, #386 .... 120- 130
Playmates, Crown, #58/I ... 295- 320
Puppy Love, Full Bee, #1 .. 142- 162
Ring Around the Rosie, Stylized Bee, #348 1,950-2,200
St. George, Full Bee, #55 .. 295- 320
School Boys, 3-line, 170/I.. 575- 590
Sensitive Hunter, Stylized Bee, #6/II 232- 262
Shining Light, 3-line, #358 . 55- 65
Singing Lesson, Full Bee, #63 .... 132- 152
Skier, Stylized Bee, #59 ... 134- 154
Soloist, Crown, #135 ...... 172- 195
Spring Dance, Stylized Bee, 353/I 299- 320
Stormy Weather, Full Bee, #71 .... 399- 460
Surprise, Crown, #94/3/O .. 220- 250
Sweet Music, Stylized Bee, #186 .... 110- 119
To Market, Crown, #49/O .. 320- 360
Umbrella Boy, Full Bee, #152/A/O 650- 750
Umbrella Girl, Full Bee, #152/B/II .... 2,400+
Visiting an Invalid, 3-line, #382 .... 121- 132
Waiter, Full Bee, 154/O 188- 198
Wayside Devotion, 3-line, 28/III.................. 220- 240
Wayside Harmony, Full Bee, 111/I 178- 188
We Congratulate, 3-line, #220 .... 75- 85
Which Hand?, Stylized Bee, #258 .... 92- 106

Madonnas

Flower Madonna, Full Bee, 10/I...................$ 800- 900
Madonna with Halo, Full Bee, #45/I 182- 192
Madonna without Halo, Full Bee, #46/I 99- 121

Music Boxes

Little Band, 3-line, #392/M .$ 210- 240
Little Band (w/candle), 3-line, #388/M 220- 240

Nativity Sets

Large set, 3-line, #260/A-R . $3,400+
Small set, Stylized Bee, #214/A-O .... 1,400+

Plaques

Ba-Bee Ring, Crown, #30/A&B...............$ 225- 260
Child in Bed, Crown, #173/B 198- 240
Madonna, Full Bee, #48/II .. 240- 260
Mail Is Here, Full Bee, #140 280- 292
Merry Wanderer, Stylized Bee, #92 .... 121- 138
Quartet, Full Bee, #134 .... 363- 374
Retreat to Safety, Crown, #126 .... 352- 362
Vacation Time, 3-line, #125 99- 108

Annual Plates

1971, Heavenly Angel, 3-line, trade ed., #264 . . . $1,300 +
1971, Heavenly Angel, 3-line, gift ed., #264 . . . . . 2,500 +
1972, Hear Ye, Hear Ye, 3-line, #265 . . . . 98- 107
1973, Globetrotter, VEE/G, #266 . . . . 162- 172
1974, Goose Girl, VEE/G, #267 . . . . 168- 172
1975, Ride into Christmas, VEE/G, #268 . . . . 99- 127
1978, Happy Pastime, VEE/G, #271 . . . . 152- 175
1980, School Girl, VEE/G, #273 . . . . 162- 178

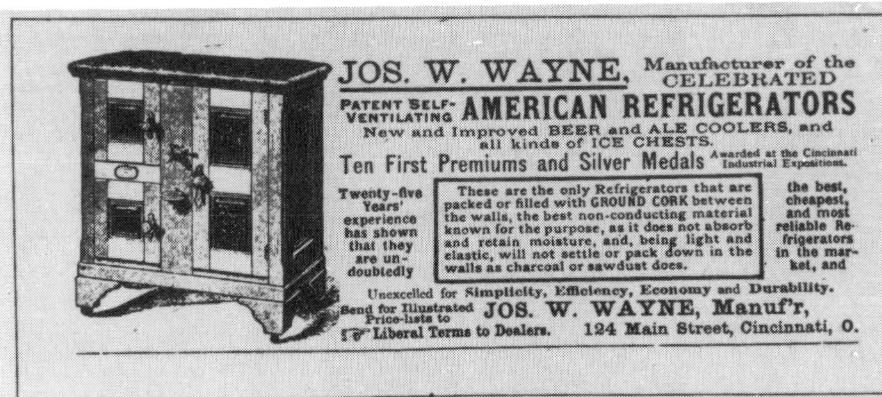

This early ad for a Jos. W. Wayne American refrigerator appeared in the Century

Ice Boxes

Ice Boxes

Usually made of oak with brass or nickel hinges, these early 1900 models make great hi-fi or stereo units. They also make great bars! If you have a summer home on a lake or in the mountains, they're still usable with a 50-pound block of ice.

They're getting more scarce every day.

Average price $295-450

Ice House Collectibles

Ice House Collectibles

It took a good man to lug a 50-pound block of ice up four flights of stairs. A horse-drawn ice wagon carried the ice before electric refrigerators came into being.

Tongs, forged iron, late 1800's (Illus.) . . . . $ 27- 35
Ice delivery cards 4- 6
Ice wagon, horse drawn 395-575

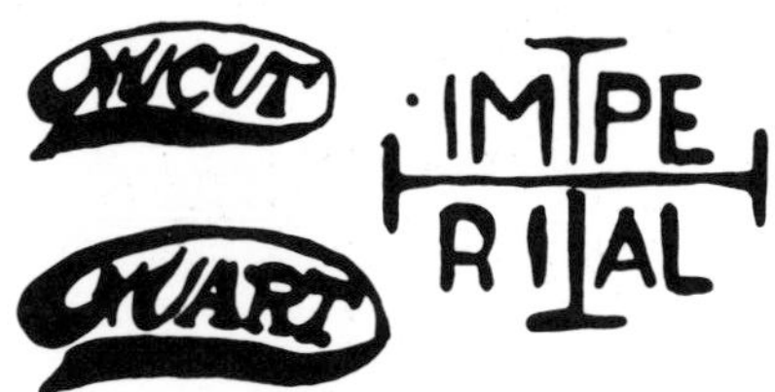

Imperial Glass

Founded in Bellaire, Ohio, in 1902, for manufacturing pressed tablewares, lighting fixtures, and shades. In 1910 they began production of an iridized glass that would become famous as Carnival Glass. NUCUT and NUART are trade names used. Imperial Art Ware and Imperial Jewels were also names used to describe an inexpensive iridescent stretch glass, in imitation of Tiffany and Aurene; also Verre de Soie. Most of these pieces were marked with the Imperial-cross trademark. Imperial purchased molds from such companies as Heisey and Cambridge, and today there are thousands of reproductions on the market that tend to confuse the beginning collector.

Bowl, clear, signed NUCUT, 5½″ wide . . . . $ 32- 37
Bowl, Imperial Jewels, blue/gold, 6¼″ high 80- 86
Bowl, Imperial Jewels, gold luster, Imperial cross mark, 6½″ high 129-137
Bowl, scalloped top, signed NUCUT, 6¼″ wide 31- 37
Candlestick, Candlewick, 3½″ high 19- 27
Compote, Imperial Jewels, blue/gold, ribbed, signed, 6″ high 80- 90
Vase, amethyst/ruby luster, 6¼″ high 143-150
Vase, green/white looping, signed, 7″ high 141-147
Vase, imitation cut glass, 7¼″ high 45- 53
Vase, signed NUCUT, 6¼″ high 23- 30

India Brass

Servicemen in the China-Burma-India Theater, WW II, brought home tons of this stuff. Usually marked "India" on

India Brass

the bottom. A lot was made from shell casings.

Incense burner, hanging type, 1940's $16-20
Lamp, hanging type, electrified . . 45-55
Vase, 14″ high, on teakwood base, 1940's 30-37
Vase, 8″ high (Illus.) 20-27

Ink Collectibles

Ink Collectibles

See **Clubs and Publications,** this Price Guide.

Blotters

These were necessary in the days when liquid ink was used in pens. Along came the ballpoint pen, out went the need for blotters. Today they're collectible.

Average price, in good condition	**50¢- 3**

Bottles

Glass, average price	**25¢-75¢**

Pads

If not dried out, average price	**50¢-75¢**

Insulators

Insulators

When the telegraph was invented in 1844, so was the insulator. Then came the telephone and more insulators. Age and color dictate the price. Clear, aqua, and green are the most common colors. The threadless type bring lots more money. See **Clubs and Publications,** this Price Guide.

A.G.M., amber	**$ 15- 19**
A.T. & T. Co., aqua or green, each	**6- 9**
Agee, clear	**14- 17**
Armstrong's DP 1, clear or green, each	**5- 8**
B.T. Co., Canada, aqua, green, or blue, each	**8- 11**
Boston Bottle Works, aqua	**46- 55**
Brookfield #9, green	**7- 10**
Brookfield #36, aqua or green, each	**13- 17**
Canadian Pacific Railroad, aqua, blue, or green, each	**44- 53**
Castle, aqua	**46- 54**
Chester, N.Y., blue (threadless)	**145-160**
Chicago Insulating Co., blue	**59- 68**
Dominion 10, 16, 42, aqua, clear, each	**3- 6**
Duquesne Glass Co., aqua or green, each	**36- 44**
Gayner No. 36-190, aqua	**12- 17**
F. W. Gregory, Pat. Apr. 7, 1893, aqua or green, each	**36- 44**
Hawley, Pa. U. S. A., aqua	**16- 23**

Hemingray No. 2 Cable, Pat. May 2, 1893, aqua or green, each	24- 29
Hemingray No. 7, aqua or green	2- 4
Hemingray Nos. 7, 9, 10, 14, 16, 19, 20, 21, 40, 42, 45, 53, 61, 71, 660, aqua or green, each	2- 4
Hemingray Nos. 8, 1-10, 11, 12, 19, 25, 43, 50, 53, 60, 72, 95, 107, Muncie, Petticoat, Lo-wex D-510, D-512, D-990, E-1, E-2, 54-A, 54-B, SB, clear, aqua, green, yellow, each	6- 25
K.C.G.W., aqua	14- 19
F.M. Locke No. 21, aqua or green	8- 12
F.M. Locke, V-29, Hi-Top 77, Victor, each	3- 10
Lynchburg Nos. 10, 30, 31, aqua or green, each	9- 14
Lynchburg Nos. 32, 36, 38, 44, aqua or green, each	6- 10
McLaughlin Nos. 10, 14, 16, aqua, clear, each	7- 11
Montreal Telegraph Co., aqua	15- 21
N.E.G.M. Co., aqua or green, each	13- 19
S.B.T. & T. Co., brown pottery, glazed	4- 9
Westinghouse Nos. 4 and 6, aqua or green, each	24- 33
Whitall-Tatum, clear or green, each	2- 4

Keep in mind that purple (amethyst, lavender) insulators may have turned that shade due to the sun's rays. On the other hand, they may have been subjected to cobalt 60 or other gamma rays.

Irons

Irons

Smoothing (or "sad") irons are the most common. There are those that operate on charcoal, gasoline, and "Norwegian steam." Fluting irons replaced the ruffles on a sleeve or petticoat. The tailor's "goose," a very heavy object, pressed the pants and the coats. Lots around for the collector. Beware of reproductions, especially the miniatures.

Acme flat iron	$33-38
Asbestos "tourist iron"	35-41
Bless & Drake, detachable handle (Illus.)	29-35
Charcoal, English, "lion"	63-70
Charcoal, Turkish	32-38
Child's flat iron	40-46
Cross Hatch, original	44-50
Curled handle, original	30-35
Fluting iron, "Geneva"	47-52
Gasoline, blue graniteware bulb	26-32
Sleeve iron	19-24
Tailor's "goose"	29-35

Ironstone

Ironstone

Ironstone is **not** porcelain. It is an earthenware mixed with slag from the steel mills. Durable, it was first patented in 1813 by C. J. Mason. A lot of what you see at Flea Markets today came from old hotels, diners, and railroad dining cars. Also being reproduced.

Bowl, covered, 6″ high, Meakin	$ 43- 50
Bowl, footed, 11″ diameter, Johnson Brothers	19- 22
Butter patties, 2″ diameter, Meakin, set of 8, all	32- 41
Dish, relish, 6″ diameter, oblong, Johnson Brothers	31- 40
Gravy boat, cable decoration, 8½″ long	23- 30
Mold, pudding, flower design inside, Wilkinson	42- 51
Pitcher, Lustre decorations, 14″ high	72- 80
Pitcher, no design, 8½″ high	44- 50
Plate, cake, 10″ diameter, flower border	22- 29
Platter, 14″ long, Oriental pattern, Clemenston	45- 51
Platter, 13½″ long, Moss Rose pattern	42- 51
Teapot, 14″ high, Meakin (Illus.)	72- 81
Teapot, embossed acorn on lid, Mason, 11¼″ high	72- 80
Toothbrush holder, complete, 4½″ high, Johnson	32- 40
Tureen, covered, paneled, 14″ diameter, Meakin	38- 47
Wash set: bowl and pitcher, Meakin, bowl, 18″ diameter, pitcher, 19″ high, both	232-242

Ivory

Ivory

Sure, you know that ivory comes from elephants, whales, walrus, hippos, even boars and elk. What do you know about **fake** ivory? Alabrite is made by pulverizing alabaster, then mixing it with a plaster, molding it, and finishing it by hand. Bone is frequently used; it's always hollow where the marrow once was. Micarta is composed of layers of cloth sandwiched under pressure with bakelite. Ivoryite is made from the sawdust of real ivory or fishbone, mixed with resin. Galolith is a curd product. Casein, the final product, is molded and hardened. Vegetable ivory is the fruit produced by several species of palm trees. When carved, the "ivory" piece will fool too many people. The illustrated figure is Alabrite and was sold as "genuine" for $75.

Suggested reading: *Is It Ivory?*, Harvey Shell, Ahio Publishing Company.

Jackson China

See **American Dinnerware.**

Jade Trees

Jade Trees

These beautiful "trees" have petals and stems made of real jade. They've been around for years. The price depends on the number of broken petals, etc. But, they are collectible.

Jade tree, new (Illus.) $43-50
This is an average price.

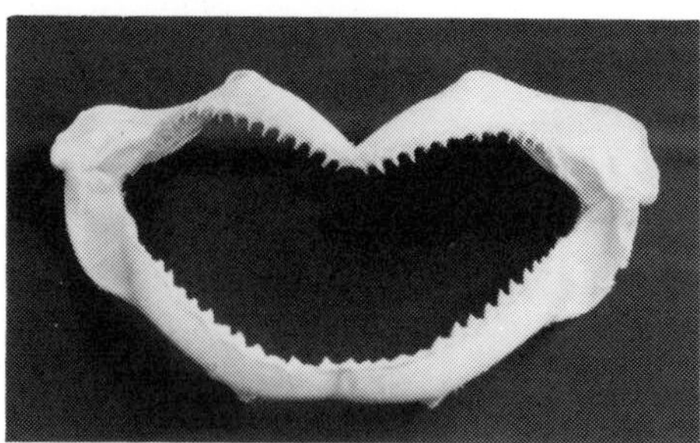

Jaws!

Jaws!

Ever since Benchley's movie scared us half to death, anything to do with this awesome creature is collectible. The jaws, belts, and sandals made from its skin, and, certainly, the teeth.

Shark's jaw, 3″ to 6″ wide (Illus.) $3-4
Shark's teeth . . . . 75¢-$1

Jewelry, Costume

Jewelry, Costume

Usually classified as "junk" jewelry, it's been popular with the masses since the Victorian era. Today, it's highly collectible. Usually, the composition is copper or brass; occasionally, gold (10K or less). Always set with paste stones. Celluloid and aluminum jewelry is also being collected. Beads of cut crystal, garnets, amber, wood, silver, and ceramics are much sought after. Price depends on condition and material. See **Clubs and Publications,** this Price Guide. The following are indicative prices; there are thousands of pieces of costume jewelry just waiting to be collected.

Bar pin, sterling silver w/blue and crystal paste stones	**$ 19- 23**
Beads, blue pressed glass, faceted, 24″ long	**34- 40**
Bracelet, enamel and paste lapis lazuli, gold wash over brass, Art Deco style	**38- 44**
Bracelet, gold wash over brass, link chain w/2 faceted, amber color stones	**20- 27**
Brooch, Art Deco, blue/white enamel on copper	**37- 42**
Brooch, enamel w/blue paste stones	**14- 19**
Brooch, sterling-silver grapes/leaf	**32- 38**

Buckle, 3-piece, imitation stones set in "silver" metal, pink "amethysts," "rhinestone" border	100-110
Clip, paste turquoise in oxidized brass frame	19- 26
Earrings, blue paste stones set in sterling silver w/screw posts	19- 24
Earrings, "emeralds" set in silver plate w/screw posts	12- 16
Necklace, inlaid turquoise, India	32- 39
Necklace, plastic cameo, 3 gold-washed hearts, gold-wash chain (Illus.)	16- 21
Pendant, celluloid cameo and chain	31- 38
Scarf pin, gold plate, horses' heads	14- 19
Watch band, imitation pearls	24- 29

Suggested reading: *Collectible Costume Jewelry,* S. Sylvia Henzel, Wallace-Homestead Book Company.

Jugtown Pottery

Jugtown Pottery

Begun in Moore County, North Carolina, in 1920, by Jaques and Juliana Bushbee. Orange was the predominant glaze used; a Chinese blue glaze is the most sought after today. The mark used is illustrated here.

Bowl, brown, signed Ben Owen, 5" high	$53-62
Bowl, brown/orange, signed, 3½" high	44-53
Mug, Chinese blue, signed	39-47
Plate, brown, signed, 5½" dia.	27-37
Plate, Chinese blue, signed Ben Owen, 6" dia.	39-47
Vase, brown, signed, 7" high	38-47
Vase, Chinese blue, 3 handles, signed, 6¼" high	46-52
Vase, green, signed Ben Owen, 4¼" high	41-50
Vase, green/tan, 2 handles, signed, 4¼" high	40-50
Vase, orange, signed, 6" high	29-38

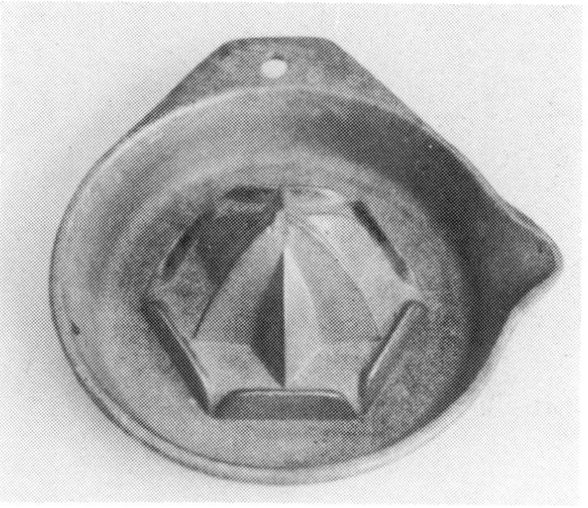

Juicers

Juicers

In the days before frozen orange juice concentrate, these juicers were found in every home. Today they're hard to find. Look for them in metal, glass, wood, even plastic.

Average price $1-5

Kewpies

Kewpies

Rose O'Neill drew pictures of these pixie-like figures for the *Ladies' Home Journal* in the early 1900's. Around 1911 Kewpie dolls began to appear on the American market. The bisque dolls came from Germany, but the most common were the ones made of celluloid. Being reproduced. Careful! See **Clubs and Publications,** this Price Guide.

Bank, glass, tin lid $127-136
Bowl, cereal, 6″ dia. 159-167
Candy container, 1915 150-160
Creamer, Kewpies playing in yard 137-142
Cup/saucer, Germany, pink lustre trim 137-146
Dish, feeding 75- 84
Doll, bisque, Japan, 4″ 68- 78
Doll, bisque, signed Rose O'Neill 140-150
Doll, composition, Rose O'Neill label, 12½″ 98-107
Doll, dressed, celluloid mark, 2½″ high 42- 50
Figurine, seated figure, 3″ high 260-270
Ice cream mold, hinged, pewter 94-103
Ice cream tray, signed Rose O'Neill 75- 85
Lamp, chalkware, fringe shade 81- 90
Pitcher, 4 action Kewpies, Royal Rudolstadt 307-315
Plate, Royal Rudolstadt, signed Rose O'Neill 68- 75
Postcard, Christmas, "We love you" 31- 39
Powder jar, signed 125-134
Teapot, creamer, sugar, signed Rose O'Neill, porcelain 162-170
Thimble 29- 37
Toothpick, "Thinker," 5½″ high 85- 93
Tray, Kewpies picking berries, signed 283-293
Vase, handled, Kewpies playing, signed 162-172

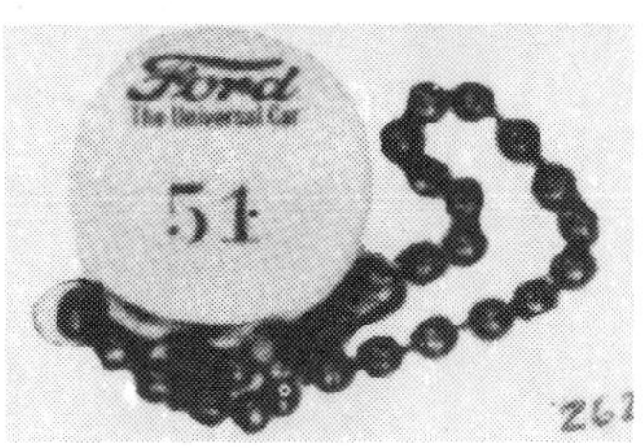

Key Chains

Key Chains

Pepsi Cola, 1940 .... $10- 12
Ford (Illus.) 3-3.50
Ruppert beer 4- 5
D.A.V., WW II 4- 5
"License plate" — D.A.V. .... 50¢-75¢

Key Holders

Key Holders

Leather, silver, gold, plastic — every style, age, and shape.

Leather holder, 1930's .... 75¢-1.25
Sterling silver ring, 1960's 4- 6

Kitchen Collectibles

Anything to do with the kitchen — the older the better. 18th- and 19th-century items tend to be expensive, but mass-produced pieces are still readily available. Three eras are involved. 18th-century kitchen — life revolved around the large fireplace; copper, brass, iron objects, all handwrought. Victorian kitchen — cast iron stoves, lots of tin, rugs on the floor, aluminum items. Early 20th-century

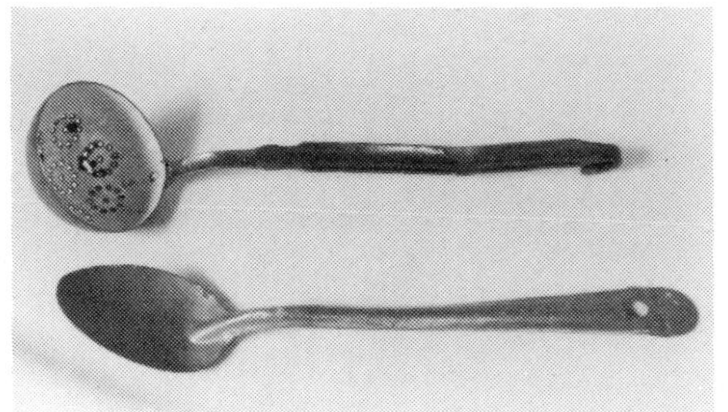

Kitchen Collectibles

kitchen — electrical appliances, gadgets galore, refrigerators, cleanliness, orderliness.

Apple Corers

All tin, 19th century	$ 7- 10

Apple Parers

Cast iron, F. A. Walker, c. 1870's	$51- 58
Rocking Table	46- 53
White Mountain	43- 51

Biscuit Cutters

Aluminum	$ 3- 4
Gold Medal, c. 1920's	3- 5
Southern Best, c. 1930's	3- 4

Bottle Openers

Acme, buttonhook end	$ 3- 5
Moxie	4- 7
Nutri-Cola, ice pick at opposite end	5- 9
Pepsi Tastes Best	4- 8

Bowls

Pine, dough	$51- 54
Rockingham, No. 2, 3 gal.	16- 19
Walnut, burl	125-150
Yellow, No. 6, 1 gal.	13- 17

Bread/Cake Boxes

Tin, brown, No. 1, 13½″ × 10½″ × 9¾″	$33- 40
Tin, crystallized, No. 2, round, 10½ × 9″	31- 37
Tin, oak, No. 3, round, 13½″ × 9¾″	33- 40

Butter Churns

Cylinder type, white cedar, 1½ gal.	$68- 77
Mak-Mor, glass, metal works, c. 1915	29- 34
Monumental, white cedar, 8 qt.	63- 71
Poplar/pine, c. 1860's	78- 84

Cake Molds

Bundt, aluminum, c. 1940's	$21- 27
Tin, F. A. Walker	23- 27
Tube type, scalloped sides, c. 1900's	24- 32

Cake Pans

Tin, Bake-A-Cake Kit, set of 3	$22- 28
Tin, Calumet Baking Powder	9- 13
Tin, F. A. Walker, c. 1880's	21- 28

Can Openers

Crocodile, also bottle opener	$ 8- 11
Never-Slip, wooden handle	7- 10
None Such, also corkscrew	7- 10
Sprague, tempered-steel blade	8- 11
Ten-in-One, also fish scaler, vegetable peeler	11- 15

Cookie Cutters

Tin (Illus.), average price, each	$ 1- 2

Cookie Molds

Depending on age and condition	$37- 47

Cork Screws

Bessemer Steel, tinned, No. 079	$ 7- 12
Champagne opener, buttonhook combination, c. 1870's	18- 22
Listerine, thin wire, c. 1930's	6- 10
Wier, Lazy Arms, c. 1880's	45- 52
Williamson's steel tempered, nickel-plated	7- 9

Dippers

Enameled ware	$ 9- 12
Gourd, 15″ handle, 1-pc., c. 1860's	27- 35

Egg Beaters

A & J high-speed beater, c. 1923	$13- 21
Cassidy-Fairbanks, c. 1930	16- 22
Holt's, Pat. 1899	12- 17
Ladd, 4 sizes, each	12- 16
Merry Whirl, c. 1916	17- 20
F. A. Walker, c. 1870's	17- 25
Whipwell, c. 1920	14- 26

Flour Sifters

Earnshaw's Patent, tin, c. 1870's	$15- 19
Tin, double lid, Uneek Utilities Co.	18- 22
Tin w/wire and screen mesh, c. 1915	14- 20
Wood, Blood's improved flour sifter, c. 1860	101-110

Food Choppers

Cast steel, C. W. Dunlop, c. 1890	$13- 16

Cast steel, J. B. Foote Foundry 9- 15
Double Action, No. 60 .... 11- 18
Nickeled steel, tubular handle, rocker blades 11- 16

Graters

BME No. 620, fastens to table, c. 1920's $14- 20
Nutmeg, Edgar, c. 1898 ...... 13- 20
Radish, wood handle, pierced tin, c. 1910 .... 13- 19
Revolving type, Enos Stimpson, c. 1880's 26- 29
Stamped and punched tin, c. 1910 .... 15- 20
Tin and wire, All-in-One, c. 1940's 9- 12

Ice Cream Freezers

Arctic $42- 50
Blizzard, single action, white cedar pail, c. 1900's 52- 60
Frezo, c. 1910, 6 qt. 45- 54
Gooch, Cincinnati 50- 57
White Mountain Freezer Co., triple motion, tin-plate pail .. 44- 51

Ice Picks

Coca-Cola $12- 19
Hurwood, c. 1910 .... 9- 13
Stanley 10- 13
White Mountain 9- 12

Juicers

Average price, each .... 75¢- 2

Kettles

Brass, wrought, c. mid-19th century $130-142
Cast iron, c. 1850's 32- 37
Cast iron, Holland's 31- 40
Copper, wrought, c. early 19th century 122-131
Enamel ware, 1 qt. 27- 37

Ladles

Brass, early $62- 70
Copper, early 61- 71
Onyx, enameled ware, 12" 20- 27

Lid Lifters

Average price .... $ 2- 4

Mashers

Beetle, maple, early $24- 29
Herb, maple, early 47- 54
Potato, aluminum, c. 1920 .... 19- 28
Potato, cherry, early 51- 60

Matchbox Holders

Aluminum, embossed, wall-type $11- 17
Brass, pedestal base, round ... 36- 41
Tin, painted, "Matches," c. 1910 .... 11- 18

Universal Stoves, cast iron, wall-type 42- 47

Miscellaneous

Apple roaster, tin reflecting oven, c. 1850's $91-100
Baller, nickel-plated, wooden handle 9- 12
Bird nest fryer, tin/wire mesh, c. 1930 .... 9- 16
Border mold, tin, fruit design .. 13- 17
Bread board, maple, 19th century 31- 37
Cabbage cutter, maple frame, steel blade 59- 66
Carpet beater, woven wire, The Niagara 28- 34
Cheese cutter, wire, c. 1920's . 9- 11
Egg glasses, F. A. Walker, c. 1870's 54- 60
Egg scale, Acme, c. 1924 ..... 18- 24
Ice shaver, Logan and Strobridge 13- 17
Ice tongs, handwrought, c. 1860's 32- 38
Pie lifter, tin, c. 1900 .... 17- 24
Pie stacker, 3-layer, c. 1920's . 19- 25
Raisin seeder, Pat. 1891 ...... 21- 26
Skillet, tin, mid-19th century .. 49- 55
Slop urn, indurated fiber, c. 1898 .... 27- 33
Vegetable skimmer, wood handle 15- 19

Pans

Cake, cast iron $34- 40
Corn stick, cast iron 29- 36
Farina boiler, tin, 3-part, 4 qt. . 23- 28
Muffin, cast iron, 8 cup 27- 33

Pot/Pan Scrapers

Babbitt's Cleanser $18- 24
Better Butter, Fairmont Creamery 26- 29
King Midas Flour 21- 27
Sunshine Finishes 23- 28

Push Handle Whippers

Galvanized, thumb handle on side $15- 20
Push-handle type, wooden handle 14- 20

Rolling Pins

Glass, screw-on tin cap $19- 25
Maple, handmade, early 30- 36
Meissen Onion pattern 45- 50

Salt Boxes

Glass w/wooden lid $37- 44
Pottery, wooden lid 31- 37

Spice Boxes

Cabinet, wood, 8 drawers $69- 77
Tin, jappaned designs, 7 round cans in large can w/lid 70- 77

Tray, japanned tin, strap handle 29- 35

Teakettles

Brass, early $82- 91
Copper, early 19th century 73- 81
Ironstone, English, c. 1870's . . 51- 60

Tinware

Available in every gadget and utensil; all sizes, shapes, and prices.

Traps

Mouse, wheel-type, c. 1890's . . $37- 47
Rat, cam, retinned, 6″ × 11″ . . . 32- 37

Waffle Irons

Crescent, wood handles $49- 58
Griswold Mfg. Co., c. 1920's . . 35- 44
Wrought iron, early 19th century 81- 86

Washboards

M. C. Cable, hardwood frame . . $26- 34
Glass Duke, glass board, hardwood frame 34- 40
Sani-Steel, sheet steel 28- 34

Suggested reading: *Kitchens and Gadgets 1920 to 1950,* Jane Celehar, Wallace-Homestead Book Company.

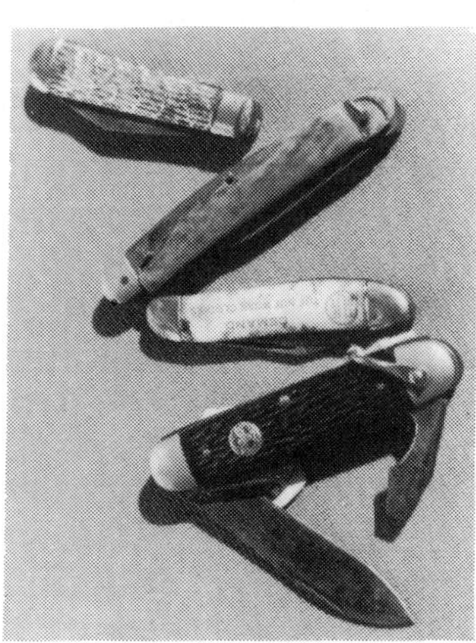

Knives

Knives

A couple of things have made knives a "hot" collectible: the 1965 government regulation that all cutlery must have the country of origin stamped on it, and the Gun Control Act of 1968 that put terrible restrictions on serious gun collectors. Whatever, knives are swapped by the tens of thousands each year and prices change almost too rapidly to mention. But we will anyway. "Cut away from your thumb!" if you don't agree with us. See **Clubs and Publications,** this Price Guide.

Anvil

3-blade (Illus.) $10- 14

Buck Knives

Pathfinder, #105, phenolic handle, 5″ long 30- 37
Woodsman, #102, phenolic handle, 4″ long 26- 33
Wrangler, #301, nonslip grip, 3¼″ long 28- 35

Camco

2-blade (Illus.) $10- 14

Case

Baby Copperhead, #62109X, rough black handle, 1940-1951 . . . . 70- 78
Barlow, #A62009½, slick bone handle, 1979 . . . . 23- 29
Barlow, #62009 SH, XX, 1940-1945, black compo handle 105-113
Copperhead, XX, green bone handle, 1950's-1965 . . . . 62- 70
Electrician's knife, #12031, walnut handle, before 1950 . . . . . 59- 67
Fisherman's knife, #32095 F SS XX, yellow compo handle, 1950-1965 . . . . 33- 41
Greenskeeper's knife, #4247K XX, white compo handle, before 1965 235-250
Hammerhead, #P159LSSP, black pakkawood handle, 1977 . . . . 42- 50
Hawkbill, XX, walnut handle, 1950-1965 . . . . 33- 40
Sharkstooth, #7197 L SS, black pakkawood handle, 1970's . . 58- 67
Sodbuster Jr., #G13755, pakkawood handle, 1970's 37- 44
Toledo Scale, #T3105SS, brass handle, 1973 . . . . 89- 97
Trapper, XX, stag handle, 1950-1965 116-124
Whittler, XX, red bone handle, 1940-1955 118-126

Cattaraugus

The Deer Slayer, #12134, stag handle $42- 50
King of the Woods, #2000, stag handle 38- 46

Ka-Bar

#5212 J, bone stag handle $56- 63
#6221, rough black handle 32- 38
#6226, bone stag handle 57- 64
#6232½, delrin handle 12- 17
#T253, celluloid handle 25- 33
Yellowstone Park, #T118, cream celluloid handle 36- 44

Maher and Grosh

Colorado stock knife, pearl handles, 4½″ long $287-295
Skinning knife, wooden handles, 4⅝″ long 72- 80

New York

Army knife, #4225, stag handle, 3⅜″ long $163-172
Corn knife, ivoryshell handle, 1 blade 52- 60
USA office knife, #200, ivoryshell handle........... 66- 73

Remington

R-698, Hawkbill $71- 80
R-892, Easy Open 163-173
R-1608, Budding knife 58- 65
R-2111, Electrician's 79- 86
R-4723, Official Girl Scout 82- 90
R-6554, Lobster 77- 85
R-6673, Congress............ 135-143

Robeson

Bulldog, #222050, rosewood handle $164-172
Office knife, #423405, white pyralin handle 37- 44
Pocketeze, #323480, black pyralin handle, 3⅜″ long 42- 48
Woodcraft, #633875, bone stag handle 142- 151

Schrade Cutlery

Equal End Jackknife, #C3-242, bone stag handle $84- 92
Esquire, #C3-709SHA, stainless steel handle............... 33- 40
Muskrat skinning knife, #C3-787, bone stag handle, 4″ long................... 83- 91
Serpentine penknife, #C3-708, stag handle, 2 blades 46- 53
Shapleigh, #E104C, striped celluloid handle 163-171

Valley Forge

Boy Scout, #0868, 4 blades, stag handle $69- 75
Junior Boy Scout, #438, 4 blades, stag handle 57- 63

Wilbert Cutlery

Dakota cowboy's knife, #6L17149, 3 blades, stag handle $91-100
Gentlemen's jackknife, #6L16807, stag handle, 3⅜″ long 70- 76
Teamster's knife, #6L16837, cocoa handle 58- 66
Texas Toothpick, #6L16939, stag handle, 3⅞″ long 77- 85

Winchester

Cattle knife, #H3646P, ebony handle, 3⅝″ long $218-230
Office knife, #2079, white celluloid handle 109-117
#2631, 2 blades, ebony handle, 3¼″ long 98-106
#2907, 2 blades, stag handle, 4¼″ long 545-565

(Note: Keep in mind that millions of knives were made and we can't mention all the companies. Colt, Empire, Excelsior, Holley, Honk Falls, Jordan, Kamphaus, Keenite . . . we could go on all day!)

Edwin M. Knowles

See **American Dinnerware**.

Koreopolis Glass

Koreopolis Glass

The vase illustrated here is shown because too many people, dealers and collectors alike, are confusing it with Lalique, a fine art glass. The illustrated vase was made in Koreopolis, Pennsylvania, in the late 1800's.

Candlesticks, cream/white, pink poppies, 10½″ high, pair $47-53
Vase, cream/white, pink poppies, 10″ high (Illus.) 54-60

IF it were Lalique, it would be worth ten times as much.

Kutani

This goes back to the 1500's. Artists who decorate this fine porcelain are known as "human treasures," they're that good. What you find today is fairly new, but it's all fine merchandise. 20th-century Kutani prices vary between $45 and $225.

Vase (Illus.) $100-108

Kutani

Lace

Lace

Filet, Irish crochet, appliqué, tatting — if you make dolls' costumes, look for it at estate sales, etc.

Homer Laughlin

See **American Dinnerware.**

Law Enforcement

F.B.I.

- G-Man badge, pot metal, 1930's .... $ 3- 4
- Melvin Purvis Secret Operators Manual (Illus.) 26-31
- Photo of J. Edgar Hoover, "signed" 3- 5

Handcuffs

- Daley's patent w/key $55-64
- Most sets w/key, working, each .. 40-47

Police Badges

- Most cities/counties, authentic, each $18-24

Sheriff

- Hat, campaign style, 1940's $35-42

Lead Crystal Ware

Simply, crystal glassware that rings when "pinged" because it contains lead oxide, a metallic element. Most of what you find is new but it's well made. See **Fostoria, Fenton,** and **Imperial.**

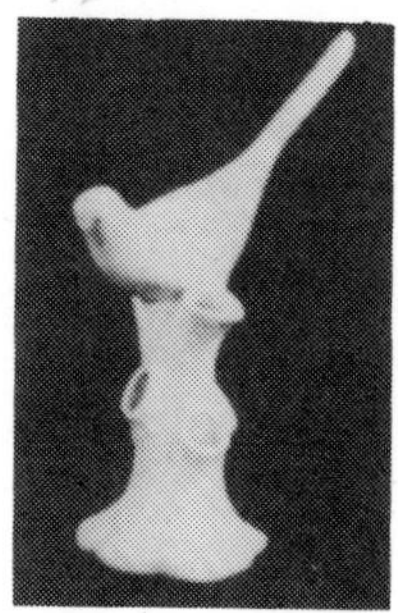

Lenox China

Lenox China

Lenox, Inc. was founded in 1906. Earlier efforts a few years before ended in failure. World War I made it difficult to obtain foreign-made china and Lenox prospered, especially after President Woodrow Wilson ordered china for the White House. The firm produced more than 3,000 different shapes by World War II. Many back marks were used.

Artware/Giftware

Ashtrays

- Shape #2030, solid coral, wreath mark 15- 19
- Shape #2399, cobalt, wreath mark 11- 14
- Shape #2427, yellow/gold trim, wreath mark 14- 18

Bouillon cups/saucers

- Shape #175, scalloped rim, fancy handles, undecorated, palette mark 17- 23
- Shape #628, transfer decorated, vegetables, gold trim, palette mark 20- 26
- Shape #633, undecorated, palette mark 11- 15

Bowls

- Shape #11, lotus leaf style, top, coral, base, white, wreath 64- 70
- Shape #23, ruffled rim, hand-painted, cupids/hearts, palette 109-116
- Shape #92, ruffled top, hand painted pink roses, red palette mark 75- 82

Shape #553, undecorated, palette mark 18- 24

Butter Pats

Item #176, gold trim, hand-painted pink roses, wreath mark 28- 33

Item #178, 3¼″, gold trim, palette mark 17- 21

Candlesticks

Shape #147, 10½″, brushed-gold trim, wreath mark, pr. . . . 84- 90

Shape #156, 1¾″, attached underplate, ring handle, ruffled rim, hand-painted flowers/blue background, palette mark 84- 90

Shape #250, 5⅛″, undecorated, palette mark, pr. 44- 51

Chocolate pots

Shape #107, 8″, undecorated, palette mark 75- 82

Shape #842, 11″, undecorated, wreath mark 49- 53

Cigarette boxes

Shape #2424, white w/Lenox rose trim, wreath mark 28- 33

Shape #3006, relief floral design on top, rose design on bottom, wreath mark 28- 33

Shape #3018, rounded corners, ribbing, apple blossom, wreath 39- 43

Shape #3033, rounded corners, Lenox rose, wreath mark 39- 43

Coffeepots

Shape #108, 8″, hand-painted yellow daffodils/green background, gold trim, artist-signed, C.A.C. palette mark . . . 56- 62

Shape #371, 10″, square base, yellow roses/buds, gold trim, no mark 19- 26

Shape #542½, 6½″, undecorated, wreath mark 29- 34

Cups/saucers

Shape #2, 2¼″, ribbed, ornate handle, gold trim, palette mark 28- 33

Shape #5, 2″, swirled rib, undecorated, palette mark 24- 29

Shape #162, 1½″, double-ring handle, large red roses, gold trim, palette mark 34- 39

Shape 633D, plain white, wreath mark 13- 17

Shape #841, gold trim, palette mark 18- 24

Ewers

Shape #33, 8¼″, gold-trimmed handle, brushed gold on rim, green wreath mark 109-115

Shape #40, 10″, undecorated, palette mark 116-125

Shape #43, 10″, beige, gold on handles and rims, C.A.C. wreath mark 262-270

Fern pots/planters

Shape #173, 3″, bulbous, ruffled rim, hand-painted violets, C.A.C. lavender palette mark . 109-117

Planter, shape #2400, white w/blue handles, wreath mark . 57- 64

Planter, shape #3019, white embossed, light pink background, wreath mark 70- 78

Horns of Plenty

Shape #70, 4½″, plain white, wreath mark 27- 33

Shape #2442, 10″, plain white, wreath mark 39- 45

Shape #2443, 8¼″, blue/white, wreath mark 56- 63

Jugs

Shape #357, 6″, grapes/blackberries, gold handle, palette mark 109-116

Shape #359, 6″, berries, gold trim on spout and handle, lavender palette mark 134-140

Shape #362, 6″, vines decor, C.A.C. palette mark 160-168

Match holders

#2425, undecorated, wreath mark 34- 39

#2425, gold trim, wreath mark . . 34- 39

Mugs

Shape #251, 4⅞″, undecorated, palette mark 19- 24

Shape #252, 5″, hand-painted grapes, gold handle, purple palette mark 55- 62

Shape #253, 5″, monk scene, palette mark 46- 53

Shape #255, 5½″, fruit decor, gold handle/trim, palette mark 83- 91

Pitchers

Shape #24, 5″, coral/white handle, wreath mark 29- 35

Shape #64, 7¼″, "mask" style, green/white, palette mark 74- 81

Shape #352, 5¼″, fruit decor, gold trim, handle inside, transition mark 262-271

Shape #467, 8″, undecorated, C.A.C., green palette mark . . . 71- 80

Salt dips

Shape #103, 1¾″, undecorated, palette mark 7-10

Shape #236, 2¼″, pale green, gold trim, C.A.C. transition . . . 13- 17

Salt shakers

Shape #215, 2½″, pink roses, gold trim, no mark 11- 15

Shape #531, 3″, roses, gold trim, palette mark 9- 14

Shape #585, 3½″, roses, gold trim, palette mark, pr. 30- 38

Sherbet cup

Shape #12, double handled, ruffled rim, floral decor, palette mark 34- 39

Sugar and creamer
Shape #38, raised gold-paste trim, C.A.C. lavender palette mark 133-140

Teapots, tobacco jars, trays, vases, and urns — many were made; look for C.A.C. (Ceramic Art Co.) and palette marks.

Dinnerware

Literally hundreds of patterns have been made and a lot are still being produced. Indicative patterns and indicative prices are listed here for the reader's benefit. If you're seriously into collecting Lenox, buy a book and study.

Adrienne; Apple Blossom; Arrowhead; Autumn; Bellevue Sea Green; Capri; Cattails; Chanson; Charmaine; Colonnade Gold; Fairmount; Firesong; Florida; Gadroon Rose; Glenthorne; Golden Gate; Imperial; Lenox Rose; Majestic; Mandarin; Meredith; Ming; Mount Vernon; Orleans; Pavlova; Pine; Princess; Rock Garden; Sonnet; Standard Plain; Trent; Washington/Wakefield; Westchester; Windsor.

Bread and butter plates, each $8.50-11.50
Chocolate pots, each 73- 90
Coffeepots, each 73- 90
Cups/saucers, set 19- 28
Demitasse cups/saucers, set 13- 18
Dinner plates, each 16- 22
Gravy boats, each 44- 59
Salad/dessert plates, each .. 11- 15
Soup/salad bowls, each 13- 20
Sugar/creamers, set 55- 70
Teapots, each 48- 60
Vegetable bowls, large, oval, each 34- 42

Figurines

Angel, shape #2764, 4⅛″, wreath mark .... $ 96-105
Birds, two shapes, crested, not crested, white, most common color: blue, pink, and green; yellow considered rare.
Jay, tail down, small, 3⅝″, #1790, blue 29- 34
Robin, tail up, small, 3⅛″, #1789, green 34- 40
Bonbon dish w/cover, bird finial, #2363, 5″, blue/pink 81- 90
Elephant, shape #2120, 9½″, white, glazed, wreath mark .. 160-170
Fish, shape #2912, green, 4½″, green wreath mark 86- 94
Flower holder, tree w/bird, #2434, 9″, white bird, coral tree, 9″ (Illus.)............. 79- 88
German shepherd, shape #3166½, 9″ white, glazed, wreath mark 158-166
Nipper (His Master's Voice), salt/peppers, set 29- 37
Penguin, shape #1827, 4⅛″, white, wreath mark......... 41- 49
Rabbit, shape #2911, 5⅜″, white, glazed, wreath mark .. 62- 71
Schnauzer, shape #2877-78 (running or sitting), blue or white, 3⅛″ or 4½″, wreath mark................... 53- 68
Seal, shape #2727, white, wreath mark 76- 84
Swan, shape #59, 2¾″, coral, wreath mark 24- 28

Swans still being made, available in 2″, 4″, 6″, and 8″; prices vary accordingly.

Toby Mugs (expensive!)

William Penn, undecorated, white, wreath mark.........$109-118
William Penn w/Bailey, Banks, & Biddle, mark 185-270
Teddy Roosevelt, decorated, letter P in shield (Edward Penfield, designer) and wreath mark 465-490
George Washington, large, undecorated, wreath mark 445-480

Letter Opener

Letter Openers

From time immemorial, every material was used to make this item, even plastic. Great fun to collect!

Average price, depending on age, condition, type of material.......$1-4

License Plates

License Plates

Since the early 1900's these have been collectible. The early plates, porcelain-on-metal, bring brisk prices today. All plates are in demand, from the 1900's until World War II. See **Clubs and Publications,** this Price Guide.

Porcelain on metal, Pennsylvania, 1907 . . . . $48-54
Tin, any state, 1900 to 1915 23-30
Tin, any state, 1920's to 1940's . . 15-23
1950's on 2- 3

Lighter Than Air Collectibles

Lighter Than Air Collectibles

Photos, menus, dishes. Anything to do with the zeppelins that flew across the Atlantic in the 1930's is being sought out by collectors.

Creamer, from Graf Zeppelin, 1930's $15-23
Menu from same airship 7-10
Post card showing the inventor of the zeppelin (Illus.) 9-11
Record, 78 rpm, describing crash of the zeppelin Hindenburg at Lakehurst, N.J., May 6, 1937 . . . 20-28

We call them dirigibles and they love to fly over football fields.

Limoges China

See **American Dinnerware.**

Limoges China

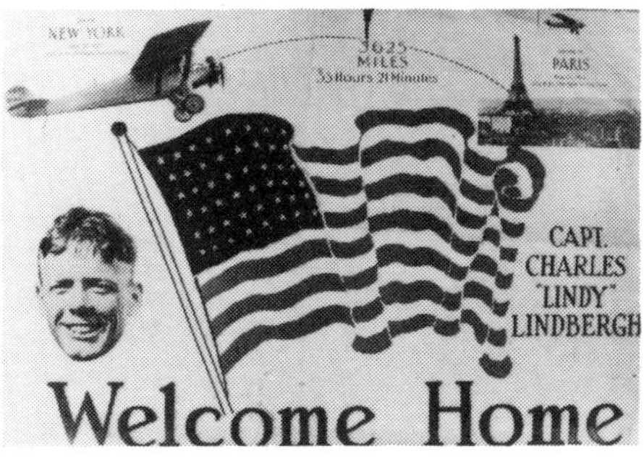

Lindbergh!

Photo Courtesy of
Hake's Americana & Collectibles

Lindbergh!

Anything to do with this **great** American is highly collectible today.

Small poster — "Welcome Home" $9-12
Kidnapping of Lindbergh baby press photos, each 7-10

Linens

Some very beautiful Irish and Portuguese linen is showing up at shows. Look for tablecloths, napkin sets, doilies, even bedspreads. Dirt can usually be removed by washing. Look for holes or worn spots by holding up to the light.

Linens

Little Orphan Annie

Little Orphan Annie

She's certainly well preserved for her age, seeing as how Annie first appeared in a comic strip in the *New York Daily News* in 1924. Since then, countless thousands of toys, comic books, television shows, movies, and books have been produced about Annie. Now a highly successful musical based on the comic strip has made everyone "Annie conscious."

Annie & Sandy, plaster, c. 1930's (Illus.) . . . . $ 9-12
Rummy cards, c. 1935 11-14
Crayon & coloring book, McLoughlin Bros. c. 1933 11-15
Ovaltine mug, plastic, c. 1930's (Illus.) 12-18
Annie kerchief, radio premium, c. 1930's 13-20
Orphan Annie "premium" comic book 15-20
Map of Simmons Corners 30-40
Sheet music, Irving Berlin, Inc. . . 8-11
1937 "Secret Society Code Book" 28-36

Little Orphan Annie

Photos Courtesy of
Hake's Americana & Collectibles

Lladro Porcelains

Lladro Porcelains

These modern-day figurines are made in Labernses Blanques, Spain. All have an "L" and a number, as well as the name "Lladro" on the bottom. They are made in a glossy finish and a matte finish.

Angel with flute, glossy finish, #L-1233 .... $140-150
Ballerina, glossy finish, #L-4855 194-203
Boy kissing, glossy finish, #L-4869 .... 55- 63
Boy thinking, glossy finish, #L-4876 .... 84- 92
Boy with dog, glossy finish, #L-4522 101-110
Boy with donkey, glossy finish, #L-1181 185-198
Coy, glossy finish, #L-5011 ... 86- 94
Devotion, glossy finish, #L-11278 262-270
Dreamer, glossy finish, #L-5008 85- 95
Eskimo boy, matte finish, #L-2007B 112-119
Eskimo girl, matte finish, #L-2008B 112-119
Feeding the ducks, glossy finish, #L-4849 172-182
Girl with bonnet, glossy finish, #L-1147 (Illus.) 104-113
Girl with geese, glossy finish, #L-4568 144-154
Girl with lamb, glossy finish, #L-4505 .... 75- 84
Hebrew student, glossy finish, #L-4684 158-167
My dog, glossy finish, #L-4893 156-165
My little pet, glossy finish, #L-4994 132-142
Naughty, glossy finish, #L-5006 85- 95
Nuns, glossy finish, #L-4611 .. 104-113
Shepherdess, glossy finish, #L-4835 144-153
Veterinarian, glossy finish, #L-4825 158-167

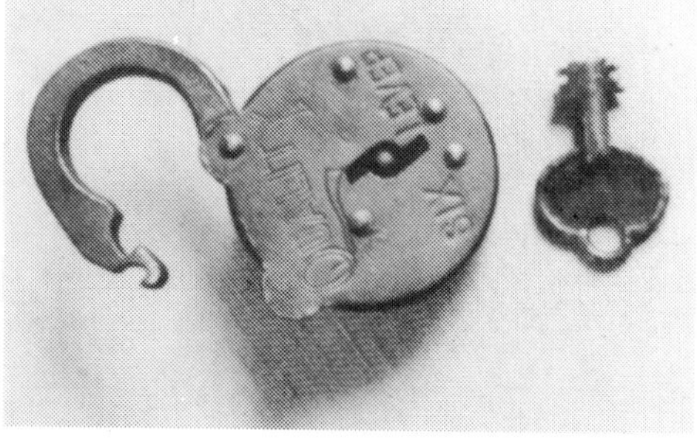

Locks/Keys

Locks/Keys

Locks

This is one of the fastest growing collectibles in the world. Some locks date back to the days of the early Egyptians. An Englishman invented the tumbler lock in the 1700's, and Lynus Yale invented the pin tumbler cylinder lock in the mid-1800's, thus changing the lock business forever. The best locks were made of brass, bronze, copper, steel, or a combination of two metals. For locks with original keys, add 20 percent to the prices listed; for railroad locks with original keys, add $6–7 more. Watch out for reproductions. See **Clubs and Publications,** this Price Guide.

Bicycle

Average selling price, depending on working condition and whether it has a key or the right combination $5- 11

Combination

American Keyless Lock Co., No-Key	$37- 46
Gougler, zinc alloy	6- 9
Miller Lock Co., iron frame	27- 34
Slaymaker, Barry Co.	9- 14
Yale & Towne Mfg. Co., Yale	9- 15

Two Lever

Corbin	$12- 19
Eagle	13- 21
Fraim, E. T. Fraim Lock Co.	8- 12
Master	8- 12
U.S. Mail	13- 20

Three Lever

Corbin	$19- 24
Eagle	11- 17
Master	9- 13
Miller, Protector	10- 17
Russell & Irwin Co., Guardian	11- 17
Yale, various sizes	9- 17

Four Lever

Corbin	$ 29- 37
Eagle	22- 30
Fraim, Western Union	37- 43
Yale, various sizes	31- 40

Six Lever

Corbin, Iron Clad	$12- 18
Edwards	11- 17
Miller, New Champion	11- 18
Quality (Illus.)	24- 33
Sargent & Co., Green Leaf	29- 36
Slaymaker, Standard	11- 19

Eight Lever

Blue Chief	$ 13- 23
Eagle, Mastadon	13- 20
Sargent	12- 19
Slaymaker	13- 20

Miscellaneous

Jailhouse, iron, large key, c. 1880	$92-107
Screw key, hand-forged, c. 1850	49- 54
Screw key, hand-forged, Mexican reproduction	12- 18
Stateroom door, *Queen Mary*	47- 55

Pin Tumbler

Corbin, various sizes	$ 11- 22

Keys

Shown here because there are thousands of different kinds. The old Spanish dungeon keys are quite collectible. Keys are a fun item to collect and decorate with. Too many to give specific prices.

Keys

Average price	$2- 3
Brass, early 1800's	8-11
Folding type, nickel-plated	7-11
Iron, jail type, large	14-20

Luggage

Luggage

Old suitcases, trunks, even steamer trunks — some folks like to collect them.

Camelback trunk, child's, mid-1800's	$ 90- 98
Steamer trunk, 4′ high, with original wooden hangers, 1930's	35- 45
Suitcase, camelback, mid-1800's (Illus.)	100-107

Lunchboxes

Some have the original thermos bottles intact; some don't. But the tin boxes make neat pocketbooks, whatever.

Average price	$ 3- 5
Batman and Robin lunchbox (Illus.)	20-24
Yellow Submarine lunchbox	15-22

Lunchboxes

Photo Courtesy of
Hake's Americana & Collectibles

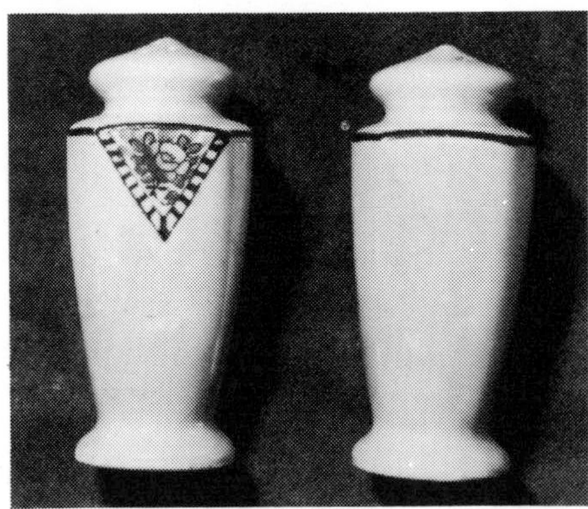

Made in Japan

Made in Japan

What **wasn't** made there? Look for pieces marked "Noritake," "Nippon," "Occupied Japan." Not as abundant as it used to be ten years ago, but you can still load your basket at most Flea Markets or shows and the price is still right on most of it. The salt/pepper set illustrated here is marked "Made in Japan" and goes for $11-15.

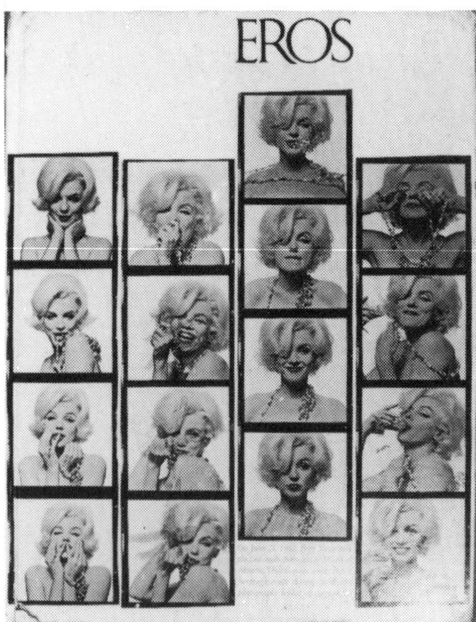

Magazines/Newspapers

Magazines/Newspapers

These are fun to collect because of their advertisements, illustrations, personalities, and articles. Usually, magazines and newspapers are sold in lots. Special collectors have a tendency to tear out special sections such as paper dolls, prints, or covers.

Magazines

The American, 1920's to 1934, each	$ 1.50- 2
American Artist, 1930's-1950's, each	4- 5
The American Boy, July 1911	3- 4
American Heritage, Vol. 1, No. 1	27-32
American Mercury, 1927	3- 5
American Pigeon Journal, 1938-1940, each	2-2.50
American Woman, Vol. 1, No. 1, March 1937	9-13
Antiques Journal, various issues, 1950's, each	1-1.50
Architectural Forum, 1940's-1950's, each	6-11
Better Homes and Gardens, 1920's, each	1- 2
Collier's, 1930's—1940's, each	2- 4
Cosmopolitan, 1930's-1940's, each	2- 7
Country Gentleman, 1930's-1940's, each	1-1.50
Eros, Vol. 1, No. 1	40-54
Good Housekeeping, 1930's-1940's, each	2- 3
Ladies' Home Journal, 1940's-1970's, each	1-2.50
Life, 1937-1939, each	6-11
Life, 1950's-1960's, each	1.75-2.75
Mechanix Illustrated, 1930's-1960's, each	75¢-1.50
New Yorker, 1930's-1940's, each	1.50- 2
Parents, 1930's, each	2.50- 3
Popular Mechanics, 1940's-1950's, each	1.50- 2
Progressive Farmer, 1920's-1930's, each	1.25-1.75
Reader's Digest, 1930's-1940's, each	75¢-1.25
Scribner's, 1920's-1930's, each	1.50- 2
Spinning Wheel, 1950's-1960's, each	1.25-1.50
Vogue, 1920's, each	2- 3
Woman's Home Companion, 1930's, each	2.50-3.50

Newspapers

Headlines establish prices here. There are countless millions of old newspapers around today. "HUN QUITS WAR!" or "EDWARD VIII ABDICATES" — that type headline makes a newspaper worth more than scrap weight.

Suggested reading: *Paper Collectibles, Identification and Value Guide, Second Edition,* Robert D. Connolly, Books Americana.

Magic

Jack Armstrong's "Magic Answer Box" (Illus.)	$12-16
"Houdini" poster, paper, 1920's	10-14
"Mandrake the Magician" coloring book	6- 8
Trick rings, metal, four in the set, 3" diameter	6- 9

Look for trick cards, wands, and anything to do with magic.

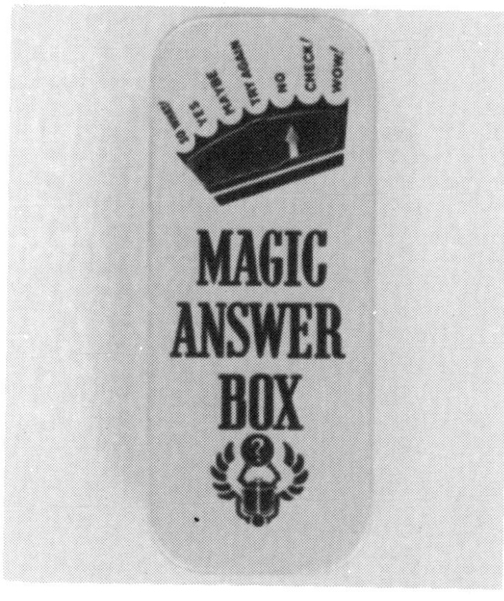

Magic

Photo Courtesy of
Hake's Americana & Collectibles

Magnifying Collectibles

Magnifying Collectibles

Three-power, round (Illus.)	$ 20- 27
Lens from old camera	8- 11
Three-power, rectangular (Illus.)	22- 26
Microscope, lab type, 1930's, 11" high	128-132

Marble

"A hard, crystalline or granular, metamorphic limestone, white or variously colored and sometimes streaked or mottled." Small statues, and bases such as the one illustrated, among other pieces, are fun to collect. Size, age, and weight set the price here.

Marble

Marbles

Glass companies in Pennsylvania and Ohio made the large glass marbles used by boys at the turn of the century. Some had colored stripes while others had animals inside. The larger are more collectible than the smaller. See **Clubs and Publications,** this Price Guide.

Agate, black/white, 1/2" dia.	$ 30- 35
Agate, brown/white, 7/8" dia.	29- 35
Agate, green/white, 3/4" dia.	25- 30
Bennington, mottled or fancy, 1 1/4" dia.	7- 9
China, bull's eye, 5/8" dia.	11- 15
China, leaves, 1/2" dia.	14- 17
China, leaves, 7/8" dia.	16- 19
Glass, 1940's on, per dozen (Illus.)	50¢-1
Goldstone, 5/8" dia.	34- 40
Kayo (comic strip), black/white	37- 42
Limestone, 5/8" dia.	9- 12
Multicolored swirl	15- 19
Sandy (comic strip), blue/white	35- 44

Marbles

Sulphide, baby (all positions) . .	125 +
Sulphide, boar	115 +
Sulphide, boy on stump	122 +
Sulphide, cat, lying down	125 +
Sulphide, cat, sitting	110 +
Sulphide, cow, grazing	122 +
Sulphide, frog	125 +
Sulphide, girl and dog	123 +
Sulphide, goat	95-103
Sulphide, lamb	88- 97
Sulphide, owl, wings spread . . .	145 +
Sulphide, ram	92-103
Sulphide, rooster, running	90-103
Sulphide, rooster, standing . . .	77- 84
Swirls, Latticinio, onionskin, each	73- 82

Suggested reading: *Collecting Antique Marbles,* Paul Baumann, Wallace-Homestead Book Company.

Mardi Gras

The trinkets that are thrown to the crowds by the people who ride on the floats are collectible, especially those items before 1941.

Beads, 1979, New Orleans (Illus.)	50¢-75¢

Mardi Gras

Mary Gregory Glass

Mary Gregory Glass

Lots of room for an argument here. Some say Mary Gregory never existed; records at the Sandwich Glass Co. on Cape Cod show that she did. Whatever, the original glass is hard to find. Delicate little children ages 5 to 12, always doing something — rolling a hoop, playing a horn, etc. **Always** white enameled figures. The European figures are **always** tinted. This is what you'll find most of today. Plus the repros! Reproduction Mary Gregory is harsh and modern-shaped.

Barber bottle, tinted figure of boy on swing, 5¼" high	$65-72
Box, silver-plated trim, tinted figure of girl picking flowers . . .	63-70

Cruet, tinted figure of boy (reproduction, 1960's) 10-14
Pitcher, tinted figure of girl on swing (harsh orange/red color, fake "cranberry," 1960's) 25-32
Tumbler, amber, tinted figure of boy w/flower, 3¾" high (Illus.) . 38-46
Vase, amber, modern shape, tinted figure, 5½" high (repro, 1950) 19-25
Vase, dark blue, white figure of girl w/hoop (repro, 1960's) 17-24
Vase, fake "cranberry," white figure of boy w/kite, 6¼" high . 19-25

So many, many fakes. DON'T buy it for old!

Masks

Photo Courtesy of
Hake's Americana & Collectibles

Masks

Paper, tin, and plastic! Halloween, birthdays, and surprise parties are **all** collectible!

"Kayo" paper mask............$ 6- 8
Wizard of Oz mask, tin 8-12
Tom Mix "premium" paper mask. 19-26
Witch from Snow White paper mask (Illus.)................. 7-10
Mickey Mouse face mask 27-34
Minnie Mouse face mask........ 26-33

Masonic Collectibles

Masonic Collectibles

Souvenirs of towns, state fairs, conventions, etc., usually made of red/clear glass. Popular from the late 1800's until World War I.

Goblet (Illus.) $24-30
Mug, Atlanta, 1907............. 27-32
Mug, 2 sword handles, Chicago, 1903 44-53

Match Boxes

Match Boxes

One, they're fun to collect; two, remove the matches.

Average price ....Free or 25¢-50¢

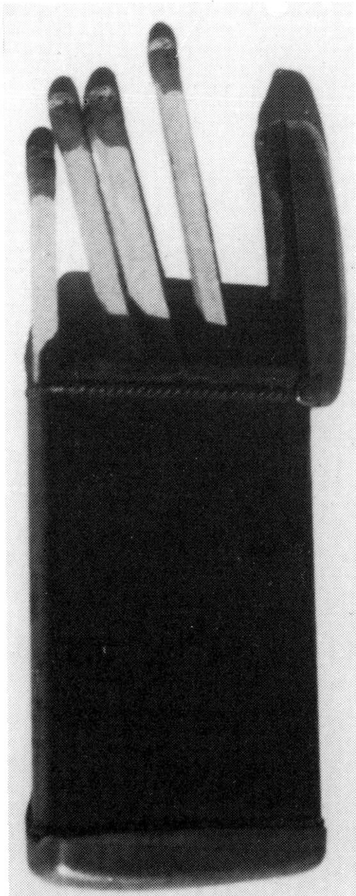

Match Holders

Match Holders

In the days of Lucifers or "house burners" (sulphur-headed matches), match holders were in vogue and were used to hold matches on the wall or the table. Used from mid-1800's until early 1930's. Many repros.

Bird, 4½" high, iron $45-52
Boots, china, green/yellow, 4½" high 47-53
Bulldog's head, porcelain, Austria 44-50
Butterfly, milk glass, 5" high 44-51
Cast iron, c. 1880's 35-42
Charlie Chaplin, clear glass (rare) 84-92
Cricket, brass, hinged lid 52-61
Dog, stump holds matches, iron . 50-60
Elephant, clear glass 50-58
Flower basket, iron 50-57
Grape leaf, 3" high, milk glass... 49-53

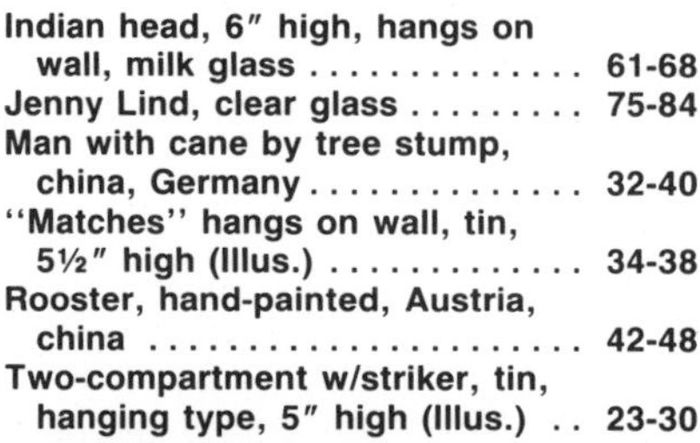

Indian head, 6" high, hangs on wall, milk glass 61-68
Jenny Lind, clear glass 75-84
Man with cane by tree stump, china, Germany 32-40
"Matches" hangs on wall, tin, 5½" high (Illus.) 34-38
Rooster, hand-painted, Austria, china 42-48
Two-compartment w/striker, tin, hanging type, 5" high (Illus.) .. 23-30

Matchbook Covers

Matchbook Covers

Remove the staple, throw away the matches, and mount the "cover" in an album. Some collectors have more than 100,000 "covers." Every restaurant, motel, business, etc. gives away matches. Great fun to collect, too.

Free or 10¢ to 50¢

Matchbox Labels

Old wooden matchboxes offer a "different" hobby for collectors.

Average price, per box with label, good condition .... 20¢-30¢

Matchbox Labels

Photo Courtesy of
Hake's Americana & Collectibles

Matchbox Toys

Matchbox Toys

Tootsietoy made thousands. The cars, trucks, and boats, whatever, come in a matchbox — thus the name.

Car and boat, 1940's $16-23
"D" type Jaguar, 1950's 19-22
Model "T" Ford, 1950's 17-21
Vauxhall Victor sedan, 1960's . . . 12-17

Hundreds of them still around and not expensive for the newer ones.

McCoy Pottery

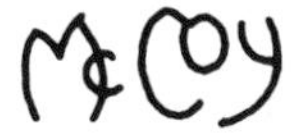

This pottery has been made in Roseville, Ohio, since 1910. In 1967 the firm was acquired by the Mt. Clemens (Michigan) Pottery Company. Early pieces are now becoming collectible. See **Clubs and Publications,** this Price Guide.

McCoy Pottery

Blossomtime 700 Line

Jardiniere, ivory, sq., 4″ tall $24-28
Planter, ivory 25-30
Vase, ivory, McCoy, 6¼″ 17-26
Vase, yellow, concave sides, 8″ . 24-31

Butterfly Line

Planter, rose (leaf relief only), 8″ $18-25
Spoon rest, green, NM USA 24-29

Cookie Jars

Bear #22 . . . . $65-70
Black antique stove 39-48
Blue windmill 28-38
Have a Happy Day (smile) 41-47
Honey bear 42-50
Mr. and Mrs. Owl 54-58
Rocking horse 57-62

Flowerpots

Dark green Double Beetle band . . $22-27
Green basketweave #2, 3¼″ 21-27
Green, long leaves and dots, 3½″ dia. × 3½″ tall, NM 19-24
Green, long leaves, two, 3 and 3¾″ dia., 2¾″, tall, NW 19-26
Orange Double Beetle band, 5″ . . 21-27

Springwood Line

Bowl, 4-ftd., pink, 6⅝″ dia., McCoy USA $17-25
Jardiniere, pink, 5⅜″, McCoy USA 26-29
Vase, green, round bottom, sq. top, 7¼″, McCoy USA 16-22

Swirl Line

Planter, orchid, ftd., 7″ long, McCoy USA $12-16
Vase, orchid, ftd., 7″ tall, McCoy USA 14-19

Tea Set Items

Creamer, pink/turquoise, matt, McCoy $11-16

Handled, ftd. vase, turquoise, Stylized Leaf and Twig, 9″ 26-32
S&H/Peppers, pr. 19-24
Swan vase, pink, 9″, McCoy..... 20-29
Leaf creamer, 2-tone green, #108 (Illus.) 15-24
Pinecone green/brown, 3-pc., McCoy 44-52
Pinecone green creamer 19-26
Pinecone green teapot and lid ... 28-32
Pinecone teapot, no lid, light crazing in and out............ 30-40
Tea set, 3-pc., green/brown 48-58
Teapot lid, as above 16-27

Vases

Butterfly vase, 7″, McCoy.......$24-29
Cornucopia, cream, light crazing, 7″, McCoy 24-32
Dark green vase, ftd., 10-sided, 7¼″ × 4½″, McCoy USA....... 22-31
Flowers and Leaf Blades, green, handled, 8″ 19-27

Medals, U.S. and Foreign

Medals, U.S. and Foreign

All countries are "medal happy." Some are valuable and others are junk.

British DSC (Distinguished Service Order).............$ 85-110
British DFC (Distinguished Flying Cross) 160-190
British, Crimea, 1854-1858 .... 14- 30
French, Croix de Guerre, 1940 . 55- 65
Good Posture, Transylvania ... 2- 12
U.S., Army, Medal of Honor, if authentic, 1862-1940 .... 650+
U.S., Army, DSC 27- 37
U.S., Navy, DSM............. 160-180
U.S., Marine Corps, good conduct 12- 17
U.S., Merchant Marine, DSM... 250-280
German, Iron Cross, 1918 (Illus.) 10- 13

Medical Items

Old instruments, bottles, prescriptions, books — all are of special interest today, especially to one allied with the field of medicine.

Ammonia Jug, c. 1863, 14″ high $6- 9
Amputating saw, mfgd. by Charrier's, wide blade, 10 oz., c. 1915 .... 45- 53
Apothecary funnel, copper, hanging ring, 9″ high 25-33
Apothecary funnel, glass, 7½″ high 14-19
Appendectomy retractor, mfgd. by Mayo, 12 oz., c. 1915 .... 19- 26
Arrow extractor, Bill's Arrow Forceps, mfgd. by Tiemann Co., c. 1895 .... 55- 65
Baume stick w/case, 10½″ long 5- 9
Betz stool, can be raised or lowered, white enamel, c. 1915 74- 83
Breast pump, rubber suction ball, 4″ high 8- 12
Bullet extractors: Bullet Seeker, Bullet Screw, American Bullet Forceps, Sayre's Vertebrated Bullet Probe, all mfgd. by Tiemann Co., 1880s to 1915, each 59- 67
Cachet kit (for making medicinal wafers), tin case, c. 1875, 12″ long................. 37- 48
Cork press, lever type, 4 different sizes, 9″ long 66- 73
Counter scale, 2 large brass pans, full set of weights 170-180
Dental forceps, Nos. 29, 31, 32, 33, 40, mfgd. by C. Ash & Sons, London, 1920, each ... 14- 23
Dentist's tooth key (or "turn key"), Spring Bolt, Rotating Fulcrum, mfgd. by Tiemann Co., c. 1888, each 73- 82
Display case, tin/wood, 3 drawers 89- 95
Doctor's bag, Pacific saddle bag, all original bottles, c. 1915 115-124
Doctor's bag, Long Drive Combination, complete 88- 94
Doctor's bag, Country Doctor, complete 75- 83

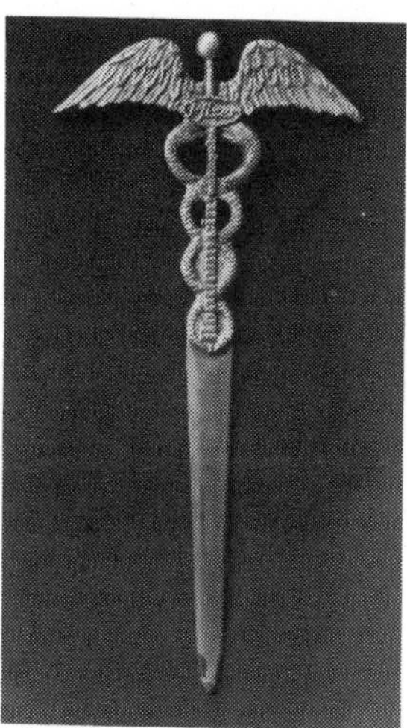

Medical Items

Drug mill 77- 86
Hand scale, wooden box, full set of weights 57- 63
Hearing aids: Currier's Duplex Conversation Tube, Ear of Dionysus, Corrugated Ear Trumpet, each 128-137
Hearing aids: Dipper Trumpet, London Hearing Horn, Conversation Tube, Dome Trumpet, each 70- 78
Hydrometer jar, hand-blown, 12″ high 24- 32
Letter opener (Illus.) 12- 17
Mentholatum lamp, brass, glass bowl, 6½″ high 27- 33
Microscope, brass, wooden case, 6″ high 31- 43
Mortar and pestle, brass 93-101
Mortar and pestle, porcelain (Illus.) 33- 42
Nebulizer, #1, wooden box, 7″ high 27- 35
Percolator, cylindrical, glass, hand-blown 9- 14
Pill machine, 16″ long 27-33
Pill roller, wood, 3″ dia. 28-34
Retractor, Fritch's, mfgd. by Tiemann Co., c. 1890 .... 8- 11
Stethoscopes: Barclay's, Burrow's, Hawksley's, Short Cedar, all mfgd. by Tiemann Co., 1880s, each 52- 63
Suppository machine, wooden case, c. 1880 .... 7- 11
Tablet mold, #10 (for making 50 1-grain tablets), box 17- 23
Urinometer, glass, c. 1905, 6″ long 5- 8
Vaporizer, steam, cardboard box, 6½″ high 18- 23

Suggested reading: ***Medical, Dental and Pharmaceutical Collectibles,*** **Don Fredgant, Books Americana.**

Mexican Glass

Mexican Glass

This glass has been around for years, cluttering up antiques shops and confusing buyers. It has been passed off as South Jersey, Sandwich, and other quality glass. Predominant colors are dark blue, amber, and light green. Always a rough pintil mark, but it's so crudely made it shouldn't fool anyone. Unfortunately, it does!

Bottle, 9″ high, dark blue (Illus.) . $33-38
Carafe, 6½″ high, amber, swirl pattern 26-30
Goblets, 4½″ high, dark blue, set of 6, all 45-52
Plates, 7½″ dia., light green, set of 12, all 72-79
Tumbler, dark blue, 4″ high, swirl pattern 9-13

Military Collectibles

Aviation

The Wright Brothers proved it could be done at Kitty Hawk, North Carolina,

Military Collectibles

1903. These are highly collectible.

Item	Low	High
Arm patches, USAF, World War II, average price, each	$ 2-	4
Charts, USAF, World War II, U.S. bases, each	6-	11
Flying helmet with goggles, World War I	45-	54
Flying jacket, Chinese/ American flag on back, World War II	240-	260
Propeller, wood, clock in center, World War I	270-	320
Rickenbacker Magazine (Illus.)	10-	13
Wings, USAF, World War II, sterling silver, pilot's	56-	74
Wings, Navy/Marines, World War II, gold-plated, pilot's	35-	45

Badges

The badges illustrated here are for British Army uniforms, World War II.

There are thousands of badges from every branch of the service. Usually $2 to $4 each.

Bayonets

Always a popular item with military buffs. Also, see Military, Japanese, Nazi Collectibles.

Item	Low	High
Illustrated: probably European, World War I	$ 38-	49

Japanese War Items

Anything to do with wars is collectible. Japanese military items are no exception. Most are from World War II.

Item	Low	High
Cigarette pack, "From Island of Attu, May 13, 1943" (Illus.)	$ 10-	15

Japanese War Items

Item	Low	High
Dagger, worn by Japanese officer, sharkskin handle	125-	135
Helmet, pith style, cork lined (Illus.)	60-	65
Japanese battle flag, white with red ball, 14″ × 19″	105-	120
Mine detector in mahogany box	145-	155
Pilot's helmet, name on peak	72-	77
Samurai sword, military issue	145-	154
Wind indicator, used on aircraft carrier (Illus.)	80-	88

Medals, U.S. and Foreign

Ever since the handmade silver medal was given by Congress to the three men responsible for the capture of a British officer connected with Benedict Arnold, the U.S. has been giving out medals for just about everything. The British, French, Italians, and Germans are also medal happy. It should be noted that any medal made of sterling silver has gone up in value, just for the silver content. See **Clubs and Publications,** this Price Guide.

Item	Low	High
British Burma Star, WW II	$ 18-	26
British Distinguished Service	145-	160
British Korea, 1950-53	31-	40
French Commemorative, WW I, sterling silver	260-	270
Imperial German Iron Cross, 1870, 2nd Class	127-	136
Italian Fascist, Eastern Front Cross, 1941-42	75-	84
Officer's blue cloth plate, 1870's, 59th Regiment	112-	119

Officer's plate, Devonshire Regiment, 1878	142- 152
Officer's plate, 16th Bedfordshire Regiment	562- 575
Polish Independence Cross, WW II	42- 51
Polish Military Service Medal, 1918-21	51- 61
Polish Monte Casion Cross (serial numbered), WW II	42- 50
U.S. Air Medal	17- 20
U.S. Army, Good Conduct	9- 13
U.S. Army, Medal of Honor, 1862-1904	1,700 +
U.S. Navy, Byrd Antarctic Expedition	240- 260
U.S. Navy, Civil War	37- 46
U.S. Navy, Medal of Honor	1,100 +
V.F.W. (Illus.), each	18- 26

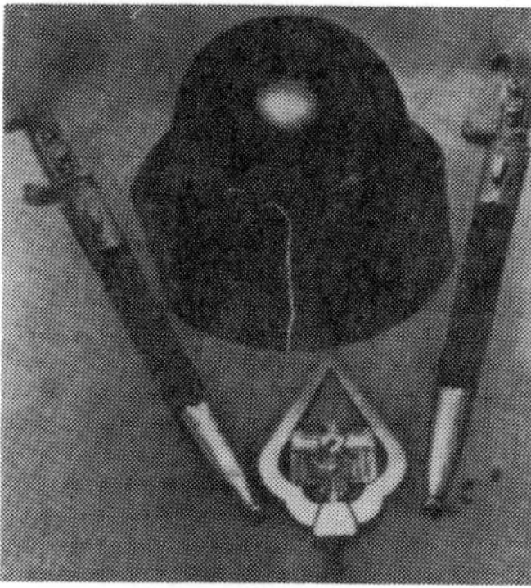

Nazi Items

Nazi Items

Hitler may have lost the war, but popularity of his military items is growing every day. They are so popular, in fact, that reproductions are beginning to appear on the market. See **Clubs and Publications (Military),** this Price Guide.

Afrika Corps Service Medal $	115 +
Armband, German Armed Forces ("Deutsch Wehrmacht"), black/yellow	77- 86
Armband, H. J. (Hitler Youth), bevo weave	86- 93
Army mess kit	92- 104
Bayonet, Nazi police eagle's head, bone-type grips (Illus.)	198- 215
Bayonet, police, eagle's head, etc. (Illus.)	188- 197
Belt buckle, swastika insignia	142- 151
Dagger, Army, w/eagle and swastika cross guard	296- 299
Dagger, carried by the Brown Shirts, wood grips, eagle, etc.	327- 333
Dagger, Hitler Youth, "Blut Und Ehre" on blade	350 +
Dagger, Luftwaffe, 1937 model, flying eagle on cross guard	385- 420
Doll, Storm Trooper, 11″ high, painted composition head	260- 270
Flag, 4′×7′, swastika and German Cross	177- 185
Helmet, Afrika Corps, tan camouflage	305- 318
Helmet, Luftschultz w/wings (Illus.)	115- 122
Helmet, Nazi police, chin strap, etc.	261- 270
Helmet, "R.L.B." (Air Defense League), parade type	475 +
Iron Cross, 2nd class	107- 112
"Kreta" cuff title — awarded to participants in battle for Crete	332- 340
Luftwaffe badge, pilot, marked "Imme"	481- 491
Mountain troops rucksack	118- 125
Peaked cap, Army infantry officer, silver cord, red piping	330- 340
Pith helmet, Afrika Corps, green felt body, both metal badges	171- 180
Tunic, Luftwaffe, officer's summer white, complete	1,100-1,300
Uniform, chaplain's Reichswehr tunic	550- 560
Uniform, medical officer's	410- 420
Uniform, Panzer Grenadier	380- 390

Milk Glass

Milk Glass

An opalescent glass, chalky white in color, some's old, some's new, and all collectible.

The piece shown here is new .... $2-3 each

So many repros it's hard to separate the wheat from the chaff. Go slow.

Miniatures

Miniatures

"The smaller the better!" Originally, miniatures were salesmen's samples because of the need to travel "light." Today, whatever suits your fancy.

Anvil, wood, ¾" high $12-17
Candlestick, brass, 2" high, 1950's 11-14
Dresser, maple, 3 drawers w/brass pulls, 14½" × 16½" × 8¼" 85-92
Elephant, ivory, 1¼" high 26-32
Frog, painted wood, 1½" high 21-27
Horse, rearing, wood, 2½" high 19-25
Owl, sterling silver, 1¼" high 28-34
Stein, ceramic, 1½" high (Illus.) 9-11
Turtle, painted wood, 2" long 13-17
Violin w/bow, carved wood, 2¼" overall 75-82
Walrus w/ivory tusks, 2½" long 45-48
Yinzell, brass, 2" high 16-22

Moonshine Collectibles

"White Lightning," "Old Pop Skull," "Splo," all describe a drink that will kill or cure you. The "Moonshiners" are still

Moonshine Collectibles

very active. They make it after dark, thus the name.

Copper coils $55-60
Copper hopper (kettle) 88-97

Don't drink it if you DON'T know its source. There is no quicker way to go blind. The paraphernalia to make it is collectible. But, don't go messin' around a man's still unless you're tired of breathing! You can get shot ten miles out of Knoxville or Pensacola or Oak Ridge.

Moorcroft Pottery

Moorcroft Pottery

W Moorcroft

This is a modern English pottery which, for some unexplainable reason, is highly collectible. Factory established in 1913

by William Moorcroft at Cobridge. Script signature.

Ashtray, red/yellow flowers, script signature	$ 55- 63
Basket, metal holder, 6″ dia., green flowers	88- 96
Bowl, blue/white decor, fruit	94-106
Bowl, pewter foot, 6¼″ dia., fruit decor, lavender/yellow/red/green (Illus.)	88- 95
Box, covered, orange/maroon, 4½″ dia.	93-102
Compote, green ground, purple flowers, 4½″ high	106-113
Cup/saucer, fruit decor, green script	75- 85
Inkwell, blue background, signed	100-107
Tea set: pot, sugar bowl, creamer, blue ground. All have pewter lids	322-332
Vase, bud, light/dark green, trees, 8″ high, script signature	240-250

Mortar and Pestle Collectibles

Mortar and Pestle Collectibles

These have been around for centuries, grinding herbs, roots, or grain into meal. What you'll find today are products of the late 19th and early 20th centuries.

Brass, late 19th century	$65-74
Cast iron, early 20th century	39-45
Drugstore type, ceramic, wood pestle (Illus.)	25-33
Maple, late 19th century	58-63
Soapstone, wooden pestle, WW I	32-38

Motorcycles

Probably this category shouldn't be in this Price Guide, but then who knows when they'll run into an ancient Harley-Davidson, an Indian, Excelsior Auto-Cycle, an Abriel, Norton, BSA, a Triumph, and even a Villiers? Well, we can all dream, can't we?

You'd pay dearly for one of the above, but it would be a classic if in any kind of condition. Keep looking.

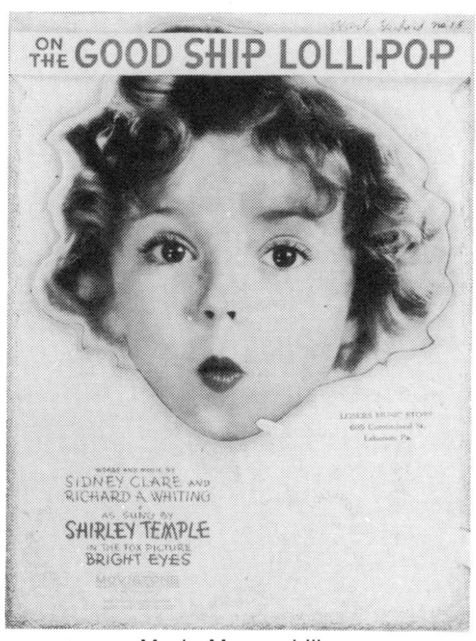

Movie Memorabilia

Movie Memorabilia

Just about everything is collectible. The stars of the 1930's and 1940's seem to stand out. Reproductions abound and the Supreme Court has just opened the door to unlimited copying by home video. See **Clubs and Publications,** this Price Guide.

Autographs

Price is for original; watch out for autopens.

Item	Low	High
Barrymore, John, signed document, 1934	$ 300-	335
Brice, Fanny, signature	300-	315
Ebsen, Buddy, signed photo, early	23-	27
Gable, Clark, signed document, contract	300-	315
Hepburn, Katherine, signed document, RKO contract	160-	170
Lowe, Edmund, signature	22-	27
Mansfield, Jayne, signature	130-	138
Muni, Paul, signed letter	36-	44
O'Brien, George, signature	13-	18
Powell, Eleanor, signed photo	21-	27
Raymond, Gene, signed photo	21-	26
Swanson, Gloria, signature	17-	22
Winters, Roland, signed photo	22-	27
Wyatt, Jane, signed photo	18-	23

Costumes/Props

Item	Low	High
Bed, brass, used in *The Unsinkable Molly Brown*	$3,100-	3,300
Bed, used by Tyrone Powers in *Blood and Sand*	700-	960
Bicycle, used in *Butch Cassidy and the Sundance Kid*	3,200-	3,400
Cape worn by Doug Fairbanks in *The Mark of Zorro*	1,900-	2,200
Chair, walnut, used by Humphrey Bogart	360-	370
Costume worn by Mary Pickford in *Little Lord Fauntleroy*	2,300-	2,450
Parasol used by Mary Pickford in *Rebecca of Sunnybrook Farm*	750-	825
Riverboat, *Cotton Blossom*, used in *Showboat*	15,000+	
Witch's hat from *The Wizard of Oz*	460-	535
Wizard's suit from *The Wizard of Oz*	665-	685

Lobby Cards

Usually 11″×14″, 8 in a set

Item	Low	High
Black Friday, Boris Karloff	$ 24-	32
Casablanca, Humphrey Bogart	83-	93
The Chase, Bob Cummings	15-	23
The Fighting 69th, James Cagney	50-	59
Flamingo Road, Joan Crawford	28-	36
The Gold Rush, Charlie Chaplin	45-	52
Good Sam, William Frawley	10-	14
Hellcats of the Navy, Ronald Reagan	23-	28
How the West Was Won, Henry Fonda	13-	18
Invisible Stripes, Leo Gorcey	9-	15
The Kiss, Greta Garbo (Illus.)	21-	27

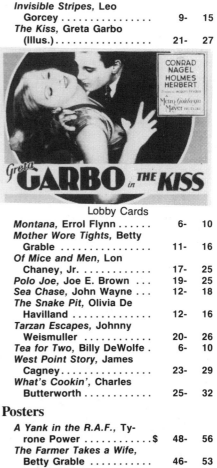

Lobby Cards

Item	Low	High
Montana, Errol Flynn	6-	10
Mother Wore Tights, Betty Grable	11-	16
Of Mice and Men, Lon Chaney, Jr.	17-	25
Polo Joe, Joe E. Brown	19-	25
Sea Chase, John Wayne	12-	18
The Snake Pit, Olivia De Havilland	12-	16
Tarzan Escapes, Johnny Weismuller	20-	26
Tea for Two, Billy DeWolfe	6-	10
West Point Story, James Cagney	23-	29
What's Cookin', Charles Butterworth	25-	32

Posters

Item	Low	High
A Yank in the R.A.F., Tyrone Power	$ 48-	56
The Farmer Takes a Wife, Betty Grable	46-	53
Gone With the Wind	1,000+	
Hellcats of the Navy, Ronald Reagan, Nancy Davis	330-	340
King Kong, 1933	1,000+	
Maltese Falcon, Humphrey Bogart	1,000+	
Million Dollar Legs, Betty Grable	51-	59
The Phantom of the Opera, Lon Chaney	5,000+	
Springtime in the Rockies, John Wayne, Betty Grable	52-	58
Tin Pan Alley, Alice Faye	53-	61
The Unknown, Lon Chaney	2,200-	2,400
The Wizard of Oz, Judy Garland	1,000+	

Sheet Music

Item	Low	High
"Awake in a Dream," 1936	$ 1.50-	2
"Bend Down, Sister," 1931	2-	3
"The Day You Came Along," 1933	1.50-	2
"Don't Give Up the Ship"	1.50-	2
"Easter Parade," 1933	2.50-	3

"Gone," 1936 .... 2- 2.50
"Here Lies Love," 1932 ... 1.50- 2
"I'd Love to Take Orders from You" 1.75- 2
"The Longest Night," 1936 1.75- 2
"Moon Crazy," 1935 ...... 2- 3
"Now I'm a Lady," 1935 ... 1.50- 2
"On the Good Ship Lollipop" (Illus.) 1.75- 2
"Pennies from Heaven," 1936 .... 1.75- 2
"Then Came the Indians," 1936 .... 1.50- 2
"Yes, My Dear," 1933 ..... 2- 3
"You're the Cats," 1931 ... 2.50- 3

Souvenir Programs

Broadway Melody, 1929 ...$ 22- 25
Cimarron, 1931 .... 23- 27
Filmex, Los Angeles, 1971 . 2.50- 3
Hell's Angels, leather-bound, 1930 .... 115- 130
New York Film Festival, 1963 .... 2.50- 3
Radio City Music Hall, 1930's, each 6- 8
Radio City Music Hall, 1940's, each 3- 4
Rain, 1932 .... 21- 25
Star Wars, 1977 .... 6.50-7.50
Wings, 1927 .... 22- 26

Mugs

Photo Courtesy of
Hake's Americana & Collectibles

Mugs

Who could drink their Ovaltine if it weren't in the "official" mug?

Uncle Wiggly china mug (Illus.) ..$11-13
Snuffy Smith mug 10-13
Orphan Annie shake-up mug 10-13
The English Pub, Miami 5- 7

Music Box

Musical

Chimes

Floor chimes, brass tubes, wooden frame, early 1900's ....$ 29- 38
Railroad dining car chimes, portable, with chiming mallet 42- 50

Music Boxes

Anri, Italy, 1970's (Illus.) ......$ 9- 14

Musical Instruments

See **Clubs and Publications,** this Price Guide.

Accordion, "Concertone," 10 keys ....$ 78- 94
Appol Harp (harp w/keyboard), 33 strings, imitation rosewood 75- 85
Banjo, 5 string, wood, 1930's.. 65- 75

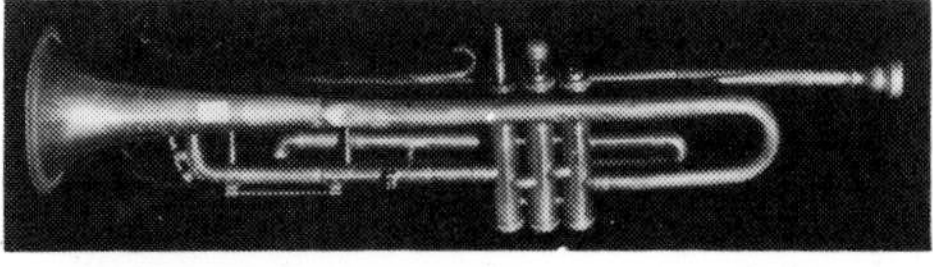

Bugle, Boy Scout, 1920's (Illus.) 65- 75
Bugle, U. S. Army, WW I 45- 53
Concertina, child's, 1920's 48- 53
Cornet, Dupont E Flat, polished brass 80- 90
Drum, toy, Mickey Mouse 245-260
Drum, toy, tin, 1920's 55- 63
Flute, German, 4-keyed, 1920's 68- 74
Guitar, "The Columbia," oak, inlaid, c. 1920 .... 95- 99
Harmonica, Bohm's Sovereign . 19- 26
Harmonica, Duss Band, c. 1920's 7- 10
Harmonica, Carl Essbach's Richter 11- 16

Harmonica, Hohner Auto	19- 26
Harmonica, "Radio Band"	9- 15
Jew's Harp, American, 2½" frame	10- 15
Jew's Harp, 4¼" frame	21- 27
Kazoo (horn whistle)	3- 5
"Kazoo Band" clarinet	5- 8
"Kazoo Band" trombone	9- 14
Nose flute	2- 3
Ocarina ("sweet potato"), various sizes, each	10- 45
Piccolo, cocoa wood, 1-key, 1920's	24- 30
Saxophone, Marceau E Flat, polished brass, c. 1910	89- 95
Trombone, Concertone B Flat Tenor Slide	155-165
Violin, "genuine" Stradivarius, Sears, Roebuck. At least 10,000 "genuine" around; I've never seen one yet that wasn't!	110-135

Phonograph Records

The 78 rpm market generally breaks down into four major groups: Popular—dance bands, combos, instrumental units; Classical—the "straights," strictly defined, operatic companies; Jazz-Blues—intimate, one-to-one, a small club, etc.; Country-Western—collect anything you can get your hands on. H-O-T! Ajax, Banner, Blue Disc, Brunswick, Capitol, Comet, Decca, Emerson, HMV (His Master's Voice), Melotone, Oriole, Regal, Varsity, and Victor are a few of the many record companies who, struggling and failing, brought music to what it is today.

Andrews Sisters, "Bei Mir Bist Du Schoen," 1937	$ 8- 11
Andrews Sisters, "Beer Barrel Polka," 1939	5- 7
Armstrong, Louis, "Heebie Jeebies," 1926	43- 49
Bailey, Mildred, "Washboard Blues," 1938	8- 10
Berigan, Bunny, "I Can't Get Started," 1937	11- 13
Blake, Eubie, "Baltimore Buzz" 1921	15- 20
Carter, Benny, "Swing It," 1933	8- 10
Dorsey, Tommy, "Song of India," 1937	6- 8
Garland, Judy, "Over the Rainbow," 1939	6- 8
Herman, Woody, "Woodchopper's Ball," 1939	8- 10
McKinney's Cotton Pickers, "Cherry," 1928	9- 11
Savitt, Jan, "720 in the Books," 1939	7- 9
Venuti, Joe, "Weary River," 1929	14- 19
Webb, Chick, "I Can't Dance," 1934	8- 11
Williams, Clarence, "Weary Blues," 1923	10- 14
Wilson, Teddy, "Rosetta," 1935	10- 14

Phonographs

Phonographs

Tom Edison invented it, among other things! Originally called a "talking machine," many firms made them and all are collectible today.

Edison, Amberola — played wax rolls (cylinders) late 1800's	$390-425
Columbia, keywind	260-280

Columbia, cylinder, with eighteen cylinders 240-260
"Morning Glory," Edison, cylinder-type, early 1900's... 350-400
Victor, Model E, table model .. 325-360
Victrola, Victor Talking Machine Co., mahogany cabinet (Illus.) 230-250

Any Victrola before 1950 is collectible and a lot of fairly new ones are being sought after, too.

Record Albums

1948 to 1977. Prices are given for those records in good to very good condition. Thousands around and most inexpensive.

Adams, Don, United Artists, "Get Smart" ....$ 4- 7
Alaimo, Steve, Checker, "Mashed Potatoes" 4- 7
Allen, Steve, Dot, "Steve Allen Sings" 3- 4
Allen, Woody, Colpix, "Woody Allen" 6- 11
Alpert, Herb and The Tijuana Brass, A & M, "South of the Border" 3- 6
Ames Brothers, RCA, "Christmas Harmony" 3- 4
Andrews Sisters, Decca, "Berlin Songs" 3- 4
Animals, MGM, "Winds of Change" 4- 6
Anka, Paul, ABC/Paramount, "My Heart Sings" 4- 7
Avalon, Frankie, Chancellor, "Frankie Avalon's Christmas Album" 4- 8
Bare, Bobby, RCA, "Cowboys and Daddys" 3- 4
Beach Boys, Capitol, "Best of the Beach Boys," Vols. 1 and 2, each 4- 6
Bennett, Tony, Columbia, "I Wanna Be Around" 3- 4
Blood, Sweat and Tears, Columbia, "Brand New Day" 3- 4
Booker T and The M.G.'s, Stax, "Green Onions" 5- 7
Boone, Debby, Warner/Curb, "You Light Up My Life"..... 3- 4
Boone, Pat, Dot, "Pat Boone Golden Hits" 3- 4
Bowie, David, Deram, "David Bowie" 8- 12
Brewer, Teresa, Coral, "For Teenagers in Love" 3- 4
Brown, Buster, Fire, "New King of the Blues" 14- 32
Bryant, Anita, Carlton, "In My Little Corner of the World" .. 3- 4
Butler, Jerry, Vee Jay, "Jerry Butler Esquire" 6- 11
Campbell, Glen, Capitol, "Best of Glen Campbell" 3- 4
Captain and Tennille, A & M, "Love will Keep Us Together" 3- 4
Cash, Johnny, Columbia, "I Walk the Line" 3- 4
Chakiris, George, Capitol, "George Chakiris" 4- 7
Cher, Imperial, "The Sonny Side of Cher" 4- 7
Chipmunks (featuring David Seville), Liberty, "Chipmunks A-Go-Go" 5- 8
Clanton, Jimmy, Ace, "Jimmy's Happy" 9- 18
Cline, Patsy, Decca, "Patsy Cline" 1.50-2.50
Clooney, Rosemary, Columbia, "Hey There" 2- 3
Darin, Bobby, Atco, "Darin at the Copa" 5- 11
Davis, Sammy, Jr., Reprise, "I Gotta Be Me" 4- 6
Dee, Joey and the Starliters, Roulette, "Doin the Twist" .. 6- 11
De Shannon, Jackie, Imperial, "Are You Ready for This"... 5- 9
Dino, Desi and Billy, Reprise, "Our Time's Coming" 5- 8
Dylan, Bob, Columbia, "Hard Rain" 3- 4
Four Freshmen, Capitol, "Voices and Brass" 3- 4
Four Lads, Columbia, "High Spirits" 4- 6
Francis, Connie, MGM, "Connie Francis Sings for Mama".... 3- 5
Griffith, Andy, Capitol, "Comedy Caravan" 4- 6
Mancini, Henry, RCA, "Music from Mr. Lucky" 3- 4
National Lampoon, Blue Thumb, "Cold Turkey" 4- 6
Rare Earth, Verve, "Get Ready" 4- 7
Ray, Johnnie, Columbia, "I Cry for You" 4- 6
Sam the Sham and the Pharaohs, MGM, "Hard and Heavy" 3- 4
Simon and Garfunkel, Columbia, "Bridge Over Troubled Water" 3- 5
Sinatra, Frank, Columbia, "Voice of Sinatra" 2- 3
Sledge, Percy, Atlantic, "Percy Sledge Away" 3- 5
Smothers Brothers, Mercury, "Think Ethnic!" 4- 8
Statler Brothers, Mercury, "Flowers on the Wall"...... 3- 5
Supremes, Motown, "Funny Girl" 3- 5
T-Bones, Liberty, "Boss Drag at the Beach" 4- 6
Turner, Ike and Tina, Capitol, "Her Man, His Woman"..... 4- 7

Vale, Jerry, Columbia, "Standing Ovation!" 3- 5
Vinton, Bobby, Epic, "Lonely Nights" 3- 4
Warren, Rusty, Jubilee, "Knockers Up!" 6- 12
Welk, Lawrence, Dot, "Mr. Music Maker" 2- 3
Williams, Andy, Columbus, "Love, Andy" 3- 4
Wilson, Flip, Atlantic, "You Devil You" 3- 4
Wonder, Stevie, Tamla, "Songs in the Key of Life" 4- 7
Young, Faron, Capitol, "Falling in Love" 3- 5
Zappa, Frank, Disc Reet, "Roxy and Elsewhere" 3- 4
Zombies, London, "Early Days" 4- 6

Suggested reading: *Record Albums, 1948-1978,* Jerry Osborne, Follett Publishing Company.

Sheet Music

Lots and lots around. Singer, song, and year dictate price here.

Average price .... 50¢-75¢

Napkin Rings

Napkin Rings

These were in vogue for less than 50 years, beginning in the 1870's. They were made of every type of material, including cut glass. Most common are those from pot metal or quadruple plate.

Cherubs, silver plate, Derby Silver Co.	$ 52- 60
Child's name engraved around chicks scratching, silver	65- 75
Porcelain, hand-painted, flowers and bees, Germany	54- 63
Silver plate, boy fishing on rock	66- 70
Silver plate, boy with hoop	55- 64
Silver plate, butterfly (Illus.)	61- 70
Silver plate, cherub, child's initials	48- 54
Silver plate, fireman's helmet, Pairpoint	88- 97
Silver plate, large boot	54- 62
Silver plate, rooster (Illus.)	50- 60
Silver plate, souvenir, Niagara Falls	54- 62
Silver plate, wild boar, barrel type, Pairpoint	94-103
Sterling silver, dog chasing cat, initialed	155-164
Sterling silver, Georgie, beaded edge	160-166
Sterling silver, owl on branch, child's name	150-160

Netsuke

Most folks know that a "netski" (that's how it's pronounced) is a miniature carving worn on a cord with a kimono. What most folks **don't** know is that literally thousands are showing up in shops and at shows and they're **brand new**! The ivory is usually genuine but the piece has been "aged" by boiling in strong tea. The difference between a genuine **old** netsuke and a "new" netsuke is about 400 percent. The piece illustrated here is "new" — it was sold in a so-called fine antiquities shop in Atlanta to an unsuspecting buyer for $275. It's worth about $55-63.

Netsuke

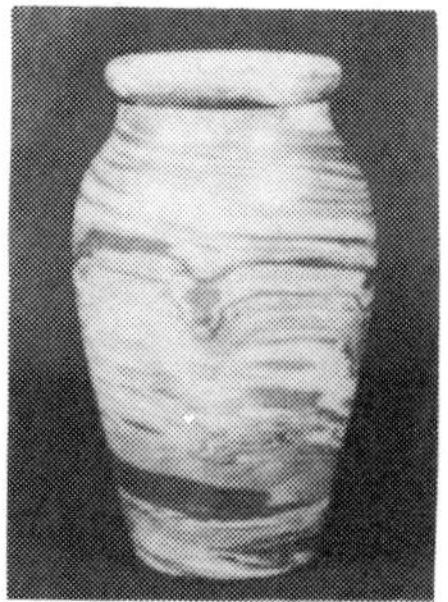

Niloak Pottery

Niloak Pottery

Niloak (Kaolin spelled backward) Pottery was founded by Charles D. Hyten in Benton, Arkansas, in 1909. Most pieces found are marked "Niloak." Swirling layers of reds, blues, browns, and buff clays describe this pottery perfectly. The firm closed in 1946.

Bowl, 4″	$ 43- 50
Bowl, 5″	28- 34
Bowl, 10″	79- 86
Candlesticks, 8¼″, pr.	165-180
Ewer, 6½″	23- 30
Jar w/lid, 4½″	33- 40
Lamp, 21″	174-182
Mug, 4½″	108-115
Pitcher, 5″	18- 25
Pitcher, 6½″	18- 25
Planter, parrot, squirrel, swan, each	16- 26
Plate, 4½″	44- 50
Stein, 7″	46- 53
Vase, 3½″	20- 27
Vase, 4½″	35- 42
Vase, 6½″ (Illus.)	47- 54
Vase, 10″	108-116

Nippon

Nippon

Hand-decorated, generally it's defined as porcelain made in Japan between 1891 and 1921 for export. It was **not** a specific type of porcelain. The name used on the back of each piece denoted the country of origin. After 1891 the U.S. required that imported items from all foreign countries be marked with the name of the exporting country. Nippon is the Japanese word for Japan, but in 1921 the U.S.A. stated that the word Nippon was no longer acceptable as a country of origin marking. Thus ended the Nippon era. See **Clubs and Publications,** this Price Guide.

Ashtray, Persian design, signed	$ 54- 61
Ashtray, scenic, Green Wreath mark	43- 50
Basket, landscape scene, Green Wreath mark, 6¼″ high	70- 78
Basket, windmill scene, Maple Leaf mark, 7″ high	80- 87
Biscuit jar, forget-me-nots, gold trim, 7½″ high	88- 96
Bowl, blue/pink flowers, gold medallion center, 6¼″	60- 68
Bowl, handled, gilt flowers, ivory ground	32- 40
Bowl, pink apple blossoms, bluebird on branch, signed	40- 48
Bowl, rope handles, farm scene, Green Wreath mark, 5¼″	40- 45
Box, covered, harbor scene, beaded edges, Noritake RC mark	62- 70
Box, covered, 2 lovers, Noritake-Nippon mark	70- 77
Cake set, roses/birds, 7 pcs., Green Wreath mark, all	99-108
Candleholder, twisted vines, 8″ high	45- 52
Candlesticks, blue, gold trim, 7¼″ high, pr.	70- 78
Candlesticks, gray/red, floral scene, 8″ high, Noritake "M" in Wreath, pr.	95-104
Chocolate set, bluebirds in tree, gold trim, Green Wreath mark	110-115
Chocolate pot, floral scene, gold beading, 10½″ high	111-118
Chocolate set, gold floral scenes, 11 pcs., all	92-101
Chocolate pot, sailboats on lake, 11″ high	125-132
Condiment set, salt/peppers, toothpick holder, mustard jar, floral scenes, all	48- 55
Condiment set, usual pieces, gold dragon motif, all	70- 78
Cookie jar, bluebirds on nest, Noritake-Nippon mark	92-100
Cookie jar, large bird in flight, 8″ high	90- 98
Cracker jar, gold flowers, RC Nippon mark	125-134
Cracker jar, raised enamel dragon, 7½″ high	128-133
Creamer, pink flowers	14- 21
Cup/saucer, cobalt, gold trim, Green M mark	20- 27
Cup/saucer, pink flowers, signed	30- 38
Cup/saucer, wild roses, gold handle, Nippon, hand-painted	22- 29
Dish, cobalt, gold trim around rim, 6½″ dia.	24- 28
Dish, handled, gold flowers, 5″ dia.	17- 24
Dresser set, pink flowers, green/white borders, all	120-130

Ewer, farm scene, gold overlay, 12" high, "M" in Wreath, Nippon 125-133
Ewer, gold overlay, blue handle, 10" high (Illus.) 140-147
Figurine, fisherman, 5½" high, signed 38- 48
Figurine, pony at fence, 6¼" high, Green Wreath mark.... 50- 57
Figurine, rearing horse, 6" high, signed 51- 60
Hatpin holder, gold dragon, blue ground, 6" high 28- 38
Hatpin holder, twining vines, gold/red, signed, 5½" high .. 29- 38
Humidor, bluebirds in tree, red trim, 7" high 110-118
Humidor, fisherman with nets, 6¼" high, Green Wreath mark 114-119
Humidor, Indian on horse, 7" high, signed 120-130
Lemonade set, pitcher, 8 mugs, floral scenes, all 160-170
Lemonade set, pitcher, 6 mugs, sailboat at sunset, all . 140-150
Match holder, green/red, gold trim, 2½" high 31- 41
Mug, blue flowers on gold ground, 5¾" high, signed ... 40- 50
Mug, gold twisted handle, dragon motif, 6" high, signed .. 38- 47
Mug, green floral scene, gold handle, 6¼" high, Green Wreath mark 48- 56
Mustache cup, Indian with pipe, signed 140-150
Mustard pot, gold flowers, blue ground, RC Nippon mark 40- 47
Mustard pot, red roses, green trim, signed 42- 50
Nut set, dragons, blue ground, bowl, 5 dishes, all 70- 76
Pitcher, floral scene, 13¼" high 71- 80
Pitcher, hand-painted roses,• gold handle, 11½" high 60- 70
Pitcher, sunset on lake, 15" high 59- 67
Planter, owl in flight, 7" high, signed 88- 97
Plaque, rearing horses, "M" in Wreath Nippon mark........ 105-109
Plaque, sailboat at sunset, 9¼" dia...................... 60- 70
Plate, boat scene, blue, red trim, 6" dia., signed 44- 52
Plate, sailboat on pond, open handles, 6¼" dia........... 43- 51
Plates, open handles, pink roses, gold borders, 6, all ... 122-130
Platter, Phoenix, gold border, 11" dia. 70- 78
Salt/pepper, blue flowers, gold trim, pr. 28- 37
Salt/pepper, green ground, gold dots, pr. 20- 27
Sugar bowl, bluebird in tree, signed 38- 47
Sugar bowl, yellow roses, Green Wreath mark 35- 40
Tankard, bear on stump, 11½" high 125-133
Tankard, Indian on horse, 12" high, RC Nippon mark 140-150
Tea set, gold dragons, blue ground, 17 pieces.......... 133-141
Tea set, red/yellow flowers, 13 pieces, all 128-133
Teapot, garden scene, 8" high, Green Wreath mark 37- 47
Teapot, hand-painted roses, gold trim, 7" high, signed ... 30- 40
Teapot, lake scene, gold trim, 7¾" high 32- 41
Tray, dragon motif, 8½" high . 44- 53
Tray, farm scene, gold trim, 9" dia. 47- 55
Vase, Art Nouveau scene, gold handles, 9¼" high 44- 53
Vase, bathing scene, beaded handles, 8" high 40- 48
Vase, twisted vines, red ground, 11" high 52- 61

Nodding Figures

Nodding Figures

Sometimes called pagods, these porcelain figures have heads and hands that are attached to the body with wires. Any movement causes the figures to move up and down.

Bird in tree, trunk sways, bisque . $20-27
Boy holding dog, dog's head moves 28-36
Chinese boy in rickshaw, head and hands move, bisque type . . 29-36
Farm couple, green/yellow/ orange, 6¾" high 32-38
Girl and boy kissing, heads nod, porcelain 29-36
Hindu, turbaned, holding basket, snake moves too, bisque 24-32
Japanese girl, Occupied Japan (Illus.) 10-14
Old lady in chair, sleeping, head nods, bisque 29-37
Rickshaw driver, Japan 10-12

Noritake China

Noritake China

Produced by the Nihon Toki Kaisha firm in Nagoya, Japan, after 1904, for export only. Azalea is the best-known pattern. It was given away as a premium by the Larkin Tea and Coffee Company in the early 1900's. More Noritake is on the market than any other mark. Look for Noritake Nippon, Noritake M in Wreath Nippon, and Noritake RC Nippon marks. They're the earliest. Modern Noritake is marked Noritake China, Japan, with the familiar "M" in the wreath above.

Basket, Azalea pattern, 5" long $ 90- 97
Berry set, 6-pc., floral scene, Green M in Wreath mark, set 80- 87
Berry set, 7-pc., Azalea pattern, all 88- 97
Bowl, Azalea pattern, 10½" dia. 40- 47
Cake plate, Azalea pattern, 7" dia. 67- 74
Cake plate, green/gold, M Mark (Illus.) 32- 38
Celery dish, Azalea pattern, 12¼" long 48- 54
Celery dish, crimson roses, 9" long, RC mark 40- 50
Chocolate set: pot, 8 cups, floral scenes, Green M mark, all 80- 90
Compote, Azalea pattern, 6½" dia. 60- 70
Condiment set, Azalea pattern, 6-pc. 45- 54
Creamer, Azalea pattern, 4½" high 47- 53
Cup/saucer, Sedalia pattern, set of 12, Green M mark, all . 92-101
Cup/saucer, Swans, gold rim, RC mark 28- 34
Dish, Azalea pattern, sauce type 12- 17
Dresser set, 7-pc. blue flowers, gold border, new mark, all . . 60- 66
Egg cup, Azalea pattern 28- 32
Figurine, boy fishing, green/ yellow, RC mark, 6" high . . . 60- 70
Mayonnaise set, 3-pc., Azalea pattern, all 80- 90
Plates, Azalea pattern, 7", 8½", 9¾" dia. 18- 22
Platter, Azalea pattern, 14" long 40- 48
Salt/pepper, Azalea pattern, pr. 30- 37
Salt/pepper, owl motif, Green M mark, pr. 32- 39
Shallow bowl, cherry blossom scene, 3-handled, Green M mark 40- 48
Tea set, garden scene, varied colors, RC mark 60- 68
Tea set, 17-pc., floral scenes, gold rims, Green M mark, all . 140-150
Tile, Azalea pattern 29- 38
Tobacco jar, horse's head, blue/red, Green M mark 60- 67
Vase, Azalea pattern, 8¾" high 70- 75
Vase, floral scenes, 7¼" high . 29- 35
Vase, salmon/pink, 8" high 44- 52

North Dakota School of Mines

North Dakota School of Mines

About 1910 a ceramics department had been established at the University of North Dakota. Margaret Kelly Cable supervised the making of pottery objects from around 1927 until 1949 when she retired. Pieces were marked with the name of the school.

Bowl, 6¼″	$ 65- 73
Dish w/cover, 3″	32- 40
Jar w/lid, 5″	44- 51
Planter, grape decor	102-114
Tile, Conestoga wagon	210-216
Vase, 7″	78- 85
Vase, cobalt, signed "M. Cable"	370-390
Vase, green, 7½″	109-116
Vase, moss green, 5½″	75- 85

Nudes

They came in all sizes and shapes, from those in the western saloons to the 20th-century "streakers." Magazine cutouts, centerfolds, oil paintings, advertisements, statuettes, and busts (head and shoulders only, silly!) are all collectible.

The price depends on the quality of the merchandise.

Nutcrackers

These have been around for years. There were more than 100 patents issued during the mid-1800's and early 1900's. Some worked, some didn't. Art Deco and Art Nouveau types are highly collectible.

Alligator, brass, 13″ long	$75-84
Bawdy lady, wood carved, 7¼″ long	13-19
Bear's head, wood carved, 8″ long	73-77
Cat, cast iron, 8″ high, tail opens mouth	43-50
Crocodile, 8½″ long	24-32
Dog, cast iron, 9″ long, tail opens mouth	42-50
Eagle's head, cast iron, 5½″ high	38-44
"Ideal," palm-type, 5″ long	9-15
"Knee warmer," fits on leg, used w/hammer	29-37
Lady's leg, 6¼″ long	18-26
Lion's head, cast iron, 6″ high	24-30
Monkey's head, brass, 7½″ long	32-39
Pliers-type, nickel-plated, 5″ long (Illus.)	16-22
Rooster, brass	18-25
Squirrel, cast iron	34-39
St. Bernard, cast iron, 5½″ long	37-44
Tiger, brass, 5″ long	67-74
Twist-screw type, wood carved	15-22
Wolf's head, cast iron, tail opens mouth	44-52

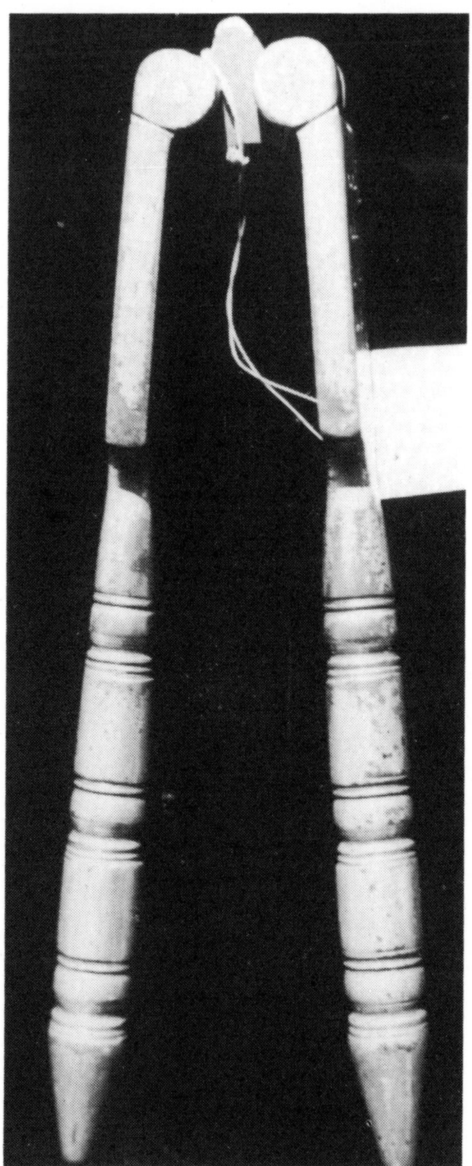

Nutcrackers

Nut Picks

When the manufacturers started to package shelled nuts, it was no longer necessary to pick out the meat with a pick. Now they're being collected.

Average price	50¢-$1

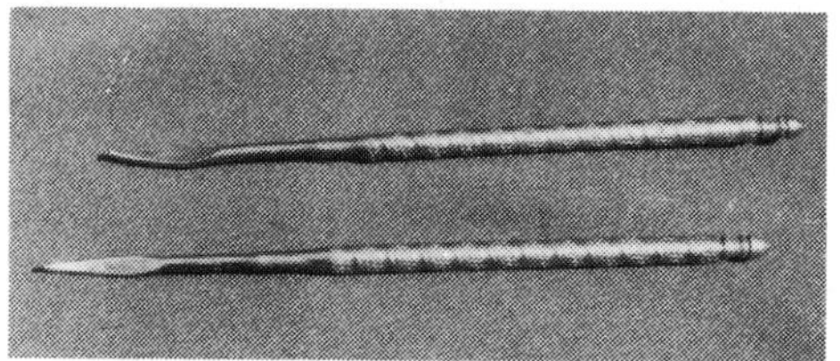

Nut Picks

Occupied Japan Items

Occupied Japan Items

The United States occupied Japan for 7 years, from August, 1945, until April, 1952. "Made in Occupied Japan" and "Occupied Japan" are the most common marks found on items manufactured for export during that 7-year period. See **Clubs and Publications,** this Price Guide.

Animals

- Dog, 4½" long $15-18
- Easter rabbit pulling egg, 4" long 11-16
- Frog playing drum, 2½" high 12-17
- Monkey playing violin, 3¼" high . 11-16
- Mother and baby swan, 2" wide . 11-15

Ashtrays

- Cherubs $11-15
- Dog and fire hydrant, 4" high ... 14-19
- Elf sitting on leaf, 4" wide 17-22
- Frog with open mouth, 3½" high 13-18

Bisque

- Boy with dog, 6" high $19-23
- Bud vase, 6" high 19-26
- Colonial couple, pr. 31-39
- Cupids on pedestals, 7½" high, pr. 26-36
- Peasant couple, 5½" high, pr. ... 30-37

Cups/Saucers

- Black, Trimont china $21-30
- Blue Willow style 21-30
- Gray, Orion china 21-30
- Green, Trimont china 21-30
- White bone 21-28

Figurines

- Court jester, 6½" high $17-23
- Dancers, 1930's style, 2¼" high, pr. 25-33
- Farm couple, 7" high 23-28
- Fisherman and mate, 5" high, pr. 35-43
- Shelf sitter, 3" high 14-19
- Victorian couple, 8" high 34-41
- Warrior, 5" high 18-24

Figurines, Children

- Boy, Hummel type, 5½" high, "American Children, I bring you greetings," on bottom $56-66
- Boy playing horn, 3½" high 16-24
- Girl, Hummel type, 5½" high, same inscription on bottom (The Hummel types are good enough to fool many collectors of the real thing.) 58-67
- Peasant girl with lamb, 5" high .. 19-24
- Pigeon-toed girl, 4½" high 15-24

Glassware and Lacquerware

- Coasters, lacquerware, set of 6 .. $37-46
- Cracker server, scalloped edges, w/glass cheese dip dish and lacquer lid, 13½" dia. 51-61
- Lighthouse, battery-operated, souvenir of Coney Island 36-45
- Niagara Falls hanging plate, lacquerware 23-33

Planters

- Angel pulling cart, 4" wide $21-31
- Donald Duck and basket, 2" wide 23-33
- Donkey and packs, 3" wide 20-29
- Elf and basket, 5¾" wide 23-30
- Owl on limb, 3½" wide 24-31
- Panda climbing tree, 4" wide 18-22

Salt/Pepper Shakers

- Chicken in nest, 3-pc., all $19-25
- Dog and chair, 2-pc. 23-31
- Elephants, 1-pc. 16-25
- Mexican boys, pr. 19-27
- Roses with butterflies, 3-pc., all . 18-24

Toby Mugs

- Captain Patches, 2¾" high $19-23
- Devil's face, 2" high (rare) 30-37
- Gent and dogs, 7" high 50-57
- Jail bailiff, 7" high 56-66
- Street peddler, 7" high 51-61

Toothpicks

- Cowboy, 4¼" high $24-29

Pixie, 3″ high 22-29
Satsuma, vase type, 2¼″, 2½″, 11″ high, each 18-24

Vases

Angel, bud type, 2¾″ high $11-17
Boy blowing horn, 2″ high 11-17
Girl on stump, 3″ high 19-24
Miniature 17-20

Oil Paintings

Oil Paintings

Skip this item unless you know that an oil painting has four layers: (1) canvas; (2) gesso — a paste-like substance to make the canvas smooth; (3) the painting itself; (4) a protective coat of varnish or shellac. You may stumble upon what looks like the dirtiest, the filthiest, the most moth-eaten painting you've ever seen. But every day, oil paintings by the famous artists are showing up at Flea Markets.

A lot of buyers go for the frames, not realizing that the oil painting is worth a small fortune. Keep a weather eye out for oil paintings.

Old Sleepy Eye Collectibles

In 1906 the Western Stoneware Company of Monmouth, Illinois, was formed to produce premium pottery for Sleepy Eye Milling Company in Sleepy Eye, Minnesota. The town and the mill were named for a Sioux Indian. His likeness, in profile, is on most of the pottery you find today. Other premiums were also given away by the mill. All are highly sought after now. The pottery is being reproduced in mugs, sugar bowls, small pitchers, salt/pepper shakers, and steins. Other reproductions are a glass jar, a large tumbler, a small advertising mirror, and the paper barrel labels. Be careful. See **Clubs and Publications,** this Price Guide.

Advertising cards, 10 in set, 5½″ × 9″, all $458-467
Advertising postcards, 9 in set, 3⅜″ × 5½″, all............. 479-488
Cookbook, Old Sleepy Eye on cover 137-145
Cookbook, shaped like the end of a bread loaf 138-146
Letter opener, bronze 110-118
Paperweight bust, bronze 160-170
Pitcher, blue-on-gray, 4″ high . 158-167
Pitcher, blue-on-white, 4″ high 108-117
Pitcher, green............... 132-141
Stein, blue-on-gray, 7″ high ... 298-315
Stein, yellow, 7¼″ high 315-322
Vase, blue-on-gray 371-380
Vase, multicolor, bullrushes, 8¼″ high 198-221

Suggested reading: *Monmouth-Western Stoneware,* Jim Martin and Bette Cooper, Wallace-Homestead Book Company.

Opera Glasses

Small binoculars, hand telescopes — call them what you will. Some were inlaid with precious gems.

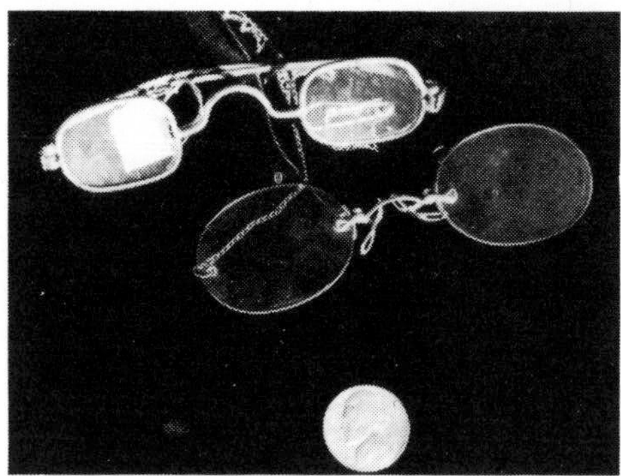

Opera Glasses

American, leather-covered, with case, early 1900's $27-36
American, ivory-covered, no case, late 1800's 45-53
French, mother of pearl — covered, late 1800's 56-64

Ornate Frames

Ornate Frames

Hundreds to choose from. The early types were made by covering a wooden frame with plaster-of-paris, then gilding it with gold leaf or gold paint. So, if it needs cleaning, use alcohol; water dissolves the paint. Spackle is good for repairing broken places.

Size, age, and condition — make your own deal.

Owens Pottery

OWENS FEROZA

Owens Pottery

The J. B. Owens Pottery Company produced this pottery in Ohio from the mid-1800's until 1933. It is comparable to Roseville and Weller.

Candleholder, Utopian, berry/leaf decor, brown glaze . . . $ 74- 83
Letter holder, floral decor, 3½" high 60- 68
Mug, Utopian, fruit on vine, 5½" high 110-118
Pitcher, flowers, green leaves, green ground, 10" high 105-112
Pitcher, orange/brown/yellow floral leaves, Utopian 115-127
Pitcher, tankard-type, berries/leaves, artist-signed 99-107
Vase, green leaves, green-to-pink flowers, 5½" high 112-117
Vase, Lincoln, brown, tan, identical to an earlier Weller vase (Illus.) 90- 98
Vase, Utopian, orange pansies, 6" high 88- 97
Vase, Utopian, pansy decor, 6½" high 91-100

Paden City Pottery

See **American Dinnerware.**

Paperbacks

In the early 1940's these came into vogue. Ian Ballentine, an Englishman, founded Bantam Books, then Ballentine Books. Since then, hundreds of publishers have popped up. As paperbacks are printed 200,000 to 600,000 at a whack, only first editions are considered collectible today. Also, find an early paperback with a

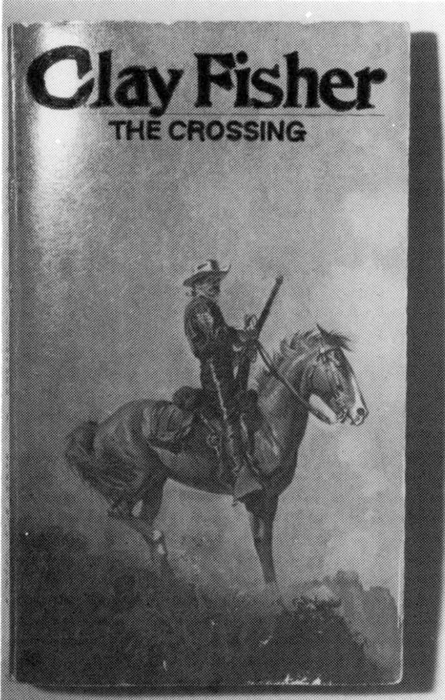

Paperbacks

cover illustration by the well-known cowboy artist, Frank C. McCarthy, and you've got something to talk about.

Average price, in good condition, before 1950 (Illus.) ...... $ 1.50-2
Average price, in good condition, after 1950 .... 50¢-75¢

Paper Dolls

The booklets of Hollywood movie stars are the most sought after. Uncut, intact, not torn — "mint" condition. They're hard to find. Most booklets have some of the pages cut or the dolls have torn costumes or bodies. Prices given are for those booklets in good to very good condition.

1930's

Charlie McCarthy, Whitman, 1938 $35-42
The Dionne Quintuplets, Merrill, 1935 36-43
Jane Withers, Whitman, 1936 or 1938, each 37-43
Shirley Temple, Saalfield, 1935, 1936, 1937, 1938, 1939, each .. 39-46

1940's

Ann Sothern, 1943 or 1944, each $31-38
Betty Grable, 1941, 1942, 1943, 1946, each 33-40
Carmen Miranda, Whitman, 1942 . 32-40
Deanna Durbin, Merrill, 1940, 1941, each 33-40
Gene Tierney, Whitman, 1947 ... 31-39
Gone With the Wind, Merrill, 1940 (Illus.) 34-40
Judy Garland, 1940, 1941, 1945, each 33-40
Lana Turner, Whitman, 1942, 1945, 1947, each 30-37

1950's

Ann Sothern, Saalfield, 1959 ....$18-24
Arlene Dahl, Saalfield, 1953 21-30
Davy Crockett, Whitman, 1955 ... 19-26
Debbie Reynolds, Whitman, 1953, 1955, each 22-26
Elizabeth Taylor, 1952-1957, each 19-27
Eve Arden, Saalfield, 1953, 1956, each 20-28
Gale Storm, Whitman, 1958 20-27
Grace Kelly, Whitman, 1955, 1956, each 36-44
Jane Powell, 1951-1957 22-28
Joan Caufield, Saalfield, 1953 ... 21-29
June Allyson, Whitman, 1950, 1953, 1955, 1957, each 20-30
Kim Novak, Saalfield, 1957, 1958, each 19-26
Loretta Young, Saalfield, 1956 ... 19-26
Oklahoma, Golden Press, 1956 .. 21-28
Polly Bergen, Saalfield, 1958 19-26
Roy Rogers/Dale Evans, Whitman, 1950, 1952, 1954, 1957, each .. 23-30
Sandra Dee, Saalfield, 1959 19-26

1960's

Annette, Whitman, 1962, 1964, each $14-21
Bewitched, Magic Wand, 1965 ... 9-14
Cleopatra, Blaise, 1963 10-14
Debbie Reynolds, Whitman, 1960, 1962, each 12-17
Donna Reed, Saalfield, 1961 11-16
Fess Parker, Art Craft, 1964 10-15
Green Acres, Whitman, 1968 9-13
Lennon Sisters, Whitman, 1963 .. 10-15
Mary Poppins, Whitman, 1964 ... 10-15
Patty Duke, Whitman, 1964, 1965, each 9-14
Tuesday Weld, Whitman, 1967 ... 9-14

1970's

Average price $4-8

Paper Money, American/Foreign

Paper Money, American/Foreign

The very same rules hold true here as with collecting American coins. Rarity, condition, and availability dictate the price in the long run. There are quite a few good currency books available. That $4 to $8 you invest could be returned ten-fold on your first purchase. Once again, know who you're doing business with.

Paperweights

Paperweights

If you're lucky you'll find a genuine Millefiori or a St. Louis or a signed La-lique. If you're smart, you'll spend your time looking for the more common ones listed below.

Acme Furniture, glass, 1930's . . . $12-17
Bilt-Well Stoves, glass, photo of stove . . . 13-17
Figural, pony/cart, Watertown Carriage Co., glass . . . 16-22
Figural, rooster, cast iron . . . 17-22
Frosted lion, round, glass . . . 51-57
Multicolored, new, India . . . 5- 9
New Coat Paints, glass, photo insert, 1930's . . . 13-17
St. Clair, apple shape (Illus.) . . . 50-58
Washington Monument, "snowflake" type, glass . . . 14-19

Parking Meters

Parking Meters

Old parking meters are being used for lamp bases, bar rails, door stops. They don't have to work.

Average price . . . $50-60

Pattern Glass

Pattern Glass

If you're a serious collector, refer to the *Wallace-Homestead Price Guide to Antiques and Pattern Glass.* Authorities consider this the finest pattern glass price guide in existence. Other than a few price guides to do with Depression glass, little information is available about pattern glass made during the 1930's, the 1940's, and on into the 1960's. A great many of the old pieces of pattern glass are being reproduced and, unfortunately, those pieces fool too many people. It's fine to say in a book, "Anyone can tell the difference!" when referring to the "new" pattern glass; but, that just isn't true. Unless you're a serious collector, you're going to be fooled.

Here are a few of the (old) patterns that have been or are being reproduced: Actress (goblet, pickle dish); Ashburton (goblet, jug, lemonade glass, sugar, wine); Baby Face (goblet); Baltimore Pear (butter dish, cake stand, celery, creamer, goblet, sugar, covered); Beaded Grape (goblet, 8¼″ plate, 4″ sauce dish, tumbler, wine); Bellflower (milk and water pitchers, flat sauce dish); Cardinal Bird (goblet); Coin, Columbian (goblet, toothpick, tumbler); Croesus (butter dish, toothpick holder, tumbler); Dahlia (water pitcher); Daisy and Button (watch out for anything here); Dew and Raindrop (goblet, wine); Diamond Quilted (goblet, tumbler); Dewdrop with Star (4¼″, 7″, and 9″ plates, footed salt, Sheaf of Wheat tray); Eyewinker (sauce, shakers, spooner, toothpick, tumbler); Holly Amber (butter dish, jelly compote, creamer, cruet, 4″ mug, nappy); Horn of Plenty (goblet, water tumbler); Inverted Strawberry (water pitcher, tumbler); New England Pineapple (goblets, both sizes, wine); Panelled Daisy (goblet, tumbler); Rose-in-Snow (goblet, 6½″ plate); Shell and Tassel (goblets, round and square); Stippled Star (creamer, goblet, sugar, wind); Texas (creamer, individual and regular, sugar, individual and regular); Thousand Eye (cruet, goblet, hat, mug, 6″, 8″, 10″ plate, water tumbler, twine holder, wine); Three in One (cracker jar); Tulip with Sawtooth (wine); Wildflower. See **Clubs and Publications,** this Price Guide.

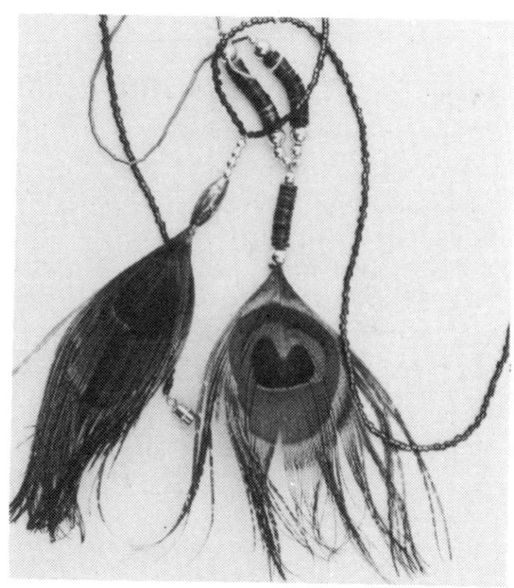

Peacock Feathers

Peacock Feathers

These feathers are used in jewelry, decorating, etc.

Peacock necklace (Illus.) $20-28
Peacock feathers, each 6-11
Live peacocks — visit your local zoo!

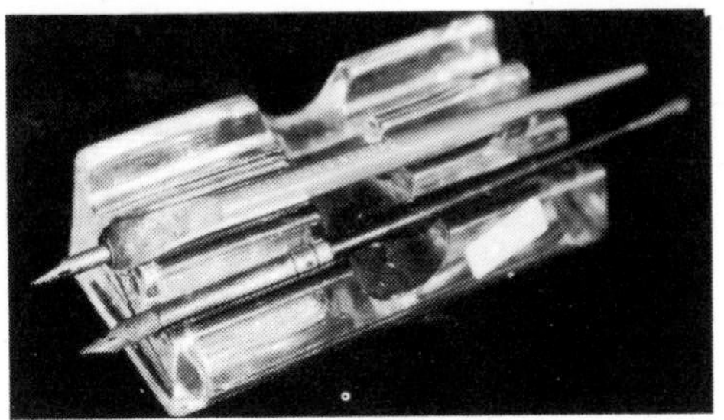
Pen Holders

Pen Holders

Brass, glass, and pot metal usually held two to four pens. Popular for years until the ballpoint pen came along.

Brass, inkwells on each side, late 1800's $45-53
Glass, slots for three pens, early 1900's (Illus.)................ 22-27

Pencil Clips

Pencil Clips

Attached to the eraser end of a pencil, they kept the pencil fastened to your shirt or coat pocket.

Ivory salt clip $1.50-2.50
7-Up clip (Illus.) 5-6
Worcester salt clip.......... 1.50-2

Pencil Sharpeners

Desk types, portables for your purse, or the wall type are all being found at Swap Meets and Flea Markets.

Pens and Pencils

The steel pen was invented in 1870 by Samuel Harrison, but Richard Esterbrook first produced it commercially in

Pencil Sharpeners

Pens and Pencils

the 1880's. Holders were made of fine materials such as gold, silver, and mother-of-pearl. George Parker and L. E. Waterman were both fountain pen pioneers, although Waterman is credited with its invention in 1884. W. A. Sheaffer invented the lever-filling pen in 1913. Wahl (later, Wahl-Eversharp) made pens after World War I. In 1929, more than 34 million dollars' worth of fountain pens were produced in this country. Mechanical pencils have been around for years, and there are thousands of "advertising" pencils available.

Pens

Conklin

Dunn, 1922, black/red, gold-filled trim ....$ 9- 11
1923, hard rubber case, gold-filled trim 14- 19
1923, Model 25R, lady's, ribbon on cap 35- 42
1925, Endura, ring top, spatter green 30- 35

Esterbrook

1928, green, gold-filled trim ...$ 14- 17
1934, red, gold-filled trim 13- 17

Eversharp

1933, Doric, Gold Seal, lady's .$ 21- 28
1933, Doric, Gold Seal, man's . 83- 91
1935, Midget, spatter green, gold-filled trim 12- 17
1944, Skyline, gold-filled trim .. 17- 23
Lady Webster, miniature 26- 31

Moore

1896, non-leakable, black case (Illus.) ....$ 17- 21
1903, non-leakable, hard rubber case 46- 54
1907, lady's, black, hard rubber case, gold rings 15- 19
1916, red/rose, etched band on cap, 14K nib 17- 24

Mother-of-Pearl

Black rubber case ....$ 13- 19
Onyx handle, 14K nib 35- 45

Parker

1895, black rubber case, 14K gold trim ....$ 46- 56
1899, Model 20, hard rubber case 32- 41
1923, Big Red, Duofold point .. 92-102
1929, Duofold deluxe, black/pearl, gold bands on cap 138-144
1942, Blue Diamond, blue/black, gold-filled trim ... 27- 37

Sheaffer

1923, White Dot, green, gold-plated trim 58- 67
1925, White Dot, ring top, black, gold-filled trim 22- 29
1932, spatter green, gold-plated trim 22- 29

Wahl

1918, silver overlay case...... 33- 40
1922, gold-plated 17- 22
1928, ball clip, gold-plated 31- 37

Waterman

1886, Model 12, spatter brown, 14K gold bands............ 42- 46
1913, Model 54, hard rubber case, silver-plated trim...... 38- 43
1918, Model 55, hard rubber case, silver-plated trim...... 75- 81
1925, Model 71, red, hard rubber case, gold-plated trim ... 74- 80
1928, Lady Patricia, sterling silver case 53- 60
1933, Model 5, black, gold-plated trim 41- 50
1943, Commando 16- 22
1947, spatter gray, silver-plated trim 11- 15

Pencils

Eversharp

1915, silver ....$ 20- 27
1920, silver-plated 9- 12
1931, silver-plated 9- 12

Mechanical, Advertising

Budweiser, whistle on end 12- 18
Castle Beer 8- 12
Dodge Autos................ 12- 17
Grand Canyon Route 9- 13
Heidlicker Beer.............. 8- 11
Kitchenware Products 8- 11
Pure Oil Company 8- 11
Quaff-A-Kola 8- 10
Whirlpool................... 8- 10

Parker

1923, Duofold senior, blue, usual mechanism 48- 55
1929, Duofold deluxe, black/pearl, gold bands 53- 60
1936, Ronson, penciliter, spatter green, rodium-plated 32- 39
1948, Model 51, gold-plated ... 24- 29

Sheaffer

1917, gold-filled case, usual mechanism 20- 27
1921, ring top, gold-filled case, usual mechanism 13- 18
1926, White Dot, gold-filled ... 17- 21
1936, White Dot, black, gold-plated trim 16- 22

Wahl-Eversharp

1924, ring top, gold-filled case. 11- 17

Waterman

1918, Model 454, sterling silver case 65- 73
1926, sterling silver case 40- 47
1933, Model 5, black, gold-plated trim 18- 22

Perfume Bottles

These have been around for centuries in all sizes and shapes. Made of glass, silver, pure gold, carved from jade, inlaid with precious stones, even "Avon calling!"

Chinese jade, dragon motif, mid-1800's $128-140
Cornucopia, 2″ long 54- 60
Cut glass, sterling silver cap with applicator attached, early 1900's 118-127

Perfume Bottles

DeVilbiss atomizer, iridescent, gold trim, flower motif	136-144
English lavender bottle	19- 26
Moser perfume bottle, multicolored enamel, Czechoslovakia, 6½″ high	240-250
Peking glass, 3″ high (Illus.)	74- 83
St. Louis, paper label, acid etched, 10¾″ high	271-280
Sterling silver/glass, 2″ long	77- 86
Tiffany glass, signed LCT Favrile	230-340

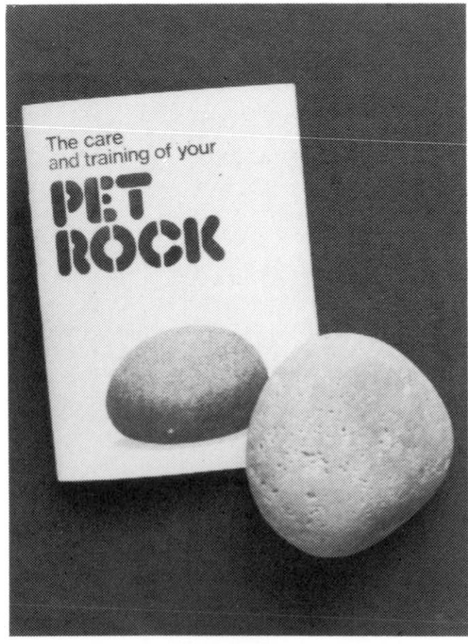

Pet Rock

Pet Rock

This object was a craze a few years ago. There's even a Pet Rock cemetery.

M.I.B. (mint, in box)	$5-7

Pewabic Pottery

Mary Chase Perry founded this pottery in 1903 at Detroit, Michigan. "Pewabic" with five maple leaves, "Pewabic PP Detroit," and "PP Detroit" were the marks generally used. The business closed in 1961. Paper labels were also used.

Ashtray, blue iridescent, signed	$133-141
Tile, Indian, iridized bronze, 6″ × 6″	173-184
Vase, amphora shape, signed, 3″	84- 92
Vase, brown/orange w/drip glaze, signed, 7½″	435-445
Vase, copper color, 7″	178-186
Vase, gold iridescent, blue ground, 18¾″	550-590

Pewter

Pewter

Don't worry about finding the very old pewter; it's either in a museum or a private collection. But, there's still lots of it around, from World War I on. Generally, pieces marked "genuine pewter" were made in the 1920's or slightly earlier.

Ashtray, elephant trunk handle . . $18-25
Box, enamel inlay, 4¼" x 7¼" . . . 38-44
Candlestick, Art Nouveau, 6" high 44-49
Candlesticks, 4" high, pr. 42-48
Coffeepot, bamboo-wrapped handle, 6½" high 57-64
Creamer 14-20
Flask, screw cap 32-39
Inkwell, glass insert 29-34
Pitcher, 9½" high (Illus.) 35-42
Plate, 7¼" dia. 24-30
Platter, 10½" long 34-40
Salt/pepper set 21-28
Spoons, 12 Apostles, 1940's, all . 48-55
Sugar bowl w/lid 14-20
Teapot 46-53

Photographs

Old black and white photographs can be found in quantity at most garage sales and Flea Markets and may have historical importance.

Average price . . . . 25¢-50¢

Photography

Mathew B. Brady, best known for his photographs of Lincoln and the Civil War, created the public's interest in photography. Today, millions enjoy this fascinating hobby. See **Clubs and Publications,** this Price Guide.

Adlake Repeater 4" x 5" plate, made by Adams & Westlake Co., Chicago, Ill. . . . . $ 96-106
Adox 35mm, made by Adox Kamerawerk, Wiesbaden, Germany, c. 1930's 57- 67
Amerex 16mm subminiature, made in Occupied Japan, 1948 . . . . 45- 55
Anscoset 35mm rangefinder, made by Ansco 120-128
Buster Brown box, made by Ansco 27- 36
Buster Brown folding, No. 2A . 23- 27
Cadet Model B2 box, made by Ansco 11- 15
Dollar Box, 1910, made by Ansco 42- 51

Photography

Klimax 5" x 7" folding plate, c. 1912, made by Butcher & Sons, London, England 74- 82
Kodak, Autographic Special No. 1A, c. 1915 (Illus.) 38- 46
Kodak, Brownie No. 1 box, for 117 film, c. 1900 360-368
Kodak, Brownie No. 3 box, for 124 film, c. 1905-34 . . . . 22- 27
Kodak No. 3, 118 film, c. 1915-26 . . . . 31- 40
Kodak No. 3A folding pocket camera 119-122
Leica B "Compur" model 35mm viewfinder, dial-set, c. 1927 . . . . 4,400 +
Leica C 35mm viewfinder 360-370
Leica G, 5/50mm, c. late 1930's 177-186
Lumiere Sinox folding, for roll-film, made by Lumiere & Co., Lyon, France 28- 35
Mason Harvard all-metal pin-hold camera for plates, c. 1890 210-220
Mendel Detective, for plates, high-speed lens 175-184
Mikut Color, for 3 color separation negatives on 1 plate, c. 1930's 360-368
Nettel Deckrullo, for 9 x 12cm plates, c. 1919 . . . . 74- 83

Plaubel Makina III folding, c. 1930 197-206
QRS Kamra, bakelite box, for 35mm film, late 1920's 67- 77
Ray box, for 30½″ × 30½″ plates 82- 91
Reflex folding focal, for plates, postcard size, c. 1912 165-174
Rex magazine, for 4″ × 5″ plates, c. late 1890's 160-170
Scovill folding view, for 5″ × 8″ plates, Waterbury lens, c. late 1880's 240-250
Seneca box, for 4″ × 5″ plates . 34- 44
Trio No. 1A folding, for 120 film 39- 46
Univex plastic box, for No. 00 film, model A, c. 1936 ...... 22- 29
Vive No. 1 box, for plates, c. 1890's, made by Vive Camera Co. 112-118
Vokar I rangefinder, for 35mm film, c. 1940 125-134
Welta folding, for 35mm film, c. 1930 .... 46- 54
Wirgin Stereo, for 35mm film, Steinheil Cassar lenses 77- 86

Suggested reading: *Jason Schneider on Camera Collecting, Book Two,* Jason Schneider, Wallace-Homestead Book Company.

Piano Stools

Piano Stools

Mahogany, mahogany-stained poplar, lots had claw and ball feet. Piano stools have four legs, organ stools have three.

Adjustable seat, early 1900's ... $98-130

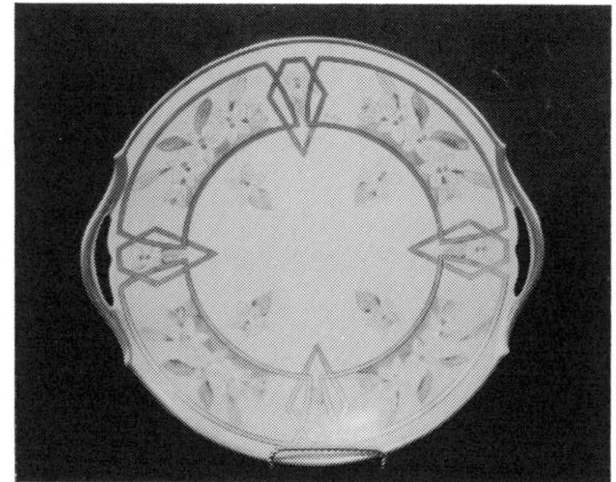

Pickard

HANDPAINTED W PICKARD A CHINA

Pickard

Wilder Pickard founded his company in Illinois around 1894. They're still in business. Once buying their pottery blanks from other firms, they now make their own.

Bowl, flowers and leaves, gold, signed ....$ 97-105
Bowl, fruit, leaves, gold fluted top, 8″ high 88- 95
Box, powder, with lid, Art Deco flowers, gold/black/cream, signed 180-188
Cake plate, hand-painted, artist-signed, 10¾″ dia. (Illus.) 70- 80
Candlesticks, etched gold, 4″ high, pr. 80- 87
Chocolate pot, pearlized ground, white, orchids, green leaves 240-250
Compote, violet/gold, artist-signed, 8″ high 240-247
Creamer and sugar, forest scene, gold handles and rim, pr. 140-148
Dish, open handles, 8″ dia. ... 44- 52
Pitcher, cider, gold color, blue trim 70- 80
Pitcher, orange poppies, signed Fuchs 80- 88

Plate, gold center, flowers, signed, 7″ dia.	40- 47
Relish dish, pink/blue, floral, signed	44- 53
Salt/pepper, all gold, 4″ high, pr.	50- 57
Teapot, gold colors, 5″ high, cover	64- 72
Tray, garden scene, signed E Challinor	410-418
Vase, floral, gold, signed, 12″ high	70- 77
Vase, peacock, multicolored, paper label, signed E, Challinor	790-815
Vase, scenic, signed Marke	100-107

Pickle Casters

Pickle Casters

Usually glass jars in a quadruple or triple-plate frame, though some were made of sterling silver. They were considered a novelty in the late 1800's. The kind of glass — cut, pressed; the type of frame — sterling, etc., has a great deal to do with how much it's worth. Handle the glass pieces carefully. If you break it, you've bought it.

Picture Frames

Go to a Flea Market! There are more sizes, shapes, and types of frames at a Flea Market than you can shake a flea at.

Sterling silver frame, square, 2½″ × 3½″ (Illus.)	$42-48
Sterling silver frame, oval, stands or hangs (Illus.)	49-56

Picture Frames

Pie Birds

At first glance they look like porcelain "whistles." During the Depression they were stuck in pies to prevent spewing over in the oven. They come in a variety of shapes, such as blackbirds, chicks, magpies, and roosters.

Average price $13-23

Pillboxes

Pillboxes

Lots of folks carry pills in their purse or coat pocket. The box illustrated here is hand-tooled sterling silver and only 1½″ long. $50-58. Look for brass, plastic, even wood.

Pin Dishes

Pin Dishes

Porcelain, silver, gold, glass — cut or pressed — all ages.

The one illustrated here is Japanese and fairly new $4-6

Who made them and when enters into the price.

Pisgah Forest Pottery

Pisgah Forest Pottery

Creamer, blue/white flowers . . .	**$ 56- 63**
Jug w/stopper, blue glaze, 4¼″	**93-101**
Pitcher, pink/green, 5″	**33- 40**
Teapot, pioneer wagon	**36- 43**
Vase, cameo/turquoise, 7″	**265-275**
Vase, crackle glaze, turquoise, pink lined	**83- 90**

Planters Peanuts

Here's a nutty collectible. Since 1916, "Mister" Peanut has been the company symbol. A 14-year-old boy originated him. Hundreds of Planters items around today. There's even a book on him!

Planters Peanuts

Photo Courtesy of Hake's Americana & Collectibles

The glass jars are scarce. The Barrel Jar with any lid brings $175-225.

Ashtray, Mr. Peanut in relief	$ 57- 66
Bag, burlap, small	16- 20
Barrel jar, glass, peanut finial on lid, 8″ (Illus.)	300-325
Blotter, peanut shape	7- 8
Book, paint, United States of America	11- 13
Bookmark, 1939 World's Fair	16- 22
Bowl, display counter, Planters	28- 35
Calendar diary, 1977	27- 31
Charm bracelet	16- 19
Clock, wall (scarce)	140-150
Cookie cutter	34- 38
Drink stirrers, set of 6	4- 6
Fork, silver plated	24- 27
Greeting card	19- 24
Jar, football	127-133
Jar, squirrel, embossed	106-114
Knife, 2-blade	8- 11
Letter opener, Mr. Peanut (scarce)	30- 38
Lighter, peanut shape	32- 37
Mirror, pocket	6- 8
Paperweight, glass	23- 27
Pencil, mechanical, celluloid	16- 19
Salad set, 4 pcs., all	54- 60
Salt/pepper set, Mr. Peanut shape	11- 14
Scale, Mr. Peanut shape	900+
Ski cap, Planters	6- 8
Spoon, Mr. Peanut, silver plated	13- 17
T-shirt	9- 12
Tennis hat	12- 15
Tin sign, store, 14″ × 20″	27- 35
Tray, Mr. Peanut	9- 11
Watch, Mr. Peanut	34- 40

Plaster Busts

Plaster Busts

Almost every Flea Market has them in all sizes, shapes, and conditions. If you like, buy. The bust illustrated here was used to advertise tobacco items at the turn of the century. $14-23.

Playboy Magazines

Playboy Magazines

This publication took over where Esquire left off when Esquire "went uptown!" in the early 1950's. Early issues are highly collectible. Prices listed are for mags in fine condition.

December, 1953, Vol. 1, No. 1 (Marilyn Monroe on cover)	$1,400-1,500
January, 1954, Vol. 1, No. 2	1,500-1,600
February, 1954, Vol. 1, No. 3	475- 490
March, 1954, Vol. 1, No. 4	325- 340
April, 1954, Vol. 1, No. 5	235- 246
June, 1955, Vol. 2, No. 6	68- 73
May, 1958–December, 1961, Vol. 5, No. 5—Vol. 8, No. 12, each	22- 26
May, 1964–January, 1966, Vol. 11, No. 5–Vol. 13, No. 1, each	9- 13

February, 1967–November, 1969, Vol. 14, No. 2–Vol. 16, No. 11, each 6- 8
February, 1973–December, 1975 (Illus.), Vol. 20, No. 2–Vol. 22, No. 12, each .. 5- 7

Playboy also publishes a yearly "playmate" calendar. The first issue, 1958, $65-73. Second through sixth issues, each $28-44. Paperbacks, hard covers, "flats," *Trump Magazine* and *Oui* were other Playboy efforts.

Playing Cards

Playing Cards

Most authorities agree that playing cards probably are an adaptation of chess, which originated in India or China around 450 A.D. They are also mentioned in the annals of a German burg in 1361. The English copied from the French; we copied from the English. The Spanish never have had a queen in their deck; the French do. *Hobbies* — the Magazine for Collectors published the various classifications of playing cards in its October 1961 issue. Here is a brief summary:

I—Early Issues: Rare museum items, U.S. and foreign, prior to 1875.

II—Special Issues: U.S. and foreign, wide and narrow, from 1837 to date.

III—Wide Pictorials: U.S. and foreign, 1875-1930.

IV—Old Flower Cards: Wide and narrow, U.S., 1910-1921.

V—Narrow Named Cards: U.S., 1913-1925.

VI—Unnamed Narrow Cards: U.S., 1925-1935.

VII—Advertising Cards: U.S. and foreign, wide and narrow, from 1885 to date.

VIII—Novelty Cards: Early and modern, U.S. and foreign, all shapes and sizes.

IX—Game Cards: Early and modern, U.S. and foreign.

X—Modern: U.S. and foreign, wide and narrow, since 1925.

Most playing cards found today were made after 1920. If you're interested in joining a playing card collectors club, see **Clubs and Publications,** this Price Guide.

Advertising

Alleghany & Western Railroad, complete, c. 1930's $10-13
Chicago & Alton Railroad, in original box, early 1900's 19-26
Delta Air Lines, "Delta is ready when you are," complete 2- 3
Delta Air Lines, seal unbroken, 1929-1979 .... 3- 4
Four Roses whiskey (Illus.)...... 5- 8
Hilton, Las Vegas, complete, in original box 1- 2
Marina Hotel, Las Vegas, seal unbroken 1- 2
Royal Crown Cola (Illus.)........ 5- 8
United Airlines, made in Hong Kong, seal unbroken 1- 2

Civil War

Army and Navy, New York, c. 1865 ....$78-83
Confederate, Picture Playing Cards, c. 1863 82-90
Union, New York, c. 1862 71-80

Clans

Anderson, Buchanan, Gordon, MacDonald; any of these decks, complete, c. 1920's, each .....$ 7-10

Comic Strips/Characters

Betty Boop, complete, c. 1930 ...$62-70
Buster Brown, c. 1907.......... 31-38
Charlie Chaplin, c. 1915 57-63
Marilyn Monroe, 2 decks, original box 74-80
Shirley Temple 14-20

Drinks/Beverages

Ayers Sarsaparilla ....$ 8-14
Coca-Cola, lady sipping Coke, 1909 62-71
Coca-Cola, lady with parasol, 1915 64-73

Coca-Cola, "Tastes Good!," 1928	54-62
Coca-Cola, lady, gold wings, 1943	27-33
Coca-Cola, lady ice skater, 1956	19-30
Coca-Cola, lady bowler, 1960	19-27
Coca-Cola, couple by fire, 1962	14-21

Souvenir

Chicago World's Fair, c. 1933	$14-22
Columbian Exposition, Columbus landing	63-71
Niagara Falls, Niagara Falls Playing Card Co.	38-44
Pan-American Exposition, c. 1901	32-41
World's Fair, New York, c. 1939	32-40

THE J. L. MOTT IRON WORKS,
NEW YORK AND CHICAGO.
1891
MOTT'S PATENT DIRECT-ACTION SYPHON JET
WATER-CLOSET,

Plumbing Accessories

Plumbing Accessories

Everything **including** the kitchen sink is collectible.

The Primo, complete	$110-120

A dealer in Atlanta, Ga., found two hundred of the above in New England and sold **every** one!

Postcards

Postcards

Austria originated the postcard in 1869; the first one was mailed in this country in 1898. Many things dictate the price in this field of collectibles: rarity, subject matter, condition (most important), age (circa), artist, and how much you want it for your collection. See **Clubs and Publications,** this Price Guide.

Actors/actresses, pre-WWI	$ 2- 3
Advertising, early	1- 2
Animals	50¢- 1
Automobiles, pre-1925	3- 4
Automobiles, post-1925	1- 2
Buses, trucks, farm equipment	75¢- 1
Christmas, New Year's	50¢- 1
Capitols, U.S., world	1- 2
Disasters, pre-1925	2- 3
Easter, embossed, pre-WW I	3- 6
Easter, general	50¢- 1
Expositions/fairs	1- 4
Fire engines, pre-1930	3- 5
Fraternal	1- 2
Girls	1- 3
Greetings, general, pre-1925	1- 2
Halloween, pre-WW I	1- 2
Horse-drawn vehicles	1- 2
Humorous (Illus.)	50¢-75¢
Indians, early	3- 7
Korea-Vietnam	25¢- 1
Leather	1- 2
Military, pre-WW I	3- 6
Military, pre-WW II	50¢- 1
Negroes	1- 2
Novelties	50¢- 1
Patriotic	50¢- 1
People (famous persons)	1- 2
Political	1- 2
Presidents, pre-WW I	2- 3

Presidents, to present	1- 2
Religious, early	2- 3
Royalty	1- 2
St. Patrick's Day, pre-WW I	2- 3
Santa Claus, early	5- 8
Santa Claus, pre-WW I	2- 3
Santa Claus, to present	50¢- 1
Ships/nautical, early	2- 4
Ships/nautical, to present	1- 2
Souvenir folders, pre-1925	2- 4
Sports, early	6- 9
Sports, Roaring 20's	5- 6
States, early	1- 3
States, pre-WW II	2- 3
Thanksgiving	50¢- 1
Thanksgiving, early	1- 3
Trains/trolley cars, early	3- 5
Valentines, early	4-15
Valentines, general	1- 3
Washington, D.C., pre-WW I	2- 3
Western/cowboys, early	2- 3
World War I	2- 4
World War II	1- 3

Precious Stones

Precious Stones

Unless you know how to positively identify a precious stone, put it down! One rule is that a 10-karat-gold setting usually doesn't have much of a stone. 14- or 24 karat gold is what to look for inside the ring. But more than one buyer has come home with a bauble that boggles the mind.

Printers' Type Cases

These old cases are great for hanging on the wall, or just use them to store small items in. Priced about $10-15 each. More for the larger ones.

Printers' Type Cases

Puzzles

Photo Courtesy of
Hake's Americana & Collectibles

Puzzles

There are lots of puzzles at every Flea Market.

Space Patrol puzzle	$ 8-10
Little Annie Rooney puzzle	3- 4
Yellow Kid puzzle	11-13
Automobile puzzle	16-19
Crusader Rabbit puzzle (Illus.)	3- 4
Raggedy Ann puzzle	8- 9
Tarzan puzzle	14-17
Snow White puzzle	9-12
Orphan Annie puzzle	9-16
Davy Crockett puzzle game	2- 3
Joe Palooka puzzle	4- 6

Quilts

Pieced and appliquéd quilts can be found at most Flea Markets, but many people don't know their value. Older quilts are bringing enormous prices. If you think you have a good one, ask a qualified dealer.

Common type, 1930's	$40- 50
Double Irish Chain	270-310
Dutch Tulip	190-230
Nine-Patch	270-310
Tobacco Leaf	350-375

Radio and Television Advertising Items

Atwater-Kent radio, jointed figure	$6-11

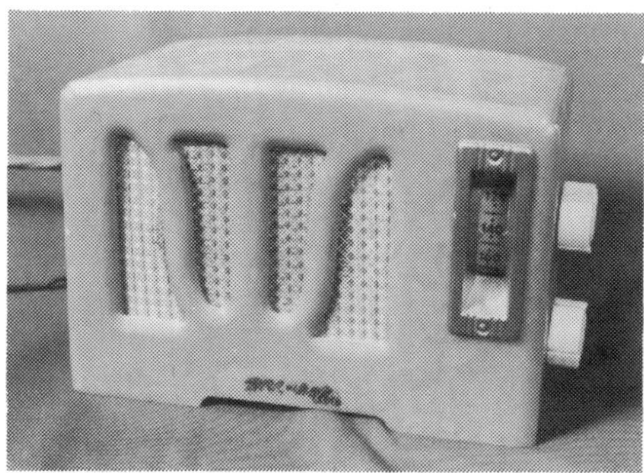

Radio/Television

Radio/Television

Don't worry too much about finding an old crystal set. But, there are a lot of 1930's through 1950's models out there that are beginning to bring decent prices. **Remember:** Have an expert check it out **before** you plug it in! See **Clubs and Publications,** this Price Guide. For tubes and parts, see **Repairs and Services.**

A. C. Dayton Co., XL71, Navigator, 1929	$225-235
Admiral, AM786 (console), 1936	38- 44
Air King, A-403, Court Jester, 1947	20- 28
Aircastle (portable), 1947	10- 17
Airline, 74BR-1053A, 74BR-1057A, 1948, each	10- 16
Alden, 1949	10- 15
Algene, AR-406 (portable), 1948	12- 16
American Bosch, 660T (multiband), 1936	19- 27
Apex, 1948	9- 16
Arvin, 78 (two-band), 1938	11- 16
Atwater Kent, 318 (console), 1934	84- 93
Belmont, 4B115, 1948	11- 17
Bendix, 416A, 1948	11- 16
Capitol, Un72 (both shortwave and AM), 1949	15- 24
Coronado, 43-8437, 1947	11- 16
Crosley, 56TN-L (both shortwave and AM), 1947	12- 17
Delco, R1408, 1947	11- 17
Echophone, S-5, 1932	199-215
Emerson, 536 (portable), 1948	11- 17
Federal, 1040TB, 1948	12- 18
Firestone, 4-A-1, 3, 10, 1948, each	11- 17
Garod, 5A1 Ensign, 1947	12- 18
General Electric	
L-740 (3-band), 1941	36- 44
YRB83-1, 1948	10- 16
357 (AM and FM), 1949	13- 18
Hallicrafters, S-53 (multiband), 1948	44- 52
Jewel, 300, 1948	16- 22
Mitchell, 1254 Madrigal, 1951	11- 16
Motorola	
47B11, 1948	9- 14
67F12 (radio/phonograph), 1948	14- 19
69L11, 1949	1- 15
Packard Bell, 5DA, 1947	10- 14
Philco	
84, 1935	80- 88
46-427 (both shortwave and AM)	16- 23
49-602 (portable), 1949	10- 15
RCA	
Victor, table model (Illus.)	27- 34
68R3, 19, 1946	11- 15
85T8 (3-band), 1947	45- 52
Remler, 5500 Scottie Pup, 1949	16- 23
Silvertone, 8005, 1948	10- 15
Tele-Tone, 150, 1948	10- 15
Westinghouse, H161 (AM/FM), 1949	12- 17
Zenith, 8-H-o61, 1946	73- 80

Suggested reading: *Antique Radios: Restoration and Price Guide,* Betty and David Johnson, Wallace-Homestead Book Company.

Railroad Collectibles

Anything relating to the Iron Horse is sought after today. Railroad silver, really just a silver-soldered product — lots of it made by Reed and Barton — is especially collectible. See **Clubs and Publications,** this Price Guide.

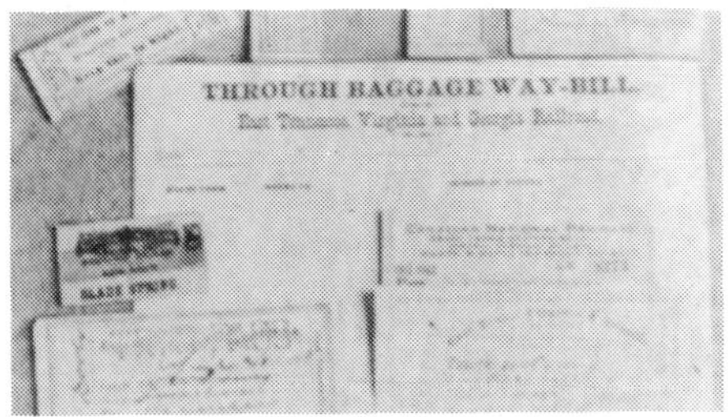

Railroad Collectibles

Miscellaneous

Attendants' and waiters' badges, most lines, each $10-15
Bonds, all railroads issued them, average price 10-16
Breast badges, each 16-20
Caboose lamp................. 67-75
Cab badges, any railroad, average price, each 20-27
Conductor's ticket punch, American brand 11-17
Cuspidor, porcelainized, Maine Central 25-32
Hand lantern, clear, Rock Island Line (Illus.) 48-56
Hand lantern, red, Southern Pacific 50-60
Inspector's lantern, Bangor & Aroostock 84-92
Journal box oil can, N.Y.N.H. & H. 37-46
Knife, fork, spoon, napkin holder, Louisville & Southern R.R., all . 57-65
Menu holder, Rock Island Line R.R. 18-23
Passes: issued to conductors, officers of the company, average 8-11
Postcards, depicting various R.R. scenes, each 1- 2
Pullman step.................. 75-83
Railroad employees' collar insignia, each 9-15
Railway Express sign, 18″ × 18″, reversible.................. 40-47
Spikes, each 1- 2
Tamping bar, 16 to 25 lbs. 19-28
Track maul, 5 to 10 lbs. 20-27
Tickets: Norfolk and Western, E. Tennessee, Virginia and Georgia R.R. (Illus.), average price, each 6- 7
Timetables, most railroads, c. 1900's, average price, each.... 3- 6

Railroad China

Railroad China

Like so many other things relating to the almost-extinct dining car, the china is now being eagerly sought after. Look for the line's name or initials on the front. Some of the firms who manufactured this china are Lenox, Maddock, Minton, Syracuse, and Warwick. Several factories in Limoges, France, also made it. Prices are for pieces in mint condition.

Ashtrays

Canadian Pacific, Banff National Park, 6½″ dia. ....$ 40- 47
Chesapeake & Ohio, Washington's bust, 7″ dia. 80- 88
New York Central, Hudson River scene, 6¼″ dia. 51- 60

Butter Patties

Baltimore & Ohio (Illus.) ......$ 25- 31
Denver & Rio Grande......... 22- 27
Great Northern 25- 31
New York Central............ 24- 33

Celeries

Erie, floral designs, Erie, diamond logo, 10″ wide	$ 64- 72
Santa Fe, Flow Blue type, 12½″ wide	79- 84

Creamers

Baltimore & Ohio, 1930's	$ 45- 53
New York Central, 1940's	43- 50
Union Pacific	44- 52

Cups and Saucers

Coffee, Denver & Rio Grande	$ 23- 29
Coffee, Florida East Coast	29- 34
Demitasse, Atlantic Coast Line	19- 25
Demitasse, Chesapeake & Ohio	18- 24

Egg Cups

Double, New York Central	$ 16- 20
Double, Union Pacific	18- 25
Single, Baltimore & Ohio	13- 17

Miscellaneous

Cereal bowl, Erie, pinstripe border, diamond logo, 6″ dia.	$ 63- 70
Compote, Boston & Albany, double logo, 4″ high	192-210
Gravy boat, New York Central	64- 73
Ice cream dish, Canadian Pacific	32- 48

Plates

Dinner, Baltimore & Ohio	$ 54- 60
Dinner, Great Northern	45- 51
Dinner, Penn Central	45- 54
Serving, New York Central	53- 61
Serving, Santa Fe	50- 60
Salad, Chicago, Burlington & Quincy	39- 49

Platters

Santa Fe	$61- 71
Southern Pacific	62- 72
Wabash	58- 68

Red Wing

Founded in Red Wing, Minnesota, in 1878, Red Wing Pottery produced stoneware items such as crocks and jugs. In the 1920's they came out with a line of art pottery, and in the 1940's, added a line of hand-painted dinnerware. Bob White was their most popular pattern. A strike in 1967 shut the plant forever. "Red Wing USA," "RW," "Red Wing Art Pottery," "Red Wing — Hand Painted," and a large wing are various marks used on their stoneware, art pottery, and dinnerware.

See **Clubs and Publications,** this Price Guide.

Art Pottery

Ashtray, blue	$18-24
Candlestick, maroon, 3″, RW	17-23
Cornucopia, ribbed/scalloped, RW USA	27-31
Pitcher, green, 8½″	27-32
Vase, brown/mottled, Red Wing USA	34-42
Vase, white/green, flowers in relief, Red Wing USA	37-42

Cookie Jars

Chef, blue or yellow, each	$35-42
Dutch girl, yellow or blue, each	26-41
Monk, blue, yellow, ivory, each	26-37

Dinnerware

Anniversary shape, 1953. There are six patterns: Capistrano, Driftwood, Pink Spice, Tweed Tex, Country Garden, and Midnight Rose. All patterns have a basket-weave texture. Each pattern has different colored accessory pieces.

Bread tray	$ 9-14
Butter dish w/cover	6-10
Casserole w/cover	9-16
Cereal bowl	5- 9
Creamer	5- 8
Cup/saucer set	7-11
Dinner plate, 10½″	5- 7
Platters, 13″, 15″, each	7-12
Salad plate, 7½″	4- 6
Salt/pepper set	5- 9
Sugar bowl w/cover	5- 9
Teapot w/cover	14-20
Water pitcher	10-17

Anniversary shape, 1955-1961. There are five patterns: Smart Set (1955), Bob White (1956), Tip Toe (1958), Round Up (1958), and Hearthside (1961).

Bread and butter plate, 6½″	$ 4- 7
Bread tray, 24″	17-32
Butter dish w/cover	11-16
Casseroles, 1 qt., 3 qt., 4 qt., each	10-22
Cocktail tray	9-20
Creamer	9-16
Dinner plate, 10½″	5-10
Gravy boat w/cover	11-23
Platters, 13″, 20″, each	13-20
Teapot w/cover	17-36
Water pitcher, 60 oz.	12-26

Concord shape, beginning in 1947. There were some eighteen patterns: Blossom Time, Bud, Chrysanthemum, Fantasy, Fruit, Harvest, Iris, Leaf Magic, Lexington, Lotus, Lanterns, Magnolia, Morning Glory (pink or blue), Nassau, Spring Song, and Willow Wind. Modified square-shaped plates, wide-lipped cups, long-handled casseroles, and "pour easy" spouts on teapots, beverage servers, and pitchers are a few of the features of Concord.

	Harvest, Nassau, Bud, Leaf Magic	Quartette	All other patterns
Bread and butter plate, 6½″	$ 6-11	3- 5	4- 6
Butter dish w/cover . .	12-17	4- 7	5- 9
Celery dish .	16-22	4- 7	5- 9
Cereal dish .	6-10	4- 7	6-10
Chop plate .	11-16	6- 9	7-12
Cream soup	9-13	4- 7	5- 8
Cream soup w/cover . .	11-16	5- 9	6-10
Creamer . . .	11-16	4- 7	5- 9
Cup/saucer set	17-26	6-11	7-11
Salt/pepper set	11-16	4- 7	5- 8
Sugar bowl w/cover . .	11-16	4- 7	6- 9
Supper tray, 10½″		6- 9	7-11
Teapot w/cover . .	27-37	7-11	7-11

Futura shape, first made in 1955, came in the following patterns: Frontenac, Tampico, Random Harvest, Crazy Rhythm, Golden Viking, Lupine, Northern Lights, Montmartre, Red Wing Rose, and Colonnes. Modified ovals and "non-splash" lips were just two of its features.

	Tampico	All other patterns
Bread and butter plate, 6½″	$ 4- 7	3- 6
Butter dish w/cover . .	7-13	6-10
Cake plate, 3 tier	22-32	17-22
Casserole w/cover . . .	13-19	10-16
Cereal bowl	6-11	5- 9
Creamer	8-15	5- 9
Cup/saucer set	14-19	8-12
Dinner plate, 10½″ . .	6-11	5- 9
Nut dish, 5 compartments	14-21	
Platter, 13″, 15″, each	8-16	7-13
Salad plate, 8½″	5- 9	4- 7
Salt/pepper set	7-11	5- 9
Sugar bowl w/cover . .	10-16	6-11

Kermis pattern was made in 1957. A "dancing jester" on turquoise and black pieces. It's considered scarce today.

Beverage server	$23-32
Creamer	10-14
Cup	8-11
Nut bowl	17-26
Plate, 8½″	10-14
Salad bowl, large	17-26
Saucer	5- 7
Sugar bowl w/cover	12-17
Tray, sandwich	17-26

Labriego pattern was made in the late 1930's and is considered very scarce. The Provincial "Oomph" pattern, made in 1943, has very scarce pieces: bowls, 6″, 8″, 10″, each $17-23. Water jug, $19-36.

Suggested reading: *Redwing Potters and Their Wares w/Price Guide,* Gary and Bonnie Tefft, Locust Enterprises.

Rhead Pottery

Founded in 1913, it was originally called the Pottery of the Camarata. The shop closed in 1917. Usual mark is Rhead Pottery/Santa Barbara. Paper labels were also used.

Jardiniere, Chinese mirror glaze, signed, 34″ high	$395-462
Tile, inlaid process, signed	72- 82
Vase, floral, blue/green glaze, signed, 9¼″ high	225-262
Vase, inlaid process, multicolored, signed, 7¾″ high .	298-342
Vase, matt green, pink/blue glaze, signed, 2¼″ high	198-240

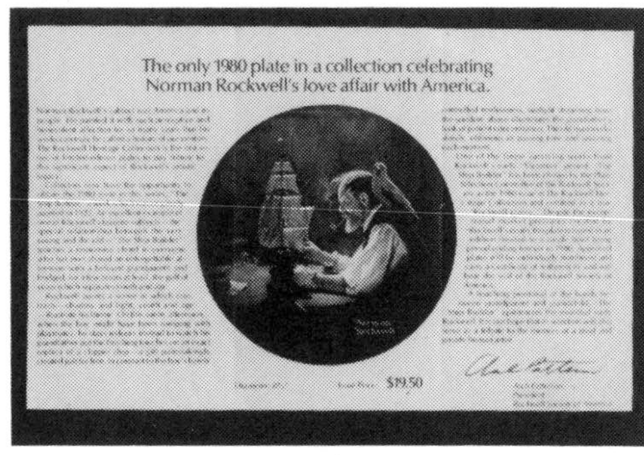

Rockwell, Norman

Rockwell, Norman

When you talk about this great artist/illustrator, you've got to look at two things: Rockwell originals, such as oil paintings and pencil sketches, **and** the thousands of reproductions flooding the market today. If you're collecting the originals, know what you're doing or engage an authority. If you're collecting reproductions, you'll have a field day. Some of the repros will one day be valuable, such as the limited edition prints, personally signed by Rockwell. See **Clubs and Publications,** this Price Guide. Carl F. Luckey's *Norman Rockwell, Art and Collectibles* is a must if you're going to collect Rockwell.

Bells

Danbury Mint Series (No. 1), 1975-1977, each .... $ 58- 64
Danbury Mint Series, 1979, each 39- 45
Gorham, 1974, first edition 87- 95
Grossman Designs, Faces of Christmas, limited edition ... 41- 50
River Shore, Ltd., children's series (No. 1), 1977, set of 4 . 340-350

Coins

Ford Motor Co., 50th Anniversary .... $ 23- 30
Kennedy Mint, Four Freedoms, set of 4 165-175

Figurines

Gorham Fine China, average price, each................. $ 53- 60
Gorham Fine China, Four Seasons, set of 4, average price, 1972-1977 450-535
Franklin Mint, 1976, limited edition, series of 10, each 158-167
Grossman Designs, Baseball, 1974 265-275
Grossman Designs, Barbershop Quartet, 1975 160-170

Ingots

Franklin Mint issues

Spirit of Scouting, sterling silver, 12 medals, 1972 .... $ 350 +
Norman Rockwell's Fondest Memories, 10, 1973 .... 350 +
As above, 1976 .... 350 +
Tribute to Robert Frost, sterling silver, 12 medals, 1974 .. 450 +
Favorite Moments from Mark Twain, sterling silver, 12, 1975 .... 450 +
The Official Girl Scout, sterling silver, 12, 1977 .... 275 +

Hamilton Mint issues

The Four Freedoms, solid silver, 4, 1974 .... $ 300 +
As above, but gold-plated ..... 300 +
The Christmas Theme, 1974-1979, pure silver, each . 47- 56
Best Loved Saturday Evening Post Covers, pure silver, 12 . 275-350
The Four Seasons, sterling silver medals, 4, 1976 95-118
Portraits of America, pure silver, 24, 1977 .... 875 +

Miscellaneous

Bottles, Beam's 1976 Bicentennial, limited edition, 6, each . $ 13- 18
Bowl, Yankee Doodle, Gorham, 8½″ dia., 1975 107-116
Cachepots (small covered bowl), Series 1, 1979; Series 2, 1980, each.............. 74- 84
Mugs, Grossman Designs, "toby" style, 4″ high, 6, 1979, each 42- 48
Music box, Schmidt Brothers, Four Seasons 34- 42
Paperweight, crystal, triple self portrait, 1980.............. 250 +
Puzzles (jigsaw), Jaymar Specialty Co. and Parker Brothers, 40 or 50 different, each 10- 15
Souvenir spoons, Grossman Designs, pewter, 12 different, each .... 35 +

Suggested reading: *Norman Rockwell, Art and Collectibles,* Carl F. Luckey, Books Americana.

Rogers, Will

Rogers, Will

Anything to do with this famous American humorist is highly collectible.

Roller/Ice Skates

The shoe-type skate is being collected.

Boot-type roller skates, pr. . . . . . . $ 9-17
Boot-type ice skates, pr. 13-22
Clamp-type roller skates, pr. 5- 9
Skate keys . . . . 75¢- 1

Rosemeade

When the Whapeton Pottery Company of Whapeton, North Dakota, was organized in 1940, Rosemeade was the name selected for the pottery. Small animals and birds were featured. "Rosemeade" in ink stamp or "Prairie Rose" paper label. In 1961 the firm closed.

Ashtray, partridge, paper label . . . $ 9-14
Basket, blue, paper label 10-14
Creamer, green glaze, ink stamp . 7-10
Flower frog, squirrel 11-15
Planter, pheasants, 5¼″ 9-13
Salt/pepper shakers, hen/rooster, pr. 10-14
Salt/pepper shakers, pheasants, pr. 12-15
Vase, blue/white, 7¼″ 24-28
Vase, pink glaze, 6½″ 21-27

Roseville Pottery

Roseville Pottery

Roseville, Ohio, 1892, this pottery firm was making stoneware jars, cuspidors, and flowerpots. In 1898 the firm moved to Zanesville but didn't make art pottery until 1900. No art pottery was ever made at Roseville. Their first art line was called Rozane. Some of the marks used were "RPCo.," "Rozane–RPCo" beneath, "Rozane Ware Royal," "Rozane Ware Mara." Paper "Roseville Pottery Co." labels were also used. This pottery was comparable to Weller. It never reached the quality level of Rookwood.

Ashtray, red, blue handles, old RV mark . . . . $ 47- 53
Bank, piggy, 4″ high, unsigned 54- 61
Basket, 6½″ high, Bittersweet, Roseville, U.S.A. in relief 55- 60
Basket, Pinecone pattern, script signature 61- 70
Bookends, Pinecone pattern, script signature, pr. 64- 73
Bowl, Donatello pattern (cherubs), cream color, beige, green 62- 72
Bowl, roses, pansies, blue/green, script signature . 57- 67
Candleholder, floral pattern, 10″ high, script signature . . . 52- 60
Cornucopia, Mock Orange, 5½″ high, Roseville, U.S.A. in relief 57- 61
Cup, 3½″ high, clover motif, Juvenile line, unsigned 44- 50
Jardiniere, 9″ high, Cameo line, unsigned 75- 82
Jardiniere, pinecone pattern, twig handles, script signature 72- 84
Letter holder, 3½″ high, brown, flowers, Rozane Ware Royal 81- 90
Mostique jardiniere, 9½″ high, unsigned 97-114
Tankard, Della Robbia line, 10½″ high, unsigned 167-175
Tankard, 11″ high, monk, brown, Rozane Ware 182-190
Tankard, 10½″ high, signed "V. Adams," Rozane Ware Royal 177-184
Teapot, creamer, sugar, flower decor, script signature, all . . . 82- 90
Teapot, 4¼″ high, Mayfair, Roseville, U.S.A. in relief 44- 50
Urn, 8½″ high, Rosecraft Vintage line, "R" containing small "v" 74- 83
Vase, Aztec, 8″ high 73- 84
Vase, Bittersweet, 6¼″ high, Roseville, U.S.A. in relief 58- 64
Vase, bud, yellow/green/blue, script signature 75- 84
Vase, double bud, 6″ high, Florentine, "R" containing small "v" 70- 78
Vase, Carnelian line, 10½″ high, blue "R" stamped on bottom 72- 82
Vase, 12″ high, flowers, Azurine, no mark (probably had paper label) 74- 83

Vase, 6″ high, Dahlrose line, unsigned	65- 73
Vase, 13½″ high, Della Robbia line, Rozane Ware	89- 94
Vase, Donatello, 15″ high	81- 90
Vase, Egypto, 11½″ high, Rozane Ware Egypto	94-102
Vase, 19¼″ high, dogs hunting, Rozane R.P.Co.	120-130
Vase, 8″ high, Florentine line, "R" containing small "v"	64- 73
Vase, 14″ high, Indian chief brown/red, Rozane Ware inside circle	155-164
Vase, 13″ high, metallic lustre line, Rozane Ware Mara	159- 164
Vase, 9″ high, Woodland, "Fujiyama" rubber stamped on bottom	110-118
Vase, 11½″ high, Woodland line, floral designs, Rozane Ware	94-100
Vase, Rozane Ware, 12″ high (Illus.)	151-161
Wall pocket, 10″ high, Donatello line	74- 82

Royal Doulton

ROYAL DOULTON ENGLAND

Royal Doulton

The art director at Royal Doulton, Charles J. Noke, developed a series of figurines, animal and bird models, and character jugs around 1913. The miniature (M) series was begun during the Depression. The K series is bird and animal miniatures. All pieces are marked Royal Doulton and bear the RD number, the registration number at the British Patent Office. Numbers for all figures are preceded by the initials HN. The numbers on the figurines are not chronological, as some numbers were skipped, while others were held in reserve for future pieces. The letters A and D appear on jugs. For some reason, those bearing the letter A bring more money than those with the letter D. Watch out for repros!

Animal and Bird Models

Alsatian, 106	$ 310- 342
American Foxhound, large, 2524	262- 281
American Great Dane, large, 2601	328- 360
Baltimore Oriole, 2542	262- 281
Bulldog, brindle, large, 1042	225- 234
Bulldog, brown and white, medium, 1046	162- 172
Cairn, black, medium, 1105	170- 180
Cat, Persian, white, 2539	158- 166
Cat, Siamese, sitting, 2665	78- 88
Cock Pheasant, 2632	520- 540
Cocker Spaniel and Pheasant, medium, 1028	148- 172
Collie, silver gray, 975	320- 340
Drake, mallard, large, 956	210- 240
Fox, on rock, 147	162- 172
Gordon Setter, small, 1081	148- 168
Hare, lying, small, 2594	56- 66
Kingfisher, small, 2573	108- 121
Mallard, 2556	240- 270
Peacock, 2577	162- 170
Pekingese, sitting, large, 1039	252- 275
Pig, asleep, 2545	277- 286
Puppy, 128	188- 199
River Hog, 2663	152- 162
Sealyham, lying, large, 1041	278- 320
Teal Duck, 229	187- 196
Tiger, 2646	887- 952

Character Jugs (all Ds)

Anne Boleyn, small, 6650, 1975	$ 74- 83
Apothecary, large, 6567, 1963	89- 104
'Ard of 'Earing, small, 6591, 1964-67	672- 720
Athos, large, 6439, 1960	94- 106
Bacchus, small, 6505, 1959	69- 75
Blacksmith, small, 6578, 1963	64- 76
Captain Ahab, miniature, 6522, 1960	44- 50
Captain Hook, large, 6597, 1965-71	332- 342
Catherine Howard, large, 6645, 1978	108- 119
Churchill, large, 6170, 1940	11,000 +
Dick Turpin, small, 5618, 1935-60	74- 83

Don Quixote, small, 6460, 1957 . . . 65- 73
Falconer, miniature, 6547, 1960 . . . 44- 51
Fat Boy, miniature, 6139, 1940-60 . . . 77- 87
Golfer, large, 6623, 1971 . . 89- 99
Gone Away, small, 6538, 1960 . . . 64- 73
Gulliver, large, 6560, 1962-67 . . . 496- 552
Izaak Walton, large, 6404, 1953 . . . 88- 101
Jockey, large, 6625, 1971-75 . . . 174- 182
Johnny Appleseed, large, 6372, 1935-69 . . . 282- 324
Long John Silver, small, 6386, 1952 . . . 73- 80
Mark Twain, large, 6654, 1980 . . . 88- 98
The Mikado, small, 6507, 1959-69 . . . 272- 299
Mr. Micawber, miniature, 6138, 1940-60 . . . 64- 73
Neptune, large, 6548, 1961 89- 99
Old King Cole, small, 6037, 1939-60 . . . 108- 118
Parson Brown, small, 5529, 1935-60 . . . 77- 87
Porthos, miniature, 6516, 1960 . . . 40- 50
Robinson Crusoe, small, 6539, 1960 . . . 62- 72
Sairey Gamp, small, 5528, 1935 . . . 67- 73
Scaramouche, miniature, 6564, 1962-67 . . . 352- 382
Smuggler, large, 6616, 1968-80 . . . 88- 98
Toby Philpots, large, 5736, 1937-69 . . . 124- 137
The Trapper, large, 6609, 1967 . . . 85- 93
Vicar of Bray, large, 5615, 1936-60 . . . 192- 221
Walrus and Carpenter, small, 6604, 1965-79 . . . 81- 90

Figurines

Adrienne—purple gown, yellow scarf, 2152, 1964-76 . . . $ 188- 229
blue gown, light green scarf, 2304, 1964 . . . 173- 188
The Afternoon Call, 82, 1918-38 . . . 2,500-2,775
A La Mode, 2544, 1964-79 . 198- 232
Alexandre, 2398, 1970-76 . . 167- 187
Annabella—orange skirt, green bodice, 1871, 1938-49 . . . 520- 570
green skirt, blue bodice, 1872, 1938-49 . . . 525- 570
red dress, 1875, 1938-49 . 552- 561
Anthea, 1526, 1932-38 . . . 820- 856
Apple Maid, 2160, 1957-62 . 468- 492
Artful Dodger, 546, 1922 . . 320- 344
At Ease, 2473, 1973-79 . . . 220- 242
The Awakening, 1927, 1927-28 . . . 2,225-2,520
Baby, 12, 1913-38 . . . 2,295-2,450
Balloon Man, 1954, 1940 . . 210- 222
Balloon Seller, 548, 1922-38 895- 970
Bather, 773, 1925-38 . . . 1,450-1,650
Beachcomber, 2487, 1973-76 . . . 220- 240
Belle, 754, 1925-38 . . . 1,400-1,600
Betsy, 2111, 1953-59 . . . 392- 452
Biddy, 1843, 1938 . . . 220- 240
Blithe Morning—pink skirt, blue bodice, 2021, 1949-71 . . . 195- 242
red dress, green/yellow, 2065, 1950-73 . . . 235- 252
Bluebeard, 1528, 1932-49 . . 1,400-1,475
Bonnie Lassie, 1626, 1934-53 . . . 352- 370
Boudoir, 2542, 1974-79 . . . 344- 359
Boy on Pig, 1369, 1930-38 . 995-1,270
Bride, 1st version, 1841, 1938-49 . . . 925- 955
Bridget, 2070, 1951-73 . . . 310- 340
Bunny, 2214, 1960-75 . . . 162- 182
Buz Fuz, 538, 1922 . . . 325- 355
Camellia, 2222, 1960-71 . . . 320- 345
Captain Hook, 2889, 1980 . . 415- 452
Carolyn, 2112, 1953-59 . . . 345- 362
Carrie, 2800, 1976 . . . 142- 156
Charley's Aunt, 1st version, 640, 1924-38 . . . 1,100-1,275
Chelsea Pensioner, 689, 1924-38 . . . 1,600-1,800
Child and Crab, 32, 1913-38 1,450-1,550
Choir boy, 2141, 1954-75 . . 128- 142
Christmas Parcels, 2851, 1978 . . . 256- 266
Cicely, 1516, 1932-49 . . . 1,500-1,650
Clockmaker, 2279, 1961-75 . 410- 432
Coachman, 2282, 1963-71 . . 575- 620
Colinette, 1998, 1947-49 . . . 542- 562
Cookie, 2218, 1958-75 . . . 118- 127
Country Lass, 1991, 1975 . . 188- 198
A Courting, 2004, 1947-53 . 752- 772
Curly Locks, 2049, 1949-53 325- 365
Debbie, 2385, 1969 . . . 141- 152
The Detective, 2359, 1977 . 196- 221
The Diligent Scholar, 26, 1913-28 . . . 1,400-1,475
Double Jester, 365, 1920-38 2,495-2,720
Drummer Boy, 2679, 1976 . 410- 432
Easter Day, 1976, 1945-51 . 528- 588
Eleanor of Provence, 2009, 1948-53 . . . 720- 790
Elyse, 2429, 1972 . . . 242- 250
Enchantment, 2178, 1957 . . 182- 192
Evening, 2814, 1977 . . . 187- 242
Faraway, 2133, 1958-62 . . . 220- 240
The Fiddler, 2171, 1956-62 . 1,100-1,250
Flora, 2349, 1966-73 . . . 225- 245
Folly, 1335, 1929-38 . . . 1,875-1,980
Friar Tuck, 2143, 1954-65 . . 462- 485
Genevieve, 1962, 1941-75 . . 252- 281

A Good Catch, 2258, 1966 . 190- 210
Grand Manner, 2723, 1975 . 278- 322
Guy Fawkes, 347, 1919-38 . 1,985-2,375
Heart-to-Heart, 2276, 1961-71 . . . . 475- 525
He Loves Me, 2046, 1949-62 . . . . 170- 180
Iona, 1346, 1929-38 2,800-3,000
Innocence, 2842, 1979 . . . . 175- 185
Jack, 2060, 1950-71 . . . . 171- 180
Janet, 1537, 1932 (Illus.) . . 130- 140
Janine, 2461, 1971 . . . . 195- 222
Jill, 2061, 1950-71 . . . . 194- 199
Judge and Jury, 1264, 1927-38 3,450-3,675
Kate, 2789, 1978 . . . . 178- 196
Katrina, 2327, 1965-69 . . . . 320- 352
Lady Betty, 1967, 1941-51 . 375- 395
Lambing Time, 1890, 1938-80 . . . . 180- 220
Long John Silver, 2204, 1957-65 . . . . 425- 456
Lucy Ann, 1502, 1932-50 . . 370- 390
Mantilla, 2712, 1974-79 . . . . 362- 392
Masque, 2554, 1973 . . . . . . 240- 260
Milady, 1970, 1941-49 . . . . . 962- 992
Newsboy, 2244, 1959-65 . . . 765- 795
Nina, 2347, 1969-76 . . . . 178- 187
Orange Seller, 1325, 1929-49 . . . . 920- 945
Past Glory, 2484, 1973-79 . . 265- 295
Pauline, 1444, 1931-38 . . . . 452- 482
Pedlar Wolf, 7, 1913-38 2,475-2,695
Picnic, 2308, 1965 . . . . 140- 150
Pirate King, 2901, 1981 . . . . 810- 880
The Potter, 1493, 1932 . . . . 362- 382
A Princess, 392, 1920-38 . . 3,200-3,400
Professor, 2281, 1965-80 . . 220- 230
Prue, 1996, 1947-55 . . . . . . 392- 422
Quality Street, 1211, 1926-38 1,375-1,475
Rendezvous, 2212, 1962-71 420- 460
Rhapsody, 2267, 1961-73 . . 262- 292
Rosabelle, 1620, 1934-38 . . 1,100-1,300
Rosemary, 2091, 1952-59 . . 522- 562
Salome, 1828, 1937-49 4,900-5,400
Seafarer, 2455, 1972-76 . . . 220- 248
Sea Sprite, 1261, 1927-38 . . 670- 690
She Loves Me Not, 2045, 1949-62 . . . . 196- 208
Shore Leave, 2254, 1965-79 230- 262
Siesta, 1305, 1928-38 2,200-2,400
Simone, 2378, 1971 . . . . 210- 242
Spirit of the Wind, 1825, 1937-49 3,900-4,400
Spooks, 372, 1920-36 1,850-2,100
Stiggins, 536, 1922 . . . . 330- 344
Summer's Day, 2181, 1957-62 . . . . 462- 479
Suzette, 1487, 1933-38 . . . . 590- 638
Sweet Lavender, 1373, 1930-49 . . . . 740- 760
Sylvia, 1478, 1931-38 . . . . . 820- 862
Thanksgiving, 2446, 1972-76 . . . . 209- 218
Tootles, 1680, 1935-75 . . . . 152- 172
Two A Penny, 1359, 1929-38 1,100-1,350
Veneta, 2722, 1974-80 . . . . . 182- 192
Victoria, 2471, 1973 . . . . 228- 310
Vivienne, 2073, 1951-67 . . . 310- 362
A Wandering Minstrel, 1224, 1927-38 1,600-1,850
Wayfarer, 2362, 1970-76 . . . 175- 235
The Welsh Girl, 456, 1921-38 2,700-2,950
West Wind, 1826, 1937-49 . 4,850-5,450
The Winner, 1407, 1930-38 . 3,570-3,690
Wistful, 2396, 1979 . . . . 385- 420
Wood Nymph, 2192, 1958-62 . . . . 285- 310
The Young Knight, 94, 1918-36 3,200-3,500
Young Master, 2872, 1980 . 362- 422
Young Widow, 1399, 1930 . 1,500-1,650

Suggested reading: *Royal Doulton Figurines and Character Jugs,* Katharine Morrison McClinton, Wallace-Homestead Book Company.

Rugs

There are Oriental rugs, hooked rugs, and just plain rugs. If you like, buy.

Salem China

See **American Dinnerware.**

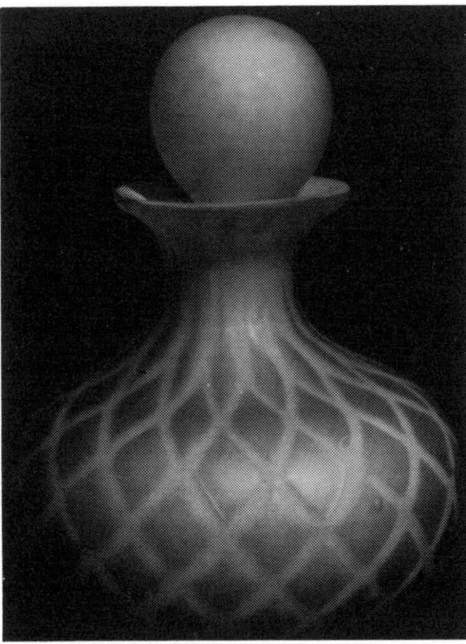

Satin Glass

Satin Glass

There is **so** much reproduction of satin glass on the market, it isn't worth collecting. The old, genuine brings high prices, but few, if any, dealers can tell it from the new. Buy if you like, but buy for NEW because that's what you're getting!

Satsuma, new

Both the old and the new are products of Japan. The original goes back to the early 1600's, but what you'll find today was made in the 1920's (see illustration) and is still being made. A simple scuff on a cement sidewalk gives you "instant age." Buy it for new; if you find it's old, voilá! Traditional colors are orange, blue, green, red, and yellow. Popular periods for modern-day collectors are Taisho and Showa.

Satsuma, new

Bowl, brown background, bird decor, 7½″ dia. $46-53
Candleholders, black background, insect decor in gilt, pr. 39-46
Cup/saucer set, brown background, molded dragon motif . . 27-33
Hotei (Buddah-like figure "combing" bald pate), various colors, c. 1940's 78-83
Lamp, yellow ground, red/blue/green, gilt trim (Illus.) 45-53
Saki set: bottle, 6 lithopane cups, typical colors, all 77-83
Teapot, dragon handle, floral decor, gilt trim, 5¼″ 57-63
Vase, black background, lotus-form handles, 7″ 64-71

School Desks

The old-fashioned kind are collectible. Mount them on runners (like skis) so they won't tip over.

Average price, wood and cast iron frames in good condition . . $70-80

Scouting Collectibles

Boy Scouts

Bank, plaster (Illus.) $12-16
Binoculars, in original case, 1930's 24-32
Bugle, brass, 1920's 65-75
Card, membership, September 1933 9-12
Compass, official, Taylor Instruments, 1939 14-18
First aid kit, official 11-15

Scouting

Photo Courtesy of
Hake's Americana & Collectibles

Flashlight	10-14
Handbook, scout master's, 1958	5- 8
Hat, campaign-type, felt	22-27
Hatchet in original scabbard	16-20
Knife, official seal, 1930's	21-27
Merit badge sash, 40 different patches, 1947, all	69-74
Scarf, official	7-10
Sundial/watch, 1930's	18-23
Uniform, complete, 1930's	44-52

Girl Scouts

Juliette Gordon Low founded the first troop on March 12, 1912, in Savannah, Georgia. The first Girl Scout convention was held on June 10, 1915, in our nation's capital. Items of interest to collectors are books, bookends, cameras, knives, handbooks, uniforms.

Sebastian Miniature Porcelains

Prescott W. Baston first produced them in 1938 at Marblehead, Massachusetts. More than 400 designs were modeled before Mr. Baston withdrew his miniatures from production in 1976. Since then, under an agreement with the Lance Corporation of Hudson, Massachusetts, 100 designs have been selected to be produced by them. The older figurines are beginning to bring brisk prices. "Sebastian" appears on all pieces. See **Clubs and Publications,** this Price Guide.

Abe Lincoln, yellow label, signed	$ 23- 27
Bringing Home the Tree, #2207	21- 26
Building Days, signed	75- 85
Coronado and Senora, #2001	16- 24
Covered Bridge	83- 93
Doctor, plate, signed	33- 42
Family Picnic, signed	39- 44
First House	133-148
First Kite, #2215	24- 28
George Washington, signed	25- 33
Henry Hudson, #2182	16- 23
John Alden	64- 73
Lobsterman, blue label	24- 29
Mount Rushmore, #6010	15- 22
Old Salt	44- 49
The Thinker	267-282
Tom Sawyer, blue label	17- 26
Will Rogers	22- 28
Yankee Clipper	57- 64

Seine (Net) Balls

Seine (Net) Balls

These were used to hold up the nets before styrofoam floats came along. Still being used in the Orient.

3″ to 5″ diameter	$ 13- 17
6″ and larger	35- 52
Very large (Illus.)	120-140

Shaving Mugs

Shaving Mugs

When the "Barber's Itch" swept this country in the late 1800's, individual shaving mugs came into demand. Lots of them around in all sizes, shapes, and quality. Some have the occupation of the former owner on them, and these are highly collectible.

Occupational

Baseball player	$160-175
Blacksmith w/anvil	155-165
Locomotive engineer	175-185
Mason	125-145

Others

Left-handed (rare), floral pattern	$ 85- 95
Silver-plated, initialed	52- 60
White w/flowers	44- 53
Milk glass	35- 44

Hundreds of repros, so watch it!

Shawnee Pottery

Zanesville, Ohio, 1935 until 1961. Inexpensive novelty ware, dinnerware, kitchenware, giveaways. Early pieces marked with an Indian on arrowhead; later, "Shawnee" and "Kenwood." Their Corn line is a popular collectible today.

Bank

Smiley pig	$10-14

Butter Dishes

Corn King	$28-34
Corn Queen	28-34

Cookie Jars

Corn King	$34-41
Miss Muffet	27-35
Owl, decorated	55-63
Sailor boy, plain	40-47
Smiley pig, clover decor	48-55

Creamers

Bo-Peep	$17-22
Corn King	10-13
Elephant	8-13
Puss 'n Boots	15-19
Smiley pig	15-20

Pitchers

Bo Peep	$28-32
Elephant, 4″ high	6-10
Smiley pig	33-37

Planters

Clown	$ 7-10
Donkey cart	16-20
Oriental lady	8-11
Rockinghorse	10-14
Rooster	13-17
Wishing well	10-14

Salt/Pepper Sets

Mugsey dogs	$17-24
Owls	11-14
Puss 'n Boots	13-16
Smiley pigs, blue bibs	19-24
Sprinkling can	9-12

Teapots

Granny	$13-17
Little Red Riding Hood	87-93
Tom, Tom the Piper's Son	36-42
Vase, bow knot, green	12-15
Vase, green/white	11-14
Wall pocket, Little Jack Horner	16-20

Shoe Lasts/Stands

You see them in various sizes at most Flea Markets. Are they collectible? They are if you collect shoe lasts/stands.

Average price (Illus.)	$8-13

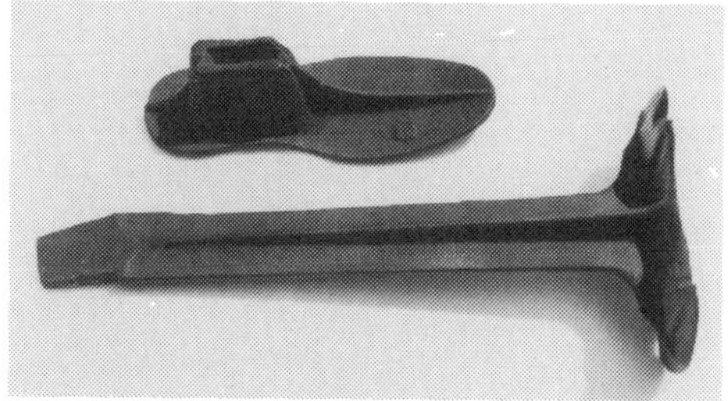

Shoe Lasts/Stands

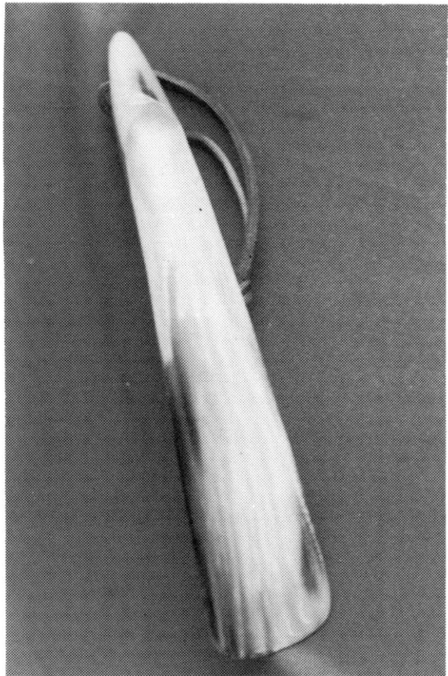

Shoehorns

Shoehorns

Metal, plastic, animal horn, trough-like in shape, they're used to help one get into one's shoes. The older ones are being collected today.

Average price . . . . 50¢-$1

Shoes

Now why would shoes be collectible? Because the old ones make great door stops when filled with cement, plaster, whatever.

Shoes

The illustrated are sabots, wooden shoes worn by the peasants of Europe, especially in Holland $20-28

Shoeshine Collectibles

Photo Courtesy of
Hake's Americana & Collectibles

Shoeshine Collectibles

Old shoeshine kits, cans of polish, shoe brushes, advertising material — all are being collected. Being a shoeshine boy was a way of surviving during our Depression years. Some of our nation's leading citizens once polished shoes.

Silhouettes

Find a Charles Peale, 1800 to 1810, and you're rich! August Edouart also made some great ones.

The kind you find today (Illus.) $4-8

Silhouettes

Silver Flatware

Silver plate is an inexpensive imitation of sterling. There are countless thousands of pieces lying around at Flea Markets, shops, garage sales, and auctions. Sterling silver means 925 parts of pure silver and 75 parts of copper per 1,000. Sterling flatware prices fluctuate with the market price of silver, generally speaking. Obviously, rare antique pieces have an intrinsic value other than bullion value. Some well-known manufacturers of silver plate flatware are International, Continental, Oneida, Rogers Bros., Gorham, National, Prestige, Reed & Barton, and Wallace. See **Repairs and Services** for silver plate and sterling matching service, this Price Guide.

Commonly used abbreviations are:

cf cocktail fork
cmf cold meat fork
cs cream (round) soup
demi demitasse spoon
fb french blade
g some wear, but still nice
gl gravy ladle
hh hollow handle
hw heel wear
ib individual butter spreader
its ice tea spoon
js jelly spreader
l/n like new
mb modern blade
ms master butter spreader
os oval soup spoon
pl f place fork
pl k place knife (hollow handle, unless marked *sh* for solid handle)
pm sp 5:00 spoon
ps pie server
pss pierced serving spoon
sf salad fork
ssb stainless steel blade
ss serving spoon
sug sugar spoon
ts tomato server
tsp teaspoon
tw tine wear
vf viande fork
vk viande or grille knife
* monogram

Silver Plate

Gorham

Kings pattern

gl . . . . $ 11-13

Lafayette pattern

pl f . . . . $ 3- 4
sug 3- 4
pickle fk 4.50- 5

Saxony pattern

pl k . . . . $ 4- 5
fruit k 4- 5
demi 4.50- 5

Other patterns are Kings, Lexington, Richmond, Shellburne, Victory, and Washington Irving. Many other patterns. Comparable prices exist.

International

Adoration pattern

pl k, mb . . . . $ 4.50- 6
pl f 5- 6
cf 6- 7
ib 5- 6

Aldine pattern

pl f . . . . $ 3.50- 4
sf ps (4 tine) 13-15
ib 6.50- 7

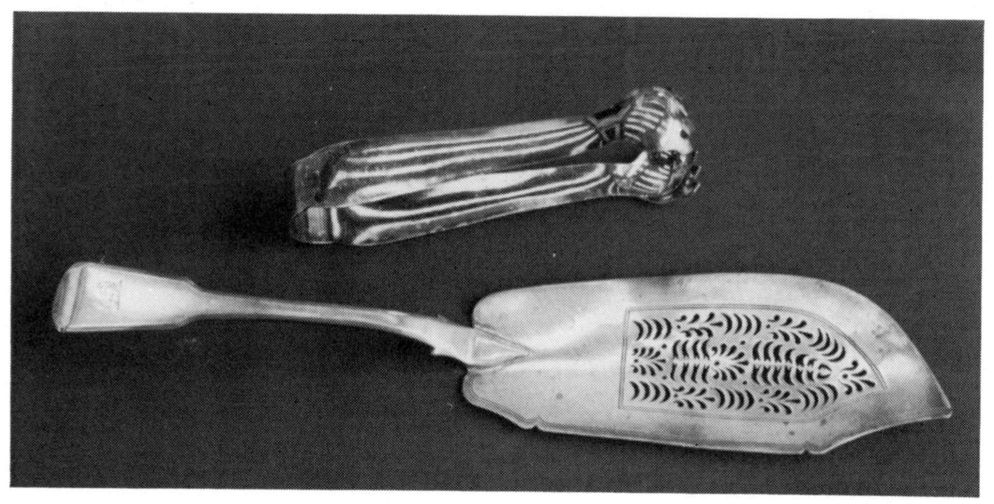

Alhambra pattern
- sf ....$ 9-10
- cs 6- 7
- ib 5- 6
- su tongs, 5″ 16-18

Ambassador pattern
- pl k, fb ....$ 6- 7
- pl f, old style 4- 5
- sf 6- 7
- cs 5- 6
- tsp 6- 7
- gl* 8.50- 9

Anniversary pattern
- pl k ....$ 5- 6
- sf 5- 6
- cmf 13-15
- gl 14-16

Avon pattern
- sug ....$ 5- 6
- lg cmf 15-17

Some other patterns in International are Beacon Hill, Berkshire, Bright Future, Cedric, Chased Rose, Chevalier, Cornell, Danish Princess, Esperanto, Faneuil, First Love, Florida, Heraldic, and Legion. There are many more. Comparable prices exist.

National

Concerto pattern
- berry sp ....$ 7- 8
- cmf 6- 7

Holiday pattern
- pl k ....$ 4- 5
- sf 4- 5
- ib 4- 5
- cf 4- 5

Moderne pattern
- pl k ....$ 3- 4
- pl f 4- 5
- sf 4- 5
- os 3.50- 4

Plume pattern
- pl f ....$ 3- 4
- sf 3- 4
- gl 4.50- 5
- cmf 4.50- 5

Other patterns are Cavalcade, Florence, King Edward, Inauguration, Martinique, Moss Rose, Narcissus, Princess Royal, and Rose and Leaf. Many other patterns. Comparable prices exist.

Oneida

Adam pattern
- pm sp ....$ 5- 6
- gl 13-15
- sug tongs, 3⅝″ 13-15

Bird of Paradise pattern
- pl k ....$ 2.75- 3
- sf 4.75- 5
- ps 17-18

Coronation pattern
- pl k ....$ 5- 6
- pl f 5- 6
- sf 5- 6
- ms 3.50- 4
- ss 6- 7
- pss 13-14.50
- berry sp 15-17

Elaine pattern
- pl k ....$ 3.50- 4
- pl f 3- 4
- cs 3- 4
- tsp 2.50- 3

Other patterns in Oneida are Evening Star, Flight, Forever, Grecian, Grenoble, Harmony, June, King Cedric, Lakewood, Louis XVI, Modern Baroque, Morning Star, and Old South. There are many other patterns. Comparable prices exist.

Prestige

Bordeaux pattern
- vk mb ....$ 5- 6
- vf 5- 6
- sf 6- 7
- tsp 4- 5

Distinction pattern
- pl k ....$ 4- 5
- pl f 6- 7

sf 6- 7
Gay Adventure pattern
pl k mb . . . .$ 7- 8
pl f 7- 8
os 5- 6
cmf 7- 8
Many other patterns; comparable prices exist.

Reed & Barton
Evangeline pattern
pl k . . . .$ 3.50- 4
pl f 3.50- 4
cs 3- 4
Grenoble pattern
vk mb . . . .$ 5- 6
pl f 5- 6
vf 5- 6
cs 5- 6
Royal pattern
pl k . . . .$ 3- 4
its 3- 4
tsp 2- 3
cs* 2-2.50
Many other patterns; comparable prices.

Wallace
Alamo pattern
pl f $2.50- 3
tsp 2.50- 3
sug 2.50- 3
Athena pattern
fruit sp . . . .$ 4- 5
ps hh 6- 7
lgcmf 6- 7
berry sp 6- 7
Floral pattern
pl k . . . .$ 9-10
egg sp 9-10
cmf* 21-23
tsp 2- 3
cs 7- 8
Sharon pattern
pl k . . . .$ 4- 5
pl f 4- 5
sf 4- 5
cmf 5- 6
Many other patterns, such as Normandy, Old London, Renaissance, Rex, Tiger Lily/Festivity, and Wisteria. Comparable prices exist.

Sterling Silver

Abbottsford by International
tsp . . . .$ 17-19
plf* 21-23
Afterglow by Oneida
sf . . . .$ 21-23
tsp 16-17
its 19-20
ss 39-41
cf 12-14
American Classic by Easterling
pl k . . . .$ 16-17
pl f 23-24
tsp 16-17
cmf 41-43
gl 39-41
ss 36-38
Aspen by Gorham
pl k . . . .$ 21-23
pl f 27-28
sf 24-25
tsp 19-21
Ballet by Weidlich
pl k fb . . . .$ 17-18
pl f 25-26
sf 19-20
tsp 15-16
cs 19-20
Blossom Time by International
pl k . . . .$ 16-17
pl f 27-29
tsp 16-17
cmf 41-43
gl 37-38
Bridal Bouquet by Alvin
pl k . . . .$ 17-18
pl f 27-29
sf 20-21
tsp 14-15
gl 39-41
Candlelight by Towle
pl k . . . .$ 21-22
pl f 39-41
sf 26-27
cs 26-27
cmf 41-43
Castle Rose by Royal Crest
cmf . . . .$ 41-43
gl 41-43
Chapel Bells by Alvin
pl k . . . .$ 16-17
gl 33-35
ss 35-37
js 21-23
Columbia by Reed & Barton
pl f . . . .$ 24-25
tsp 15-16
cs 19-21
Corinthian by Wallace
cmf . . . .$ 34-36
ss 39-41
Debutante by Wallace
pl k . . . .$ 16-17
pl f 24-25
sf 21-22
cs 20-21
cmf 39-41
gl 39-41
Enchanted Orchard by Westmoreland
pl k . . . .$ 16-17
sf 19-20
ss 41-43
cheese k 15-16
Fiddle Shell by Frank Smith
sf . . . .$ 27-28
gl 43-45
Francis I by Alvin
pl k . . . .$ 17-18
pl f 22-23
sf 20-21
gl 41-43

su tongs 28-30
pickle f 13-14

Francis I by Reed & Barton
pl k ....$ 23-24
sf 24-25
pss 76-78

Georgian Maid by International
cmf ....$ 40-42
ss 38-40
js 20-21

Horizon by Easterling
pl k ....$ 15-16
sf 18-19
tsp 13-14
cs 18-19

Lafayette by Towle
gl ....$ 55-57
ss 50-52
ice cream f 24-25

Mary II by Lunt
pl k fb ....$ 18-19
pl k 30-31
sf 20-21
tsp 15-16

There are so many different patterns with comparable prices, such as Old English (Towle), Old English (International), Old Maryland (S. Kirk), Olympia (Watson), Persian (Tiffany), Princess Mary (Wallace), and Royal Danish (International). If you're trying to match a pattern, see the introduction to this category.

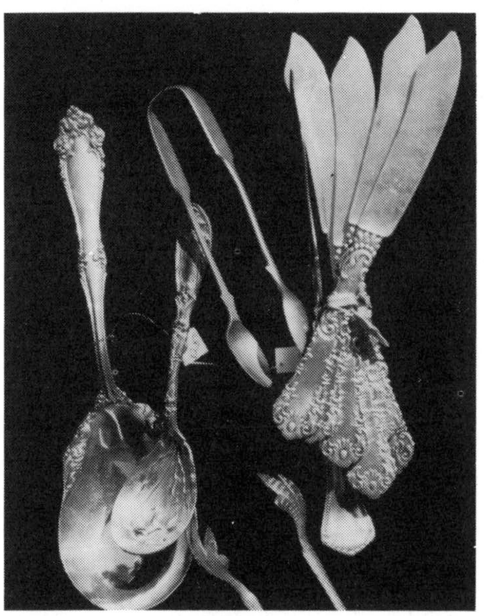

Silverware

Silverware

Coin, plated, Sheffield, sterling, EPNS, EPWM, quadruple-plate, African silver, Brazil silver, Siberian, etc. If you don't know the definition for **all** of those types of silver, learn or be prepared to get nicked.

Skate Boards

Is skate boarding a sport? A few hundred thousand enthusiasts think so. The older boards are "hot dogging" at Flea Markets.

Average price $7-20

Skate Keys

Skate Keys

Remember when your skates fastened to your shoes and everyone carried a key? Well, they're a collector's item today.

Average price ....75¢-$1

Smurfs

Someday these ridiculous characters will be as collectible as the Walt Disney items.

Soap Collectibles

Advertising posters, hand bills, and especially old soap in its original container are all collectible!

Black Soap Baby, in original container, early 1920's $7-11
Dutch hand soap advertisement, cardboard, 1920's (Illus.) 5- 7

Soap Collectibles

Photo Courtesy of
Hake's Americana & Collectibles

Lilac-Rose advertisement, cardboard, 1900's	5- 9
Lux soap, in original box, 1930's	4- 6
Ivory soap, four bars in original wrapper, 1930's, all	4- 7
Lye soap, large bar, homemade, 1900's	4- 7

And, don't overlook the wrappers — great for framing!

Soapstone

Soapstone is actually a mineral called steatite. It was used to make a variety of items during the 19th and early 20th centuries. Lots of "new" soapstone is showing up at Flea Markets **and** antique shows. Careful.

Bed warmer, wire handle	$37-44
Bookends, footed urns, reddish brown, pr.	42-48
Figurine, elephant, 4″ high	44-49
Figurine, Hoti, 6″ high	56-63
Figurine, man w/fish, 4¼″ high	47-51
Flower holder, floral motif, 5″ high	58-61

Soapstone

Incense burner, dragon motif, 3¼″ high	38-42
Paperweight, 3 monkeys	43-51
Rooster, 4″ high	62-71
Toothpick holder, dragon's head, 3½″ high	25-31
Vase, floral decor, 8″ high	65-73
Vase, Kuan Yin figure, 7¾″ high	68-72
Wise men, c. 1950's (Illus.)	20-28

Songbooks

Songbooks

Military marches, religious, jazz, swing, the old songbooks with the words to "just follow me, folks!" are popping up here and there in ever-increasing numbers. Fun to display on the family piano or organ.

A general price for one in good condition $2-4

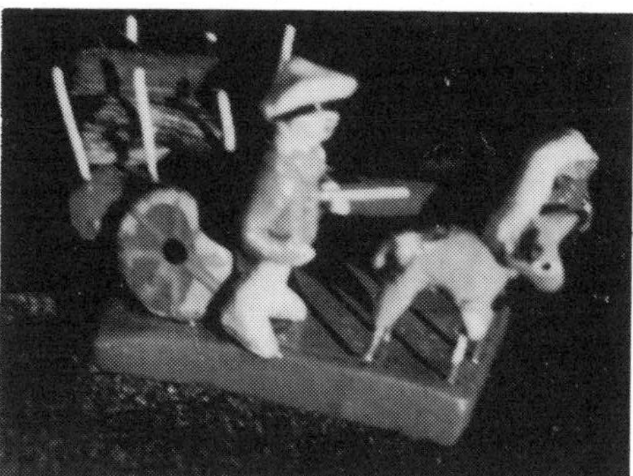

South of the Border Collectibles

South of the Border Collectibles

Mexican, Guatemalan — everyone brings back souvenirs from Central and South America.

Clay donkey cart (Illus.) . . . . 75¢-1.50
Clay burro . . . . 75¢-1.50
Clay tea set . . . . 75¢-1.50
Straw handbags, hats, belts, shoes, average price 2-4
Wood carvings — jewelry boxes, crosses, etc., average price 3-8

Souvenir Medals

Souvenir Medals

Some were made of solid silver, others of 14 karat gold; most were pot metal. All are collectible today.

Columbus Centennial, Columbus, Ohio, 1912 (Illus.) $10-13
Average price, depending on metal and age 4- 8

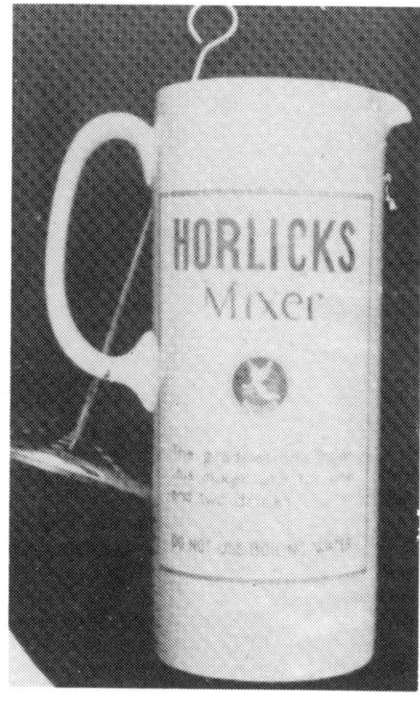

Souvenir Mugs

Souvenir Mugs

"Try our Platinum Cow and keep the mug as a souvenir!" When was the last time you heard that? Pat O'Brien's in New Orleans must have sold two million glasses because you see them in every state in the Union! That historical fact not withstanding, mugs that advertise a restaurant, club, bar, etc., are being bought every day at every Flea Market.

Average price . . . . 75¢-1.50

Sports Collectibles

Autographs

Keep in mind that thousands were signed by autopen. Unless you know the source or are an expert at detecting fakes, be careful! This also holds true for "signed" baseballs. A genuine "Babe" Ruth ($225-240), a genuine Jackie Robinson ($65-74). During the 1930's the bat boys earned "pin" money affixing "genuine" signatures to baseballs.

Baseball Schedules

Today, a million are printed at a time, making them virtually worthless as a collector's item.

1875-1900, each	$ 13-26
1900-1920, each	9-16
1920-1940, each	6-11
1940-1960, each	2- 5
1960-1970, each	65¢-1.50
1970-1984, each	10¢-15¢

Basketball Schedules

Early NBA and BAA are getting scarce.

Pre-1950, each	$2.50 up
1950-1970, each	1- 5
1970-1984, each	10¢-55¢

Boxing Items

From knuckles wrapped with leather strips (early Roman) to leather mitts to draft dodgers, boxing has been around awhile. "Putting in the fix" sent more than one "tank" boxer into same — thus, "Tank towns." For my money, no greater boxer **and** gentleman ever lived than Joe Louis!

James J. Corbett cabinet photo, early	$ 8-12
Boxing gloves, "Wearever" brand, 1930's, red leather, pair	12-16
Kangaroo leather shoes, lace-up type, 1930's pr.	12-20
Training bag, sawdust-filled, 5′ high, 1930's	19-27
Punching bag with platform, working condition	47-56
Program of Louis-Sharkey fight	8-12
Signature of Joe Louis on fight program	12-16

Equipment

Too many fakes here to establish realistic prices. Once-serious collectors have turned to other categories. Look for original labels; look for wear around the collar, under the sleeves; look for sizes such as 44, 46, etc. Today, everything is S-M-L-XL.

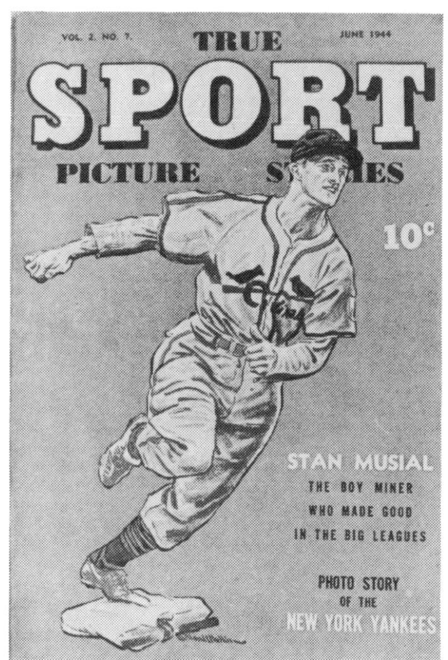

Sports Collectibles

Hartland Statues

Hartland Plastics Company, Hartland, Wisconsin, made these lifelike statues from around 1958 until the end of 1963. Nineteen baseball statues were made — twenty-eight football statues.

Aaron, Hank	$ 75- 95
Aparicio, Luis	105-130
Banks, Ernie	105-125
Berra, Yogi	85- 97
Colavito, Rocky	285 +
Drysdale, Don	175-185
Fox, Nellie	95-105
Groat, Dick	300-318
Killebrew, Harmon	200-218
Little League	138-146
Mantle, Mickey	73- 82
Maris, Roger	153-160
Matthews, Eddie	52- 60
Mays, Willie	72- 80
Musial, Stan	63- 70
Ruth, Babe	69- 75
Snider, Duke	128-135
Spahn, Warren	52- 60
Williams, Ted	67- 73

Hockey Schedules

Early NHL are hard to find, especially in the United States.

Pre-1940, each	$ 2- 5
1940-1960, each	1- 6

Matchbook covers, Pennants, Programs, Scorecards, Sheet Music, Ticket Stubs, Stadium Postcards, see *The Sports Collector's Bible*, Bert Randolph Sugar.

Stangl Pottery

Stangl Pottery

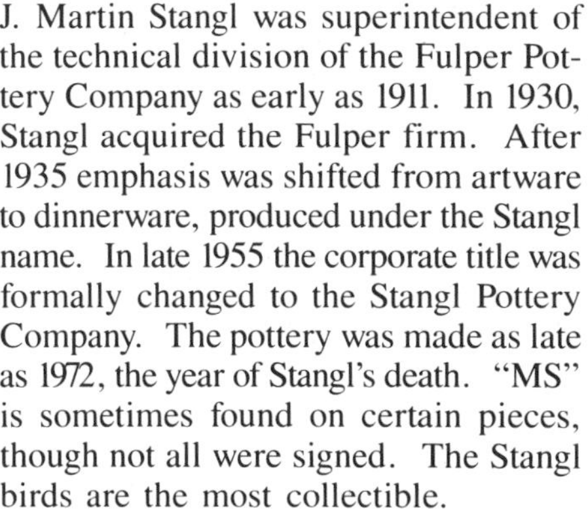

J. Martin Stangl was superintendent of the technical division of the Fulper Pottery Company as early as 1911. In 1930, Stangl acquired the Fulper firm. After 1935 emphasis was shifted from artware to dinnerware, produced under the Stangl name. In late 1955 the corporate title was formally changed to the Stangl Pottery Company. The pottery was made as late as 1972, the year of Stangl's death. "MS" is sometimes found on certain pieces, though not all were signed. The Stangl birds are the most collectible.

Bird of Paradise	**$ 80- 90**
Bluebird, signed	**52- 61**
Bowl, white, flower shape, 8″ dia.	**28- 37**
Cardinal on stump	**61- 71**
Cockatoo, marked Jacobs	**230-240**
Double bluebirds	**130-150**
Double cockatoos	**83- 93**
Double hummingbirds	**260-272**
Gray cardinal	**45- 53**
Hummingbird, signed "STANGL POTTERY COMPANY" (Illus.)	**65- 75**
Oriole, signed as above	**61- 71**
Parrot eating worm	**120-130**
Rooster, signed as above	**70- 80**

Stanley Products

Comparable to the Fuller Brush products. Stanley parties are now in vogue. Like Amway, you sell to your friends and neighbors. People are collecting the early products.

Stanley Products

Star Wars

Three movies have made this a highly collectible category. Like Buck Rogers in the 1930's, one day Star Wars items will bring high prices.

Steins

Steins

The Westerwald area of Germany in the 17th century made the finest steins ever made. Mettlach also made fine steins, as did Dresden at Meissen, Germany. These are old steins. Today, there are thousands of "new" on the market (Illus.). Average price, $8-22. See **Clubs and Publications,** this Price Guide.

½ liter, flower motif, forest scene, pewter lid $412-420
½ liter, green/buff, Liberal Arts Palace, St. Louis Exposition, 1904 410-420
½ liter, roses, castle scene, porcelain, pewter lid........ 394-398
1 liter, etched decor, porcelain lined, pewter lid 452-461
1 liter, musicians, barmaid, drinking scene, pewter lid ... 420-440
2 liter, blue and buff, pewter cap, 17″ high 522-540
3 liter, brewery wagon and horse, advertising item, 1890's 240-250
Bardolph and Falstaff, #614, Germany, 9½″ high, pewter cap, 1½ liter 226-240
Character steins, plain 205-215
Crystal deer, forest, hunters, pewter cap, 11½″ high 340-350
Etched and art glass 275-285
Family crest, pewter lid, dated 1863, Germany 282-292
Fraternal, glass or pottery 220-229
Geschut, #1102, ½ liter....... 330-348
HR, etched 275-282
Hand-painted glass 210-240
Hunt scene, wild boars, pewter lid, 3 liter, 16″ high 340-350
Lithophane bottom, nude, pewter top, Germany, 10″ high, new 173-182
Merkelback & Wick, 7″ high ... 184-192
Musterschutz, Bismarck, multicolored.................. 405-415
Musterschutz characters 305-315
Occupational porcelains 240-250
Pewter, scene in relief 274-283
Plain crystal 227-235
Pottery, scene in relief 194-205
Schultz and Dooley, Utica club beer, advertising item, 1900's 193-202
Stoneware, 3 liter, pewter cap, 16″ high................. 218-227

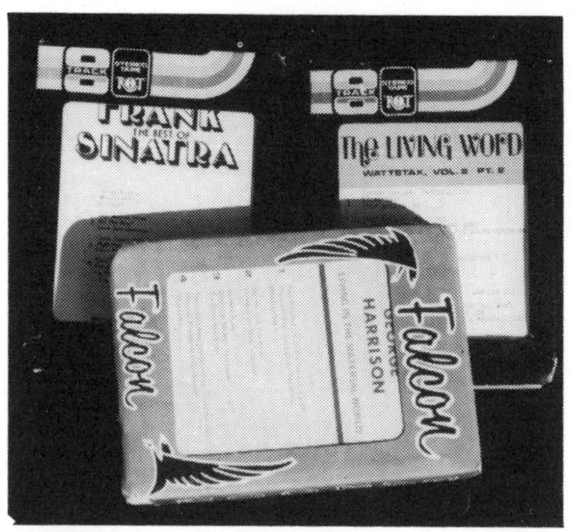

Stereo Tapes

Stereo Tapes

Just plug 'em in and away you go! Like paperback books, tapes come in all styles of music.

Average price, in playing condition, used, each ....50¢-$2

Steubenville Pottery

See **American Dinnerware.**

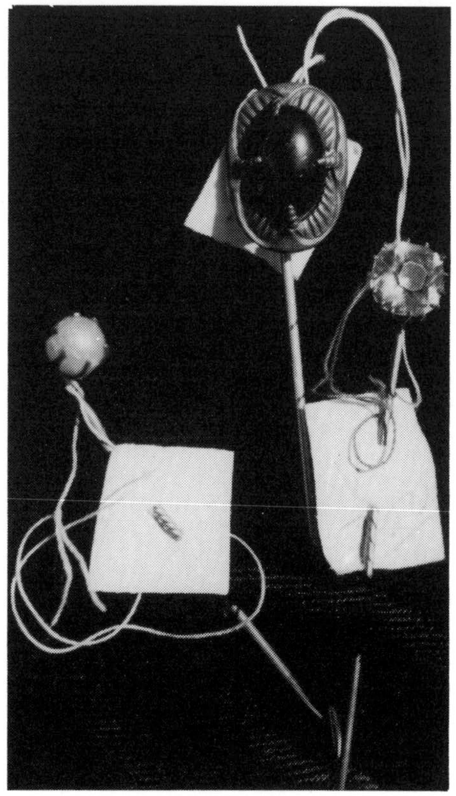
Stickpins

Stickpins

Never know when you'll find a genuine diamond or ruby. Most of what you see is in the $4 to $7 range. More if it's a 14-karat-gold stem.

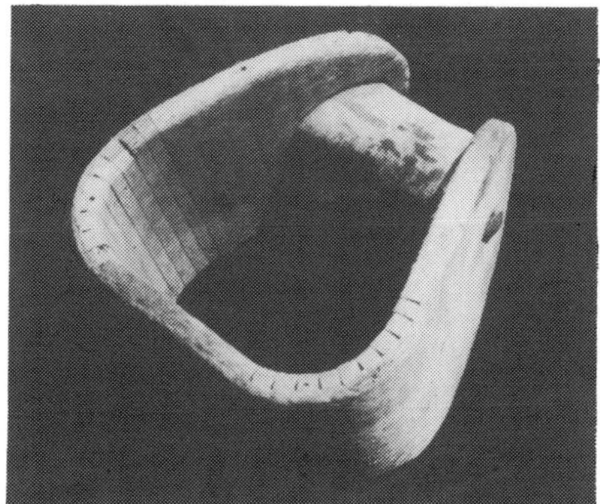

Stirrups

Stirrups

Shown here because they make handy napkin holders or wall decorations. The metal ones are perfect for holding a kitchen towel.

Wooden (Illus.) $8-11
Metal 9-14

Stocks and Bonds

After the crash of the stock market in 1929, countless millions of stock certificates weren't worth the paper they were printed on. Today — a new hot collectible. If the certificate hasn't been perforated to cancel it, you may have a winner. Ask your friendly banker how to trace old certificates. Average price, each, $3-10. Old stock certificates are great for wall decorations. Some of the finest engravers did the scrollwork.

Allied Stores, Delaware, 1950's
Alma Lincoln Mines, Idaho Springs, Colo., 1930's
American Telephone and Telegraph, 1960's
Basic Resources, Utah
Canada General Funds, 1950's
Cambridge Garage Co., Massachusetts
Centennial Mines, Washington
Dayco Corp., Ohio
Dahl Uranium Mines, 1950's
Dison Chemical Co., New Jersey, 1950's
Erleme Corp., early 1900's
Golden Cycle Mines, Colorado, 1920's
Great Northern Railway
Gulf Mobile and Ohio Railroad, 1940's
Louis Rothenblum, Inc., New York
Plastic and Fibers, Inc.
Publicker Industries, 1970's
Southern Railroad, 1960's
Spokane National Mines, Washington
Woodward Iron Co., Alabama
WS Lockman Construction Co.

"Stradivarius" Violins

NO, no, no! You DO NOT own a genuine unless you're wealthy and/or famous. There are few unknown Strads still lying around. Antonio Stradivari, Italian, 1644-1737, made them. But there are thousands of fakes made from remnants of mahogany cigar boxes. Fake Strads usually have a "Strad" label inside the sound box. Sears Roebuck sold thousands of them, Model No. 12R214, at $2.45 each, 1900's!

Average price $90-120

Stretch Glass

The outer surface of this iridized glass looks like onion skin. Unknowing collectors think they're buying Steuben's Verre De Soie — "glass of silk" — or Tiffany when they're really buying Carnival Stretch glass. Look for mold marks.

Sugar Packs

Sugar Packs

You'll find these in restaurants, diners, and at all the popular drive-ins. Thousands of different pictures.

Teddy Bears

Teddy Bears

Supposedly, Teddy Roosevelt refused to shoot a bear cub while on a hunting trip in Mississippi, c. 1902. Actually, a political cartoon in *The Washington Post* on November 16, 1902, started the American craze for these cuddly toys. Rose and Morris Michtom made the first (c. 1907), calling their company the Ideal Novelty and Toy Company. Margaret Steiff, Germany, also made some of the originals in 1902-1903. Teddy bears are highly collectible and bring brisk prices.

Bears

5″, mohair, straw stuffed, button eyes and nose, Germany (Illus.) .... $ 28- 35
5½″, gold mohair, straw stuffed, black sewn mouth and nose, jointed limbs, Steiff, early 1900's 118-127
5½″, white mohair, shoe button eyes, Steiff, early 1900's 108-121
6″, brown mohair, straw stuffed, jointed limbs, head swivels, sewn nose and mouth, Steiff 127-142
8½″, brown mohair, roller skating windup, Made in U.S. Zone — Germany 299-340
9″, gold mohair, black sewn nose and mouth, jointed limbs, original ruffled collar and clown hat, Steiff, early 1900's 262-272
9½″, original felt jacket and pants, windup arms, bear somersaults, German, c. 1920's 368-382
11″, mohair, shoe button eyes, jointed limbs, red felt jacket and hat, dressed as bellhop, tail movement moves head .. 396-422
12″, brown plush, jointed limbs, swivel head, English .. 88-107
12″, mohair, shoe button eyes, black sewn mouth and nose, swivel head, Ideal, early 1900's 440-470
13″, soft brown mohair, glass eyes, black sewn mouth and nose, jointed limbs, swivel head, stomach squeaker, early 1900's 228-242
14″, brown plush, shoe button eyes, black sewn mouth and nose, felt paws, jointed limbs, swivel head, c. 1930's 162-177
15″, orange mohair, straw stuffed, glass stickpin eyes, black sewn mouth and nose, pink felt paws, stomach squeaker, c. 1940's 118-126
15″, white mohair, straw stuffed, glass stickpin eyes, linen paws, jointed, swivel head, early 1900's 168-182
16″, brown plush, special edition box, original tag, 75th anniversary 35- 45
18″, Beefeater outfit, English, modern.................. 77- 87
19″, gold mohair, glass stickpin eyes, sewn mouth and nose, swivel head, hump, jointed limbs, early 1900's... 328-348
20″, brown mohair, glass eyes, velvet paws, jointed limbs, Knickerbocker, c. 1938 142-152
22″, mohair, glass eyes, felt paws, tail moves head up and down, side to side, Roddy on tag, English 462-482
24″, white mohair, soft stuffed, glass eyes, felt paws, jointed limbs, swivel head, stomach squeaker, c. 1930's 236-246

Jewelry

Charm, ruby eyes, 14K gold ...$318-347
Child's coffee set: pot, 2 cups/ saucers, tray, c. 1920, all ... 112-127
China vase, green/white, 2 bears inside, c. 1900 91-107
Paper doll, E. I. Horsman, 5 outfits, complete, early 1900's, 10½″ 410-446
Stickpin, sterling silver 42- 52

Miscellaneous

4-wheeler, brown mohair, glass eyes, growler operates when wire pulled, Steiff, modern, 20″ high..................$328-372

4-wheeler, mohair, glass eyes, swivel head, squeaker, Steiff, 8″ high 162-177
Kellogg bears, printed fabric, soft stuffed, company premium, 3 in set, c. 1920's, all ... 142-152
Muff, gray mohair, glass eyes, black sewn nose, felt paws, early 1900's, 15″ 328-347
Perfume holder, mohair, jointed limbs, hinged body w/mirror, early 1900's, 3¾″ high .. 187-196

Suggested reading: *The Teddy Bear Catalog,* Peggy and Alan Bialosky, Workman Publishing Company.

Telegraph Collectibles

The old sending keys, headsets, Western Union forms, and uniforms are all collectible.

Telephones

Telephones

Don Ameche and Alexander Graham Bell made the telephone famous. The oak and walnut wall-types are highly collectible, as are the candlestick types of the early 1920's and 1930's. See **Clubs and Publications,** this Price Guide.

American Electric, 1905	$250-260
Candlestick, 1930's (Illus.)	45- 53
Chicago, 1899	265-275
Dearborn Electric, 1902	255-265
DeVeau, 1898	85- 95
Eureka, 1899	240-250
Kellogg, 1901	240-250
Leich, 1909	85-100
Phoenix, 1898	90-107
Stromberg-Carlson, 1912	235-250
Sumpter, 1902	240-250
Varney, 1902	235-245
Wheeler, 1897	95-110
Whitman and Couch, 1898	275-284
Williams, 1901	230-240

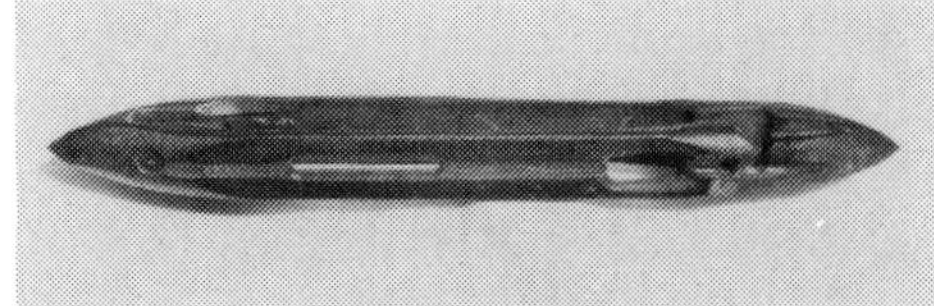

Textile Bobbins

Textile Bobbins

These were used in mills to weave cloth. They make attractive wall decorations.

Average price $4-7

Thermometers

Galileo and Sanctorius devised these instruments for measuring temperature. The three most widely used are the Fahrenheit, the Centigrade (Celsius), and the Reaumur (used to some extent in parts of Europe). Today, collectors avidly seek them out, especially the decorative ones.

AB Co., pot metal, Greek child, brass scale, permacolor, 4½″ $ 31- 36
American Thermometer, heavy wood/porcelain, permacolor, 11″ 135-143
Bargess Reversible Box, brass scale, oak box, mercury, 5½″ 25- 32

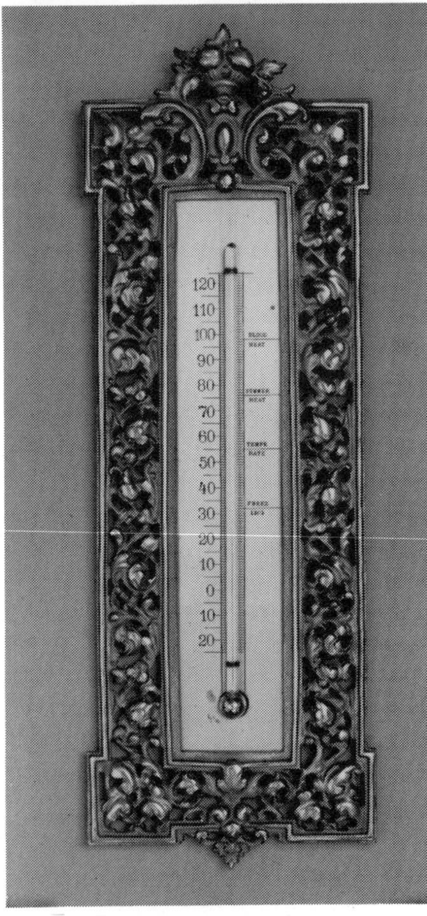

Thermometers

Photo Courtesy of
Hake's Americana & Collectibles

Barnes, figural, brass, mercury or pointer 29- 34
Bradley & Hubbard, engraved, gold plate on iron, mercury, 15″ 60- 68
Fahrenheit, black brass on mahogany, ornate bulb protector, 9″ 23- 28
Freeborn, desk-type, bronze w/lead decor, brass scale, mercury, 8″ 39- 45
Germanow Simon, Tel Tru model, octagonal, pointer, 3″ 21- 26
Gladstone, oak foldout box, bakelite scale, mercury, 2½″ 21- 25
Graphic (Illus.) 7- 8
Grimes Co., blue glass obelisk, mercury, 4″ 24- 28
Helmut, desk-type, scroll edge, stainless steel/plastic, easel pedestal, 6″ 32- 39
Hiergelsell Bros., cabinet, oak back, blue permacolor, indoor type, #159 . . . . . 42- 50
Hiergelsell Bros., self-registering, magnet, permacolor, #153 150-157
Hohmann Maurero Co., steel Fahrenheit and Celsius scales, mercury, 12″ 28- 34
Hughes Co., bakelite on wood, mercury, 10″ 19- 24
Hygro Automatic, 2 magnifying tubes w/stand, mercury, #T5558 . . . . . 45- 52
Ill. Mfg. Co., outdoor-type, rotating aluminum scale, permacolor, 9½″ 250-258
L. C. Tower, Weather Prognosticator, cherry/brass scale, mercury 19- 25
C. E. Lange, The Modern Thermometer, kitchen-type, tin, permacolor 145-153
Pace Mfg. Co., Cottage Barometer, storm glass, permacolor, 8½″ 25- 31
R & G, Battleax, 4″ stainless scale, mercury, c. 1904, 18″ . 560-570
Reynolds Branson & Leeds, brew-master's-type, mahogany/brass, 34″ 135-144
Siegel, Weather Prophet, German cottage figural, mercury, 10″ 750-763
Taylor, Comfortmeter, brass scale on green back, permacolor, 7″ 21- 26
Taylor, desk/mantel, mahogany w/metal scale, permacolor, #5340S 29- 36
Taylor, indoor-type, cabinet, brass/wood, permacolor, #T5121 SW, 6″ 17- 24
Tiffany, Honeywell, stainless and glass ball, pointer, 2½″ . 58- 64

Tycos, Hygrodeik, wet and dry bulb hygrometer, hanging, 10″ 43- 49
Tycos, maximum/minimum, japanned tin/brass, mercury, #T5452 ..... 18- 25
Tycos, outdoor/indoor, brass/white metal, permacolor, #T5115S 15- 21
Tycos, Temprite, indoor-type, black/white lithograph, permacolor, #T5145S, 5″ 23- 28
Tycos, Weather Station, brass case housing, revolving drum recorder, 7″ 90- 97
C. Wilder Co., bear and billboard figural, brass, mercury, 6½″ 41- 48
World's Fair Key, 1939, brass scale, permacolor, 8″ 19- 25

Tin Containers

Tin Containers

The type that held tobacco, spices, talcum, etc. The very early ones are all but gone; those made after World War I are still around.

Azurea Talcum, floral decor ..... $ 5- 8
Ben Hur Spice, ginger 8-12
Bulwark Cut Plug, 3″ high, sailor 26-33
Dream Girl Talcum 24-27
Eight Bros. Tobacco, pail 41-50
El Roi Tan Cigars, 5″ high 11-15
Huxley's Plasma Powder, floral decor 9-14
Kugler Chocolates, 10″ high, horses/carriage 15-19
Loose Wiles Biscuits, octagonal, Santa Maria ship 22-28
Love's Harmonicas, 5″ high, musician, king/queen 21-29
Mennen's Sen Yang Talcum, duck flying 24-30
Piso's Tooth Powder, floral decor 13-18
Raptco Wafers, flat tin, embossed leaf on lid 25-32
Royal Baking Powder 9-14
Schinasi Bros. Natural Cigarettes, 6″ high 14-21
Songster Needles, bird decor 23-30
Surbrug's Navy Cut 21-30
Tudor Coffee, castle, paper label. 22-28
Union Leader Tobacco, Uncle Sam decor 34-40
Vantine Incense, Art Deco style .. 24-31
Victor Needles, Nipper/ phonograph 31-38
Watkins Ginger 8-14
White House Coffee, paper label . 18-26
Ying Mee Tea Co., birds/flowers . 14-19

Tobacco Collectibles

Tobacco Collectibles

Sir Walter Raleigh got it from the Indians. He took it to England and the rest is history. Sports and political heros were immortalized on cigar box labels. Nearly every kid in the 1920's wore a cigar band ring, and the cigarette rage of the 1930's and 1940's swept millions of Americans into the nicotine habit. The Surgeon General warns. . . . Anyway, see **Clubs and Publications,** this Price Guide.

Ashtrays

These were popular in the 1920's and 1930's. The glass tray was removable; the base was pot metal, "brassed," or "coppered."

Average price ....$ 30-40

Cigars

Cigar bands, paper, depending on age, each .... 10¢-1.50

Cigar box labels, paper, in mint condition

Betsy Ross ....$	7-10
Clipper	11-15
Cuban Cousin	14-19
Daniel Defoe	38-45
Du Barry	11-16
Franklin D. Roosevelt	13-17
John C. Calhoun	12-16
Judge Best	13-18
La Sabilla	18-25
La Sciencia	32-38
My Duena	22-28
Prima Lucia (Illus.)	3- 5
Red Cloud	18-24
Rudolph Valentino	11-15
Sherlock Holmes	5- 8
Three Twins	4- 7
Uncle Jake's Nickel Seegar .	5- 8

Cigar boxes, wood; paper label in fine to excellent condition.

Airliner (San Telmo Cigar Co.)	$6- 9
Call Again (J. A. Doll Cigar Co.)	7-10
Da Vinci (Salvador Rodrigues, Inc.)	6- 9
Dick Custer	8-11
Franklin D. Roosevelt	7-10
Irvin S. Cobb (Yorkana Cigar Co.)	6-10
Lincoln Bouquet	10-14
Sea Robin (W. B. Lenz, Manufacturer)	7-10
William Tell	6- 9
Cigar mold, 2-pc., maple, early 1900's	31-39
Cigarette case, sterling silver, 1930's	85-93
Cigarette holder, carved ivory, 1920's	32-40
Cigarette lighters, Zippo-type, pre-WW II, each	3- 7

Pipes

Pipe bowls were carved from briar roots, meerschaum, or molded in porcelain and clay. When or who lit up the first one is lost to history.

Alpine, porcelain bowl, 21″ long, marked "Holland" ....$	84- 93
Beethoven, briar, carved	75- 85
Briar, carved, sea captain	77- 87
Deer's head carved into bowl, curved 10″ stem	118-125
Elk's head bowl, B.P.O.E. and date, straight 6″ stem	81- 91
Face of monk in bowl, curved 7″ stem, clay	62- 72
Lion devouring prey, curved stem, 11″, briar	88- 98
Meerschaum, bearded Turk, case	65- 75
Meerschaum, deer pursued by dog, 9″ curved stem	70- 80
Meerschaum, horse's head, trees, 9½″ curved stem	80- 90
Opium pipe, Chinese figures, 14″ long, old	88- 98
Panther's head, glass eyes, 10″ straight stem	72- 82
Porcelain bowl, painted decor .	71- 88
Satyr, briar, carved	75- 84

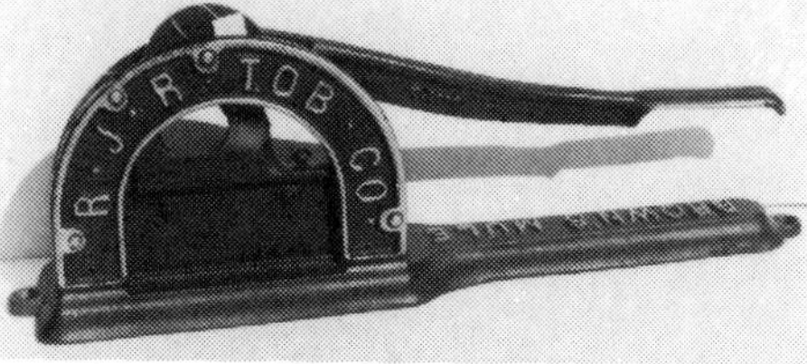

Tobacco Cutters

Tobacco Cutters

Black Beauty	$49- 56
Brown Mule	42- 48
Imp thumbing nose	86- 93
R. J. R. Tobacco Co. (Illus.) ...	67- 72
Star	64- 70
Triumph	42- 48

Being reproduced in several models.

Tokens

Tokens

These were used in place of money for many different purposes.

Bawdy house, brass, 1900's (look out for repros!)	75¢-$1
Bus, Philadelphia Transit Co. ...	25¢-50¢
Ration, during WW II the government issued them through the O.P.A. Usually, pressed fiber, blue or red, each	5¢-10¢

State Sales Tax, during the 1930's just about every state used them; 95 percent were made of aluminum, each . . . . . 10¢-15¢
Subway, average price, each . . . 10¢-15¢
Trolley, c. 1895, Philadelphia (Illus.) 2-3

Toothbrush Holders

Photo Courtesy of
Hake's Americana & Collectibles

Toothbrush Holders

A lot of companies sold these holders along with their toothbrushes.

Orphan Annie and Sandy toothbrush holder (Illus.) $24-29
Mickey, Donald, and Minnie toothbrush holder 29-36

Toothpick Dispensers

Most restaurants have them; some use a hot pepper bottle with the small opening.

Diner type, metal, push-down $3-5

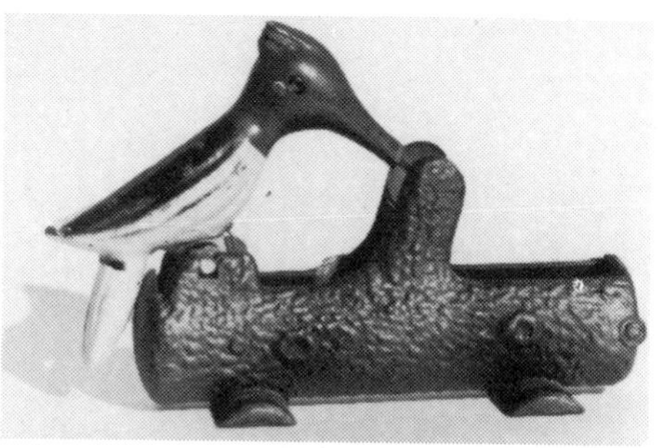

Toothpick Dispensers

Woodpecker — push his head down, "beak" stabs toothpick (Illus.) 3-6

Average prices depend on age and condition.

Toothpick Holders

Toothpick Holders

Metal, glass, wood, plastic, old, and new. Take your choice.

Loving cup style, pressed glass . . $ 8-11

Pressed glass (Illus.) 8-11
Tumbler style, iridized glass (Illus.) 19-24

Tortoiseshell Items

Tortoiseshell Items

Combs, each $11-14
Jewelry box, inlaid mother of pearl 20-26
Fan, tortoiseshell ribs, 9″ long, ostrich feathers 23-28
Bracelet, silver links, silver figures set into shell 23-31
Buttons, set of six, ½″ diameter, brass sewing loops, set 21-28

Toys

Carved from wood, stone, cast from iron, machine-pressed, soldered, the very old, and the not-so-old — all highly collectible today.

Airplane, by Marx, tin mechanical windup, 1940's ....$ 72- 80

Charlie McCarthy Radio

Photo Courtesy of
Hake's Americana & Collectibles

Howdy Doody

Photo Courtesy of
Hake's Americana & Collectibles

Amos 'n' Andy Fresh Air Taxicab, tin mechanical windup, 1930's 475-500
Amos 'n' Andy radio script, "Amos' Wedding," 1935 162-172
Amos walking toy, tin mechanical windup, 1930's 162-170
Andy walking toy, tin mechanical windup, 1930's 198-230
Animated cow, 1920's, moving the tail made it "moo" 68- 74
Baby carriage, tin, cloth top, 2½′ long, 1920's 95-105
Balky mule, tin mechanical windup, 1920's, by Lehmann 102-111
Bear-on-a-ball, composition, mechanical windup, 1940's .. 90- 98

Jazzbo Jim

Photo Courtesy of
Hake's Americana & Collectibles

Joe Penner

Photo Courtesy of
Hake's Americana & Collectibles

Bus, cast iron, Arcade Mfg. Co., 1920's 290-310
Busy Bee seesaw, tin mechanical, sand operated, litho, 1920's 135-144
Calliope, cast iron, Hubley, 1920's, 16″ long 352-361
Cannon, "Big Bang" type, 3″ barrel, 1930's, carbide type .. 84- 93
Car, VW, cast iron, 1950's 64- 72
Casey Jones, rider type, metal, late 1930's 271-281
Cash register, tin, "Benjamin Franklin," by Kamkap, 1930's 101-112
Cat with ball, tin mechanical windup, U.S. Zone, Germany, 1940's 49- 57
Charlie Chaplin squeeze toy, Germany, 1920's 345-355

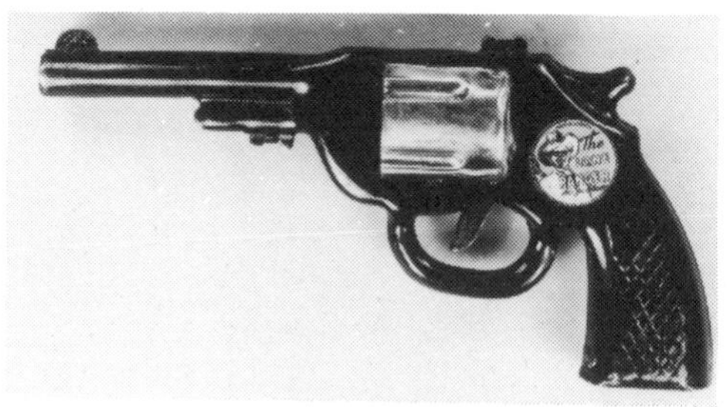

Lone Ranger Popgun

Photo Courtesy of
Hake's Americana & Collectibles

Charlie McCarthy radio by Majestic, c. 1930's, price if radio works (Illus.) 150-160
Chicken in a basket, tin mechanical windup, 5½″ high, 1920's............... 145-154
Clown and monkey, celluloid/ tin mechanical windup, 1930's 96-104
Crapshooter, by Cragston, tin windup, 1930's 101-112
Double-decker, friction toy, 1930, 13″ long 270-274
Greyhound bus, cast iron, 1930's, 9″ long 108-117
Gyroscope, pot metal, complete with instructions, 1930's 91-100
Harmonica, Original Emmet Richter, tin/wood, 1920's 74- 83
Howdy Doody tumbling toy, tin windup, c. 1950's (Illus.) 91-100

Mickey Mouse Band

Photo Courtesy of
Hake's Americana & Collectibles

Jazzbo Jim, tin windup, Straus, c. 1921; dances on tin roof when activated; in original box (Illus.) 310-320

Joe Penner, tin windup, lithographed, Marx, early 1930's; walks, carrying Goo Goo, his duck; hat and cigar move up and down; carrying basket of ducks with "Wanna buy a duck? Sincerely Joe Penner," on large tag (Illus.) 362-370
Kid Sampson, tin mechanical windup, B & R trademark, 1921 441-451
Little Daisy sweeper, made by Bissell for give-aways, 28½" long, 1920's............... 109-118
The Lone Ranger popgun, c. 1930's (Illus.)............. 53- 62
Matchbox fighter planes, 6 in set, 1940's, each 12- 19
Mickey Mouse Band pull toy, Fisher-Price, beats drum when toy is pulled (Illus.) ... 128-138
Monkey, tin mechanical windup, mohair coat, Japan, 1920's 95-105
Moon Mullins (and Kayo) Railroad Handcar, by Marx, deluxe model.............. 660-668
Moon Mullins (and Kayo) Railroad Handcar, by Marx, regular model 470-480
Motorboat, tin mechanical windup, 1920's 130-140
Motorcyle, cast iron, 6" long, 1920's 91-100
"Oh, Boy" bus, No. 105, 1920's 161-170
Overland Circus, animals in cage, iron, 1920 490-505
Pail, wood handle, lithograph on tin, 1920's 73- 82
Phaeton, cast iron, 1901, 11" long, pony type........... 295-303
Popeye and the Parrot Cages, Marx, tin mechanical windup, 1930's 240-250
Projector, hand-operated, concave mirror at rear, 6" high, 1920's 196-205
Roller skates, hard rubber wheels, child's, 1950's...... 77- 87
Singing bird, tin mechanical windup, 4" high, Germany, 1950's 136-145
Sled, wood/metal, child's handpainted, 1920's, 33" long ... 140-150
Speedboy 4, tin mechanical windup, 1920's 150-160
Steamroller, tin, Buddy L, rider type, 1930's, 12½" high 232-252
Streetcar, tin, friction, doors open and close, c. 1920's ... 287-295
Superman Fighting Airplane, tin mechanical windup, litho, Marx, 1940................ 310-342
Taxi, cast iron, by Arcade, painted, 5" long, 1928 277-285
Teddy bear, miniature, by Steiff, 1920's, 2½" high 151-160
Tin Lizzie, 1920's, friction type 250-260
Toy soldier, friction type, 1920's 131-140
Traffic B squad car, tin mechanical windup, Marx, 1930's 294-303
Truck, metal Buddy "L", 1920's 300-312
Truck, tin, Metalcraft Corp., St. Louis, 1930 275-284
Walking-on-hands clown, by Chien, 1920's 111-120
Wells Fargo stagecoach, Tootsietoy, 1920's 108-117
Wheelbarrow, tin, 29" long, 1920's 93-102
Wheelbarrow, wooden, 1920's, 18" long................. 63- 72

Trains

Trains

You simply don't find trains in mint condition unless you're terribly lucky **or** you're buying a repro! Prices here are for good to very good condition.

American Flyer

Baggage car, American Express .$14-22
Caboose, No. 1127 6-10
Gondola, No. 3013............. 6-10
Passenger car, No. 3153........ 11-17

Lionel

Caboose, No. 17 ....$ 8-16
Locomotive, No. 224 26-34
Locomotive, No. 248 28-35
Pullman car, No. 337........... 16-23
Tank car, Sunoco (Illus.)........ 15-22
Turbo missile launching car 14-19
TV monitor car 14-19

Marx

Box car, Rock Island ....$ 5- 9
Caboose, NY Central 4- 7
Crane car, NY Central 3- 6

Dump car, side, NY Central 3- 6
Gondola, Pennsylvania Railroad .. 3- 6
Hopper, Northern Pacific 3- 6
Locomotive, tin litho 5- 9
Tank car, Utility 4- 7
Tender, NY Central 3- 6

Tootsietoy

Train, 6-pc., all $17-24

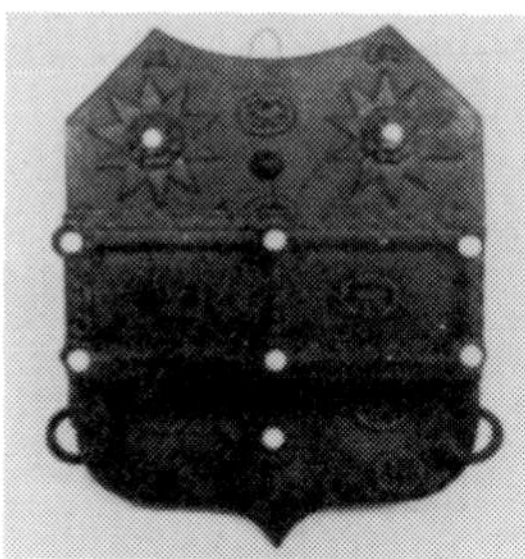

Tramp Art

Tramp Art

There is little evidence that tramps (or hobos) or "knights of the road," if you will, made these glued-together pieces. Popular from the 1870's until World War II, most of the workmanship is crude and the wood seems to be from cigar boxes, fruit crates, or anything else that was lying around. Chip-carved designs prevail.

Box, rectangular, stained ..... $ 75- 85
Clock case, chip-carved designs, stained 180-190
Corner shelf, porcelain knobs, stained 88- 96
Desk, kneehole, 22" 395-415
Frame, 12" × 15" 28- 35
Magazine rack, wall type, stained 115-124
Mirror frame, 8" × 10" 43- 50
Planter, hanging type 68- 75
Rack, wall type, porcelain knobs (Illus.) 98-107

Traps

These have been around for years and now collectors are showing an interest. Prices for traps are based on legibility of the maker's name on the pan. Prices listed are for those in very good to fine condition. There are literally thousands around!

A.M.T. Throw-Away, mouse type $7- 10
Acme mole choke 5- 9
Adirondack (Instant Death) wire trap 1- 3
Aldrich (Snare) spring loaded, fox type 9- 13
Alligator (Trapper's Supply), No. 1 coil spring 35- 43
Austin Humane, flat loop, No. 1 14- 19
Barnes Jar Trap, insect type .. 5- 9
Bell Spring, No. 1¼ 54- 60
Bigelow (Killer Trap), Nos. 1, 1½, 2, 3, coil spring, each .. 5- 9
Bigelow (Killer Trap), Nos. 4, 5, 6, 6S, coil spring, each 7- 11
Blake & Lamb bear trap, No. 5, long spring 365-380
Blake & Lamb, hand forged, Nos. 1, 1½, long spring, each 27- 32
Blake & Lamb, Nos. 0, 1, 1½, jump spring, each 5- 9
Bug-Popper, electric, insect, 15 watt 42- 48
California Gopher, No. 44 ..... 3- 6
Champion "B" (by Briddell), Nos. 1, 1½, jump spring, each 5- 8
Clap Net (Christensen, 1962), bird type 11- 15
Davenport Choker, No. 4 ..... 78- 85
Delusion Live Mouse, mouse type 16- 22
Easy Set, round jaw, Nos. 1, 1½, 2, coil spring, each 3.50- 6
Easy Set, square jaw, Nos. 1, 1½, 2, 3, 4, coil spring, each 3- 9
Elisco (Cone and Cage), Japanese beetle 5- 8
Flygon Electric Killer, Fly No. 150 .... 47- 53
Garrote (Thompson), snare type 26- 32
Getsum Gun Trap (mole), .45 caliber, blank type 47- 52
Gibbs Single Grip, Nos. 0, 1, 2, 3, 4, coil spring, each 5- 12
C. Hart, hand forged, bear type, No. 5 215-240
Hawley & Norton (cast pan), Nos. 1, 1½, 2, 3, long spring, each 5- 10
Hawley & Norton (riveted pan), Nos. 0, 1, 1½, 2, 3, long spring, each 5- 10
Herter's Hudson Bay, Nos. 2, 3, 4, double-coil spring, each 4- 7
Hoffman Canada (snare type), No. 0, rabbit 1- 3
Hoffman Canada (snare type), Nos. 1, 2, 3, 4 (mink, fox, beaver, coyote), each 1.50- 4
Kompakt (Oneida Community), No. 3, jump spring (or under-spring) 16- 22

Master Killer (Wilderness Corp.), No. 5	3- 5
Montgomery (Stake 'n Take), No. 110M	4- 7
Newhouse (hand forged), No. 1, long spring	37- 42
Non-N-Jack bird trap, pigeon type	7- 10
Northwoods, fox type, No. 1¾, double-coil spring	6- 9
Oneida Community (cast iron jaws), No. 0, jump spring	6- 9
Oneida Community Wood Choker, 4-hole, round, mouse type	5- 7
Peck, Stowe & Wilcox, jaws bolted, straight chain, Nos. 1, 1½, 2, long spring, each	5- 9
Pioneer Snap Trap (Taiwan), mouse type	1.50- 2
Prott (Lodi, Wisconsin), pan, Nos. 1¼, 1½, each	11- 14
Quick Catch (Triumph), mouse killer	5- 7
Sargent & Co., Wire Link Chain, No. 21, long spring	32- 37
Simmons Clincher, mouse type	4- 6
Snappy, mouse type	4- 6
Victor (Oneida Community), Pat. 5/28/11, figure-8 chains, Nos. 0, 1, 1½, 2, 3, 4, long spring, each	2- 6
Waredick (Niles, Michigan), mole, spear type	6- 8
"X" Best (England), rabbit type, long spring	16- 19
Young's Barrel Ell Trap, wire type, 3′ long	30- 38

Trays

Photo Courtesy of
Hake's Americana & Collectibles

Trays

Serving trays, change trays, and souvenir trays are all collectible. Look out, though, the Coca-Cola trays and a few others are being reproduced.

N.Y. World's Fair, 1939, tin (Illus.)	$8-10
St. Louis Exposition, 1904, souvenir tray	9-12

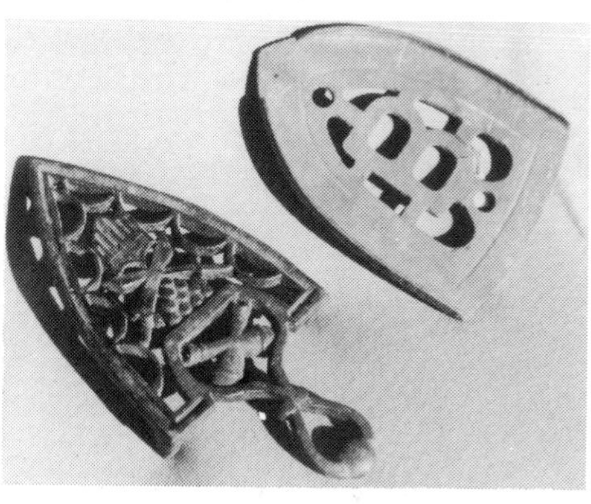

Trivets

Trivets

Like so many other antiques, these are being reproduced. A three-legged one is called a "spider;" six-legged, "cat." Usually made of cast iron or brass, the new are made of pot metal. Used to hold sadirons in the early 1800's until early 1900's.

Diamond T, iron, mid-1800's	$19-24
George Washington, brass, if authentic	49-58
"B" Brand (Illus.)	21-26
Military — cannon, crossed swords (Illus.)	24-32
Order of Odd Fellows, iron	31-37
Snake/Eagle, iron, mid-1800's	29-38

Trolls

These are even uglier than the Cabbage Patch Kids. Marti and Helena Kuuskoski designed them in Tampere, Finland, in 1952. Early versions with the horseshoe or DAM mark are considered collectible. They've been reproduced many times. The Wishniks by Uneeda Doll Co. are considered the best. The animals are considered scarce today.

Batman	$ 9-13
Boy, felt outfit, 1″, marked "DAM"	47-52
Clown	15-19
Cow, marked "DAM"	54-60

Eccky, 1964, 12″ 80-87
Frankenstein, 3½″ 15-19
Gorilla, marked "DAM" 16-20
Leprechaun, 11″ 36-42
Vampire, 3″ 7-10
Wishnik bride, 5½″ 9-12
Wishnik doctor 8-11
Wishnik hula girl 21-26

Trophies

Trophies

Any trophy is a find, especially the older ones. This sterling silver bowl was a 1934 Westchester County Diving Champion trophy.

Sterling bowl (Illus.) $40-47

Turquoise

Turquoise

Too much fake turquoise around today — plastic or synthetic. The illustrated pieces are fake and new. Know what you're doing. "Handmade by the Indians." Which — Cleveland, Hoboken, or Zuni?

TV Games

Everything from the early "Winky Dink" kit, 1950's, to the kind that connect to your boob tube are showing up at swap meets, garage sales, etc. It's better if they work, but they're all being bought.

Average price $3-7

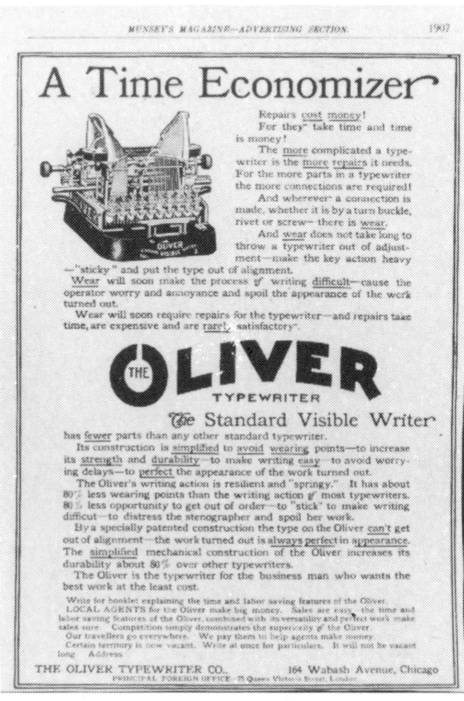

MUNSEY'S MAGAZINE—ADVERTISING SECTION. 1907

A Time Economizer

Repairs cost money!

For they take time and time is money!

The more complicated a typewriter is the more repairs it needs. For the more parts in a typewriter the more connections are required!

And wherever a connection is made, whether it is by a turn buckle, rivet or screw—there is wear.

And wear does not take long to throw a typewriter out of adjustment—make the key action heavy—"sticky" and put the type out of alignment.

Wear will soon make the process of writing difficult—cause the operator worry and annoyance and spoil the appearance of the work turned out.

Wear will soon require repairs for the typewriter—and repairs take time, are expensive and are rarely satisfactory.

THE OLIVER TYPEWRITER

The Standard Visible Writer

has fewer parts than any other standard typewriter.

Its construction is simplified to avoid wearing points—to increase its strength and durability—to make writing easy—to avoid worrying delays—to perfect the appearance of the work turned out.

The Oliver's writing action is resilient and "springy." It has about 80% less wearing points than the writing action of most typewriters. 80% less opportunity to get out of order—to "stick" to make writing difficult—to distress the stenographer and spoil her work.

By a specially patented construction the type on the Oliver can't get out of alignment—the work turned out is always perfect in appearance. The simplified mechanical construction of the Oliver increases its durability about 80% over other typewriters.

The Oliver is the typewriter for the business man who wants the best work at the least cost.

Write for booklet explaining the time and labor saving features of the Oliver.

LOCAL AGENTS for the Oliver make big money. Sales are easy—the time and labor saving features of the Oliver, combined with its versatility and perfect work make sales sure. Competition simply demonstrates the superiority of the Oliver.

Our travellers go everywhere. We pay them to help agents make money.

Certain territory is now vacant. Write at once for particulars. It will not be vacant long. Address

THE OLIVER TYPEWRITER CO., 164 Wabash Avenue, Chicago

Typewriters

Typewriters

"Does it work?" If the answer is affirmative and you collect these mechanical pencils, well, buy it! For some unexplained reason, old typewriters never die, they just keep showing up at Flea Markets. I know a gal who planted ivy amongst the keys of an old Royal and it's as purty as a speckle-nosed pup!

Oliver typewriter $69-76
Underwood, early 60-70
Smith-Corona, early 41-48
Royal 40-50

Umbrellas (Parasols)

Umbrellas (Parasols)

The older the better. Some even had porcelain/gold handles.

Black silk, ebony shaft, late 1800's	$12-21
Average price, in working condition	4- 8

Union Cap Badges

Most unions issue a new button or badge each month. The earlier ones are now being sought by button/badge collectors.

Average price	75¢-2

Universal Potteries

See **American Dinnerware.**

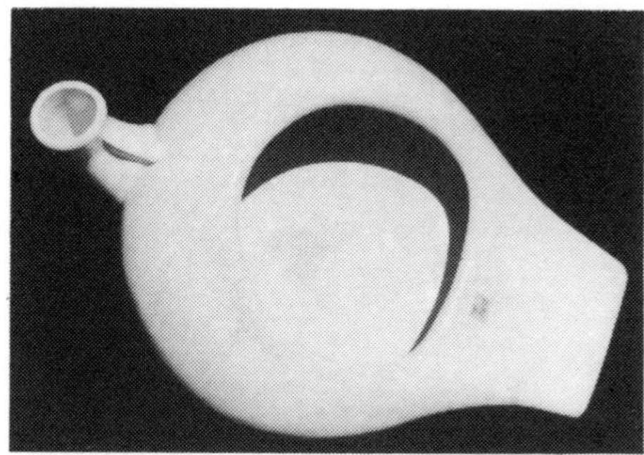
Urinals

Urinals

The ironstone kind make great planters for flowers, ivy, etc. The porcelainized hospital-type are common.

Glass, Civil War	$25-30
Ironstone, late 1800's	22-26
Porcelainized, hospital-type	8-13

Valentines

Valentines

"Won't you be my ----?" If there's anything more beautiful than the valentines of around the turn of the century — these tired old eyes haven't seen it. Love and devotion were just that when Ma and Pa were sparking, courting, and "going together." If you're lucky enough to "luck up" on an album of old valentines, grab same and run for your life! Pay for it first, though.

Large, fancy valentine .... $ 5- 8
Small valentines, old 4- 6
Buster Brown valentine, rare 43-51
A token of love (Illus.) 6-13

Van Briggle Pottery

Van Briggle Pottery

Artus Van Briggle worked at Rookwood Pottery in the late 1800's, then moved to Colorado Springs for his health. The company is still in business. Van Briggle's work at Rookwood was far superior to anything he ever made in Colorado. He died in 1904.

Bookends, maroon/green, pr. . . $105-115
Bowl, blue, 1924, paper label . . 58- 64
Bowl, Persian Rose, dated 1918 in bottom, 3″ dia. 66- 74
Candleholder, red/brown 65- 73
Candlesticks, Persian Rose, 3¾″ high, Pat. #733, signed . 64- 74
Creamer, blue, Grecian Key ... 70- 80
Figurine, Indian maiden, turquoise 157-165
Lamp, Art Deco style, figural lady, Oriental, 10½″ high, monogram mark 74- 83
Pitcher, maroon, 5″ high, 1932 (Illus.) 82- 90
Planter, oval shape, green/blue, incised signature 63- 69
Plaque, Indian maiden, blue, signed 81- 90
Tulip bowl, turquoise, 8½″ long, 3″ high, signed 65- 73
Tulip flower frog, 20 holes, signed 44- 51
Vase, floral decor, Colorado Springs mark 66- 71
Vase, plum color, handled, incised signature, 1934 .... 72- 81
Vase, red/green, Greek Key, 6″ high 64- 69
Vase, turquoise, daffodils, 9½″ high, signed 93-101
Vase, turquoise, 2½″ high, scalloped rim, signed 55- 64

Vases

Vases

Take your choice — thousands to choose from.

Pink pottery vase, new (Illus.) ...$ 4- 7
Haviland, hand-painted vase, 1860's, 8″ high (Illus.) 49-55

Video Cassettes, Games

PacMan, Centipede, you name it — bargains at every garage sale or swap meet.

Wade Ceramics

Wade Ceramics

George Wade and Son, England, makes these ceramic figures that are put in packages of rose tea. Little Creatures, Nursery Favorites, and Nursery Rhyme Characters are three of the lines produced. Signed "Wade, England."

Little Creatures

Angel fish	$ 3- 4
Brown turtle	9-11
Crocodile	7- 9
Fawn	3- 4
Green frog	9-11
Kangaroo	3- 4
Poodle	9-11
Sea lion	9-11
Zebra	3- 4

Nursery Favorites

Goosey Gander	$ 8- 9
Jack Horner	8- 9
Miss Muffet	8- 9
Old King Cole (Illus.)	8- 9
Queen of Hearts (Illus.)	8- 9
Tom the Piper	8- 9

Nursery Rhyme Characters

Cat and the Fiddle (Illus.)	$ 5- 7
Gingerbread Man	5- 7
Jack and Jill, each	5- 7
Mother Goose	5- 7
Puss in Boots	5- 7
Red Riding Hood	5- 7

Wagon Wheels

Light fixtures, yard decorations, fences — you name it, someone's using a w.w. to good advantage. Start around $40 for the cheapest, and expect to pay upwards of $175-$200 for the larger, more ornate wheels.

Wagon Wheels

Walking Sticks (Canes)

Walking Sticks (Canes)

Stylish in Europe for centuries. Men of means in America used them from the 1840's until around World War I.

Carved animal's head, 1920's	$7- 10
Gold-headed, glass tube inside for ¼ pint of booze, 1920's	115-130

"Wanted!" Posters

Ask your local postmaster to save them for you.

Warwick China

Warwick China

WARWICK CHINA

Made in Wheeling, West Virginia, from 1887 until 1951. Much of their ware was decal-decorated.

Ale set, pitcher, 10½" high, 6 mugs, 5" high, "B.P.O.E., Akron" on all pieces, brown ground, all $540-554
Bookends, Indian head, 7" high, pr. 28- 33
Creamer, dairy maid, 5½" high 27- 32
Dish, floral decor, 7" dia. 19- 24
Ewer, floral decor, 8¼" high .. 51- 60
Humidor, monk's head, brown, 6½" high 161-170
Mug, Indian head, brown, 5" high 72- 81
Mug, monk holding beer stein, brown 63- 70
Mugs, various fraternal orders, 4½" high, each 42- 44
Pitcher, cows, blue 47- 50
Pitcher, floral decor, 6¼" high (Illus.) 46- 51
Pitcher, monk, brown, 8½" high 53- 60
Plate, Indian, 8¼" dia. 71- 80
Platter, floral decor, blue/gold border, 16" long 41- 50
Spittoon, English village scene, flared top 171-178
Vase, "B.P.O.E., Cincinnati," 8¼" high 68- 74
Vase, gypsy lady, 10" high 71- 80
Vase, pine needles/cones, 7¼" high 68- 77
Vase, poppies, brown/green, Helmet mark, 8" high 79- 85
Vase, portrait of dog, 9" high . 78- 85
Vase, portrait of woman, twig handles, 11" high 138-145

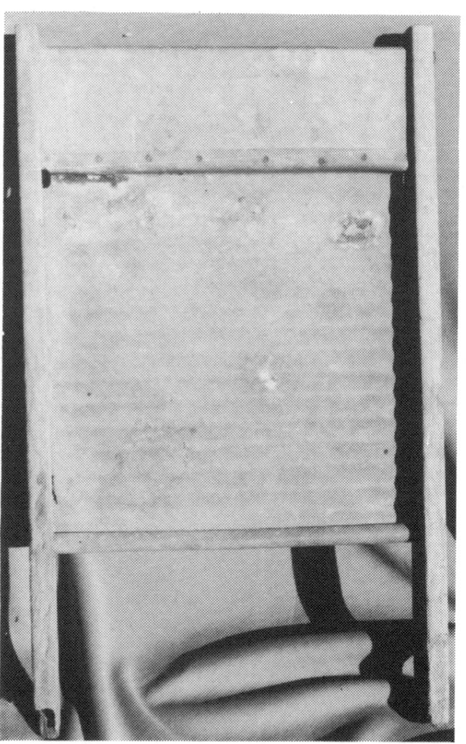

Washboards

Washboards

Average price in good condition .. $8-14

Washing Machines

Before Grandma got electricity, she did everything by hand. The one illustrated worked like a pogo stick. Pushing up and down on the handle "agitated" Grandpa's longjohns in the wooden tub. It really worked.

Hand-operated washer (Illus.), copper, wood handle $35-42

Washing Machines

Washington, George

Washtubs

Washington, George

Our 200th anniversary is behind us, so **anything** with George's face or name on it will bring above-average prices.

Washtubs

Usually the tub was copper and the top a cheaper metal with a wooden handle. Popular before the washing machine came upon the scene.

Tub w/lid, if polished and in good condition $99-130

Watch Fobs

These have been around for years. Popular until World War I when the wristwatch came into vogue. Whitehead & Hoag, Newark, New Jersey; Robbins Co., Attleboro, Massachusetts; St. Louis Button Co., St. Louis, Missouri — just a few of the companies that manufactured the thousands of fobs from the late 19th century until the mid-1930's.

Most popular to collectors are the old machinery type, but those to do with advertising, transportation, politicians, patriots, sports, and fraternal organizations are also collectible. Just about every metal was used to make them. Those with enamel blended into the surface are more collectible than the usual run-of-the-mill types. They've been reproduced for a good number of years; most of the repros don't have any advertising on the reverse side.

Advertising

Battle Axe Shoes, silver color, c. 1908 ....$13-19
Brown's Shoes, multicolored, c. 1905 16-22
Gillette Tires and Tubes, silver color, c. 1950's 9-15
H & M Paints, silver color, c. 1915 10-15
The Malleable Range, silver color, c. 1910 19-24
Rio Coffee, bronze color, c. 1909 14-19
State Automobile Insurance Association, bronze color, c. 1920 9-15
Walk-Over Shoes, silver color, c. 1915 10-14

Clubs/Organizations

A. F. of L., bronze color, c. 1932 .$ 5- 9
B.P.O.E., bronze color, c. 1926 .. 6-10
C.I.O., bronze color, c. 1930's ... 6-10
K of C, bronze color, c. 1914 6-10
The Rochester Club, bronze color, c. 1912 7-10
Sons of American Revolution, bronze color, c. 1919 6-11
The Taddood Melkite Catholic Society, multicolored, c. 1912 8-11

Fire/Police

City of Troy, N.Y. (police) 3000, silver color, c. 1940's.........$ 7-10
Firemen's Convention, bronze color, c. 1936 6-10
Pennsylvania Fire Convention, silver color, c. 1935 7-11

Machinery

Cat engines D334, silver color, c. 1970's ....$ 5- 8
Caterpillar DW 2, bronze color, c. 1950's 7-10
Highway Equipment Co., silver color, c. 1960's 6- 9
Ingersoll-Rand, bronze color, c. 1960's 5- 9
Joy Ram track drill, bronze color, c. 1950's 5- 9
Worthington Blue Brute, hand-held rock drills, silver color, c. 1930's 13-18

Miscellaneous

American Legion, New York, bronze color, c. 1937 ....$ 5- 8
I Bring Good Luck, multicolored, c. 1920's 7-10
Izaak Walton League of America, silver color, c. 1915 18-24
Peace Bridge, Toronto, bronze color, c. 1930 7-10
United Spanish War Veterans, bronze color, c. 1940 .... 5- 9

Patriotic

George Washington, 1732-1932, silver color, c. 1932 ....$ 9-14
Miss Liberty, bronze color, c. 1918 8-11
Union Veterans, bronze color, c. 1917 8-12

People

Boy Scouts, silver color, c. 1915 .$ 7-11
Count Casimir Pulaski, silver color, c. 1930 6-10
John Deere, bronze color, c. 1937 12-18
Luther Burbank, bronze color, c. 1912 8-12

Political

Franklin D. Roosevelt, silver color, c. 1940 ....$19-26
G.O.P., bronze color, c. 1912 7-11
Lincoln, 1809-1865, bronze color, c. 1930 9-14
Republican Convention, Ohio, bronze color, c. 1932 8-12
Taft and Sherman, bronze color, c. 1908 20-27

Sports

Baseball, silver color, c. 1925 ...$ 8-13
Football, bronze color, c. 1925 .. 6-10
Golf, bronze color, c. 1920 8-12
Hockey, silver color, c. 1920 6-10
New York vs. Chicago, Golden Gloves, bronze color, c. 1941 .. 8-12

Transportation

Aviation, silver color, c. 1920's ..$ 9-15
Bessemer & Lake Erie Railroad, silver color, c. 1930's......... 12-16
Buy It Because It's A Studebaker, silver color, c. 1930's......... 33-41
New York to Paris, Lindbergh, silver color, c. 1928 19-27
The Speed Demon, silver color, c. 1910 26-33

Interested in collecting watch fobs? Join the International Watch Fob Association, Inc., 35½ North Old State Rd., Norwalk, OH 44857.

Wedgwood

Some old and some new; all are confusing to the uninformed. Turn the piece over, and if it has "Wedgwood" incised in the bottom, start dickering.

Wedgwood

Ashtray, new, Jasperware, green (Illus.) . . . . $ 6- 9
Creamer, old, has British Registry Mark on bottom, 1870's (Illus.) . 47-54

As confusing as Haviland, so read up or save your money!

Weller Pottery

Baskets

Blossom pattern, 6″ (Blossom has a blue or green matte background, pink blossoms, green leaves, late period) . . . $ 27- 34
Delsa pattern, 7″ (Delsa has flowers and leaves in relief on a matte background of different colors) 38- 44
Florenzo pattern, 5½″ (Florenzo has tinted flowers at the base of ribbed ivory background; many w/scalloped tops, c. 1928) 60- 68
Patra pattern, 5½″ (Patra has pebbled leaves, scalloped top, mottled colors, matte finish, middle period) 82- 90

Bowls

Atlas pattern, 4″ (Atlas has an angular, star-shaped top, in various colors, late period) . . $ 49- 52
Cornish pattern, 4″ (Cornish has leaves w/clusters of berries in relief, small handles, middle period) 39- 44
DuPont ware, 2½″ (DuPont has roses in relief on a background of various colors, middle period) 54- 61
Pumila pattern, 3½″ (Pumila has a matte glaze, leaves or blossoms extending to a serrated top, various colors) . . . 30- 37

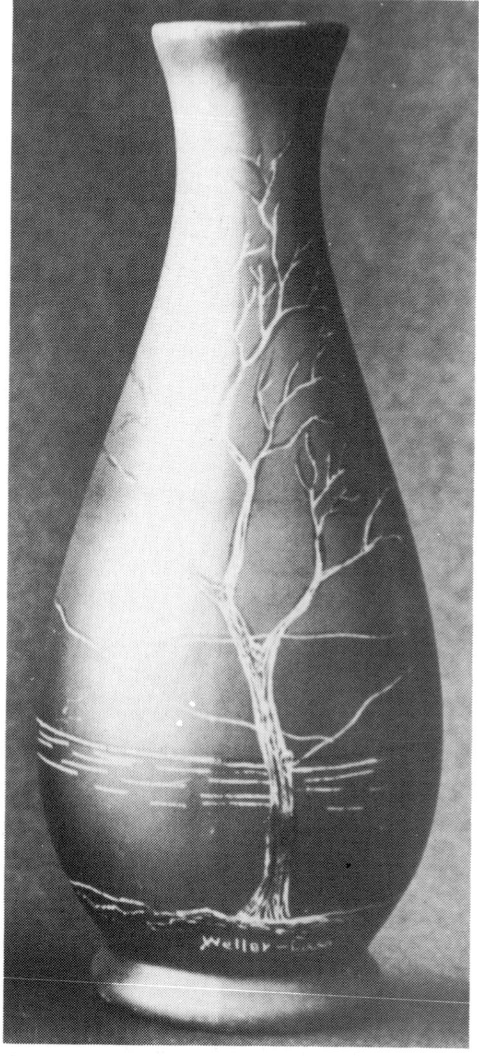

Weller Pottery

Candle Holders

Ardsley, 3″ high, pr. (Ardsley has tall cattails and slender leaves rising from water lilies, matte finish, 1928) . . . . $ 75- 84
Clarmont pattern, 10″ high, pr. (Clarmont has a dark brown background w/flowers, grapes, and vines) 212-221

Hobart pattern, nude, 6″ (Hobart is finished in a vellum, viridis green and white, human and animal figures) . . 116-124

Cornucopias

Blossom pattern, 6″ . . . .$ 29- 35

Loru pattern, 4″ (Loru has vertical ribs, angular scallops at the top and a sprig of leaves at the base, matte finish, late) 24- 30

Sydonia pattern, 8½″ (Sydonia has a flaring shell effect from a "leaves" base, some have scalloped tops, middle period) 72- 80

Ewers

Dickens 2nd Line pattern, Mr. Micawber/streets, 11″ (Dickens 2nd Line are scenes from Charles Dickens' novels. Incisions in soft clay, matte background) $485-550

Floretta pattern, roses, 6″ (Floretta has brown and pastel backgrounds, slip-decorated on molded fruit and flowers, early) 88- 96

Louwelsa pattern, floral, 5″ (Louwelsa gets its name from the first 3 letters of Sam's Daughter, Louise, the first 3 letters of his surname, and his first 2 initials. It's a shaded brown ware with underglaze decoration of flowers, birds, fruit, dogs) 78- 87

Jardinieres

Blue Ware, classic figure, 10″ (Blue Ware has a blue matte background embossed w/classic figures, middle period) $113-122

Chengtu pattern, 5½″ (Chengtu has a plain red matte glaze, 1920-1925) 84- 93

Forest pattern, 7″ (Forest is polychrome forest scenes w/tinted colors, matte finish) 117-125

Jap Birdimal pattern, blue trees, 9″ (Jap Birdimal is outlines of white slip on white ground) 325-345

Pitchers

Coppertone pattern, fish handle, 8″ (Coppertone is yellow mottled w/green and decorated w/animals, fish, plants, middle period) . . . . . .$ 57- 65

Etna pattern, daisies, 6″ (Etna has underglaze decorations slip-painted on low relief w/background in light colors, early) 154-164

Oak Leaf pattern, 14″ (Oak Leaf has oak leaves and acorns on various shades of matte background, late period) 104-122

Planters

Blue Drapery pattern, 4″ (Blue Drapery has sprigs of red roses, molded folds, dark blue matte glaze, middle period) . . . .$ 39- 47

Dupont Ware, 4″ square 57- 64

Pastel pattern, 7½″ (Pastel pieces have modernistic shapes, pastel colors, matte glaze, late period) 42- 50

Roba pattern, 6″ (Roba has loops of flowers and leaves, various colors, matte glaze background, late period) 35- 43

Vases

Blo' Red pattern, 7¼″ (Blo' Red is blue w/red splotches of glossy glaze, middle period) . . . .$ 79- 86

Cretone pattern, cream w/white figures, 7½″ (Cretone is decorated with human figures, late period) 345-365

Greora pattern, 11½″ (Greora has splashes of light and dark green w/a semigloss finish, middle period) 142-150

Ivoris pattern, small handles, 6¼″ (Ivoris has flowers in relief on an ivory background) 37- 44

LaMar pattern, 7¼″ (LaMar is decorated with black trees on a red overglaze, middle period) 144-152

Sicardo pattern, 12½″ (Sicard or Sicardo was invented by a Frenchman, Jacques Sicard. He worked for Weller around 1902) . . . . 1,900+

There's so much Weller around, especially the "script" signature.

Whiskey Bottles, Miniature

These "baby" bottles have been around for years. Railroads, then airlines, sold them. Thousands around. Prices given are for unopened, seal unbroken, tax stamp intact. Empty, 30 to 40 percent less.

U.S.A.

Ancient Age, 1960's, 86 proof, 1/10 pt., brown bottle $2- 3

Antique, 1913, 100 proof, 1/4 pt., brown bottle 11.75-12.50

Antique, 1936, 100 proof, 1/10 pt., brown bottle 7.50- 8.50

Bard's Town, 1939, 90 proof, 1/10 pt., brown bottle 9.75-10.50

Bard's Town Bond, 1940, 100 proof, 1/10 pt., brown bottle 17.25-18.50

Beam's Choice, 1970's, 90 proof, clear bottle 2.50- 3.50

Belle of Boston, 1933, 90 proof, 1/10 pt., clear bottle 5.75- 6.50

Bellows Special Reserve, 1940's, 86 proof, 1/10 pt., clear bottle 4- 5

Belmont, 1941, 86 proof, 1/10 pt., brown bottle 4.75- 5.50

Bourbon Springs, 1939, 93 proof, 1/10 pt., brown bottle 18-19

Brigadier, 1930's, 80.6 proof, 1/10 pt., clear bottle 5- 6

Broad Ripple, 1934, 100 proof, 1/10 pt., brown bottle 6- 7

Broadmoor, 1930's, 90 proof, 1/8 pt., clear bottle 5- 6

C & G Old Reserve, 1937, 93 proof, 1/10 pt., clear bottle 4.75- 5.50

Calvert Reserve, 1950, 86.8 proof, 1/10 pt., brown bottle 3.25- 3.75

Carstairs Harmony, 1957, 85 proof, 1/10 pt., brown bottle 4.75- 5.50

Carstairs White Seal, 1958, 86 proof, 1/10 pt., brown bottle 2.75- 3.50

Clover Hill, 1970's, 80 proof, 1/10 pt., clear bottle 3.75- 4.50

Cobbs Creek, 1936, 90 proof, 1/10 pt., clear bottle 5.25- 6

Colonel Lee, 1970's, 80 proof, 1/10 pt., clear bottle 2.25- 2.75

Duffy's Tavern, 1940's, 42 proof, clear bottle 1.75- 2.50

Early Times, 1940's, 86 proof, 1/10 pt., clear bottle 3.50- 4.50

8-Ball Whiskey, 1940's, 80 proof, 1/10 pt., brown bottle 6.50- 7.50

Family Club, 1940's, 86.8 proof, 1/10 pt., clear bottle 5.50- 6.50

Four Decades Brand, 1941, 100 proof, 1/10 pt., clear bottle 5.75- 6.75

Geo. T. Stagg, 1950's, 86 proof, 1/10 pt., clear bottle 3.25- 4

Gold Crown, 1970's, 80 proof, 1/10 pt., clear bottle 1.50- 2

Glenmore, 1930's, 100 proof, 1/10 pt., clear bottle 6- 7

Glenmore Silver Label, 1965, 86 proof, 1/10 pt., clear bottle 5.75- 6.50

Golden Mash, 1935, 93 proof, 1/10 pt., clear bottle 7.25- 8

Gordon's Distilled Dry Gin, 86 proof, 1/10 pt., clear bottle (Illus.) 1.50- 1.75

Grand Sire, 1930's, 90 proof, 1/10 pt., clear bottle 7- 8

Green River, 1934, 90 proof, 1/10 pt., clear bottle 6.50- 7.25

Guckenheimer Reserve, 1960's, 86 proof, 1/10 pt., clear bottle 2-2.50

Heaven Hill, 1960's, 86 proof, 1/10 pt., clear bottle 2.75- 3.25

Hill and Hill, 1940's, 93 proof, 1/10 pt., clear bottle 4- 4.50

Hotel Maples, 1964, 86 proof, 1/10 pt., clear bottle 4- 4.75

I. W. Harper, 1960, 100 proof, 1/10 pt., clear bottle 3.50- 4

Jack Daniel's No. 7 Brand, 1968, 90 proof, 1/10 pt., clear bottle 2- 2.50

James E. Pepper, 1950, 86.8 proof, 1/10 pt., clear bottle 3.50- 4

Jim Dant, 1950's, 86 proof, 1/10 pt., clear bottle 3.50- 4

Kentucky Life, 1970's, 86 proof, 1/10 pt., clear bottle 2- 2.50

Kentucky Pride, 1936, 90 proof, 1/10 pt., clear bottle 5.25- 5.75

Laird's Apple Jack, 1964, 80 proof, 1/10 pt., brown bottle 2.25- 2.75

Lewis 66, 1930's, 90 proof, 1/10 pt., clear bottle 6.75- 7.50

Lord Calvert, 1941, 86.8 proof, 1/10 pt., brown bottle 5.50- 6.50

Maker's Mark, 1960's, 90 proof, 1/10 pt., clear bottle 2.25- 2.75

Miller's Deluxe, 1936, 90 proof, 1/10 pt., brown bottle 4- 4.50

National's Eagle, 1941, 90 proof, 1/10 pt., clear bottle 5- 6

Nevada Centennial, 1964, 86 proof, 1/10 pt., clear bottle 4.50- 5.25

Old Cask, 1935, 90 proof, 1/10 pt., clear bottle 7.75- 8.75

Old Charter, 1962, 86 proof, 1/10 pt., clear bottle 2- 2.75

Old Classic, 1954, 86 proof, 1/10 pt., brown bottle 5.50- 6.25

Old Crow, 1935, 93 proof, 1/10 pt., clear bottle 4.75- 5.50

Old Dover Brand, 1940's, 90 proof, 1/10 pt., clear bottle 4.75- 5.50

Old Fitzgerald, 1959, 100 proof, 1/10 pt., clear bottle 3.25- 4

Old Forester, 1961, 86 proof, 1/10 pt., brown bottle 11.25-12.25

Old Grand-Dad, 1917, 100 proof, 1/10 pt., clear bottle 25-28

Old Harmon, 1918, 100 proof, 1/10 pt., brown bottle 23-25

Old Hickory, 1930's, 90 proof, 1/10 pt., clear bottle 5.50- 6.50

Whiskey Bottles, Miniature

Old Kentucky Tavern, 1970, 86 proof, ⅒ pt., clear bottle 1.75- 2.50
Old Medley, 1939, 100 proof, ⅒ pt., clear bottle 6- 7
Old Mr. Boston Rocking Chair, 1940's, 86 proof, ⅒ pt., clear bottle 5.50- 6.25
Old Stagg, 1952, 86 proof, ⅒ pt., clear bottle 2.75- 3.50
Old Taylor, 1972, 86 proof, ⅒ pt., clear bottle 2- 2.75
Old Treasure, 1930's, 90 proof, ⅒ pt., clear bottle . 5.50- 6.25
Old Velvet Brand, 1940's, 90 proof, ⅒ pt., brown bottle 5.25- 5.75
PM De Luxe, 1947, 86 proof, ⅒ pt., brown bottle 4.50- 5.50
Paul Jones, 1937, 90 proof, ⅒ pt., brown bottle 3.75- 4.50
Red Horse, 1940's, (?) proof, (?) capacity, brown bottle . 6.50- 7.50
Royal Oak, 1930's, 86 proof, ⅒ pt., clear bottle 5.25- 6
S. S. Pierce Number 6, 1970's, 86 proof, ⅒ pt., brown bottle 3.50- 4
Schenley Reserve, 1947, 86 proof, ⅒ pt., clear bottle . 3.50- 4
Silver Dollar, 1938, 90 proof, ⅒ pt., clear bottle 2.25- 3
Sweep Stakes, 1940's, 90 proof, ⅛ pt., green bottle . 6- 6.75
21 Brand, 1936, 90 proof, ⅒ pt., clear bottle 6.25- 7
Union Leader, 1937, 85 proof, 4⅜ pt., clear bottle . 8- 9
Very Old Barton, 1960's, 90 proof, ⅒ pt., clear bottle . 2.25- 2.75
Hiram Walker's Ten High, 1958, 86 proof, ⅒ pt., clear bottle 2.75- 3.50
Washington Club, 1939, 90 proof, ⅒ pt., clear bottle . 6.25- 7
Wild Turkey, 1964, 101 proof, 1.6 oz., clear bottle. 2- 2.50
Yellowstone, 1954, 100 proof, ⅒ pt., clear bottle . 3.50- 4

Foreign

Albany Club, Argentina, 86 proof, 50 cm., clear bottle. 4.25- 5
Black Opal, Australia, 86 proof, ⅒ pt., clear bottle . 4- 4.50
Canadian Club, Canada, 1934, 90.4 proof, ⅒ pt., brown bottle 5- 5.50
Canadian MacNaughton, Canada, 1964, 86.8 proof, ⅒ pt., brown bottle 2.50- 3
DH-Bourbon, Italy, 80 proof, 30 cc., clear bottle 3- 3.50
Don Granger, Argentina, 86 proof, 50 cm., clear bottle. 4.25- 4.75
Green River, Canada, 1928, 100 proof, ⅒ pt., clear bottle 6- 6.75
Hobo's Delight, Argentina, 86 proof, 50 cm., clear bottle 4.50- 5
Jacob Stuck, Germany, 86 proof, (?) capacity, brown bottle 5- 5.75
John Jameson & Son, Ireland, 86 proof, ⅒ pt., brown bottle 3- 3.50
Kohut Whiskey, Germany, 96 proof (?) capacity, clear bottle 4.75- 5.50
Old Bushmills, Ireland, 86 proof, ⅒ pt., clear bottle . 2.75- 3
Old Herold Whiskey, Czechoslovakia, 85 proof, clear bottle 5.25- 5.75
Robert Brown Deluxe, Japan, 1978, 86 proof, 50 ml., clear bottle 3.50- 4
Robert Brown's Special, Argentina, 86 proof, 50 cc., clear bottle 3.50- 4
Royal Label Extra, Mexico, 1976, 86 proof, 47 ml., clear bottle 3- 3.50
Waterfill and Frazier, Mexico, 1930's, (?) proof, ⅓ liter . . 4.50- 5

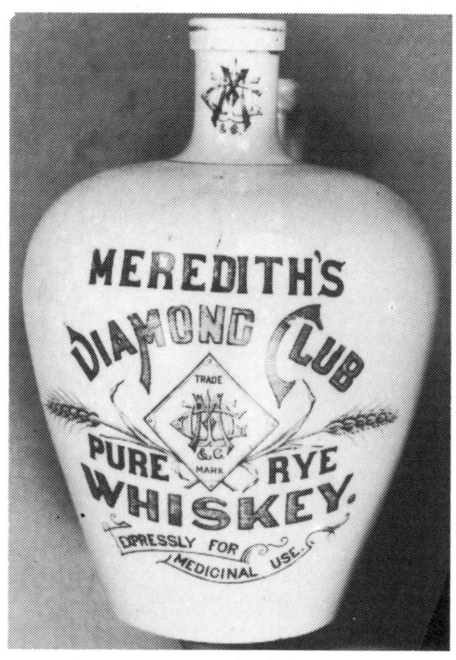

Whiskey Jugs/Flasks

Photo Courtesy of
Hake's Americana & Collectibles

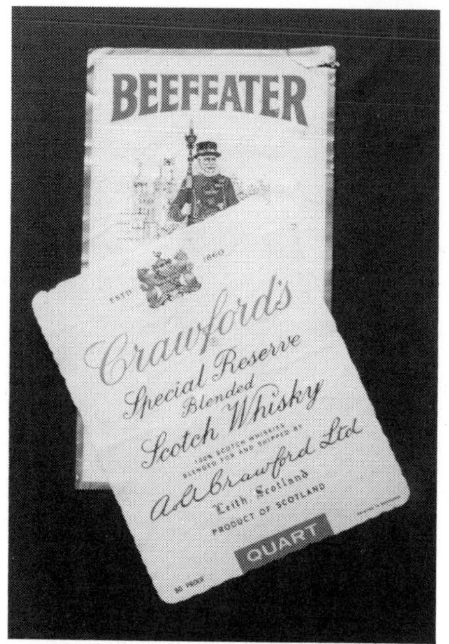

Whiskey Labels

Whiskey Jugs/Flasks

If it's marked "Federal Law Prohibits the Reuse of this bottle," the bottle was made after 1933, when the U.S.A. repealed the 18th amendment, again making liquor legal in certain states.

Meredith's whiskey jug (Illus.) . . $19- 25
Old Grey Mare whiskey flask . . . 84- 93
Whitney Glass Works whiskey flask . . . 77- 87
Small earthenware jug . . . 5- 8
Doulton jug, marked "JRD," late 1800's . . . 92-101
Large earthenware jug, corn stobb . . . 21- 37

Whiskey Labels

Soak them off with water. Thousands to choose from.

Average price . . . 10¢-25¢

Whiskey Sample Glasses

Whiskey Sample Glasses

Drummers (salesmen) carried these little "shot" glasses to convince their customers that their booze was the best!

Habanero "Piza" tabasco, ½ ounce . . . $11-14
Big 6 gin, 1 ounce . . . 16-19
Hanover rye, 2 oz. (Illus.) . . . 20-23

Wicker Items

Wicker Items

Wicker is a name used to describe many types of materials, such as willow, cane, rattan, reed, and rush, even twisted paper. At one time it was quite common. Now, too many collectors have driven prices up, and many pieces are being reproduced worldwide. Most pieces were handwoven or loom-woven from the materials mentioned or from man-made fibers. Prices are for pieces in good to fine condition.

Baby Furnishings

Baby carriage, willow, handwoven, complete $875-966
Bassinet, reed, handwoven 150-170

Bird Cages

Reed, metal stand, handwoven $178-188
Willow, hanging type, handwoven 170-180

Chairs

Child's high, reed, handwoven . $104-115
Child's, rocking, willow, man-made fibers 86- 94
Fireside, cane, handwoven 265-280
Fireside, willow, loom-woven . . 300-325
Rocking, ornate, willow, handwoven (Illus.) 365-400
Rocking, willow, handwoven . . 270-280
Straight, cushioned seat and back, willow, handwoven 340-350
Straight, magazine racks at arms, reed, handwoven 365-400

Chaise Lounges

Grass, handwoven $430-440
Reed, loom-woven 440-450

Davenports

Cushioned back and seat, reed, handwoven $540-557
Cushioned back and seat, willow, handwoven 475-500

Desks

Reed, handwoven $340-360
Rush, loom-woven 310-320
Man-made fibers, handwoven . . 290-310

Fern Stands

Box-type, w/hanging bird cage, reed, handwoven $375-400
Box-type, willow, loom-woven . 240-260
Floor-type, reed, handwoven . . 215-225

Lamps

Floor, reed, handwoven $310-335
Hanging, willow, handwoven . . 235-250
Phonograph cabinet, floor model, willow, handwoven . . 460-470
Table, reed, handwoven 195-218

Settees

Grass, handwoven $410-420
Reed, loom-woven 408-417

Sewing Stands

Man-made fibers, handwoven . . $155-168
Reed, handwoven 165-175

Swings

Porch, reed, handwoven $360-375
Porch, willow, handwoven 365-375

Tables

Bridge, reed, handwoven $290-320
Dining, willow, handwoven 410-430
End, reed, handwoven 115-124
Library, reed, handwoven 270-280
Parlor, reed, loom-woven 170-188

Tea Carts

Reed, removable tray, solid rubber tires, handwoven $365-400
Willow, removable tray, solid rubber tires, handwoven 420-440

Umbrella Stand

Reed, handwoven $115-132

Willow Ware

Willow Ware

This was first made in England in 1772, in America about 1880. It was made in every quality, from Spode and Minton to the 5¢ and 10¢ store variety. Chinese legend says two escaping lovers were turned into doves. Found in light and dark blue, also in pink and green. Red is rare. Lots of scenes other than the dove bit were used. Maker, year, and quality dictate prices here. See **Clubs and Publications,** this Price Guide.

Bowl, Ridgway, 8″ dia. $26-31
Bowl, soup, marked Allerton, England, 6″ dia. 19-25
Bowl, vegetable, 9¾″ dia. 35-40
Butter pat, marked Allerton 8-12
Butter pat, Ridgway 8-12
Butter pat, Wedgwood.......... 10-15
Creamer, Buffalo Pottery, 4¼″ high 16-23
Creamer, Johnson Bros., 4½″ high 14-20
Creamer, Made in Japan, 4″ high 12-17
Cup/saucer, Japan 19-25
Cup/saucer, marked Allerton 31-35
Cup/saucer, Ridgway........... 29-34
Cup/saucer, Wedgwood 37-45
Egg cup, Japan 8-14
Egg cup, marked Allerton 11-16
Pitcher, Buffalo Pottery, 10½″ high 35-42
Pitcher, bulbous, Japan, 7″ high . 27-33
Pitcher, miniature, 3″ high 19-24
Pitcher, Ridgway, 8½″ high 36-39
Plate, Japan, 6″ dia. 16-21
Plate, marked Allerton, 7¼″ dia. . 26-31
Plate, marked Ridgway, 7¼″ dia. 27-30
Plate, marked Wedgwood, 7″ dia. 27-33
Plate, Royal Worcester, 7¼″ dia.. 27-33
Plate, unmarked, 7″ dia. 19-23
Plates, 8″, 8½″, 10″ dia., made in Ohio, each (Illus.) 32-38
Platter, Buffalo Pottery 39-44
Platter, England 28-31
Platter, Japan 25-33
Platter, marked Ridgway 38-41
Relish, Japan 11-16
Relish, marked Ridgway 17-25
Sauce, England 12-19
Sauce, Japan 9-12
Sugar/creamer, England 59-63
Sugar/creamer, Japan 38-42
Tea set, child's, Japan, 22 pcs. .. 40-48
Tea set, England, 25 pcs. 59-66
Tea set, Occupied Japan, 10 pcs. 42-52

Wine Glasses

Wine Glasses

They come in crystal, regular glass, and in every shape. Leaded crystal means it'll ring when pinged; lead oxide in the glass batch. Neat shelf items.

Average price, each $6-9

Engraved and/or cut: a few bucks more.

Wine Labels

After you've enjoyed the bubbly, soak off the label. Foreign wine labels are fascinating to use for decorations on pocketbooks, etc. And they're not expensive.

Average price (Illus.) .... 50¢-$1

Wine Labels

Commemorating the best-loved, most-seen motion picture of all time

Wizard of Oz

Wizard of Oz

Ever since Dorothy skipped down that yellow brick road, anything to do "wiz" the Wiz is sought after.

Wood Carvings

Carrying on probably the oldest form of art, whittlers have been around since the days of the Romans. European wood-carvers, especially the German and French, decorated many of the finest palaces in the world. What we find today usually was carved in the mid-1800's. See **Clubs and Publications,** this Price Guide.

Drunk under lamp post, 10" high; removable head is a bottle opener, lamp a corkscrew $47-53
Japanese God, rosewood, 6" high (Illus.) 65-74
Mother with child, Italian, 7" high 60-68
Swiss couple, 5" high, early 20th century, pr. 66-74
Wine maker, French, 8" high 60-68

Wood Carvings

Wooden Nickels

Wooden Nickels

"Don't take any wooden nickels!" is an expression from the 1930's. What it means is beyond me. But, you see them at most Flea Markets.

Average price . . . . 50¢-75¢ each

Woodenware

All sizes, all ages, and all types of wood. Few things you can't do with them.

Mixing bowl, wooden straps, mid-1800's (Illus.) $38-44
Basket made from oak strips, late 1800's (Illus.) 33-40

Woodenware

Stirrup (great for holding napkins) (Illus.)	15-21
Large keg, probably for cider or molasses, early 1800's (Illus.)	61-70
Rolling pin, early, hand-carved	20-28

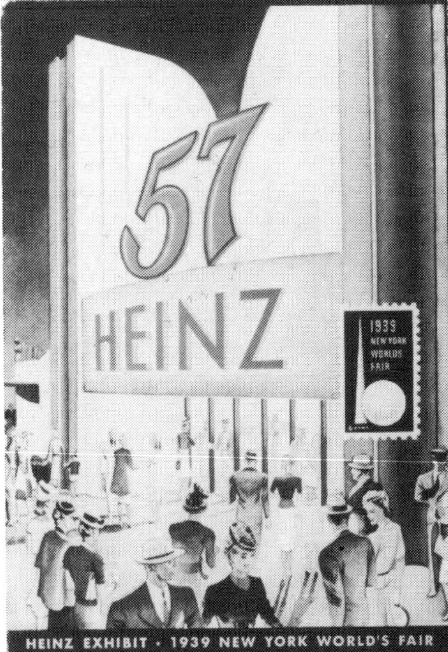

World Expositions

World Expositions and Fairs

The first exhibition opened at the Crystal Palace in London in 1851. The first World's Fair opened at the Crystal Palace in New York City in 1853. The first exposition opened in Philadelphia in 1876. Mementos of these great events are highly collectible today — the older the better. What you find in shops is from the late

World Expositions and Fairs

Photo Courtesy of Hake's Americana & Collectibles

1800's in the form of spoons, glass mugs, toothpick holders, in metal or glass. These items stayed in vogue until the Sesquicentennial Exposition in Philadelphia, 1926. See **Clubs and Publications,** this Price Guide.

Ashtray, 1933, pot metal, sky ride	$ 5- 7
Ashtray, 1939, brass	10-13
Bank, 1939, Trylon & Perisphere, glass	12-15
Banner, 1933	10-13
Book, 1933, Official Guide	7-10
Book, 1939, Official Guide, Grover Whalen's "signature"	10-14
Bottle, 1939, milk glass	24-32
Compact, 1939, Trylon & Perisphere	10-14
Lock, 1933, Master Lock Co.	30-36
Match holder, 1939	21-27
Paperweight, 1933	11-16
Pin, Simoniz, 1933 (Illus.)	3- 4
Plate, 1939, Trylon & Perisphere, 10½"	26-33
Salt/pepper set, 1939, plastic	8-11
Sewing kit, 1964, complete (Illus.)	11-14
Teapot, 1939, ceramic, Trylon & Perisphere	20-25
Teaspoon, 1939, Empire State Building	8-11
Tumbler, 1939, Trylon & Perisphere	6- 9

Message du Président Roosevelt au Peuple Français

Voici le texte d'un message important radiodiffusé par le Président des Etats-Unis d'Amérique au peuple français, au moment où le Corps Expéditionnaire Américain débarquait en Afrique française du Nord.

MES AMIS—mes amis qui souffrez jour et nuit sous le joug accablant des Nazis! Je vous parle comme celui qui en 1918 était en France avec votre Armée et votre Marine. J'ai conservé toute ma vie une amitié profonde pour le peuple français entier. Je retiens et je garde soigneusement des centaines d'amis français en France et en dehors de la France. Je connais vos fermes, vos villages, vos villes. Je connais vos soldats, vos professeurs, vos ouvriers. Je sais bien

F.140

World War II Propaganda Leaflets

World War II Propaganda Leaflets

We dropped them, the Japs and Germans dropped them, and all had the same message: "Surrender!" Some did and some didn't, but because of the texture of the paper, they were good for more than one thing.

Average buying price, good condition $5-12

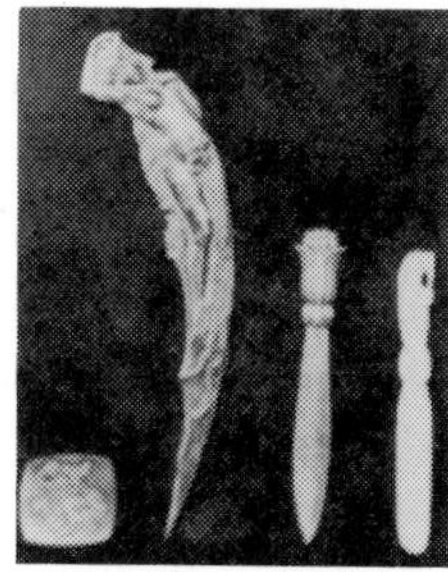

Writing Collectibles

Writing Collectibles

Ink blotters
Acme Moving Co., 1930's . . . .$ 2- 3
Arm & Hammer baking soda . . 1- 2
Morton's Salt (Illus.) 3- 4
Ink bottle, glass . . . . .50¢-75¢
Ink pad, still usable . . . . .25¢-50¢
Inkwell, glass, pewter cap, 1920's 4- 7

Yellow Ware

Yellow Ware

This heavy earthenware varies in color from a rich orange to lighter shades of tan. Most of what you find are kitchen pieces, although occasionally you will find other items. English pieces have a harder body.

Bowl, blue band at top, 12½" dia. . . . .$ 60- 63
Bowl, plain, 7½" dia. (Illus.) . . . 18- 25
Bowl, relief exterior, 9" dia. . . . 40- 48
Crock, covered, large, brown bands 70- 77
Crock, small, white bands 40- 44
Custard cup, small, blue band . 10- 13
Mold, Grape pattern, large 40- 44
Mold, Sunflower pattern, medium 41- 50
Pie plate, 8" dia. 40- 47
Pie plate, 9½" dia. 50- 58
Pitcher, blue band, 7" high . . . 110-115
Pitcher, 5" high 91- 98
Rolling pin, wooden handles, 8" long 56- 63

Zoo Collectibles

Most zoos sell souvenirs. The camel (Illus.) came from Cairo, Egypt's, zoo. Programs, admission tickets, photo albums — all sought after.

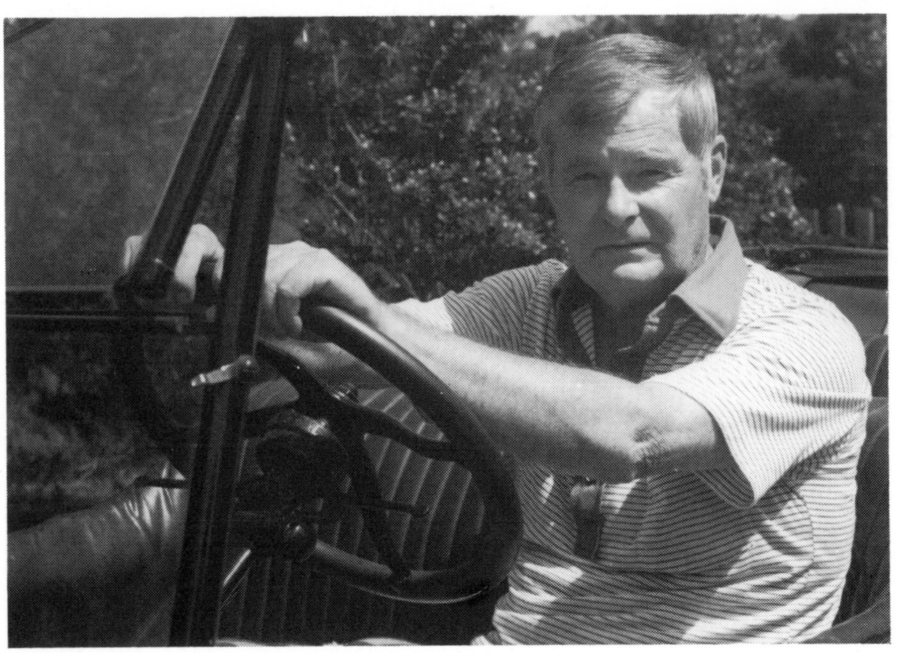

About the Author

A collector of old cars for more years than he cares to remember, Robert W. Miller enjoys the subjects he loves best, antiques and collectibles.

Television and radio personality, author, lecturer, and museum consultant, Mr. Miller has traveled throughout the world for thirty-five years buying and selling antiques and collectibles.

Past editor of the *Antique Trader Weekly,* he holds memberships in most of the world's major organizations to do with antiques and collectibles. Since 1971 he's written twenty-six books, and when asked which book he enjoyed writing the most, he answers, without hesitation, *The Flea Market Price Guide*!

When asked why, he smiles and says, "Because flea marketeers have more fun than anybody!"